HALAKHIC HERMENEUTICS

Jacob Neusner

BARD COLLEGE

Studies in Judaism

University Press of America,® Inc.
Lanham · New York · Oxford

BM
503.7
.N45
2003

⊖™ The paper used in this publication meets the minimum
requirements of American National Standard for Information
Sciences—Permanence of Paper for Printed Library Materials,
ANSI Z39.48—1984

Studies in Judaism

TABLE OF CONTENTS

Preface

A distinguished historian of religion once said, "The history of religions is the exegesis of exegesis." In a profound sense, that judgment animates an entire field of learning. In this project in the history of religions, I undertake an inductive account, through systematic inquiry into data, of the hermeneutics — both specific and generic — of the Halakhic documents of Rabbinic Judaism. I offer a hypothetical-logical reconstruction of the thought-processes that generated the category-formations of the Halakhah, that is, the exegesis of the hermeneutics of Halakhic exegesis. To do so, I ask whether a determinate theory of interpretation guides the sages in their exposition of the topics, the category-formations, of Rabbinic Judaism in the documents that expound those formations. My answer is, a hermeneutics of comparison and contrast yielding the hierarchical classification of data governs the selection of data and the interpretation thereof for the entire corpus of category-formations of the Halakhah. The rest of this project sets forth cases that spell out the meaning and effect of that sentence — six cases in all. Hence "Halakhic hermeneutics" here bears the primary meaning, "a hermeneutics of analogical-contrastive analysis."

I use the word "hermeneutics" to refer to the process of interpretation — the selection and interpretation of data, their systematization, rationalization, configuration and representation — that governs the native category-formations of the Halakhah. Rather than beginning with the whole — the Halakhah, or the Halakhah as represented by the Mishnah — I work, as is my way from bottom up, not top down. I find my way back from details of the Halakhic documents to their exegetical program, meaning, what do the Rabbinic sages wish to find out about a given topic, the information they systematize, and thence — from the exegesis — to the rules of interpretation that govern the document's presentation of one topic, then of all topics. Finally, within the framework of the documentary theory of the Rabbinic corpus, I undertake the comparison and contrast of the rules of interpretation realized in the respective documents (so far as these vary, as they do occasionally). So I set forth the comparative hermeneutics of the Rabbinic Judaism: the rules for interpreting the topics that all together comprise the Halakhah, the norms of actuality, of that Judaism.

What issue falls into the category of hermeneutics, the theory of interpretation of a received document? To begin with, the hermeneutics determines how random data fall into classifications and form coherent compositions. Hermeneutics in guiding the formation of organizing categories thereby defines the rules of coherence. It guides reading the received and holy scriptures. It selects the information, both of Scripture and of nature, as well as of tradition in Israel's social order, that requires inclusion. It defines the laws that dictate questions that will be raised and those that will not be raised. Hermeneutics here forms the theory that guides the formulation and transmission of tradition from generation to generation.

How do I conceive hermeneutics to relate to the detailed work of exegesis? Common usage suffices: hermeneutics forms the governing process of interpreting data, mediating chaos into order, and exegesis takes up the consequent, episodic challenges to harmonious reason, coherence, cogency. First comes the theory of interpretation, then its application to specific problems. Accordingly, hermeneutics defines the exegetical task, that is, the work of dealing with detail in a consistent, rational manner. That is because hermeneutics identifies what, within a received piece of writing, requires attention, framing problems for exegetical inquiry in a particular setting. Defining rationality, hermeneutics explains the coherence of the bits and pieces of the writing.

But that is not the direction of this project, which starts with small things and aims at a few large generalizations. I know how to move only by starting from the patient sifting of large aggregates of textual data and proceeding to the patterns and constructions that inhere therein. In the present context, as is always my way, I progress from detail to generalization. That is to say, I progress from the results of a process of exegetics to what I conceive to form the generative hermeneutics, from the manner of the exegesis of details to the guiding hermeneutics of the whole.

This I do in an encompassing framework, reading first the Halakhic documents — the Mishnah, Tosefta, Yerushalmi, and Bavli — in sequence, then the entire corpus of authoritative writings viewed whole. That involves a process of comparison and contrast. Here, if "hermeneutics" derives from the theory of exposition of a given topic that sustains the successive writings of the authoritative Rabbinic sages of late antiquity, "comparative hermeneutics" concerns itself with the logical next step. That is, the comparison and contrast of the respective theories of the exposition of a single program of topics in cognate documents. How a given topic is expounded, the issues people deem to inhere therein and to require exposition — description, analysis, and interpretation — these rules of interpretation in particular terms embody the general theory of how to make sense of a received, determinate tradition, that is, the Torah or "Judaism."

What, exactly, do I promise to do in producing the information required for this inquiry? After much labor over many topics, I offer in Chapter Seven a few generalizations about how any given topic is likely to be expounded in a given document, and what characterizes the theory of interpretation characteristic of the respective documents. Some may reasonably think that that is a rather modest result for a formidable effort, and I concur. But it is more than we have now. More to the point, along with everyone who has studied from start to finish all of the documents treated here (and there are not many), I have formed some impressions. Now I seek to transform general impressions into specific knowledge.

In Chapters One through Six, for the specified tractates that define the category-formations, I present a systematic comparison of Mishnah-Tosefta-Yerushalmi-Bavli. This permits me to account for how each document determines what it wants to know, and say, about a shared agendum of specified subjects. What may we expect the Mishnah to do with its topic? What then does the Tosefta want to accomplish in the presentation of the same topic, whether in dialogue with the Mishnah or not (that is an autonomous question)? When the Yerushalmi takes up the same topic, what interests its framers? Finally, how does the Bavli recapitulate the subject, and what are the traits of its mind in addressing a common heritage? I do not know a systematic account of these matters, and that is what I am trying to achieve. Chapter Seven then asks about the generic hermeneutics of the Halakhah, which pertains to all category-formations, that is, the general hermeneutics transcending the particular topics of tractates.

This book presents a condensation of a much larger project, covering all the Halakhic category-formations, which is as follows:

The Comparative Hermeneutics of Rabbinic Judaism. Volume One. *Introduction. Berakhot and Seder Mo'ed.* Binghamton, 2000: Global Publications. ACADEMIC STUDIES IN ANCIENT JUDAISM series

The Comparative Hermeneutics of Rabbinic Judaism. Volume Two. *Seder Nashim.* Binghamton, 2000: Global Publications. ACADEMIC STUDIES IN ANCIENT JUDAISM series.

The Comparative Hermeneutics of Rabbinic Judaism. Volume Three. *Seder Neziqin.* Binghamton, 2000: Global Publications. ACADEMIC STUDIES IN ANCIENT JUDAISM series.

The Comparative Hermeneutics of Rabbinic Judaism. Volume Four. *Seder Qodoshim.* Binghamton, 2000: Global Publications. ACADEMIC STUDIES IN ANCIENT JUDAISM series.

The Comparative Hermeneutics of Rabbinic Judaism. Volume Five. *Seder Tohorot.* Part *Kelim through Parah.* Binghamton, 2000: Global Publications. ACADEMIC STUDIES IN ANCIENT JUDAISM series.

The Comparative Hermeneutics of Rabbinic Judaism. Volume Six. *Seder Tohorot. Tohorot through Uqsin.* Binghamton, 2000: Global Publications. ACADEMIC STUDIES IN ANCIENT JUDAISM series.

The Comparative Hermeneutics of Rabbinic Judaism. Volume Seven *The Generic Hermeneutics of the Halakhah. A Handbook.* Binghamton, 2000: Global Publications. ACADEMIC STUDIES IN ANCIENT JUDAISM series.

Here I have selected a single case from each of the six volumes at the shank of the original work; and I have also reproduced the chapter of generalizations set forth in Volume Seven.

There is an eighth volume in the original work, which I have condensed and reproduced in the following way:

Why This, Not That? Ways Not Taken in the Halakhic Category-Formations of the Mishnah-Tosefta-Yerushalmi-Bavli. Lanham, 2003: University Press of America. Second printing, revised, of *The Comparative Hermeneutics of Rabbinic Judaism.* Volume Eight. *Why This, Not That? Ways Not Taken in the Halakhic Category-Formations of the Mishnah-Tosefta-Yerushalmi-Bavli.* Binghamton, 2000: Global Publications. ACADEMIC STUDIES IN ANCIENT JUDAISM series.

All of my research enjoys the support of my research professorship at Bard College, for which I express thanks.

JACOB NEUSNER
BARD COLLEGE
ANNANDALE-ON-HUDSON, NEW YORK 12504
neusner@webjogger.net

Introduction

The goal of this study is to define the main lines of the hermeneutics of the Halakhah, as that hermeneutics governs the formation of native-categories out of a mass of data, some deriving from Scripture, some from natural reason, some from tradition, and that further guides the interpretation and articulation of each of those native-categories.[1] A subsidiary goal is comparative. That entails an effort to identify evidence of variation within the hermeneutics of the native-categories as these categories are set forth in the successive documents of the Halakhah, from the Mishnah, ca. 200, which is primary, to the Tosefta, ca. 300, Yerushalmi, ca. 400, and Bavli, ca. 600. Here, therefore, we deal with the hermeneutics of the Halakhic documents, within a very particular framework: the native-categories of the Halakhah.

I analyze the topical framework within which the Halakhic compilations conduct their discourse, the entire Halakhah being organized by subject-matter and within a logic comprised by two components. First, the organizing logic imputes coherence to the requirements of topical exposition. Second, the logic insists, within the concrete case, abstract principles are to be encapsulated in details alone. Specifically, in this protracted exercise — illustrated one time for each of the second

---

[1]I stress, I deal with hermeneutics, not exegesis, the technology of problem-solving. That distinction is standard and need not detain us. A considerable body of literature on what the authors call "hermeneutics" that deals with rules for the exegesis of Scripture, comparable to Graeco-Roman rules of rhetoric on interpreting mythic or legal writings, plays no role in my inquiry. I do not regard as problems of hermeneutics, but only as exercises of exegesis, the relationship between a verse of Scripture and the explanation of that verse of Scripture by Rabbinic exegetes. Using "hermeneutics" for the rules by which the Torah is expounded (hammiddot shehattorah nidreshet bahen) errs. Those rules are exegetical in classification, and not hermeneutical; they propound no large-scale theory of mediation and interpretation of a received corpus, only ad hoc rules for concrete cases, a very different matter. Exegetics can go forward (if in an intellectual coarse manner) without theology; hermeneutics forms a chapter in theology. But, we cannot forget, hermeneutics is the father of exegetics properly executed.

through the fifth of the six divisions of the Halakhah, and two times for the sixth[2]
— I identify the theory of how a given topic is to be interpreted, specifically moving
backward from exegesis of cases to hermeneutics of topics, that is, from the evidence
of the consequent exegesis that gives actuality to that theory backward to the theory
of interpretation itself. Since Rabbinic Judaism in its normative corpus comes to us
in four documents, the Mishnah, the Tosefta, the Yerushalmi (Talmud of the Land
of Israel), and the Bavli (Talmud of Babylonia), documentary hermeneutics enters
in. Therefore I further compare and contrast the theory of presenting a given topic
that dictated the character of the one document with the theory that governed in
another of the cognate writings of Judaism.

I

In the beginning is the chaos of data, incoherent clouds of data. In the aggregate
these are formed by bits of information bearing no intelligible shape, deriving we
know not whence. Out of chaos comes order, effected, in the case of the Halakhah,
through sorting out data by subject-matter. The topic subject to discussion, the
principal categories of a given cultural system — these organize facts in one structure
rather than in some other, with one consequence for meaning, rather than another.
The intrinsic, inherent traits of the facts joined by topic then bring about their own
ordering. These categories, fixed by the authoritative formulations of a culture,
then require interpretation, an account of how the categories cohere, the components
of which they are comprised, the inner principles and rules of logic that permit the
categories to be augmented and reconfigured. Then the interpretive process works
through the traits of things — their common task or purpose or point of coherence
— and appeals to their nature, their teleology. What is interpreted is a vast corpus
of established facts, some deriving from Scripture, some from nature, some from

---

[2] The complete presentation of the Halakhah in the present context is in my *The Halakhah:
An Encyclopaedia of the Law of Judaism*. Volume I. *Between Israel and God*. Part A. *Faith,
Thanksgiving, Enlandisement: Possession and Partnership*. Leiden, 1999: E. J. Brill. THE
BRILL REFERENCE LIBRARY OF JUDAISM; *The Halakhah: An Encyclopaedia of the Law of
Judaism*. Volume II. *Between Israel and God*. Part B. *Transcendent Transactions: Where
Heaven and Earth Intersect*. Leiden, 1999: E. J. Brill. THE BRILL REFERENCE LIBRARY OF
JUDAISM; *The Halakhah: An Encyclopaedia of the Law of Judaism*. Volume III. *Within Israel's
Social Order*. Leiden, 1999: E. J. Brill. THE BRILL REFERENCE LIBRARY OF JUDAISM; *The
Halakhah: An Encyclopaedia of the Law of Judaism*. Volume IV. Inside the Walls of the
Israelite Household. Part A. *At the Meeting of Time and Space. Sanctification in the Here
and Now: The Table and the Bed. Sanctification and the Marital Bond. The Desacralization
of the Household: The Bed*. Leiden, 1999: E. J. Brill. THE BRILL REFERENCE LIBRARY OF
JUDAISM; *The Halakhah: An Encyclopaedia of the Law of Judaism*. Volume V. *Inside the
Walls of the Israelite Household*. Part B. *The Desacralization of the Household: The Table.
Foci, Sources, and Dissemination of Uncleanness. Purification from the Pollution of Death*.
Leiden, 1999: E. J. Brill. THE BRILL REFERENCE LIBRARY OF JUDAISM.

logic. How these are to be interpreted — organized into intelligible constructions and compositions and recast, then, into structures and composites — forms the issue of hermeneutics.

By hermeneutics, people mean, "the science or art of interpretation."[3] But the word is used in this project in a somewhat unconventional manner, as I shall explain. Usually, what is subjected to interpretation is written material, scripture, or, in antiquity, "the interpretation of written material pertinent to legal cases, such as laws, wills, and contracts:"

> In the course of these treatments... rhetoricians considered such
> seemingly current hermeneutical questions as the nature of meaning
> and the role of context in the quest for this meaning.[4]

At issue were modes of argument and analysis, rhetorical media of advocacy, and similar matters. Matters of style are portrayed (only after treating matters of proof."[5] In the context of the study of Judaism, by "hermeneutics," people mean, the rules of Scriptural exegesis, how one gets from here (Scripture) to there (the meaning imputed to Scripture). Numerous reliable studies composed from the formative age of Rabbinic Judaism itself and on down to our own day spell out these exegetical rules ("hammiddot shehattorah nidreshet bahen").

But hermeneutics as the theory of interpretation may cover other sorts of things that are to be interpreted, besides received documents, their grammar, rhetoric, and meaning. In the case of Rabbinic Judaism in its Halakhic writings, a received construction of category-formations and *their* exposition constituted the field of interpretation that was explored by the Rabbinic sages of the Mishnah, Tosefta, Yerushalmi and Bavli.[6]

---

[3] I follow Jean Grondin, *Introduction to Philosophical Hermeneutics* (New Haven and London, 1988: Yale University Press). Translated by Joel Weinsheimer, p. 1.

[4] Kathy Eden, *Hermeneutics and the Rhetorical Tradition. Chapters in the Ancient Legacy & its Humanist Reception* (New Haven & London, 1997: Yale University Press), p. 2.

[5] Eden, p. 10.

[6] I omit the Tannaite Midrashim, except within the framework of the Halakhic exposition of the Mishnah (and the Tosefta), because so far as I can tell they present very little Halakhah that is not set forth in the Mishnah and the Tosefta. My systematic analysis of those documents in *The Components of the Rabbinic Documents: From the Whole to the Parts.* Volume I. *Sifra.* Atlanta, 1997: Scholars Press for USF Academic Commentary Series, *The Components of the Rabbinic Documents: From the Whole to the Parts.* VII. *Sifré to Deuteronomy.* Atlanta, 1997: Scholars Press for USF Academic Commentary Series, *The Components of the Rabbinic Documents: From the Whole to the Parts.* VIII. *Mekhilta Attributed to R. Ishmael.* Atlanta, 1997: Scholars Press for USF Academic Commentary Series, and *The Components of the Rabbinic Documents: From the Whole to the Parts.* XII. *Sifré to Numbers.* Atlanta, 1998: Scholars Press for USF Academic Commentary Series, left the impression that the systematic program of the Tannaite Midrash-compilations involved secondary expansion of details, not primary exposition of the principles of the law through cases, such as we find in

At issue here are the rules of interpretation of the native categories within which the Halakhah, the body of normative rules of conduct, of Judaism is set forth. The Halakhah represents a different sort of text for interpretation from the documentary ones of law and rhetoric, myth and poetry, and received Scripture,[7] that occupied the ancient expositors of rules of interpretation. For the Halakhah — the corpus of law — transcends the tangible representations of cases and rules that embody it. The Halakhah takes shape in category-formations of a topical character and spins out in concrete terms quite profound and abstract reflection on issues of a theological and metaphysical character. The exegesis of the cases then adumbrates an animating hermeneutics. I deem the native-categories and the way in which these are instantiated and articulated to represent a response to interpretative conventions, which I propose to identify, and the continuation of which in the successive documents I propose to examine as well.

On what basis? The evidence of a corpus of rules of interpretation comes to us in the results of interpretation, in the legal texts, but the rules respond to the data that are being interpreted, structured and proportioned and endowed with significance in one way, rather than in another. So the field of interpretation I wish to explore is not textual in an ordinary sense but in an unusual sense: the text is constituted by the laws, themselves formed into coherent patterns and made to yield cogent knowledge. Here I work back from the laws to the constitutive principles, the hermeneutics of the laws, not of the rhetoric of the texts of the laws (the Mishnah, Tosefta, two Talmuds, not to mention the Torah of Moses). The comparative aspect focuses attention on how four documents, continuous with one another at various levels, define the labor of interpreting the same set of category-formations.

We begin with a native-category and ask how it is mediated, what rules govern its articulation and extension, into the normative Halakhah. Take the native-category of religion in general, the one that stands at the head of the repertoire of the Halakhah, "prayer," and the counterpart within native-category-formation of Rabbinic Judaism that corresponds to "prayer." That category bears the title, Berakhot, and deals

---

the Mishnah and the Tosefta. Admittedly, that is an impression, but it is based on a systematic examination. I should welcome studies on the Halakhic contribution of the Tannaite Midrash-compilations, which would show fundamental Halakhic categories and conceptions, not just secondary and tertiary clarifications, e.g., of the relationship of a rule to Scripture. Such studies, if constructed along the systematic lines of my *Religious Commentary to the Halakhah*, would clarify the matter on which, at this time, we are left to rely on mere impressions.

[7] The rules of scriptural interpretation guiding Rabbinic exegetes form a separate problem, one that has received considerable attention; it does not require attention in this project. Those who investigate how sages derived from Scripture the laws that they put forth in the Mishnah and related compilations, by contrast, have investigated that matter — from antiquity onward, as a matter of fact. It is not under discussion in these pages.

with obligatory prayers required of the individual on an everyday, secular basis. What is it about "prayer" in that particular context that — within the hermeneutics governing the articulation of the native category, Berakhot — we wish to discuss, meaning, what are the aspects or qualities or traits of the act or phenomenon of "prayer," once defined, that shape our understanding and interpretation of that act or phenomenon? What rationality or logic do we deem implicit in that act of phenomenon, which allows us to identify and organize and harmonize the data that are organized within that category? The answers to those questions define the hermeneutics of "prayer." They determine the meaning we find in the generative category of "prayer," and the exegetics of prayer as well, the specific, detailed problems that require attention.[8]

Since my usage is unconventional, why use the word "hermeneutics" at all? The reason is that, viewed in generous proportions, hermeneutics transcends its documentary origins in the study of rhetoric and language. Rather, as a mode of learning, hermeneutics defines the logic or rationality that lends consequence to inert, raw data. It would not exaggerate to propose that hermeneutics embodies the logic of exegesis. Exegesis then dictates the articulation of the details of the data in accord with that governing logic. The document as a whole in its propositional presentations of topics coheres within the match of exegesis to generative hermeneutics. We compare the hermeneutics that are realized in the exegesis of cognate writings when we set side by side documents that take up the same topic and analyze their respective reading of the same data. That allows us to compare the hermeneutics of the one with that of the other. To address the hermeneutical question in this manner to the representations of the Halakhah in concrete terms will not have puzzled the Rabbinic sages.[9]

Accordingly, I use "hermeneutics" with special reference to the rules of interpretation that have generated a received category-formation, as that category-formation is articulated by the foundation-documents of formative Judaism for its normative law. Stoic philosophy "worked out a procedure for systematic, rationalizing, and hence allegorical interpretation of myth."[10] Working our way

---

[8] This matter is made concrete in Chapter One.

[9] though the language lay beyond their intellectual boundaries: "The idea of an art of interpretation can be traced much farther back, at least to the patristic period, if not the Stoic philosophy (which developed an allegorical interpretation of myth) or even to the tradition of the Greek rhapsody (Grenadine, p. 1). More broadly, synonyms for "hermeneutic" such as "interpretation, explication, exegesis" serve not uncommonly, so Grondin. But I use the term here in a most limited sense: the rules of interpretation.

[10] Grondin, p. 24.

back from what they said to the rules that guided their representation of matters, we may say that the Rabbinic sages, for their part, followed a fixed procedure for systematic interpretation of the native-categories of the Halakhah and their contents. By a detailed survey of the Halakhic compilations, I show that a few fixed rules dictated the character of interpretation and exposition of matters, as much as, in the exposition of the Aggadah, a hermeneutics guided exegesis of detail.[11]

But in the case of the Halakhah, sages dealt with a problem much different from that confronting Philo and Origen. Theirs was not a corpus of fixed Scripture (or myth) that required mediation into the sense accessible to philosophically-trained minds. Theirs was a vast corpus of norms in the form of rules of behavior and belief, some deriving from Scripture, some not, some of recent venue, some attested in remote antiquity. The intellectual problem faced by the Rabbinic sages and solved by the Mishnah-Tosefta-Yerushalmi-Bavli, then, was, how to systematize, organize, rationalize, and derive sense from, that received corpus of rules. From the time of the formation of the Deuteronomic Code, the Priestly Code (Lev. 1-15) and the other scriptural codes of law, so far as extant evidence suggests, few such systematic and encompassing efforts to accord a context to the diverse texts of law — statements of rules about this, that, and the other thing — had imposed such a task on Israelite sages.[12] In the codes of Exodus, Leviticus, Numbers, and Deuteronomy that select and organize data for the purposes accomplished therein, a theory of interpretation functioned.

Such a theory — and we need not undertake to define it — told the sages who did the work what belonged here and with what consequence, what there, and with what result. From the closure of the Written Torah's codes, regnant theories on the systematization and interpretation of the category-formations deemed to pertain produced no imitators or continuators, though other constructions by Israelites, each group with its own focus and system, were undertaken. But from the earliest phases of work that resulted in the Mishnah, a counterpart labor, as universal in scope, as ambitious in intent, as weighty in effect, did commence. And that labor, I

---

[11] But the problematics of the Aggadic hermeneutics requires a shift from the reading of passages or stories to the exposition of category-formations of the Aggadah, as I shall suggest in a moment. And that poses a separate set of problems, not addressed in these pages. On Philo as the father of allegory and a principal figure in ancient hermeneutics, see Grondin, pp. 26ff. But it is not inconsequential that Origen (185-254) was framing a Christian hermeneutics just when the Rabbinic sages were engaged in the realization of a Judaic-Halakhic hermeneutics (Grondin, pp. 29ff.) But his rules of interpretation, like those of Philo, concerned themselves with the reading of Scripture, while the rules of interpretation treated here dealt with the reading of a corpus of category-formations, an immeasurably more abstract problem of thought than faced Philo or Origen.

[12] Some texts found at Qumran, e.g., the Temple Scroll, are at least as large in scope as the Priestly Code or the Deuteronomic Code, but nothing found at Qumran compares in scope and coverage with the Mishnah, with or without the Tosefta!

show in these pages, invoked an original composite of category-formations and followed rules of interpretation of those category-formations that produced, in countless details, the same cogent result: interpretation in accord with rules, mediation of details in response to fixed laws. That labor of interpretation, as I said, overcame obstacles of abstract thought vastly more formidable than those presented by Scripture to the allegorists. Here then I spell out how the Mishnah-Tosefta-Yerushalmi-Bavli embody that hermeneutics: a hermeneutics of category-formations, their explanation, extension, and articulation.

Can I compare their solution to their problem to Augustine's solution to his? At the risk of trespassing where I do not belong, I cite a passage of Grondin and articulate what I conceive to be the Rabbinic sages' counterpart mode of interpretation. Writing about Augustine's reflection on the relationship of signs to the word and thought, Grondin states (and I quote somewhat lavishly, since I cannot pretend to speak in my own name about the matters under discussion here:

> The conclusion of the third book alludes to a relations between sign (signum) and word (verbum) that needs to be elaborated by reference to Augustine's De trinitate... Augustine conceptualizes this relation within a religious context: how can the son of God be understood as verbum or logos, without conceiving the verbum simply as the sensible utterance of God, and thus implying an anti-Trinitarian subordination of son to father? In answering this question, Augustine recurs in the fifteenth and last book of De trinitate to the Stoic distinction between an inner (endiathetos) and an outer (prophorikos) logos or verbum. Original speaking and thinking, says Augustine, is inner: a language of the heart. This inner speech does not yet have a sensible or material form; it is purely intellectual and universal — that is, it has not yet taken on the form of a particular sensible or historical language. *When we hear a human word in a particular language, it is clear that we attempt to understand not its specific, accidental form but rather the verbum or reason that is embodied in it... Thus it is necessary to transcend sensible, uttered language in order to reach the true human word. What the listener strives to understand is the verbum which no ear can hear; yet it dwells within every language and is prior to all the signs into which it can be 'translated.'*[13]

The words that I have italicized capture, for words, what I conceive to have been the power of the Halakhah. The details transcend their particularity, when the Rabbinic sages display them in such a way as to reveal the principle or law embodied in the detail. The Mishnah is so arranged and so formulated as to show us how to transcend the particularities of details in order to reach the true principles of being that are contained therein. In my presentations of the six category-formations treated here, I articulate precisely what I mean by "true principles."

---

[13] Grondin, p. 35f.

Now what I am going to show, specifically, is a comparable process of *interpreting the particular as exemplary of the general*. I shall establish beyond any doubt that a principle of interpreting the structure of a received corpus of data will require the presentation of cases that realize rules, rules that are subject to abstract reconfiguration so as to pertain to a broad variety of data other than those that to begin with make the rule manifest as a case. Working backward, then, from the "particular sensible or historical language," we shall learn how the Rabbinic sages made the specificities of rules serve into the medium for a vast set of abstract principles. Then the hermeneutics of the Halakhah will conform to those of the age of the Halakhah, for Judaism, and the founding of theology, for Christianity. The statement, "it is necessary to transcend sensible, uttered language in order to reach the true human word," speaks for the Rabbinic sages with this revision: it is necessary to transform the sensible, specific case into a rule, and the rule into a means for penetrating into the true foundations of the social order. But that shift is perfectly familiar, with Israel's social order forming the medium that bears what Christianity knows as the logos, the inner construction and structure of that reality that, in this world, embodies God (Christianity) or God's plan for humanity (Judaism).

II

How does the Halakhic hermeneutics impart form to a mass of inchoate information. The hermeneutics transforms random facts into a topic, linking datum to datum, turning the whole into active, formed knowledge. Hermeneutics guides the work of category-formation, and, categories in hand, determines what reasoned knowledge inheres in the category at hand. That theory in hand concerning what is there to be known, exegetical problems present themselves. In the engagement with the topic read in one way, rather than in some other, the logic of exegesis dictates the application of the regnant hermeneutics. Then, a comprehensive theory in hand, comes the writing. Recording the results of topical exegesis, sentences translate the topic into propositions that cohere and impart to the topic particular meaning.

That theory, stated in abstract language, moves from the hermeneutical precipitant or cause to the exegetical result, which in actuality rarely defines the course of learning. In the present study of the way in which diverse documents' authors devise hermeneutical rules for the presentation of one and the same topic, I start from the end-product. Specifically, from the way in which a sequence of related documents portray one and the same subject, I work my way back to the logic that governs in the reading of data and the formation of data into useful knowledge, the point at which we began. I offer an exercise in the comparison of the hermeneutics of kindred writings as they converge upon the presentation of one and the same topic.

On the foundation of a dense corpus of detailed evidence, I seek a few generalizations concerning the hermeneutics of Rabbinic Judaism in its formative writings. I am trying to understand the category-formations of that Judaism and how they work.[14] By that I mean, I propose to account for the traits in rationality and logic of a highly rational and disciplined corpus of the writing down of normative rules. I mean to show that we may make sense, in our terms and intellectual context, of the Rabbinic sages' rules, viewed as a coherent system. Identifying the rules of analysis and exposition that governed in the category-formations of Rabbinic Judaism and their coherent construction allows us to assess that rationality by both their rules and by our own. That explains my resort to the language of hermeneutics. Hermeneutics mediates an ancient text to the contemporary intellect, building a bridge across the ages for intellects to meet. Both parties, ancient and contemporary, participate in the construction of meaning. In this study I propose to give voice to the first of the two parties, those that formed the ancient texts.

The manner in which the authors or framers of the ancient texts shaped information into (to them) consequential, therefore worthwhile, knowledge attests to their program and intent. When we know how they consistently defined what they wished to know about a given topic, we gain access to the principle of interpretation that guided them. It is for us inductively to form a theory of the rules of interpretation that the initial authors adopted for themselves. We do so by working our way back from the result to the substrate of questions that produced that result and at the level beneath that to generalize about the character of those questions. That theory of how the authors wished their statements to form intelligible and persuasive propositions for future ages — their logic of intelligible discourse broadly construed — emerges from the indicative traits of the document itself. Specifically, from how they made their statements on any given topic, we may intuit the larger theory of intelligible intent that governed their modes of thought about topics. And for our part, granted access to those modes of thought, we may match and meet them with our own. In the end a shared rationality sinks deep into bed-rock. A logic common to us all forms the piles of that bridge that stretches from age to succeeding age.

III

These observations about how we gain access to the ancient texts of an alien world by means of the entry afforded by the authors of the texts themselves brings us to the particular problem to which this project is dedicated. That is, how the writers of the respective normative texts of Judaism, the Halakhic corpus of late

---

[14] I further wish to complete the demonstration of the documentary hypothesis of Rabbinic Judaism in its formative age, but that is the inevitable consequence of answering the question, how do the Mishnah, Tosefta, Yerushalmi, and Bavli, respectively define, each in a distinctive way, the presentation of a shared native category? Once we have seen that each compilation in fact exhibits its own characteristic hermeneutics, the final demonstration of the documentary hypothesis will have come to its successful conclusion.

antiquity, defined their work of topical exposition, analysis, and interpretation. In comparing and contrasting 'he successive presentations of the same topics, I identify the hermeneutics — the rules of interpretation of an established topical program — of Rabbinic Judaism in its formative writings, the Mishnah, Tosefta, Yerushalmi, Bavli, and pertinent parts of the Tannaite Midrash-compilations. The Halakhic sector of Rabbinic Judaism is comprised by a structure of category-formations — topics — that deal with norms of behavior and belief, classifications of actions and convictions, that all together constitute the statement of that Judaism in action and actuality. To state the purpose with heavy emphasis:

I undertake to investigate the rules of interpreting the categories of normative conduct: how, over all, do the documents that constitute the system uniformly describe, analyze, and interpret the generative categories of behavior.

To do so I take up a determinate and precise matter: what are the documentary rules of exposition of the generative category-formations of that Judaism? I seek to define the principles that dictate how a given topic or problem will be expounded and the general rules that guide us in making sense of that exposition. That is why, in vast detail, I answer the questions,

[1] how does the Mishnah, in dialogue with Scripture,[15] define and expound its generative categories,

[2] sometimes in dialogue with the Mishnah, sometimes not,[16] how does the Tosefta define what bears consequence in the exposition of these same categories,

[3] generally in dialogue with the Mishnah and sometimes with the Tosefta as well as with the baraita-corpus (which awaits its analyst), how does the Yerushalmi take up the task of tradition and what does the Yerushalmi deem to require exegesis within its theory of topical presentation,

---

[15] For a systematic account, see *The Law and the Torah: The Four Relationships.* Lanham, 2003: University Press of America. Second printing, condensed and revised, of *Scripture and the Generative Premises of the Halakhah. A Systematic Inquiry.* I. *Halakhah Based Principally on Scripture and Halakhic Categories Autonomous of Scripture.* Binghamton, 2000: Global Publications. ACADEMIC STUDIES IN ANCIENT JUDAISM series. *Scripture and the Generative Premises of the Halakhah. A Systematic Inquiry.* II. *Scripture's Topics Derivatively Amplified in the Halakhah.* Binghamton, 2000: Global Publications. ACADEMIC STUDIES IN ANCIENT JUDAISM series. *Scripture and the Generative Premises of the Halakhah. A Systematic Inquiry.* III. *Scripture's Topics Independently Developed in the Halakhah. From the Babas through Miqvaot.* Binghamton, 2000: Global Publications. ACADEMIC STUDIES IN ANCIENT JUDAISM series. *Scripture and the Generative Premises of the Halakhah. A Systematic Inquiry.* IV. *Scripture's Topics Independently Developed in the Halakhah. From Moed Qatan through Zebahim.* Binghamton, 2000: Global Publications. ACADEMIC STUDIES IN ANCIENT JUDAISM series.

[16] That the Tosefta cites verbatim and glosses the Mishnah establishes that the framers of the Tosefta conducted a dialogue with the Mishnah. But that accounts for only part of the compositions and composites of the Tosefta, my rough estimate is, a sixth. Another sixth of the document stands topically and conceptually independent of the Mishnah, and about

[4] and, also in dialogue with the Mishnah and occasionally with the Tosefta and with the baraita-corpus too, how does the Bavli at the end impose the imprint of its intellectual character on those same classifications of correct conduct?

I can ask about the rules of describing, analyzing, interpreting the native categories of Rabbinic Judaism because that Judaism is comprised by writings that systematically expound those categories and shape them into a coherent system of a propositional character. These writings embody a system open to on-going exegesis in later times and different circumstances. And how is that so? It is because the Rabbinic writings do not simply set forth rules. They form of those rules coherent statements of grand dimensions. Theirs is a purposive and propositional, not merely an illuminating, discourse. When we find ourselves able to identify the rules of rationality, the generative logic, of the system in its authoritative initial statement, we come closer to identifying the sources of intellectual vitality that have sustained, and that now sustained, the Judaism realized in the Halakhah. So beneath the surface of the exposition a substrate of rules of description, analysis, and interpretation governs. And, as the definition of the hermeneutical task, working backward from the details, I want to know the rules that guide the organization of the data and information in the formation of those expositions distinguish purposive sense from what is merely random.

IV

Why categorize the work, in the original project that is epitomized here, as that of "comparative hermeneutics" — the exegesis of exegesis, in language used just now?

By hermeneutics, as is now clear, I mean, the general theory that tells us how to make sense of a given piece of writing, conveying the rules of interpreting that writing. Such a theory tells us — in advance of dealing with any given document or (in the present context) topic — what we are likely to find out and how we are to identify as consequential and intelligible the statement that is before us. A hermeneutics may emerge from a document, which guides readers to the right way of making sense of what is written, or it may derive from a theory independent of the writing and imposed thereon. Since the problem at hand is to define the governing principles of interpretation characteristic of an entire Judaism in its successive

---

two-thirds of the Tosefta's compositions and composites go over topics treated by the Mishnah but do so in their own terms. That the Tosefta overall pursues its own program, not only comments on the Mishnah's, seems to me an established fact, and that explains why I wish to read the Tosefta in its own terms, not only in relationship with the Mishnah, and to define just what those terms are. In seeing matters in this way, I am indebted to Professor Ithamar Gruenwald for a long debate by correspondence on this problem, and, by extension, interchange with the students of his seminar at Tel Aviv University.

documentary formulations of topics, the direction of the work is clear. We begin in the detailed writings and through a labor of comparison and contrast between and among those writings, we undertake to generalize.[17]

I specify the indicative hermeneutical traits of a given document. I aim at a simple outcome, the identification of the documentary mark, the footprint, the fingerprint, the imprint. Specifically, if we know what an unidentified unit of discourse ("paragraph") says about a subject, we should readily identify the document in which that exposition is located — or, at least, the ones in which it is not located. That forms a test of the facticity of our proposed generalizations: this document does this, that document does that, with a given topic. Comparing the hermeneutics of a given topic that characterize one document with that that characterizes some other will then allow a clear definition of the indicative traits of each.[18] That accounts for my describing the project as one of comparison.

What is at stake in comparative hermeneutics is identifying the rationality of a logical system as it conducts its intellectual labor. What I shall show in vast detail is how people knew what they wanted to know about a given topic, what they deemed to require exposition and amplification, generating a vast exegetical work on details. The theory by which successive Rabbinic writings define and spell out one and the same subject thus will define for us the hermeneutics of those writings, one by one and in sequence. And the consequences for our understanding of Judaism in its origins as an intellectual construction have already been indicated.

V

Now we turn to the concrete plan of the original work, which guides Chapters One through Six. To do the work on the successive topics that comprise the system,

---

[17] But (as shown in connection with the Aggadic theology) one may with equal reason bring *to* the evidence a theory of the governing hermeneutics and undertake to validate that theory in other media of investigation altogether.

[18] That the hermeneutical problem and its solution form a component of the larger documentary reading of the Rabbinic corpus that I have devised is self-evident. I see no need to go over the larger project; a few of the more important components are these: *Midrash as Literature: The Primacy of Documentary Discourse.* Lanham, 1987: University Press of America *Studies in Judaism* series. *Sifra in Perspective: The Documentary Comparison of the Midrashim of Ancient Judaism* Atlanta, 1988: Scholars Press for Brown Judaic Studies. *Rabbinic Judaism. The Documentary History of the Formative Age.* Bethesda, 1994: CDL Press. *The Documentary Form-History of Rabbinic Literature.* I. *The Documentary Forms of the Mishnah.* Atlanta, 1998: Scholars Press for USF Academic Commentary Series, and *The Documentary Foundation of Rabbinic Culture. Mopping Up after Debates with Gerald L. Bruns, S. J. D. Cohen, Arnold Maria Goldberg, Susan Handelman, Christine Hayes, James Kugel, Peter Schaefer, Eliezer Segal, E. P. Sanders, and Lawrence H. Schiffman.* Atlanta, 1995: Scholars Press for South Florida Studies in the History of Judaism.

I first describe and then analyze the successive topical treatments of the Mishnah, Tosefta, Yerushalmi, and Bavli in dialogue with Scripture. The Mishnah as a matter of fact forms the source of the sixty category-formations of the norm of conduct that order the Halakhah and that classify all of its data. The Mishnah's mode of organization governs the Tosefta's, Yerushalmi's, and Bavli's presentation of the same topics. Only Scripture's own, different mode of presenting the same topics competes. So for each topic I commence with an account of how the Mishnah defines the topic. I answer the question, what is the information that the Mishnah deems necessary, and how is that information organized, in its topical exposition? From description I turn to analysis, which requires not only comparison but contrast. In many instances we have an alternative way of presenting the same topic, and that is Scripture's.

So the first analytical exercise requires the comparison and contrast of Scripture's and the Mishnah's reading of the same topic. The initial, and paramount exegetical work on any given topic, beyond the Mishnah's, comes to us in the Tosefta.

The second analytical exercise demands that we compare the Tosefta's with the Mishnah's presentation of the same topic. Does the Tosefta constitute an exegesis of the Mishnah's presentation of the topic or of the topic itself, and, if the latter, how does the Tosefta reshape the formation of the matter? We want to know whether the Tosefta undertakes its own theory of what is at stake in a given topic, and if so, what traits commonly characterize the Tosefta's distinctive theory of matters.

The third analytical problem carries us to the Yerushalmi's recapitulation of matters: what does that document identify as its task, so far as that task undertakes the presentation of the topic of the Mishnah (not only the exegesis of the laws of the Mishnah and the Tosefta)?

And, finally, the Bavli frames its own statement of the topic common to the four documents and, often, to Scripture as well. Here again, what interests us is, does the Bavli's "take" on the established topic reshape, or merely reprise, the received account of said topic? The strategy of exposition that governs in this project aims at a simple provision of the facts required to produce the besought data. For that purpose I cite texts seldom, rather, I ordinarily provide a précis of them.[19]

---

[19] Any other mode of presentation would require citing nearly the whole of the Mishnah, Tosefta, Yerushalmi, Bavli, and large tracts of the Tannaite Midrash-compilations. That is not necessary. I have already made all of those texts available in English, and my translations are readily accessible. Readers who compare my translations into English with other English translations, or with the counterpart translations into German, Spanish, and Hebrew, will not find a great many points of difference in the basic wording of matters, though all translations are easily criticized in matters of taste and judgment.

In the case of the Mishnah, my account of its topical presentation takes the form of an outline of a given tractate. In that way I define both the principal parts of the Mishnah's parsing of the topic and also the sequence that dictates which of those parts comes first, which later on. I ask whether a logic dictates the order of the presentation of the subdivisions of a subject; I invoke the criterion: if we re-ordered matters in some other way, would we still understand the presentation, or would confusion result? So we deal with the components of the Mishnah's topical exposition and the order that they follow. Our theory of the Mishnah's hermeneutics then will invoke the general traits that for the mind of the Mishnah's framers apparently defined sense, order, and rationality upon the raw data of a given topic.

When we come to the Tosefta, our question concerns not the documentary traits of the Tosefta but the Tosefta's mode of presenting the topic. Here we do have to compare the Mishnah's to the Tosefta's presentation of the same topic. To do so, I utilize my recapitulation of both, in abbreviated form, in my *Halakhah: Encyclopaedia of the Law of Judaism.* There I cite, sometimes verbatim, sometimes in précis, the Mishnah in relationship to the Tosefta, using bold face type for the Mishnah, italics for the Tosefta. In examining those matters, we shall see how the later compilation conceives it necessary to portray the subject at hand. We shall not read the Tosefta as a commentary to the Mishnah but as a statement of an autonomous character. Therein we shall identify its theory of interpreting the Halakhah at hand.

The Yerushalmi lays itself out as a commentary to passages of selected Mishnah-tractate. But it also constitutes a presentation of the topic of the Mishnah (encompassing also of the Tosefta). Here I shall want to know, beyond recapitulating the Mishnah's and the Tosefta's presentation of the topic, does the Yerushalmi propose to portray the topic in a distinctive manner, and, if so, what does the Yerushalmi's authorship contribute?

The Bavli forms the pinnacle of Rabbinic Judaism and its summa. When it approaches a topic, the Bavli will be seen to bring an original and important perspective on matters. Here once more we ask, what does the Bavli contribute that is unique to the Bavli? In answering that question, we shall point toward the solution to a still more critical question of the history of Rabbinic Judaism. That is, what accounts for the Bavli's hegemony over the mind of that Judaism? I have already conducted a systematic comparison of the two Talmuds, outlining each, then bringing the outline of the one into juxtaposition to that of the other.[20] In so doing, I have shown how the Talmuds differ, as they do profoundly and fundamentally, in their

---

[20] That work is accomplished in three phases. First I outlined each Talmud, then I systematically compared the outlines, providing a research tool for others to use over time. Preparing for the complete comparison, I did a series of probes, following a logical program of my own, choosing diverse composites to test a series of propositions on the differences between the two Talmuds; this was *The Bavli's Unique Voice*, which led to the systematic outlining.

capacities for the reading of the Mishnah. In the present exercise, by contrast, I ask a correlative, but distinct question: how do the two Talmuds define the rules of interpretation of a category-formation treated by each? That question — different from the one taken up in my *Bavli's Unique Voice* and *The Two Talmuds Compared,* animates my reading of the Bavli in the hermeneutical context.[21]

VI

Having specified the goals of the project and the means for reaching them, let me now spell out with some precision the procedures that, in the shank of the book, I follow to elicit the information that I seek. Here are the issues and how I investigate the data pertinent to them, following the outline that governs Chapters One through Six.

[1]THE DEFINITION OF A CATEGORY-FORMATION: what topics are covered within an established category-formation, corresponding to a tractate of Mishnah-Tosefta-Yerushalmi-Bavli? How is the encompassing formation defined, and what principles of selection govern the selection of data that are encompassed? Here the character of Rabbinic Judaism, defined by its dialogue with Scripture and (in some measure) the dialectics of its relationship therewith, defines the logically-consequent question: the hermeneutical stimulus, Scripture or some logic perceived internal to the native-category itself. And that leads to the second issue.

[2]THE FOUNDATIONS OF THE HALAKHIC CATEGORY-FORMATIONS: Two sources for category-formations present themselves: Scripture and some kind of autonomous logic, e.g., the organization of data through the identification of species of a common genus. In the former case these questions emerge: Does a category-formation correspond to one of Scripture, e.g., a passage of Scripture that systematically expounds a topic? An example of an affirmative case is the category-formation Negaim, which corresponds to Leviticus 13-14. An instance of a negative case is the category-formation Berakhot, which occasionally utilizes data supplied by the Written Torah but entirely on its own identifies a large category of activity and defines, divides, and organizes the pertinent data. In the later case — the working of autonomous logic — can we specify the workings of that logic? An instance of an affirmative answer comes to us from Berakhot, which organizes around the

---

[21] I do not make reference to the baraita-corpus. I have not worked on the Yerushalmi's and the Bavli's collections of statements bearing the signal, TNY, TNN, TNW RBNN, and their variations, which collectively are classified as *baraitot.* I do not have a theory on the standing of that corpus, or even whether it forms a coherent corpus. If I were working on the pre-redactional sources of the Halakhah, I should have had to examine those data in a thorough and systematic way. But my problems have been defined by the documents viewed whole, in their condition of closure, and not the sources that some maintain are taken over in the formation of the documents. I cannot point to rigorous and systematic work of any critical sophistication on the baraita- corpus.

classification of data within the genus, the individual's obligations to Heaven, a variety of species, carefully limited to those that share common traits dictated by the genus.

[3]THE EXPOSITION OF THE COMPONENTS OF A GIVEN CATEGORY-FORMATION BY THE MISHNAH-TOSEFTA-YERUSHALMI-BAVLI: This brings us to the heart of the matter. That is, the hermeneutical core of the category-formation. Here I systematically ask, how is the topic expounded in the successive documents, and what traits of mind, what theory of consequence and significance, in those documents dictate the course of exposition? Here I have to present the Halakhah, in abbreviated form, but in a comprehensive manner. I undertake to describe what each document contributes to the exposition of the Halakhic category-formation. That is where I find the data that tell me what hermeneutical principles are in play, how successive sets of sages represented by the four documents of the Halakhah mediate the category-formation in their literary labor.

I did exactly that — a presentation of the successive documentary treatments of one and the same topic — for a different purpose in my *The Halakhah. Encyclopaedia of the Law of Judaism.* There I constructed a précis of the Halakhah. articulated in detail in the four successive documents of the Halakhah. These are signaled in the following type-faces: **the Mishnah**, the Tosefta, *the Talmud of the Land of Israel,* and THE TALMUD OF BABYLONIA. Here I draw upon, but have revised, that presentation

I cite, from the Tosefta, Yerushalmi, and Bavli, only those passages that represent fresh initiatives, but not those that merely take up and amplify what has already been said. This requires a labor of selection, sorting through the types of Halakhic expositions in the Tosefta, Yerushalmi, and Bavli, with special interest in the approach to Halakhic presentation, analysis, and reconstruction particular to the successive documents in sequence. The outcome is to specify a documentary hermeneutics, e.g., the Bavli's characteristic way of analyzing a problem, the Yerushalmi's typical manner of disposing not of a passage of the Mishnah (which does not concern us here) but of a native-category received from the Mishnah.

In my repertoire for the Tosefta, Yerushalmi, and Bavli, therefore, I omit glosses and clarifications of the Mishnah's initial presentation of the Halakhah. I stipulate in advance that the successor-documents have made integral to their hermeneutics a theory of tradition that encompasses a labor of clarification. I find no need to give a great many demonstrations of that established fact. So I make no reference to what merely recapitulates the received formulation of the Halakhah in the Mishnah. I lay stress, rather, upon what is not only characteristic of the successor-compilations in sequence but original to each of them, again in sequence. Here I do not elaborately cite what the documents say, but rather describe their contribution in a few words, based on an abstract of the text.

It follows that, since the successor-documents undertake to amplify the received statement of the Halakhah that the Mishnah sets forth, my portrayal of matters omits reference to that fact. Where the Tosefta pursues its own program, where the Yerushalmi and the Bavli raise fresh questions of Halakhic description, analysis, and interpretation, there I cite, in as brief a form as possible, what is said. In general, therefore, I cite just so much of the texts as is absolutely necessary in order to make the point at hand. So while I start with already-completed work, the articulation of the project requires a very different presentation of the Halakhah from the one that served in the *Encyclopaedia.*

[4]DOCUMENTARY TRAITS: For each category-formation I conclude with some remarks upon the traits of the respective documents' expositions, seeking to generalize out of the particularities we shall have examined. That is the point at which results pertinent to the purpose of this project will emerge. I aim at laying a very, very solid foundation in data for the generalizations that I shall systematically set forth in the category-formations and then recapitulate at the end. These summary-remarks will prove fairly succinct, but well-founded. My initial experiment told me that I should work in pairs of documents, each set bearing its own distinctive task: the Mishnah and the Tosefta, then the two Talmuds.

Chapter Seven then summarizes the principal generic hermeneutics of the Halakhah, providing the generalizations that emerge from the detailed reconstructions.

1

Tractate Sukkah

I. THE DEFINITION OF THE CATEGORY-FORMATION

Called simply "the Festival," the festival of Tabernacles, Sukkot, commencing on the fifteenth of Tishré, the first full moon after the autumnal equinox, forms the counterpart, in the autumn, to the festival of Passover in the spring. Scripture links both to the Exodus, Passover in detail, Sukkot in general terms, e.g., Israel dwelt in booths in the wilderness, Lev. 23:40. A single pattern of exposition governs, preparation of the home, activity in the Temple. The festival of Sukkot is observed in the home in the construction and use of the Sukkah, and in the Temple, in the offerings for the occasion, just as the exposition of Passover takes up preparation of the home through removal of leaven and offerings in the Temple. Passover places Israel's freedom into the context of the affirmation of life beyond sin, Sukkot returns Israel, which has just atoned and starts a new cycle of life, to the fragility of life at God's grace, abiding in the wilderness.

Sukkot as sages portray the Festival is to be seen only in the context of the penitential season that begins with Elul, reaches its climactic moment with the judgment and atonement of the New Year and Day of Atonement, and then works its way to an elegant conclusion in Sukkot. The Aggadah, as we shall see, picks up on this very theme and makes it immediate and particular. In the rhythm of the Torah's time, Sukkot forms a meditation in deeds upon the uncertain life still open to judgment even beyond the penitential season. Israel recapitulates the life of the wilderness, after Egypt and before the Land, in Halakhic terms, beyond death, before eternal life. Then Israel takes up residence in the fragile present, not yet in the perfected life that will take place in the Land when Israel regains Eden.[1]

---

[1] In this context, we readily see the rhythm from Passover to Tabernacles and how the Halakhah identifies the foci of greatest emphasis. But why the Halakhah of the Oral Torah does not accord to Pentecost a counterpart statement is unclear to me. Perhaps the special domestic,

II. The Foundations of the Halakhic category-formations

As to the Halakhah, Scripture supplies nearly all of the pertinent facts of Sukkot, the feast of booths of tabernacles, so Lev. 23:33-43, though leaving to the Oral Torah the work of defining details:

> And the Lord said to Moses, "Say to the people of Israel, On the fifteenth day of this seventh month and for seven days is the feast of booths to the Lord. On the first day shall be a holy convocation, you shall do no menial labor. Seven days you shall present offerings by fire to the Lord; on the eighth day you shall hold a holy convocation and present an offering by fire to the Lord; it is a solemn assembly; you shall do no menial labor....On the fifteenth day of the seventh month, when you have gathered in the produce of the land, you shall keep the feast of the Lord seven days; on the first day shall be a solemn rest and on the eighth day shall be a solemn rest. And you shall take on the first day the fruit of goodly trees, branches of palm trees and boughs of leafy trees and willows of the brook; and you shall rejoice before the Lord your God seven days. You shall keep it as a feast to the Lord seven days in the year; it is a statute for ever throughout your generations; you shall keep it in the seventh month. You shall dwell in booths for seven days; all that are native in Israel shall dwell in booths, that your generations may know that I made the people of Israel dwell in booths when I brought them out of the land of Egypt; I am the Lord your God."

Numbers 29:12-38 specifies the offerings on the occasion of the festival of Sukkot, and Deuteronomy 16:13-15 specifies the use of the booth:

> "You shall keep the feast of booths seven days, when you make your ingathering from your threshing floor and your wine press; you shall rejoice in your feast, you and your son and your daughter, your manservant and your maidservant, the Levite, the sojourner, the fatherless and the widow who are within your towns. For seven days you shall keep the feast to the Lord your God at the place that the Lord will choose; because the Lord your God will bless you in all your produce and in all the work of your hands, so that you will be altogether joyful."

---

extra-cultic requirements of Passover, with the offering and leaven in mind, and of Tabernacles, with the Sukkah and the Temple rites to take up, find no counterpart in Pentecost, where nothing happens in the home. That would explain the failure to present Pentecost as a principal category of the Halakhah alongside Passover. But that does not strike me as a compelling reason, and I can think of no other, since Purim has no home rites — it is the Halakhah's only synagogue-celebration, lacking all Temple activity.

Deuteronomy assigns the feast to Jerusalem, at the same time arranging for rejoicing in the towns elsewhere.

III. The exposition of the components of the given category-formation by the Mishnah-Tosefta-Yerushalmi-Bavli.

I set forth the main points of **the Mishnah (in bold face type)**, then at the appropriate place add the Tosefta's own presentation (I repeat: not merely the clarification or amplification of the Mishnah's Halakhah) (in ordinary type), thereafter *the Yerushalmi's (in italics)*, and finally, THE BAVLI'S (IN BOLD FACE LOWER CASE TYPE). These are paraphrased and epitomized, they are not cited in full. I insert my observations on the points of special interest at the conclusion of each topical sub-unit. The units and sub-units derive from my own outline of the Mishnah-tractate, encompassing also the Tosefta-tractate; then the outline of the Yerushalmi, finally that of the Bavli.

I. The Appurtenances of the Festival of Sukkot: The Sukkah, the Lulab

A. THE SUKKAH AND ITS ROOFING

M. 1:1 **A Sukkah taller than twenty cubits is invalid. And one that is not ten handbreadths high, one that does not have three walls, or one, the light of which is greater than the shade of which, is invalid. A superannuated Sukkah is invalid. And what exactly is a superannuated Sukkah? Any which one made thirty days [of more] before the Festival [of Sukkot]. But if one made it for the sake of the Festival, even at the beginning of the year, it is valid.**

T. 1:2 A Sukkah, the light of which is greater than its shade, is invalid [M. Suk. 1:2E-F]. Under what circumstances? [When that is the case for the] upper surface. But if that is the case for the sides, even if the whole of it is full of light, it is valid.

T.1:3 If one spread Sukkah roofing on top of a bed or on top of a tree, which are ten handbreadths high, if its shade was greater than its light, it is valid. And if not, it is invalid [cf. M. Suk. 1:1C, E].

T. 1:4 The Sukkah made by shepherds, the Sukkah made by field workers in the summer, or a Sukkah which is stolen is invalid [cf. M. Suk. 1:1L]. If one made a Sukkah roofing of ropes, or with sheaves of grain, it is valid.

B. SUK. 1:1 I.11/3B-4A [IF A SUKKAH] WAS TALLER THAN TWENTY CUBITS AND ONE ATTEMPTED TO DIMINISH ITS HEIGHT BY PLACING ON THE GROUND BLANKETS AND PILLOWS, THAT DOES NOT CONSTITUTE A VALID ACT OF DIMINUTION AND THAT IS SO EVEN THOUGH THE OWNER DECLARED THE OBJECTS TO BE ABANDONED [AND NULL, OF NO VALUE WHATSOEVER] SO FAR AS ALL PARTIES ARE CONCERNED. IF HE DID SO WITH STRAW AND NULLIFIED [ITS VALUE], THIS DOES INDEED CONSTITUTE AN ACT OF VALID DIMINUTION, AND ALL THE MORE SO IF HE DID IT WITH DIRT AND NULLIFIED [ITS VALUE]. [IF A SUKKAH] WAS HIGHER THAN TWENTY CUBITS, BUT PALM LEAVES WERE HANGING DOWN WITHIN THE TWENTY CUBITS, IF THE SHADE THAT THEY CAST IS GREATER THAN THE SUNLIGHT THEY LET THROUGH, THE SUKKAH

IS VALID, AND IF NOT, IT IS INVALID. [IF A SUKKAH] WAS TEN HANDBREADTHS HIGH, AND PALM LEAVES WERE HANGING DOWN INTO THE SPACE OF TEN HANDBREADTHS, [IF] IT WAS HIGHER THAN TWENTY CUBITS, BUT THE OWNER BUILT A LEDGE IN IT ACROSS THE ENTIRE FRONT OF THE MIDDLE [OF THE THREE] WALLS OF THE SUKKAH, AND [THE LEDGE] HAS SUFFICIENT SPACE TO CONSTITUTE A VALID SUKKAH, IT IS A VALID SUKKAH. [IF THE OWNER] BUILT THE LEDGE ON THE SIDE WALL, IF FROM THE EDGE OF THE LEDGE TO THE [OPPOSITE] WALL OF THE SUKKAH IS A SPACE OF FOUR CUBITS [OR MORE], THE SUKKAH IS INVALID. IF THE SPACE FROM THE LEDGE TO THE WALL IS LESS THAN FOUR CUBITS, IT IS A VALID SUKKAH. [IT IS VALID BECAUSE THE ROOF ABOVE THE AREA BETWEEN THE LEDGE AND THE OPPOSITE WALL IS REGARDED AS A CONTINUATION OF THAT WALL WHICH THUS SERVES AS A THIRD WALL FOR THE LEDGE.] [IF A SUKKAH] WAS TALLER THAN TWENTY CUBITS, AND THE OWNER BUILT A LEDGE IN THE MIDDLE OF THE SUKKAH, IF FROM THE EDGE OF THE LEDGE TO THE WALL IS A SPACE OF FOUR CUBITS IN ALL DIRECTIONS, THE AREA IS INVALID TO SERVE AS A SUKKAH. BUT IF IT IS LESS THAN THAT SPACE, IT IS VALID. [IF A SUKKAH] WAS LOWER THAN TEN HANDBREADTHS, AND ONE MADE A HOLE IN THE GROUND OF THE SUKKAH SO AS TO FILL OUT THE SUKKAH ['S REQUISITE SPACE, FROM GROUND TO ROOF] UP TO TEN HANDBREADTHS, IF FROM THE EDGE OF THE HOLE TO THE WALL THERE IS A DISTANCE OF THREE OR MORE HANDBREADTHS, THE SUKKAH IS INVALID. IF THE DISTANCE IS LESS THAN THIS, IT IS VALID. IF A SUKKAH WAS HIGHER THAN TWENTY CUBITS, AND THE OWNER BUILT IN THE SUKKAH A PILLAR TEN HANDBREADTHS IN HEIGHT, WITH SUFFICIENT SPACE [FOUR CUBITS BY FOUR CUBITS] TO CONSTITUTE A VALID SUKKAH.

B. 1:1 IV.5/B A SUKKAH OF [BUILT BY OR FOR] GENTILES, WOMEN, CATTLE, AND OR SAMARITANS FALLS INTO THE CATEGORY OF A SUKKAH ON ALL ACCOUNTS [AND IS] VALID, SO LONG AS IT HAS SUKKAH-ROOFING IN ACCORD WITH THE LAW APPLYING TO IT.

M. 1:2 He who makes his Sukkah under a tree is as if he made it in [his] house. A Sukkah on top of a Sukkah — the one on top is valid. And the one on the bottom is invalid.

M. 1:3 .[If] one spread a sheet on top of [a Sukkah] on account of the hot sun, or underneath [the cover of boughs] on account of droppings [of the branches or leaves of the bough-cover], or [if] he spread [a sheet] over a four-post bed [in a Sukkah], it is invalid [for dwelling or sleeping and so for fulfilling one's obligation to dwell in the Sukkah]. But he spreads it over the frame of a two-poster bed.

M. 1:4 [If] one trained a vine, gourd, or ivy over it and then spread Sukkah-roofing on [one of these], it is invalid. But if the Sukkah-roofing exceeded them, or if he cut them [the vines] down, it is valid. This is the general rule: Whatever is susceptible to uncleanness and does not grow from the ground — they do not make Sukkah-roofing with it. And whatever is not susceptible to uncleanness, but does grow from the ground [and has been cut off] — they do make Sukkah-roofing with it.

T. 1:5 If one made a Sukkah roofing of stalks of flax, it is valid. [If one made a Sukkah roofing of] processed stalks of flax, it is invalid [cf. M. Suk. 1:4].

T. 1:6 [If one made a Sukkah roofing] of reeds or spears, even though one makes them adhere to one another, [the Sukkah] is valid. If one made a Sukkah roofing with sheaves, if the straw was more abundant than the grain, it is valid. And if not, it is invalid.

M. 1:5 Bundles of straw, wood, or brush — they do not make a Sukkah-roofing with them. But any of them which one untied is valid [for use as Sukkah-roofing]. And all of them are valid [as is] for use for the sides [of the Sukkah].

M. 1:8 He who makes a roof for his Sukkah out of spits or with the side-pieces of a bed — if there is a space between them equivalent to their own breadth, [the Sukkah] is valid. He who hollowed out a space in a haystack to make a Sukkah therein — it is no Sukkah.

M. 1:9 He who suspends the sides from above to below — if the [the partitions] are three [or more] handbreadths above the ground, [the Sukkah] is invalid. [If he builds the sides] from the ground upward, if [they are] ten handbreadths above the ground, [the Sukkah] is valid. [If] one sets the Sukkah-roofing three handbreadths from the walls [of the Sukkah], [the Sukkah] is invalid.

M. 1:10 A house, [the roof of] which was damaged, and on [the gaps in the roof of which] one put Sukkah-roofing — if the distance from the wall to the Sukkah-roofing is four cubits, it is invalid [as a Sukkah]. And so too, [is the rule for] a courtyard which is surrounded by a peristyle. A large Sukkah, [the roofing of which] they surrounded with some sort of material with which they do not make Sukkah-roofing — if there was a space of four cubits below it, it is invalid [as a Sukkah].

T. 1:8 A large courtyard which is surrounded by pillars — lo, the pillars are tantamount to sides [for a Sukkah] [cf. M. Suk. 1:10C]. One may make his fellow into the side of a *Sukkah, so* that he may eat, drink, and sleep in the *Sukkah* [formed with his fellow as one of the sides]. Not only so, but a person may lean a bed on its side and spread a sheet over it, so that the sunshine will not come either onto food or onto a corpse.

M. 1:11 He who makes his Sukkah in the shape of a cone or who leaned it up against a wall — it is valid. A large reed-mat, [if] one made it for lying, it is susceptible to uncleanness, and [so] they do not make Sukkah-roofing out of it. [If one made it] for Sukkah-roofing, they make Sukkah-roofing out of it, and it is not susceptible to uncleanness.

T. 1:10 A reed mat of wicker or of straw, [if it is] large, they use it for Sukkah roofing. [If it is small], they do not use it for a Sukkah roofing. And one made of [one kind of] reeds or of [another kind of reeds, [if it is] large, they use for a Sukkah roofing. [If it is] woven, they do not use it for a Sukkah roofing.

M. 2:1 He who sleeps under a bed in a Sukkah has not fulfilled his obligation.

M. 2:2 He who props his Sukkah up with the legs of a bed — it is valid. A Sukkah [the roofing of which] is loosely put together, but the shade of which is greater than the light, is valid. The [Sukkah] [the roofing of which] is tightly knit like that of a house, even though the stars cannot be seen from inside it, is valid.

M. 2:3 He who makes his Sukkah on the top of a wagon or a boat — it is valid. And they go up into it on the festival day. [If he made it] at the top of the tree or on a camel, it is valid. But they do not go up into it on the festival day. [If] two [sides of a Sukkah] are [formed by] a tree, and one is made by man, or two are made by man and one is [formed by] a tree, it is valid. But they do not go up into it on the festival day. [If] three are made by man and one is [formed by] a tree, it is valid. And they do go up into it on the festival day. This is the governing principle: In the case of any [Sukkah] in which the tree may be removed, and [the Sukkah] can [still] stand by itself, it is valid. And they go up into it on the festival day.

M. 2:4 He who makes his Sukkah among trees, and the trees are its sides [but do not form its roofing] — it is valid.

The Sukkah, open to the elements, must be freshly constructed for the occasion, counterpart to the designation of the Passover beast for the particular household and occasion. The Sukkah cannot be too tall or the roofing will not serve the contained space in particular. The roofing must leave more shade than light, and the principal validating characteristic is the correct condition of that roofing (sekhakh). The sides or walls may be supplied unconventionally, e.g., by existing pillars. The roofing must be insusceptible to uncleanness and derive from natural growth. We shall in due course have much to say about the Halakhah of the *sekhakh*, the Sukkah-roofing.

B.   THE OBLIGATION TO DWELL IN THE SUKKAH

M. 2:4 Agents engaged in a religious duty are exempt from the requirement of dwelling in a Sukkah. Sick folks and those who serve them are exempt from the requirement of dwelling in a Sukkah. [People] eat and drink in a random manner outside of a Sukkah.

T. 2:2 Sick folk and those who serve them are exempt from the requirement of dwelling in a Sukkah [M. Suk. 2:4C], and [this is the case] not only of one who is seriously ill, but even if someone has a headache or a pain in the eye.

T. 2:3 Waste matter which protrudes from a Sukkah is judged equivalent to the Sukkah. City guards by day are exempt from the religious requirement of dwelling in a Sukkah by day, but they are liable by night. City guards by night are exempt from the religious requirement of dwelling in a Sukkah by night, but they are liable by day. City guards by day and by night are exempt from the religious requirement of dwelling in a Sukkah by day and by night. Those who are out on a trip are exempt from the religious requirement of dwelling in a Sukkah by day, but they are liable by night. Garden guards and orchard guards are exempt by night, and liable by day.

M. 2:6 There is no fixed requirement, covering the number of meals one is obligated to eat in the Sukkah except for the first two nights of the festival alone.

M. 2:7 He whose head and the greater part of whose body are in the Sukkah, but whose table is in the house — it is a valid arrangement.

M. 2:8 Women, slaves, and minors are exempt from the religious requirement of dwelling in a Sukkah. A minor who can take care of himself is liable to the religious requirement of dwelling in a Sukkah.

M. 2:9 All seven days a person treats his Sukkah as his regular dwelling and his house as his sometime dwelling. [If] it began to rain, at what point is it permitted to empty out [the Sukkah]? From the point at which the porridge will spoil.

T. 2:4 [If] one was eating in a Sukkah and it rained and he went and stood somewhere else [cf. M. Suk. 2:9B], even though the rain let up, they do not obligate him to go back, until it completely stops. [If] he was sleeping in a Sukkah and it rained and he got up and went away, even though the rain let up, they do not obligate him to go back, until it is dawn.

The main point is, during the Festival, one's house is his Sukkah; he is eat, sleep, and live there, so far as possible, and to use his permanent house in a random, not in an ordinary and regular, manner. The religious obligation of the Sukkah concerns, in particular, eating there; that is the act, we recall from tractate Erubin, which establishes one's location or dwelling. At no point do we find the Tosefta's or the Bavli's reading of the topic to diverge from the Mishnah's program.

C.   THE LULAB AND THE ETROG 3:1-15

M. 3:1 A stolen or dried up palm branch is invalid. And one deriving from an asherah or an apostate town is invalid. [If] its tip was broken off, or [if] its leaves were split, it is invalid. [If] its leaves were spread apart, it is valid. Thorn-palms of the Iron Mountain are valid. A palm branch which is [only] three handbreadths long, sufficient to shake, is valid.

T. 2:7 A palm branch which is shaped like a fan, or one, most of the leaves of which were split, is invalid [vs. M. Suk. 3:1C]. A willow branch grown in a field, and one grown in the mountains, is valid. If so, why is it said, Willows of the brook (Lev. 23:40)? This is meant to exclude the kind which grows in the mountains. What is the kind which grows in the mountains? One which has teeth like a saw. What is a valid willow branch? One which has a red stem and an elongated leaf. What is an invalid willow branch? One which has a white stem and a round leaf.

M. 3:2 A stolen or dried up myrtle branch is invalid. And one deriving from an asherah or an apostate town is invalid. [If] its tip was broken off, [or if] its leaves were split, or if its berries were more numerous than its leaves, it is invalid. But if one then removed some of them, it is valid. But they do not remove [some of them] on the festival day.

2:8 A. A myrtle branch and a willow branch, of which the berries which grow on the inner side are removed, are valid [M. Suk. 3:2F]. The requisite measure of the length of a myrtle branch and a willow branch is three handbreadths, and of a palm branch, four. These four species — just as they do not diminish from their number, so too they do not add to them [other species].

M. 3:3 A stolen or dried up willow branch is invalid. And one deriving from an asherah or an apostate town is invalid. [If] its tip was broken off, [if] its leaves split, or [if it was] a mountain-willow, it is invalid. [If] it was shriveled, or [if] some of the leaves dropped off, or [if it came] from a [naturally watered] field [and did not grow by a brook], it is valid.

M. 3:5 A stolen or dried up citron is invalid. And one deriving from an asherah or from an apostate town is invalid. [If it derived from] 'Orlah-fruit, it is invalid. [If it derived from] unclean heave-offering, it is invalid. [If it derived from] clean heave-offering, one should not take it up. But if he took it up, it is valid.

And one in the status of second tithe in Jerusalem one should not carry. But if he carried it, it is valid.

T. 2:9 If one does not have a citron, he should not use a pomegranate, a quince, or any other sort of fruit. If [the four species] were wrinkled, they are valid. If they were dried up, they are invalid [cf. M. Suk. 3:1A, 2A, 3A, 5A].

T. 2:11 On the first day of the Festival a person does not fulfil his obligation to wave the lulab by using the lulab of his fellow [M. Suk. 3:13C], unless he gives it over to him as an unconditional gift.

M. 3:6 (1) [If] scars covered the greater part of it, (2) [if] its nipple was removed, (3) [if] it was peeled, split, had a hole and so lacked any part whatsoever, it is invalid. (1) [If] scars covered the lesser part of it, (2) [if] its stalk was removed, (3) [if] it had a hole but lacked no part whatsoever, it is valid. A dark-colored citron is invalid.

M. 3:9 And at what point [in the Hallel-psalms, 113-118] did they shake [the lulab]? At "O give thanks unto the Lord" (Ps. 118), beginning and end; and at, "Save now, we beseech thee O Lord" (Ps. 118:25). He who was on a trip and had no lulab [with which] to carry [out his religious duty] — when he reaches home, should carry the lulab at his own table. [If] he did not carry his lulab in the morning, he should carry it at dusk, for the entire day is a suitable time for the palm-branch.

M. 3:10 He for whom a slave, woman, or minor read answers after them by saying what they say. But it is a curse to him. If an adult-male read for him, he answers after him [only] "Hallelujah."

M. 3:11 Where they are accustomed to repeat [the last nine verses of Ps. 118], let one repeat. [Where it is the custom] to say them only once, let one say them only once. [Where it is the custom] to say a blessing after it, let one say a blessing after it. Everything follows the custom of the locality. He who buys a lulab [palm-branch, myrtle-branch, willow-branch] from his fellow in the Seventh Year — [the seller] gives him a citron as a gift. For one is not permitted to buy [the citron] in the Seventh Year. [Transactions in certain produce may not be carried on in the Seventh Year, so the citron cannot be sold or bought. The restrictions do not affect the other components of the lulab.]

M. 3:15 A woman receives the lulab from her son or husband and puts it back into water on the Sabbath. A minor who knows how to wave the lulab is liable to the requirement of waving the lulab.

Y. 3:12 I:1 *[If a minor] knows how to wave the lulab, he is liable to the requirement of waving the lulab. If he knows how to wrap himself up in a cloak, he is liable to put show-fringes on his garment. If he knows how to speak, his father teaches him the language of Torah. If he knows how to watch out for his hands, people may eat food in the status of heave-offering relying on his hands [if he touched it]. [If he knows how to keep] his body, they eat food prepared in conditions of cultic cleanness relying on his person [if the food touched it]. But he does not go before the ark [to lead the congregation in prayer], raise up his hands, or stand on the platform [as a Levitical singer], until his beard has filled out.*

The palm branch that is waved must belong to the person who does the waving and therefore carries out his religious duty therewith. This once more underscores that the obligation of the Festival is personal and individual, involving each Israelite male, his person and his property. It corresponds to the "registering" on the lamb for the Passover. The law makes provision for a number of persons to utilize the same object by having ownership transferred from one to the next by means of a gift. Hence a stolen palm branch is invalid. It must, moreover, derive from a valid tree and location, not from an asherah-tree or an apostate town. The various appurtenances are waved during the Hallel-psalms.

II.   THE RITES AND OFFERINGS OF THE FESTIVAL 4:1-5:8

A.   THE FESTIVAL RITES CARRIED OUT ON VARIOUS DAYS OF THE FESTIVAL 4:1-5:4

M. 4:1 [The rites of] the lulab and the willow-branch [carried by the priests around the altar, M. 5:5] are for six or seven [days]. The recitation of the Hallel-Psalms and the rejoicing are for eight [days]. [The requirement of dwelling in the] Sukkah and the water libation are for seven days. And the flute-playing is for five or six.

M. 4:2 The lulab is for seven days: How so? [If] the first festival day of the Festival coincided with the Sabbath, the lulab is for seven days. But [if it coincided] with any other day, it is for six days.

M. 4:3 The willow-branch [rite] is for seven days: How so? [If] the seventh day of the willow-branch coincided with the Sabbath, the willow-branch [rite] is for seven days. But [if it coincided] with any other day, it is for six days.

M. 4:4 The religious requirement of the lulab [on the Sabbath]: How so? [If] the first festival day of the Festival coincided with the Sabbath, they bring their lulabs to the Temple mount. And the attendants take them from them and arrange them on the roof of the portico. But the elders leave theirs in a special room. They teach them to make the following statement: "To whomever my lulab comes, lo, it is given to him as a gift." On the next day they get up and come along. And the attendants toss them before them. They grab at lulabs and hit one another. Now when the court saw that this was leading to a dangerous situation, they ordained that each and every one should take his lulab in his own home.

Tosefta-tractate Berakhot 6:9-10 One who makes a lulab for himself says, "Praised [be Thou, O Lord ...], who gave us life and preserved us and brought us to this occasion." When he takes it [in hand] to carry out his obligation, he says, "Praised [be Thou, O Lord ...] who has sanctified us through his commandments and commanded us concerning the taking of the lulab." And though he has said a blessing on the first day, he just recite the benediction over [the lulab] all seven [days of the festival]. One who performs any of the commandments must recite a benediction over them. One who makes a Sukkah for himself says, "Praised [be Thou, O Lord ...] who has brought us to this occasion." [One who] enters to dwell in it says, "Praised [be Thou, O Lord ... [who has sanctified us through his commandments and commanded us to dwell in the Sukkah." Once he recites a benediction over it on the first day, he need not recite the benediction again [or remaining days of the festival].

M. 4:5 The religious requirement of the willow-branch: How so? There was a place below Jerusalem, called Mosa. [People] go down there and gather young willow-branches. They come and throw them up along the sides of the altar, with their heads bent over the altar. They blew on the Shofar a sustained, a quavering, and a sustained note. Every day they walk around the altar one time and say, "save now, we beseech thee, O Lord! We beseech thee, O Lord, send now prosperity (Ps. 118:25)." And on that day [the seventh day of the willow-branch] they walk around the altar seven times. When they leave, what do they say? "Homage to you, O altar! Homage to you, O altar!"

M. 4:6 As the rite concerning it [is performed] on an ordinary day, so the rite concerning it [is performed] on the Sabbath. But they would gather [the willow-branches] on Friday and leave them in the gilded troughs [of water], so that they will not wither.

T. 3:1 The rite of the lulab overrides the prohibitions of the Sabbath at its [the festival of Sukkot's] beginning [that is, when the Sabbath coincides with the first festival day of Sukkot], and the rite of the willow branch at the end [when the seventh day's rite of the willow branch is to be done on the Sabbath].

M. 4:7 They take their lulabs from the children's hands and eat their citrons.

M. 4:8 The Hallel-Psalms and the rejoicing are for eight days: How so? This rule teaches that a person is obligated for the Hallel-Psalms, for the rejoicing, and for the honoring of the festival day, on the last festival day of the Festival, just as he is on all the other days of the Festival. The obligation to dwell in the Sukkah for seven days: How so? [If] one has finished eating [the last meal of the festival], he should not untie his Sukkah right away. But he brings down the utensils [only] from twilight onward — on account of the honor due to the last festival day of the Festival.

T. 3:2 On eighteen days in the year and on one night do they recite the Hallel psalms, and these are they: On the eight days of the Festival [of Tabernacles] [M. Suk. 4:8H], on the eight days of Hanukkah, on the first festival day of Passover and on the night preceding it, and on the festival day of Pentecost.

M. 4:9 The water-libation: How so? A golden flask, holding three logs in volume, did one fill with water from Siloam. [When] they reached the Water Gate, they blow a sustained, a quavering, and a sustained blast on the Shofar. [The priest] went up on the ramp [at the south] and turned to his left [southwest]. There were two silver bowls there. They were perforated with holes like a narrow snout, one wide, one narrow, so that both of them would be emptied together [one of its wine, flowing slowly, the other of its water, flowing quickly]. The one on the west was for water, the one on the east was for wine. [If] he emptied the flask of water into the bowl for wine, and the flask of wine into the bowl for water, he has nonetheless carried out the rite. And to the one who pours out the water libation they say, "Lift up your hand [so that we can see the water pouring out]!" For one time one [priest] poured out the water on his feet. And all the people stoned him with their citrons.

T. 3:14 There were two silver bowls on top of the altar [M. Suk. 4:9E], one for water, one for wine. The one on the west was for water [M. Suk. 4:9J]. In the normal course of approaching the altar, the one on the east was for wine [M. Suk. 4:9J], [since the priest would meet up with the one for wine as he approached the altar].

[If] he emptied the flask for water into the bowl for wine, or the bowl for wine into the flask for water, he has nonetheless carried out the rite [M. Suk. 4:9K].

T. 3:16 At what time do they pour out the water libation? Along with the offering up of the limbs of the daily whole offering. For there already was the case of the Boethusian who poured out the water on his feet, and all the people stoned him with their citrons [M. Suk. 4:9N O]. And the horn of the altar was damaged, so the sacred service was cancelled for that day, until they brought a lump of salt and put it on it, so that the altar should not appear to be damaged. For any altar lacking a horn, ramp, or foundation is invalid.

M. 4:10 As the rite concerning it [was carried out] on an ordinary day, so was the rite [carried out] on the Sabbath. But on the eve of Sabbath one would fill with water from Siloam a gold jug, which was not sanctified, and he would leave it in a chamber [in the Temple]. [If] it was poured out or left uncovered, one would fill the jug from the laver [in the courtyard]. For wine and water which have been left uncovered are invalid for the altar.

T. 3:17 The water used for the water libation on the Festival [of Tabernacles] — one is liable on its account by reason of violation of the laws of remnant, refuse, and uncleanness. Therefore if it was kept overnight or contracted uncleanness, it goes forth to the place of burning. But the jug and flask themselves are subject to the laws of sacrilege [if filled from the laver, M. Suk. 4:10D], for they themselves are holy [cf. M. Suk. 4:10B].

M. 5:1 Flute-playing is for five or six [days]: This refers to the flute-playing at the place of the water-drawing, which overrides the restrictions neither of the Sabbath nor of a festival-day.

M. 5:2 At the end of the first festival day of the Festival [the priests and Levites] went down to the woman's courtyard. And they made a major enactment [by putting men below and women above]. And there were golden candle-holders there, with four gold bowls on their tops, and four ladders for each candle stick. And four young priests with jars of oil containing a hundred and twenty logs, [would climb up the ladders and] pour [the oil] into each bowl.

M. 5:3 Out of the worn-out undergarments and girdles of the priests they made wicks, and with them they lit the candles. And there was not a courtyard in Jerusalem which was not lit up from the light of *bet hasho'ebah.*

M. 5:4 The pious men and wonder-workers would dance before them, with flaming torches in their hand, and they would sing before them songs and praises. And the Levites played on harps, lyres, cymbals, trumpets, and [other] musical instruments beyond counting, [standing, as they played] on the fifteen steps which go down from the Israelites' court to the women's court. corresponding to the fifteen Songs of Ascents which are in the Book of Psalms — on these the Levites stand with their instrument and sing their song. And two priests stood at the upper gate which goes down from the Israelites' court to the women's court, with two trumpets in their hands. [When] the cock crowed, they sounded a sustained, a quavering, and a sustained blast on the Shofar. [When] they got to the tenth step, they sounded a sustained, a quavering, and a sustained blast on the Shofar. [When] they reached the courtyard, they sounded a sustained, a quavering, and a sustained blast on the Shofar. They went on sounding the Shofar in a sustained blast until they reached the gate which leads out to the east. [When] they reached the gate which goes out toward the east, they turned around toward the west, and they said, "Our fathers who were in this place turned with their backs toward the Temple of the Lord and their faces toward the east, and they worshipped the sun toward the east (Ez. 8:16). "But as to us, our eyes are toward the Lord."

T. 4:7 And Levites [played on] harps, lyres, cymbals, and all sorts of musical instruments [M. Suk. 5:4C]. What did they sing? A song of ascents. Come, bless the Lord, all you servants of the Lord who stand by night in the house of the Lord (Ps. 134:1).

T. 4:8 Some of them would sing, Lift up your hands to the holy place and bless the Lord (Ps. 134:2).

T. 4:10 And two priests stood at the upper gate which goes down from the Israelites' court to the women's court, with two trumpets in their hands [M. Suk. 5:4G]. When the cock crowed, they sounded a sustained, a quavering, and a sustained note on the Shofar [M. Suk. 5:4I].

Having completed the exposition of the way in which all Israel participates in the Festival, the Halakhah turns to the counterpart activities of the Temple. The premise that "Israel" is located in Jerusalem sustains the presentation, e.g., M. 4:4: bringing the lulabs to the Temple, counterpart to dealing with the Passover. We note at T. 3:2 the Tosefta's tendency to recast discussion in general terms and away from the particulars of the category-formation at hand, Sukkah. Once the activities in the Temple but not at the altar are set forth, the offerings themselves are logged in.

B.   THE OFFERINGS 5:5-8

M. 5:5 They sound no fewer than twenty-one notes in the Temple, and they do not sound more than forty-eight. Every day there were twenty-one blasts on the Shofar in the Temple: three at the opening of the gates, nine at the offering of the daily whole-offering of the morning, and nine at the offering of the daily whole-offering of the evening. And on [days on which[an additional offering [is made], they would add nine more. And on the eve of the Sabbath they would add six more: three to make people stop working, and three to mark the border between the holy day and the ordinary day. On an eve of the Sabbath which came during the festival there were forty-eight in all: three for the opening of the gates, three for the upper gate and three for the lower gate, three for the drawing of the water, three for the pouring of the water on the altar, nine for the offering of the daily whole-offering in the morning, nine for the offering of the daily whole-offering of the evening, nine for the additional offerings, three to make the people stop work, and three to mark the border between the holy day and the ordinary day.

T. 4:11 Three to make the people stop working [M . Suk. 5:5F] — how so? The minister of the synagogue takes a trumpet and goes up to the top of the highest roof in town. He begins to sound the trumpet. Those [workers] nearest town stop work, and those near the Sabbath limit come together and go inside the Sabbath limit. Now they did not go in right away, but they waited until all of them came together, then all of them came in at one time. When did he go in [to mark the Sabbath]? Once he had filled a jug of water, roasted a fish, and kindled the Sabbath light.

T. 4:12 Three to mark the border between the holy day and the ordinary day [M. Suk. 5:5F] — how so? The minister of the synagogue takes a trumpet and goes up to the top of the highest roof in town. He begins to sound the trumpet. They take the cooked dish off the stove and cover it with a warm pot and light the candle. Once he has completed sounding, even if the warm pot is in his hand, he may not cover it [the cooked dish], but he leaves it on the ground. Even if the candle is in his hand, he may not put it into the candle-holder, but he leaves it on the ground. The minister of the synagogue leaves the trumpet up there on the roof and climbs down and goes his way.

M. 5:6 On the first festival day of the Festival there were thirteen bullocks, two rams, and one goat [Num. 29:13, 16]. There remained fourteen lambs for the eight priestly watches. On the first day, six offer two each, and the remaining two, one each. On the second day, five offer two each, and the rest, one each. On the third day, four offer two each, and the rest, one each. On the fourth day, three offer two each, and the rest offer one each. On the fifth day, two offer two each, and the rest offer one each. On the sixth day, one offers two, and the rest offer one each. On the seventh, all of them are equal. On the eighth, they go back to drawing lots, as on the [other] festivals. They ruled: "Whoever offered a bullock one day should not offer one the next day. "But they offer them in rotation."

T. 4:15. All the priestly courses repeat the offering of a bullock during the seven days of the Festival a second and a third time, except for the last two, which repeat it but do not do it a third time [cf. M. Suk. 5:6].

M. 5:7 Three times a year all the priestly watches shared equally in the offerings of the feasts and in the division of the Show Bread. At Pentecost they would say to him, "Here you have unleavened bread, here is leavened bread for you." The priestly watch whose time of service is scheduled [for that week] is the one which offers the daily whole-offerings, offerings brought by reason of vows, freewill offerings, and other public offerings. And it offers everything. On a festival day which comes next to a Sabbath, whether before or after it, all of the priestly watches were equal in the division of the Show-Bread.

M. 5:8 [If] a day intervened [between a festival-day and a Sabbath], the priestly watch which was scheduled for that time took ten loaves, and the one that stayed back [in the Temple] took two. And on all other days of the year, the entering priestly watch took six, and the one going off duty took six. The ones going on duty divide at the north, and the ones going off duty divide at the south. [The priestly watch of] Bilgah always divided it in the south, and their ring was fixed, and their wall-niche was blocked up.

T. 4:19 Daily whole offerings, the offerings brought by reason of vows and ,freewill offerings land the other public offerings] [M. Suk. 5:8C], firstlings, tithes of cattle, and additional offerings of the Sabbath, sin offerings of the community and their burnt offerings, the obligatory burnt offering of an individual — the work of offering them up, and eating them, [are to be done] by the scheduled priestly watch.

T. 4:20 The Two Loaves — the work of offering them and eating them are by all the priestly watches, because they are brought as an obligation of the festival [at which time all the priestly watches are present].

T. 4:21 The Show Bread — the work of offering it is done by the scheduled priestly watch. But eating it is by all the priestly watches

T. 4:22 What does he do? He gives a half a loaf [of the twelve] to each priestly watch [of the twenty four]. And they divide it up among themselves

4:24 The outgoing priestly watch offers the morning's daily whole offering and the additional offerings.

4:25 The incoming priestly watch then offers the evening's daily whole offering and the Show Bread. On what account does the incoming priestly watch divide up its share at the north? Because that area is close to the place in which they carry out the labor [liturgy].

The Tosefta's glosses of M. 5:5 and T. 4:11, 12, show the Tosefta at its best: providing systematic, orderly clarifications of the Mishnah's succinct statements. The concluding unit, on the details of the priests' assignments, M. 5:7f., is not particular to Sukkah but is relevant.

IV. DOCUMENTARY TRAITS

As explained at the outset, what I propose to describe are those traits distinctive to the documents as autonomous statements, not those characteristics of the later documents' reception of the earlier one(s).

A. THE MISHNAH AND THE TOSEFTA

Both documents follow a single theory on the exposition of the topic; with the modest variations already noted, the Tosefta closely follows the Mishnah's program. So far as we may hope to compare the hermeneutics of Rabbinic Judaism in its various components, it is not a comparison along documentary lines.

B. THE YERUSHALMI AND THE BAVLI

I find nothing to suggest that a reading of the topic, Sukkah, in all its dimensions, different from that of the Mishnah and the Tosefta impressed the compilers of the Yerushalmi or the Bavli, let alone the authors of the Halakhic compositions that they have assembled for us. But, as before, there is a considerable hermeneutical initiative taken by the Bavli's compilers in their Aggadic composition, as we shall now see.

C. THE HALAKHAH AND THE AGGADAH IN THE BAVLI

All but one of the Talmud's important, free-standing composites provide appendices to the Mishnah's own topics. With one important exception, examining the composites that do not serve as Mishnah-commentary pure and simple hardly yields a very strong case that the framers of the Talmud, in their commentary to the Mishnah, have vastly redefined the topic of the Mishnah. In no way have they imparted to it dimensions not clearly contained within the Mishnah's own presentation, or otherwise given to the Mishnah's topic a character different from that defined by the Mishnah itself. That exception is an important one, and it occupies a prominent position in context. In *Rationality and Structure,* the jarring juxtaposition serves M. 5:2 and in context is labeled XLIII.C. To understand the importance of XLIII.C, not only in size but in substance, we have to glance at my characterization of the item:

> XLIII.C: Here we deal with a genuinely important composite, and one that moves considerably beyond the limits of the Mishnah's program. Specifically, the Mishnah has invited some comments on the "evil inclination," which in this context refers to libido in particular. Then we have at XLIII.C a rather substantial discussion of sexuality. But a second look shows us that the composite concerns not sexual misbehavior or desire therefor, so much as the Messiah-theme. And that theme is not invited by the Mishnah's formulation of matters. Here are the principal propositions: [1] The Messiah son of Joseph was killed because of the evil inclination; [2] the Messiah son of David will be saved by God; [3] the evil inclination then is made the counterweight to the Messiah and a threat to his survival. It is overcome, however, by study of the Torah. The composite is hardly coherent in detail, but its thematic program — Torah, Messiah, in the context of the Festival of Tabernacles — imposes upon the topic of the Mishnah-paragraph a quite different perspective from that set forth in the Mishnah itself.

That is what I mean by the Aggadah's fresh hermeneutical theory on the reading of a Halakhic topic. Here we have an invitation greatly to enrich the Mishnah's topic — the saints' and sages' conduct in song and dance at the bonfire. But apart from the enigmatic but clearly celebratory saying attributed to Hillel, I see nothing that strays outside of the Mishnah's own framework. By contrast, XLIII.B explains why the men were located below, the women above, and, when C forthwith introduces the matter of the Messiah, the issue of improper sexual desires falls away almost at once. At that point we are given a huge and complex composite on the evil impulse, the coming of the Messiah, and the power of Torah to overcome that evil impulse. For none of these propositions has the Mishnah prepared us.

A rapid recapitulation of the propositions in the large composite tells us what the Talmud has added to the Mishnah's topic, which is, the Festival of Tabernacles. None of them has any bearing at all on the topic at hand, but by introducing the set of propositions into the present context, the topic before us is recast:

1. God created the impulse to do evil but regrets it: there are four things that the Holy One, blessed be he, regrets he created, and these are they: Exile, the Chaldeans, the Ishmaelites, and the inclination to do evil.

2. The impulse to do evil is weak at the outset but powerful when it becomes habitual. The inclination to do evil to begin with is like a spider's thread and in the end like cart ropes. In the beginning one calls the evil inclination a passer-by, then a guest, and finally, a man of the household. The impulse to do evil affects one's status in the world to come.

3. The Messiah was killed on account of the impulse to do evil. That is why the Messiah, son of David, asked God to spare his life and not allow him to be killed the way the Messiah son of Joseph was killed.

4. The impulse to do evil is stronger for sages than for others. But they possess the antidote in the Torah: "For it has done great things" (Joel 2:20): "And against disciples of sages more than against all the others." A man's inclination [to do evil] overcomes him every day. A man's inclination to do evil prevails over him every day and seeks to kill him. If that vile one meets you, drag it to the house of study. If it is a stone, it will dissolve. If it is iron, it will be pulverized.

Now, if we did not know that the Festival of Tabernacles was associated with an autumnal celebration of the advent of rain and the fructifying of the fields, on the one side, and also identified as the occasion for the coming of the Messiah, on the other, then on the strength of this extrinsic composite, we should have formed the theory that those two protean conceptions governed. As is common in Rabbinic sources, we treat in one and the same setting private life and public affairs, this world and its concerns and the world to come as well. The private life — the role of the sexual impulse in one's persona affairs and fate — and the destiny of Israel in the world to come and the Messianic future correspond. God governs in both dimensions, the personal and the political. And sages then represent the realm of affairs: suffering more than others from the desires to sin, but better able than others to resist those desires.

v. The Hermeneutics of Sukkah

a. What fuses the Halakhic data into a category-formation?

The temporary abode of the Israelite, suspended between heaven and earth, the Sukkah in its transience matches Israel's condition in the wilderness, wandering between Egypt and the Land, death and eternal life. Passover marks the differentiation of Israel, expiating sin through the Passover offering and so attaining life, from Egypt, expiating sin through the death of the first-born. For its part too Sukkot addresses the condition of Israel. It is the Israel comprised by the generation of the wilderness with which we deal, that is, the generation that must die out before Israel can enter the Land. So entering the Sukkah reminds Israel not only of the fragility of its condition but also — in the aftermath of the penitential season — of its actuality: yet sinful, yet awaiting death, so that a new generation will be ready for the Land. So it is that interstitial circumstance, between death in Egypt and eternal life in the Land,[2] that the Festival recapitulates. The now-abode of Israel-in-between is the house that is not a house, protected by a roof that is open to the elements but serves somewhat: Israel en route to death (for those here now) and then eternal life (for everyone then).

What can we say about the Halakhic hermeneutics of the Festival? It is at the Sukkah itself that I find the center of the Halakhic repertoire concerning the Festival. Without the Sukkah, all we have for the Halakhah is the log of the offerings and related Temple rites, which, we recall, the Halakhah does not supply for Pesahim (all the more so, for the absent category-formation, Pentecost!). Israel in the wilderness, replicated annually from the first New Moon after the autumnal equinox, lived in houses open to the rain and affording protection only from the harsh sunlight, shade, but not the continuous shadow such as a roof provides. Their abode was constructed of what was otherwise useless, bits and pieces of this and that, and hence, as we noted in examining the generative problematics of the Halakhah, insusceptible to uncleanness. And, we note, that is the abode in which Israel is directed to take up residence. The odd timing should not be missed. It is not with the coming of the spring and the dry season, when the booth serves a useful purpose against the sun, but at the advent of the autumn and the rainy one, when it does not protect against the rain. And it is immediately following the remarkable exaltation of the Day of Atonement: Said Rabban Simeon ben Gamaliel, "There were no days better for Israelites than the fifteenth of Ab and the Day of Atonement" (M. Ta. 4:7A).

Now the Sukkah forms an abode that cannot serve in the season that is coming, announced by the new moon that occasions the festival. Israel is to take shelter, in reverting to the wilderness, in any random, ramshackle hut, covered with what nature has provided but in form and in purpose what man otherwise does not value. Israel's dwelling in the wilderness is fragile, random, and transient — recalling the condition of Israel in the wilderness. Out of Egypt Israel atoned and lived, now, after the season of repentance, Israel has atoned and lived — replicating the situation only of the Israel of the wilderness, like the generation that, after all, had to die out before Israel could enter the Land and its intended-eternal life.

Reminding Israel annually by putting the Israelites into booths that Israel now lives like the generation of the wilderness then, sinful and meant to die, the

---

[2]Sages maintain that had Israel not sinned, the Torah would have contained only the Pentateuch and the book of Joshua, a neat way of stating in a few words the conviction that permeates the Aggadic reading of the Land as counterpart to Eden, Israel as counterpart to Adam. It is on that basis that I see the wilderness as I do: the interval between death in Egypt and eternal life in the Land. These matters do not require amplification, because they are spelled out at great length in *The Theology of the Oral Torah: Revealing the Justice of God.*

Halakhah — in its remarkable symbolic system recapitulating the Aggadic gloss of the Halakhah itself! — underscores not only transience. It emphasizes the contemporaneity of the wilderness-condition: the Sukkah is constructed fresh, every year. Israel annually is directed to replicate the wilderness generation — Scripture says no less. The dual message is not to be missed: Israel is en route to the Land that stands for Eden, but Israel, even beyond the penitential season, bears its sin and must, on the near term, die, but in death enjoys the certainty of resurrection, judgment, and eternal life to come. What we are dealing with here is a re-definition of the meaning of Israel's abode and its definition. All seven days a person treats his Sukkah as his regular dwelling and his house as his sometime dwelling. On the occasion of the Festival, Israel regains the wilderness and its message of death but also transcendence over death in the entry into the Land. Only in the context of the New Year and the Day of Atonement, only as the final act in the penitential season and its intense drama, does Sukkot make sense. It is the Halakhah that draws out that sense, in the provisions that define the valid Sukkah upon which I have laid such heavy emphasis.

True, the Written Torah tells more about the observance of the Festival of Sukkot than about the occasion for the Festival. But what it does say — "that your generations may know that I made the people of Israel dwell in booths when I brought them out of the land of Egypt" — suffices. The reversion to the wilderness, the recapitulation of the wandering, the return to Israel's condition outside of the Land and before access to the Land, the remembrance of the character of that generation, its feet scarcely dry after passing through the mud of the Reed Sea when it has already built the Golden Calf — that is the other half of the cycle that commences at Passover and concludes at Sukkot. Who can have missed the point of the Festival, with Scripture's words in hand, "that I made the people of Israel dwell in booths"? The rabbis of the Halakhah certainly did not.

Let us return to the eternal present established by the Halakhah and compare the provisions for the principal Halakhic moments in lunar-solar time, Pesahim and Sukkah. Viewing the Festival of Tabernacles in the model of the Festival of Passover, we find that three elements require attention, in two divisions: what happens in the home, what happens in the Temple, and what happens in the home that connects the home to the Temple? Passover has the home cleansed of leaven, with the result that the bread of the holiday corresponds to the bread served to God in (most of) the meal offerings. What happens in the Temple is the sacrifice of the Passover offering. What happens in the home that connects the home to the Temple is the eating of the portions of the Passover offering that the ordinary Israelite on Passover eats, just as the priest in the Temple eats portions of the sin-offering (among other Most Holy Things). So, as we have seen, Passover marks the moment at which the home and the Temple are made to correspond, the whole taking place within the walls of Jerusalem.

That perspective turns out to clarify the divisions of the Halakhah of Sukkah as well: what happens in the Temple is a celebratory rite involving the utilization of certain objects (lulab, etrog) and the recitation of the Hallel-Psalms. What happens in the home? The home is abandoned altogether, a new house being constructed for the occasion. During the Festival, the Israelite moves out of his home altogether, eating meals and (where possible) sleeping in the Sukkah, making the Sukkah into his regular home, and the home into the random shelter. Just as, in the wilderness, God's abode shifted along with Israel from place to place, the tabernacle being taken down and reconstructed time and again, so, in recapitulating the life of the wilderness, Israel's abode shifts, losing that permanence that it ordinarily possesses. What happens in the home that connects the home to the Temple? At first glance, nothing, there being no counterpart to the Passover Seder. But a second look shows something more striking. To see the connection we must recall that during the Festival a huge volume of offerings is presented day by day. There he will consume the festal offering (*Hagigah*) and other sacrificial meat, e.g., from the freewill offering. Israel removes to the housing of the wilderness to eat the Festival meat, doing in the Sukkah what God did in the Tabernacle in that epoch.

To find the religious meaning of the Halakhah of Sukkot, therefore, we must ask, what, then, does the abode in the wilderness represent? To answer that question within the framework of the Halakhah, we have to introduce two well-established facts. First, I cannot over-stress that as the Halakhah knows Sukkot, the Festival continues the penitential season commencing with the advent of Elul, reaching its climax in the season of judgment and atonement of the Days of Awe, from the first through the tenth of the month of Tishré, the New Year, and the Day of Atonement. Sukkot finds its place in the context of a season of sin and atonement. And since, as the rites themselves indicate, it celebrates the advent of the rainy season with prayers and activities meant to encourage the now-conciliated God to give ample rain to sustain the life of the Land and its people, the message cannot be missed. Israel has rebelled and sinned, but Israel has also atoned and repented: so much for the first ten days of the season of repentance.

At the new moon following, having atoned and been forgiven, Israel takes up residence as if it were in the wilderness. Why so? Because in the wilderness, en route to the Land, still-sinful Israel depended wholly and completely on God's mercy and good will and infinite capacity to forgive in response to repentance and atonement. Israel depends for all things on God, eating food he sends down from heaven, drinking water he divines in rocks — and living in fragile booths constructed of worthless shards and remnants of this and that. Even Israel's very household in the mundane sense, its shelter, now is made to depend upon divine grace: the wind can blow it down, the rain prevent its very use. Returning to these booths, built specifically for the occasion (not last year's), manipulating the sacred objects owned in particular by the Israelite who utilizes them, as the rainy season impends, the particular Israelite here and now recapitulates his total dependence upon God's mercy.

Accordingly, requiring that everything be renewed for the present occasion and the particular person, the Halakhah transforms commemoration of the wandering into recapitulation of the condition of the wilderness. The Sukkah makes the statement that Israel of the here and now, sinful like the Israel that dwelt in the wilderness, depends wholly upon, looks only to, God. Israelites turn their eyes to that God whose just-now forgiveness of last year's sins and acts of rebellion and whose acceptance of Israel's immediate act of repentance will recapitulate God's on-going nurture that kept Israel alive in the wilderness. The Halakhah's provisions for the Sukkah underscore not so much the transience of Israel's present life in general as Israel's particular condition. The Halakhah renders Israel in the Sukkah as the people that is en route to the Land, which is Eden. Yes, Israel is en route, but it is not there. A generation comes, a generation goes, but Israel will get there, all together at the end.

So in defining the Sukkah as it does, the Halakhah also underscores the given of God's providence and remarkable forbearance. In a negative way the Halakhah says exactly that at M. 2:9: "[If] it began to rain, at what point is it permitted to empty out [the Sukkah]? From the point at which the porridge will spoil. They made a parable: To what is the matter comparable? To a slave who came to mix a cup of wine for his master, and his master threw the flagon into his face." No wonder, then, that in the Aggadah Sukkot is supposed to mark the opportunity for the Messiah to present himself and do his assigned duty, which is, to bring Israel back to the Land for the raising of the dead.

B. THE ACTIVITY OF THE CATEGORY-FORMATION

The Halakhah takes as its task the presentation of three topics: [1] Temple rites, [2] home obligations, [3] special media for, and modes of, the celebration of the Festival. First comes the home rite: building the Sukkah; then we consider the media for the celebration, the lulab and etrog; finally we come to the Temple rites in their own terms and context. But the quality of the Halakhah, its intellectual energy, varies, some topics proving complex and profound, others merely interesting. So we ask, where does the Halakhah transcend the merely informative and descriptive and ask its own questions? There, where a topic is investigated through searching questions and the application of abstract principles, treated as dense and many-layered and rich in implications, we identify the focus of the Halakhah's intense interest. In the present Halakhic unit, the merely informative part concerns Temple rites, with information organized but not analyzed in the expository part of the Halakhah, the Mishnah's, the Tosefta's, and the *baraitas'* part.

We begin with the amplification of the practical requirements of how the Sukkah is constructed, defining what marks an invalid one. The Sukkah is to resemble a house but not replicate one. It is the abode of the wilderness: impermanent but serviceable under the circumstances. So the main point is, the Sukkah must resemble a dwelling, casting a shadow and affording protection from the sun. But it does not shelter from the rain, and a strong wind will knock it over. More important and definitive traits distinguish the Sukkah from the house. It must be constructed out of doors, not under a tree; it must be built for that particular holiday, meaning, the roofing *(sekhakh)* must be put up for the occasion, just as the Passover lamb must be designated for a particular sacrifier, a particular Passover-occasion (by definition, since it has to have been born after the last Passover). The roofing moreover forms the center of interest, the walls not having to be modeled on conventional housing, and the key is that the shade must exceed the light but cannot by definition block out all light. The main purpose of the impermanent abode, like that in the wilderness, then is shelter from the sun. But, as the Tosefta specifies, the form scarcely matters: If one spread Sukkah roofing on top of a bed or on top of a tree, which are ten handbreadths high, if its shade was greater than its light, it is valid. And if not, it is invalid, meaning, the walls may be provided by the most unconventional arrangements. So the ordinary house supplies not so much a model as an analogy.

What are the key provisions? The upshot is that the Sukkah must derive from man's artifice and intent; it cannot be formed of what is attached to the ground, but must be made of what has grown from the ground, what is insusceptible to uncleanness, and what has been cut down. It must come about through the deliberate action of man, a natural Sukkah being an oxymoron, and it must represent an occasion, not a permanent arrangement, a permanent Sukkah being another oxymoron. The Sukkah-roofing must afford shelter by means of what derives from nature but has been detached from nature; human intervention then is required.

But the roofing also must be insusceptible to uncleanness. That requirement hardly figures routinely, for why people should build the Sukkah, at home, out of insusceptible *sekhakh* is not self-evident. What has to be at issue, when questions of susceptibility to cultic uncleanness enter in, involves eating, specifically, eating consecrated food such as the family's portion of an offering for the holy day. So, after all, the Halakhah makes provision for the Passover offering to be eaten in a condition of uncleanness, so it is not a given of the festival seasons that appurtenances pertaining to them must be insusceptible. But if we recall that the ordinary house in which an Israelite dwells will is attached to the ground and therefore insusceptible, while important components of the Sukkah need not be attached to the ground at all — the walls may be suspended some handbreadths off the ground — we may make some sense of the rule. The insusceptibility of the *sekhakh* accommodates the separation of the abode from the earth. The temporary abode of the Israelite, where he is going to eat his share of the sacrifices to God — the peace offerings and freewill offerings occasioned by the Festival — is comparable in its function to the Temple. The Sukkah should therefore be constructed out of insusceptible materials.

But the definition of the kind of materials to be used adds a dimension to the layers of meaning attached to the Sukkah. Edible vegetation is susceptible to uncleanness as food, e.g., when someone intends to eat it. Insusceptibility to uncleanness in this context finds its definition in what is useless and not edible as food (as the Tosefta's amplification makes explicit: If one made a *Sukkah roofing* with sheaves, if the straw was more abundant than the grain, it is valid. And if not, it is invalid). Once more the Sukkah crosses lines of definition. The *sekhakh* therefore is to be the produce of nature, which man has turned to his own purpose, but produce of nature that is inedible and deemed useless and therefore insusceptible to uncleanness. A good case in point is the difference between bundled and loose straw, wood, or brush. Bundled straw or wood or brush may not serve, since in that form the straw, wood, or brush are formed into useful composites; undone, in natural form, they do serve. The upshot is, not only is the Sukkah to be fragile and makeshift, but it also is to be constructed out of materials that otherwise serve no useful purpose. In that way the random and fragile character of the dwelling is underscored.

So what serves to make a structure into a Sukkah, commemorating the dwelling of Israel in the wilderness and bringing Israel back into the wilderness for the week? It is harvested vegetable matter that man ordinarily deems useless, e.g., for food, and that in form serves no particular purpose (bundles of straw undone). Israel's abode in the Festival, then, forms the mirror-image of its ordinary abode: the walls matter only for formal reasons, the roof must serve to keep out not the rain but the sun, a temporary shelter that scarcely serves at all, a house that is not a house, a house that resembles a house in only a loose and generic way: walls that scarcely reach the ground or the roofing suffice, for instance. It is a house constructed out of otherwise valueless fragments.

To dwell in the abode of the Sukkah forms a religious obligation, an act of acceptance of God's dominion. Those engaged in carrying out other religious duties are exempt. The main point is the act of eating in the Sukkah. People eat and drink in a random manner outside of a Sukkah, but have their regular meals therein. That is principally the obligation of the first two nights of the festival. Women, slaves, and minors are exempt from the commandment of dwelling in the Sukkah, because it is an obligation that is temporally defined; women, slaves, and minors are subject to the will of others and cannot be required to do a defined deed at a particular moment, since at any given time the householder may impose upon them some obligation that prevents their complying at that specific hour.

The Halakhah's regulations treat as the counterpart to the Passover offering the lulab and etrog. The latter are utilized in the Temple, just as is the former. Just as the animal designated for the Passover offering must belong to the sacrifier and be subject to his particular ownership and will, so the palm branch, willow, and etrog must belong to the person who utilizes them; they may not be stolen or lost or borrowed, and they must meet a particular standard as to their form, just as the animal for a sacrifice must be free of blemishes. Just as, in connection with eating the Passover meat, the sacrifier recites the Hallel-Psalms, so in the utilization of the lulab and other objects, the worshipper recites those Psalms. (The former takes place at home, the latter, it is assumed, in the Temple.)

C. THE CONSISTENCY OF THE CATEGORY-FORMATION

The Halakhic hermeneutics of the Sukkah-hut itself yield the interpretative theory of the Festival as a whole; where the message of the Sukkah does not figure, I find nothing contradictory, but not much that pertains either. The category-formation of Sukkah encompasses all of the topically-relevant data but imparts its hermeneutical imprint only part of those data. And the Bavli's Aggadic hermeneutics, as we have already noticed, is still more precisely focused upon the central issue: sin and judgment and resurrection. What could better match the season of renewal brought by the autumn rains, the sure sign, as the Halakhah of Taanit will tell us, that sin has been forgiven and life renewed.

D. THE GENERATIVITY OF THE CATEGORY-FORMATION

The topic, Sukkah, requires a variety of data for a complete exposition of the rules and their meaning; but the hermeneutics of Sukkah — living now as though in the wilderness then, therefore embodying now the situation of the generation fated to die in the desert and not to enter the Promised Land that is Israel's Eden — shows its full generative power in the Aggadic juxtapositions devised by the Bavli's compilers.

2

Tractate Qiddushin

I. THE DEFINITION OF THE CATEGORY-FORMATION

Israel is sanctified in two ways: by nature, through genealogy; and by conviction realized in deed, through adherence to the Torah. Sanctification by nature comes about when an Israelite man consecrates an Israelite woman who is available to him, and when the woman consents to becoming sanctified to him. That is, she is one not married or betrothed to someone else, the governing analogy being the consecration of the offering, as we shall note. She also is not forbidden to him by reason of incest taboos or caste regulations, the governing analogy being the consecration of the priesthood. Then sanctification by nature is passed on when that union produces offspring. In these two conditions for a valid betrothal, we discern the analogical-contrastive hermeneutics of Qiddushin, as will be seen presently. Sanctification by actualized conviction, on which we dwell elsewhere (e.g., Ketubot, Sotah) but not here, takes place when through those actions specified in connection with, e.g., correct food-selection and preparation, the Israelite sustains life as life is sustained at the altar. So in creating and sustaining life Israel both *is* holy and *acts* — behaves — so as to sanctify itself. In other words, Israel both is genealogically holy and also nourishes itself in the manner required by holiness.

Here we focus on the former of the two media of sanctification, the genealogical one. To undertake the required analogical-contrastive analysis of the category-formation, Qiddushin, we begin not with the abstraction conveyed by the title, Qiddushin, "sanctification," but with the concrete matters encompassed within the native category. We work our way from these surfaces to the subterranean, interior sources of the Halakhah. The data coalesce in two matters: the procedures of betrothals and the rules of marriage between Israelite castes, with the usual heavy component of the Halakhah's generic exegesis, e.g., cases of doubt, impaired documents, and other standard issues:

I.   BETROTHALS
     A.   Rules of Acquisition of Persons and Property
     B.   Procedures of Betrothal: Agency, Value, Stipulations
     C.   Impaired Betrothal
     D.   Stipulations
     E.   Cases of Doubt

II.   CASTES FOR THE PURPOSES OF MARRIAGE
     A.   The Status of the Offspring of Impaired Marriages
     B.   Castes and Marriage Between Castes
     C.   Cases of Doubt

We deal with [1] a transaction (betrothal) and [2] its outcome (intermarriage between Israelite castes, e.g., priest to Israelite). These extend outward to the comparison and contrast of acquiring a woman and acquiring (other) property, procedures, and the usual generic-exegetical concerns with impaired results, stipulations and the fulfillment thereof, and cases of doubt; then the issue of intra-Israelite marriage across caste-lines. At stake therefore is the formation of valid marital unions, such that Heaven approves the outcome, the progeny as suitable for holy Israel. That is in two aspects: [1] correct procedure, and [2] correct partnerships, the "how" and the "who" in the formation of a marriage for the procreation of holy Israel.

What happens when the Halakhah registers is not that Israel is sanctified, but that Israelites through procreation activate and transmit their *pre-existing* condition of sanctification. Then — within the hermeneutics of analogical-contrasting analysis — to what genus and what species of said genus do the categorical data belong? For answers to that question I see two candidates. Both serve. Neither excludes the other. They work together to form of the data an integrated system of interpretation. The "how" of the formation of the marital bond that will yield holy progeny finds its Halakhic formulation in the first of the two candidates that follow, and, self-evidently, the "who" in the second, The "who" and the "how" form components of the still larger genus: sustaining and transmitting life in conditions of holiness. In both genera, holiness is understood as incarnate, physical, whether in the natural media of nourishment and procreation, whether in the social media of Israel's own genealogy and that of the nations.

[1] NATURE: PROCREATION/NOURISHMENT: The first is the genus, "the preservation and transmission of the status, sanctification through processes of nature." The comparison and contrast between species of the genus, sanctification, encompasses [A] procreation, that is, the marital bond at outset and end (as Gittin has already shown us), the act of sanctifying a woman to an Israelite man and [B] nourishment, modeled on an offering to the altar (the one requiring intentionality of both parties, the other not), and the like. The hermeneutics yielded by the analogy produces the comparison and contrast of sanctifying a beast for the altar and a woman for a man. The outcome presents no surprises, recapitulating much that we learned in our encounter with Gittin. Fundamental to the first, and the more important,

genus then are activities for sustaining life and how these are conducted in conditions of sanctification. These activities — the species of the genus — are only two, eating and sex. What is compared is the table and the bed, and what is contrasted are rules of sanctifying acts of nourishment with rules of sanctifying acts of procreation. In a moment we shall address a concrete comparison of the species of this genus, the table and the bed as media for sanctification of the woman and the crop, respectively. The language of sanctification in the present analogical-contrastive exercise thus overspreads the household in its principal functions, creating and sustaining life, in the bed as much as the table.

[2] SOCIETY: GENEALOGICAL ISRAEL AND THE NATIONS: A distinct, but correlative, genus accommodating analogy and contrast is, the genealogy of humanity, encompassing Israel and the nations: how the correct participants in procreation transmit the status of sanctification. The species of the genus, humanity, Israel, and the other species, "everybody else" ("the nations"), form a striking contrast, each linked to its respective ancestors and descendants. Here we compare and contrast holy Israel with the generality of mankind. The genus is easily speciated: one species being heavily differentiated (sub-speciated by castes, as we shall see), the other not. Then the primary task is contrastive: how are these classifications of data different? That will encompass those classes of gentiles that can enter Israel, differentiated from those that cannot; those classes of Israelites that through marriage can enter the priesthood or the Levitical caste or Israel, differentiated from those that cannot; and the like. Then the contrastive process takes two parallel paths with entry into Israel the common goal, the one differentiating among nations, the other, among Israel.

In both sets of comparisons and contrasts, "holy seed," the incarnation of the status, sanctification, figures. How in the exercises of analogical-contrastive analysis does genealogy ("the bed") in fact enter in? Transmission of caste-status provides the model. The sanctification of the priesthood is passed on through the male line, a principal consequence of genealogy. But, more broadly speaking, the Halakhah imputes to birth to an Israelite mother the caste-status of the offspring within holy Israel. If Israel is to form a kingdom of priests and a holy people, and if belonging to the holy people (without speciation in caste-status) comes about "naturally," that is, by birth to a Jewish mother, as the Halakhah everywhere takes for granted, then genealogy will take its place beside theology as arbiter of the validity of acts of betrothal.

So the native-category, Qiddushin, bears an apt and appropriate name, sanctification, in reference to its subject matter, the formation of the Israelite family, securing the transmission of Israel's sanctification genetically. The category is formed by [1] the woman who consents [2] to the man at hand and agrees to enter into a sacred relationship with him, to maintain the domestic order of the household and bear and raise children in the condition of holiness. When that relationship is characterized as holy and the result of an act of sanctification, the man's of the consenting woman, the act then confirmed by Heaven, the intent is not figurative or merely symbolic but material and concrete, and for its part genealogy is physical, genetic, not merely symbolic or "figurative," whatever that might mean. Within the walls of the Israelite household through betrothal an act of incarnate sanctification takes place that bears as weighty consequences as does an act of sanctification of an animal for an offering to God in the Temple. The transaction at hand defines the locus at which Israel attains the sanctity that God proposes to bestow on it.

What links the issue of the preservation of Israel's sanctity through the consecrated seed of Israelites together with the issue of Israel's unique genealogy and standing among the nations? It is the activity of sexuality, defined by the conditions under which sexuality is legitimately carried on. And that leads to the more encompassing question, how is sanctification "physicalized" or made incarnate within Israel? Both nourishment and procreation serve. Then how to explain in particular terms the focus on genealogy, that is, to say why genealogy (sexuality properly governed) forms the medium for transmission of Israel's holy condition? To answer that question we shall have to cross the boundaries of the Halakhah and turn to an Aggadic category, and that we shall do in due course. It suffices here to note that we deal with yet another category-formation that can be fully understood, its hermeneutics entirely set forth, only when the Aggadah and the Halakhah join together.

But, remaining entirely within the limits of the Halakhah, we ask how and where, precisely, does the transformative act of sanctification take place? Gittin has already prepared us for the answer: sanctification is always particular, this woman to this man, just as the writ of divorce must correspond to the specificities of the exchange. The governing principle of Qiddushin, comparable to that of Gittin, focuses upon the singularity of the transaction of betrothal that is compared to one with the altar and the individuality of its effects. In the Halakhah what is at issue is sanctifying a particular woman to a particular man, comparable to sanctifying a given beast to the Lord for a given, particular purpose, e.g., this animal for this classification of offering, and, in the case of a sin-offering, for this specific sin committed inadvertently in particular.

That is because in the Halakhah to "sanctify" means "in full deliberation to select in a concrete way, for a distinctive sacred purpose, not in a general way or for a generic purpose." Precision of intentionality finds its match in precision of language. The act of selecting a beast for sacrifice on the altar involves setting that beast aside from all others and designating it for the unique purpose of an offering for the sacrifier (the one who benefits, e.g., expiates sin, through the offering) carried out by the priest. The animal must be designated ("consecrated") for an offering for a singular purpose; it must be a specific type of offering, e.g., sin-offering; and the particular sin that the sacrifier has in mind must be articulated, there being no such thing as a sin-offering in general. So the act of sanctification finds its definition in the specificity of the selection, designation for a unique purpose, and performance of those rites that effect the selection and designation and carry out the purpose. Out of these concrete exchanges of intentionality matched to circumstance the transaction of sanctification produces a relationship of sanctity. Here one exercise in analogical-contrastive analysis modifies the result of another, sanctification through deed confirming intentionality being imposed on sanctification through correct genealogy. The latter, status within holy Israel, sets the necessary condition for the procreation of sanctification through genealogy. But it is not sufficient. It is the intentionality of the Israelite man that realizes the potential of sanctity inhering in the woman's capacity to procreate with him, and the consent of the Israelite woman to that realization.

The upshot is simply stated. The man possesses the power to effect consecration when he wishes to do so; his will determines. The woman is potentially sacred to any appropriate Israelite; her will decides which one, among those that present themselves. She is then made actually holy to that particular one when he asks and she agrees. So according to the details at hand by an act of will what is potential becomes real. The transaction of Qiddushin therefore involves the actualization, by the Israelite man, of the potential of sanctification inherent in the Israelite woman. If this reading of matters is valid, then the hermeneutics of analogical-contrastive analysis has produced a very particular result, and what we wish to know is whether that result — the actualization, through an act of will, of what is potential — is unique to the case or more broadly present in the system throughout? More simply stated, the question is, does the Halakhah afford other cases in which Israelite man's specific intentionality evokes in that which is subject to his will an inherent, but latent, holiness? These are the conditions we have identified: [1] the woman is subject to sanctification, but [2] until the man sanctifies her as his own and she affirms his act, her inherent status is not actualized; then it is. Not only so, but [3] the woman contains within herself the potentiality of producing holy Israel, but [4] until the man contributes the holy seed, her potentiality is not realized. To what, then, is the transaction comparable?

The realization of a potential of sanctification through an act of will finds its counterpart when we turn to the disposition of the crops of the Land of Israel raised by Israelite householders. It is the act of will confirmed by specific deeds by the Israelite householder that imparts the status of sanctification to the crop and imposes the obligation upon the householder to remove God's share in the crop, so securalizing the remainder of the crop for private use. Within the analogy afford by that Halakhic category-formation — tithing, Ma'aserot, and its companions, e.g., Terumot, Hallah, and the like — the Israelite householder through his act of will realizes in the Israelite woman her potential for sanctification, with the proviso that she join in the willful transaction by consenting. In the one case, the produce is made holy by the householder's will and made available by his separating the holy part for God; in the other, the woman is already holy, being Israel, but her sexuality is sanctified by the man's act of will to which she responds.

To spell out the comparable Halakhic category-formation: when Israel — the Israelite householder — asserts rights of possession of the crop of the Land of Israel, God's interest is aroused and he as the owner of the Land lays claim to his share in the crop, the ownership of which is held in partnership between God and the Israelite farmer. Then the rest follows, a vast exercise in how the will of God and the will of the Israelite meet in concord, Israel obeying God's laws about the disposition of the abundance of the Land. The basic principle is that when the produce is suitable for use by its owner, then it becomes subject to tithing and may not be used until it is tithed. The halakhah then indicates the point in the growth of various species at which tithes may be removed. That is the moment at which the produce is deemed edible. If someone picks and eats unripe produce, that does not impose the obligation to tithe, since the commonality of people do not regard unripe produce as food and do not eat it. Only when people ordinarily regard the produce as edible does consideration of tithing arise. Then there are two stages in the process, votive and obligatory. Crops *may* be tithed when the produce ripens. Then the produce becomes useful, and it is assumed that the farmer values the produce. But crops *must* be tithed when, by his action confirming his attitude, the farmer claims the produce as his own.

So what makes the difference? It is not the condition of the produce at all, but, rather, the attitude toward the produce that is taken by the farmer who has grown it. That attitude takes effect through the farmer's act of ownership, beyond possession. Asserting ownership takes place when he brings untithed produce from the field to the courtyard or prepares it for sale in the market. At that moment, the farmer having indicated his claim to the produce and intent to use it for his own purposes, God's interest is aroused, his share then is due. God responds to man, specifically, God's attitudes correspond to those of man: when (Israelite) man wants to own the crop and dispose of it as he wishes, then, God demands his share. God asserts his ownership when Israel proposes to exercise its rights of usufruct: when the tenant takes his share of the crop, he must also hand over to the Landowner (and to those designated by him to receive his share) the portion of the crop that owing. And until the tenant, in possession of the Land, does pay his rent, he may not utilize the crop as owners may freely do. Human actions that reveal human intentions provoke God: when the farmer indicates that he plans to dispose of the fruit, God wants his share. Martin Jaffee expresses this matter in the following *language (The Mishnah's Theology of Tithing*, p. 5):

> The fundamental theological datum of Ma'aserot...is that God acts and wills in response to human intentions. God's invisible action can be discerned by carefully studying the actions of human beings....the halakhah of Ma'aserot locates the play of God's power...in an invisible realm immune from the hazards of history...the realm of human appetite and intentions...God...acts and wills...only in reaction to the action and intention of his Israelite partner on the Land... Those who impose upon

themselves the task of reconstructing the human and social fabric of Israelite life make effective the holiness of the Land and make real the claims of its God.

From these remarks, the point of the analogy is clear. The inherent sanctification is actualized when God responds to man's will. The specific analogy is readily drawn:

[1] The woman's sexuality compares with the Land's fecundity, both bearing latent sanctity;

[2] the woman's status as a medium of sanctification is comparable to the Land of Israel's equivalent status, both bearing the power to make manifest what is latent;

[3] the man's intentionality to sanctify this woman is like the householder's intentionality to make his own the produce of the Land, and

[4] God's confirmation of the woman's sanctification to that man is comparable to the God's sanctification of the produce that the householder has designated as God's share.

God by an act of will — claiming his share — and the Israelite man by an act of will — declaring his desire — accomplish the same transformation of status, from secular to sacred. But there is an important, indeed a decisive contrast. The Land need not consent for its crops to be sanctified. But the woman must consent to enter into the relationship of sanctification to this man. So in a critical component, Israel's power of the realization of sanctity is vested in both the man and the woman. And from that contrast flows much of the Halakhah of Qiddushin that is particular to the category-formation and not generic to the Halakhah.

We see then the ultimate result of analogical-contrastive analysis: in attitude and emotion, Israelite man possessed of the power of intentionality (what he wants makes a difference) is like God. In the concrete case, the Israelite farmer and God see matters in exactly the same way when it comes to assessing the value and use of the Land and its crops, the woman and her offspring. Both parties — Israel and God — value the Land. Both furthermore regard the Israelite woman as embodying (latent) sanctification. Man's desire for the crop precipitates God's interest and effects the sanctification of the crop. Man's intentionality to sanctify that woman precipitates God's confirmation that the potential for sanctification in that woman has been realized and is now actual.

II. THE FOUNDATIONS OF THE HALAKHIC CATEGORY-FORMATIONS

No Halakhic passage of Scripture contributes to the Halakhic transaction described here.

III. THE EXPOSITION OF THE COMPONENTS OF THE GIVEN CATEGORY-FORMATION BY THE MISHNAH-TOSEFTA-YERUSHALMI-BAVLI

As always, I set forth the main points of **the Mishnah (in bold face type)**, then at the appropriate place add the Tosefta's own presentation not merely the clarification or amplification of the Mishnah's Halakhah) (in ordinary type), thereafter *the Yerushalmi's (in italics),* and finally, the Bavli's (in bold face lower case type). These are paraphrased and epitomized, they are not cited in full. I insert my observations on the points of special interest at the conclusion of each topical sub-unit. The units and sub-units derive from my own outline of the Mishnah-tractate, encompassing also the Tosefta-tractate; then the outline of the Yerushalmi, finally that of the Bavli.⁼

I.   BETROTHALS

A.   RULES OF ACQUISITION OF PERSONS AND PROPERTY

M. 1:1 A woman is acquired [as a wife] in three ways, and acquires [freedom for] herself [to be a free agent] in two ways. She is acquired through money, a writ, or sexual intercourse. And she acquires herself through a writ of divorce or through the husband's death. The deceased childless brother's widow is acquired through an act of sexual relations. And acquires [freedom for] herself through a rite of removing the shoe or through the levir's death.

T. 1:1 A woman is acquired [as a wife] in three ways, and acquires herself to be a free agent in two ways. She is acquired through money, a writ, and sexual intercourse [M. Qid. 1:1A-B]. By money — how so? [If] he gave her money or something worth money, saying to her, "Lo, you are consecrated to me," "Lo, you are betrothed to me," "Lo, you are a wife to me," lo, this one is consecrated. But [if] she gave him money or something worth money and said to him, "Lo, I am betrothed to you," "Lo, I am sanctified to you," "Lo, I am a wife to you," she is not consecrated.

T. 1:2 By a writ [— how so?] Must one say it is a writ which has a value of a perutah? But even if one wrote it on a shard and gave it to her, on waste paper and gave it to her, lo, this one is consecrated.

T. 1:3 By sexual intercourse [— how so?] By any act of sexual relations which is done for the sake of betrothal is she betrothed. But if it is not for the sake of betrothal, she is not betrothed.

T. 1:4 A man should not marry a wife until the daughter of his sister grows up or until he will find a mate suitable for himself, since it is said, "[Do not profane your daughter by making her a harlot lest the land fall into harlotry and the land become full of wickedness" (Lev. 19:29).

B. 1:1 III.51/8B [A WRIT:] A WRIT: HOW SO? IF ONE WROTE ON A PARCHMENT OR ON A POTSHERD, EVEN THOUGH THEY THEMSELVES WERE OF NO INTRINSIC VALUE, "LO, YOUR DAUGHTER IS BETROTHED TO ME," "YOUR DAUGHTER IS ENGAGED TO ME," "YOUR DAUGHTER IS A WIFE FOR ME" — LO, THIS WOMAN IS BETROTHED.

M. 1:2 A Hebrew slave is acquired through money and a writ. And he acquires himself through the passage of years, by the Jubilee Year, and by deduction from the purchase price [redeeming himself at this outstanding value (Lev. 25:50-51)]. The Hebrew slave girl has an advantage over him. For she acquires herself [in addition] through the appearance of tokens [of puberty]. The slave

whose ear is pierced is acquired through an act of piercing the ear (Ex. 21:5). And he acquires himself by the Jubilee and by the death of the master.

T. 1:5 How does [he redeem himself] by deduction from the purchase price [at his outstanding value] [M. Qid. 1:2B]? [If] he wanted to redeem himself during these years, he reckons the value against the years [left to serve] and pays off his master. And the hand of the slave is on top [in estimating the sum to be paid]. How is usucaption [established in the case of] real estate? [If] he locked, made a fence, broke down a fence in any measure at all, lo, this is usucaption. How is usucaption [established in the case of] slaves? [If] he [the slave] tied on his [the master's] sandal, or loosened his sandal, or carried clothing after him to the bathhouse, lo, this is usucaption.

M. 1:3 A Canaanite slave is acquired through money, through a writ, or through usucaption. By money paid by himself or by a writ taken on by others, on condition that the money belongs to others.

B. 1:3 I.5/22B HOW IS A SLAVE ACQUIRED THROUGH AN ACT OF USUCAPTION? IF THE SLAVE FASTENED THE SHOE OF THE MAN OR UNDID IT, OR IF HE CARRIED HIS CLOTHING AFTER HIM TO THE BATHHOUSE, OR IF HE UNDRESSED HIM OR WASHED HIM OR ANOINTED HIM OR SCRAPED HIM OR DRESSED HIM OR PUT ON HIS SHOES OR LIFTED HIM UP, THE MAN ACQUIRES TITLE TO THE SLAVE.'

M. 1:4 Large cattle are acquired through delivery [of the bit or bridle]. Small cattle are acquired through an act of drawing [the beast by force majeure].

T. 1:8 What is an act of delivery [M. Qid. 1:4A]? Any act in which he handed over to him the bit or the bridle — lo, this is an act of delivery. Under what circumstances did they rule, Movables are acquired through drawing? In the public domain or in a courtyard which does not belong to either one of them. But if it is the domain of the purchaser, once he has taken upon himself [to pay the agreed upon sum], he has acquired the thing. [And if it is] in the domain of the seller, once he has raised up the object or after he has taken it out from the domain of the owner [it has been acquired]. In the domain of this one in whose hands the bailment is located, an act of acquisition is carried out when he [the owner] will have taken it upon himself [to allow the buyer a portion of the premises to effect an acquisition] or when he [the purchaser] will have rented their place for himself.

M. 1:5 Property for which there is security is acquired through money, writ, and usucaption. And that for which there is no security is acquired only by an act of drawing [from one place to another]. Property for which there is no security is acquired along with property for which there is security through money, writ, and usucaption. And property for which there is no security imposes the need for an oath on property for which there is security.

M. 1:6 Whatever is used as payment for something else — once this one has effected acquisition [thereof] the other has become liable for what is given in exchange. How so? [If] one exchanged an ox for a cow, or an ass for an ox, once this one has effected acquisition, the other has become liable for what is given in exchange. The right of the Most High is effected through money, and the right of ordinary folk through usucaption. One's word of mouth [dedication of an object] to the Most High is equivalent to one's act of delivery to an ordinary person.

T. 1:9 If one exchanged with another person real estate for other real estate, movables for other movables, real estate for movables, movables for real estate, once this one has made acquisition, the other has become liable for what is given in exchange [M. Qid. 1:6B-C]. The right of the Most High is effected through money [M. Qid. 1:6G] — how so? The Temple-treasurer who paid over coins of the Sanctuary for movables — the Sanctuary has made acquisition wherever [the movables] may be located. But an ordinary person has not made acquisition until he will have drawn [the object]. One's word of mouth [dedication of an object to the Most High is equivalent to one's act of delivery to an ordinary person [M. Qid. I:6H] — how so? "This ox is sanctified," "This house is sanctified" — even if it is located at the end of the world, the Sanctuary has made acquisition wherever it is located. But in the case of an ordinary person, he makes acquisition only when he will effect usucaption.

T. Arakhin 4:4 If a common person performed the act of drawing when the beast was worth a maneh but did not suffice to redeem the beast, paying the money, until the price rose to two hundred zuz, he must pay the two hundred. How come? Scripture says, "And he will pay the money and depart," meaning, if he has given the money, lo, these belong to him, but if not, they do not belong to him. If he performed the act of drawing when it was worth two hundred zuz but did not suffice to redeem it before the price fell to a maneh, he still has to pay two hundred zuz. How come? So that the rights of a common person should not be stronger than those of the sanctuary. If he redeemed it when it was worth two hundred but did not suffice to draw the beast before the price went down to a maneh, he has to pay the two hundred zuz. How come? Scripture says, "And he will pay the money and depart." If he redeems it at a maneh and did not suffice to perform the act of drawing before it went up to two hundred zuz, what he has redeemed is redeemed, and he pays only a maneh.

M. 1:7 For every commandment concerning the son to which the father is subject — men are liable, and women are exempt. And for every commandment concerning the father to which the son is subject, men and women are equally liable. For every positive commandment dependent upon the time [of year], men are liable, and women are exempt. And for every positive commandment not dependent upon the time, men and women are equally liable. For every negative commandment, whether dependent upon the time or not dependent upon the time, men and women are equally liable, except for not marring the corners of the beard, not rounding the corners of the head (Lev. 19:27), and not becoming unclean because of the dead (Lev. 21:1).

T. 1:10 What is a positive commandment dependent upon the time [of year, for which men are liable and women are exempt (M. Qid. 1:7C)]? For example, building the Sukkah, taking the lulab, putting Tefillin. What is a positive commandment not dependent upon the time [of year (M. Qid. 1:7D)]? For example, restoring lost property to its rightful owner, sending forth the bird, building a parapet, and putting on *Sisit*.

T. 1:11 What is a commandment pertaining to the son concerning the father to which men and women are equally liable (M. Qid. 1:7B)]? Giving him food to eat and something to drink and clothing him and covering him and taking him out and bringing him in and washing his face, his hands, and his feet. All the same are men and women. But the husband has sufficient means to do these things for the child, and the wife does not have sufficient means to do them, for others have power over her. What is a commandment pertaining to the father concerning the son [M . Qid. 1:7A]? To circumcise him, to redeem him [if he is kidnapped], and to teach him Torah, and to teach him a trade, and to marry him off to a girl. And there are those who say, "Also: to row him across the river."

M. 1:8 [The cultic rites of] laying on of hands, waving, drawing near, taking the handful, burning the fat, breaking the neck of a bird, sprinkling, and receiving [the blood] apply to men and not to women, except in the case of a every commandment which is dependent upon the Land applies only in the Land, and which does not depend upon the Land applies both in the Land and outside the Land, except for 'Orlah [produce of a fruit tree in the first three years of its growth] and mixed seeds [Lev. 19:23, 19:19], the meal-offering of an accused wife and of a Nazirite girl, which they wave.

M. 1:10 Whoever does a single commandment — they do well for him and lengthen his days. And he inherits the Land. And whoever does not do a single commandment — they do not do well for him and do not lengthen his days. And he does not inherit the Land. Whoever has learning in Scripture, Mishnah, and right conduct will not quickly sin, since it is said, "And a threefold cord is not quickly broken" (Qoh. 4:12). And whoever does not have learning in Scripture, Mishnah, and right conduct has no share in society.

T. 1:17 Whoever occupies himself with all three of them, with Scripture, Mishnah, and good conduct, concerning such a person it is said, And a threefold cord is not quickly broken (Qoh. 5:12) [cf. M. Qid. 1:10E-G].

Once more the comparison of the situation of the woman to that of the slave (Hebrew, Canaanite) figures in the Halakhah, with M. 1:1 compared to M. 1:2. The analogy is, both voluntarily surrender their will to the householder, the difference, the one is sanctified, the other merely acquired as a worker. The exposition proceeds to other classifications of the acquisition of property, now to animals and real estate and movables. Once the genus, acquisition, has been speciated into its species, woman, Hebrew slave, Canaanite slave, animals, real and movable property, we proceed to the woman's status as to her husband's and God's will. The issue is liability to keep the commandments, and these are immediately divided. The key is that for man, God's will is unmediated, but for woman, God's will and man's will both come into play. Negative commandments apply equally, positive ones do not, because a woman has obligations that take priority over commandments dependant upon a particular time or occasion, namely, caring for her children and feeding her family. M. 1:8 is tacked on, but, as my account of the comparability of woman to the Land has suggested, it is pertinent in its way.

B. PROCEDURES OF BETROTHAL: AGENCY, VALUE, STIPULATIONS

M. 2:1 A man effects betrothal on his own or through his agent. A woman becomes betrothed on her own or through her agent. A man betroths his daughter

when she is a girl on his own or through his agent. He who says to a woman, "Be betrothed to me for this date, be betrothed to me with this," if [either] one of them is of the value of a penny, she is betrothed, and if not, she is not betrothed. [If he said to her,] "By this, and by this, and by this" — if all of them together are worth a penny, she is betrothed, and if not, she is not betrothed. [If] she was eating them one by one, she is not betrothed, unless one of them is worth a penny.

T. 2:1 Just as a man does not effect a betrothal for his son, either on his own or through his agent, so a woman does not effect a betrothal for her daughter, either on her own or through her agent [cf. M. Qid. 2:1C].

T. 2:3 "Be betrothed to me with this and this," and she was eating [the pieces of fruit] one by one [M. Qid. 2:1H-I], if there remained in his possession produce worth a perutah, she is betrothed, and if not, she is not betrothed. "Be betrothed to me with this cup," if the value of the cup and of what is in it is a perutah, she is betrothed, and if not, she is not betrothed. And she has acquired both it and what is in it. "With what is in this cup," if what is in it is worth a perutah, she is betrothed, and if not, she is not betrothed . And she has acquired only what is in it alone.

M. 2:2 "Be betrothed to me for this cup of wine," and it turns out to be honey — "...of honey" — and it turns out to be of wine, "...with this silver denar" — and it turns out to be gold, "...with this gold one" — and it turns out to be silver — "...on condition that I am rich" — and he turns out to be poor, "...on condition that I am poor" — and he turns out to be rich — she is not betrothed.

T. 2:5 "Be betrothed with a sela," and after she took it from his hand, she said, "I was thinking that you were a priest, but you are only a Levite," "…that you were rich, but you are only poor," lo, this woman is betrothed. This is the principle: Once the tokens of betrothal have fallen into her hand, whether he deceived

T. 2:6 "Be betrothed to me with this sela, with this cow, with this cloak," once she has taken the sela, and drawn the cow, and made use of the cloak, lo, this woman is betrothed.

T. 2:7 "Collect this sela for me," and at the moment at which it was given over, he said to her, "Lo, you are betrothed to me," lo, this woman is betrothed. [If this happened] after she has taken it from his hand, [however,] if she agrees, then she is betrothed, but if she does not agree, she is not betrothed . "Here is this sela which I owe you," [if] at the moment of giving it over, he said to her, "Lo, you are betrothed to me," if she concurs, she is betrothed, and if she does not concur, she is not betrothed. [If this happened] after she has taken it from him, even though both of them concur, she is not betrothed. "Be betrothed to me with the sela of mine which is in your hand" — she is not betrothed. What should he do? He should take it from her and then go and give it back to her and say to her, "Lo you are betrothed to me."

T. 2:8 "Be betrothed to me with this sela," [if] after she took if from his hand, she tossed it into the ocean or into the river — she is not betrothed. "Be betrothed to me with this maneh," and she said to him, "Give it to so-and-so" — she is not betrothed. ["Give it to Mr. So-and-so,] who will receive it for me," lo, she is betrothed. [If] he gave her her tokens of betrothal but did not say to her, "Lo, you are betrothed unto me," "Be betrothed to me with this maneh," and it turns out to be a maneh lacking a denar — she is not betrothed. [If] it was a bad denar, let him exchange it for a good one.

T. 3:10 "...with this silver denar," and it turns out to be gold, she is not betrothed [cf. M. Qid. 2:2]. What should he do? He should take it back from her and go and give it to her again and say to her, "Lo, you are betrothed to me."

Y. 2:1 IV:8 "Be betrothed to me with this maneh," and it turns out to lack a denar — she is not betrothed [since she expected a whole maneh]. If there was a counterfeit denar in it, lo, this woman is betrothed, on condition that he exchange the counterfeit for a valid coin. If he was counting out the coins one by one into her hand, she has the right to retract until he completes counting out the entire sum.]

M. 2:3 "...On condition that I am a priest," and he turns out to be a Levite, "...on condition that I am a Levite," and he turns out to be a priest, "...a Netin," and he turns out to be a mamzer, "...a mamzer," and he turns out to be a Netin, "...a town dweller," and he turns out to be a villager, "...a villager," and he turns out to be a town dweller, "...on condition that my house is near the bath," and it turns out to be far away, "...far," and it turns out to be near: "...On condition that I have a daughter or a slave girl who is a hairdresser"' and he has none, "...on condition that I have none," and he has one; "...on condition that I have no children," and he has; "...on condition that he has," and he has none — in the case of all of them, even though she says, "In my heart I wanted to become betrothed to him despite that fact," she is not betrothed. And so is the rule if she deceived him.

T. 2:2 He who says to a woman, "Lo, you are betrothed to me, on condition that I am [called] Joseph," and he turns out to be [called] Joseph and Simeon, "...on condition that I am a perfumer," and he turns out to be a perfumer and a tanner, "...on condition that I am a town-dweller," and he turns out to be a town-dweller and a villager [M. Qid. 2:3E-F], lo, this woman is betrothed. [If he said, "Lo, you are betrothed to me, on condition that] I am only Joseph," and he turned out to be Joseph and Simeon, "...that I am only a perfumer," and he turned out to be a perfumer and a tanner, "...that I am only a town-dweller," and he turned out to be a town dweller and a villager, she is not betrothed.

T. 2:4 [If a man said to a woman, "Be betrothed to me] on condition that I am poor," and he was poor but got rich, "...on condition that I am rich" and he was rich and became poor, "...on condition that I am a perfumer," and he was a perfumer but became a tanner, "...on condition that I am a tanner," and he was a tanner but became a perfumer, "...on condition that I am a town-dweller," and he was a town dweller but he moved to a village, "...on condition that I am a villager," and he was a villager, but he moved to a town, "...on condition that I have children," and he had children, but then they died, "...on condition that I have no children," and he had no children, and afterward children were born to him — lo, this woman is betrothed. [If he said, however,] that he was only poor, and he was rich and became poor, that he was only rich, and he was poor and became rich, ". . .that I am only a perfumer," and he was a tanner and became a perfumer, "...that I am only a tanner," and he was a perfumer and became a tanner, "...that I am only a town-dweller," and he was a villager and became a town-dweller, "...that I am only a villager," and he was a town-dweller and became a villager, that he had no children, and he had children, but afterward they died, that he had children, and he did not have any, but afterward children were born to him, she is not betrothed. This is the principle: In the case of any condition which is valid at the moment of betrothal, even though it was annulled afterward, lo, this woman is betrothed. And in the case of any condition which is not valid at the moment of betrothal, even though it was validated afterward, lo, this woman is not betrothed.

M. 2:4 He who says to his messenger, "Go and betroth Miss So-and-so for me, in such-and-such a place," and he went and betrothed her for him in some other place, she is not betrothed. [If he said,] "...lo, she is in such-and-such a place," and he betrothed her in some other place, lo, she is betrothed.

T. 4:2 He who says to his agent, "Go and betroth for me Miss So-and-so in such-and-such a place," and he went and betrothed her in some other place — she is not betrothed. "...lo, she is in such and such a place," and he went and betrothed her in some other place, lo, this woman is betrothed [M. Qid. 2:4].

M. 2:5 He who betroths a woman on condition that she is not encumbered by vows, and she turns out to be encumbered by vows — she is not betrothed. [If] he married her without specifying and she turned out to be encumbered by vows, she goes forth without collecting her marriage contract. ...On condition that there are no blemishes on her, and she turns out to have blemishes, she is not betrothed. [If] he married her without specifying and she turned out to have blemishes, she goes forth without collecting her marriage contract. All blemishes which invalidate priests [from serving in the Temple] invalidate women.

T. 2:9 [If] he was counting out and putting into her hand one by one, she has the power to retract up to the time that he completes [counting out the specified sum]. [If in a dispute about how much was specified for a betrothal,] this one says, "With a maneh," [a hundred zuz] and this one says, "With two hundred zuz," and this one went home and that one went home and afterward they laid claim against one another and effected betrothal, if the man laid claim against the woman let the claims of the woman be carried out. And if the woman laid claim against the man, let the claim of the man be carried out. And so in the case of him who sells an object, and he was counting out [the objects] into the hand of the buyer, he has the power to retract. [If] this one claims, "[You sold it for] a maneh," and that one claims, "[You bought it for] two hundred zuz," and this one went home and that one went home, and afterward they laid claim against one another, if the purchaser laid claim against the seller, let the claim of the seller be done, and if the seller laid claim against the purchaser, let the claim of the purchaser be done.

We proceed to the generic analytical program of the Halakhah. We start with issues of procedure and agency. The token of betrothal has to bear a specific, minimal value, hence the issues of M. 2:1. The inclusion of stipulations in the husband's language, familiar from Gittin, is then addressed, M. 2:2-3; here the wife must have given consent to the actuality, and if the language of the husband has misrepresented the facts, it is an act of sanctification that has taken place in error and is null. The rules of agency recur at M. 2:4, once more with reference to the husband's statement. M. 2:5 introduces other stipulations that the husband imposes, now on the condition of not himself but his prospective wife.

    C.   IMPAIRED BETROTHAL

M. 2:6 He who betroths two women with something worth a penny, or one woman with something worth less than a penny, even though he sent along [additional] presents afterward, she is not betrothed, since he sent the presents later on only because of the original act of betrothal [which was null]. And so in the case of a minor who betrothed a woman.

T. 4:4 He who betroths a woman in error, or with something of less than the value of a perutah, and so a minor who effected an act of betrothal — even though he sent along presents afterward, she is not betrothed. For it was on account of the original act of betrothal that he sent the gifts [M. Qid. 2:6].

M. 2:7 He who betroths a woman and her daughter, or a woman and her sister, simultaneously — they are not betrothed.

M. 2:8 He [who was a priest] who betroths a woman with his share [of the priestly gifts], whether they were Most Holy Things or Lesser Holy Things — she is not betrothed.

T. 4:5 He who effects an act of betrothal by means of something which is stolen, or with a bailment, or who grabbed a sela' from her and betrothed her with it — lo, this woman is betrothed. [If] he said to her, "Be betrothed to me with the sela' which is in your hand," she is not betrothed. What should he do? He should take it from her and go and give it back to her, and say to her, "Lo, you are betrothed to me."

T. 4:6 He who betroths a woman with meat of cattle of tithe, even if it is after slaughter — she is not betrothed. [If he does so] with its bones, sinews, horns, hooves, blood, fat, hide, or shearings, lo, this woman is betrothed.

T. 4:7 He who betroths a woman, whether with Most Holy Things or Lesser Holy Things — she is not betrothed [M. Qid. 2:8A-B].

M. 2:9 He who betrothed a woman with (1) Orlah fruit, (2) with fruit which was subject to the prohibition against Mixed Seeds in a vineyard, (3) with an ox which was to be stoned, (4) with a heifer the neck of which was to be broken, (5) with birds set aside for the offering of a person afflicted with the skin ailment [Lev. 13-14], (6) with the hair of a Nazir, (7) with the firstborn of an ass, (8) with meat mixed with milk, (9) with unconsecrated animals [meat] which had been slaughtered in the courtyard [of the Temple] — she is not betrothed. [If] he sold them off and betrothed a woman with the money received in exchange for them, she is betrothed.

M. 2:10 He who consecrated a woman with food in the status of heave-offering, tithe, or gifts [to be given to the priest], purification water, purification ash — lo, this woman is betrothed, and even if she is an Israelite.

T. 4:8 He who betroths a woman by means of libation-wine, an idol, a city and its inhabitants which are slated for destruction [for rebellion], hides with a hole cut out at the heart, an asherah and its produce, a high place and what is on it, a statue of Mercury and what is on it, and any sort of object which is subject to a prohibition by reason of deriving from idolatry — in the case of all of them, even though he sold them and betrothed a woman with their proceeds — she is not betrothed [cf. M. Qid. 2:9A-C]. [If he did so] with purification-water and with purification-ash, she is betrothed [cf. M. Qid. 2:10A]. [The Israelite may not benefit from the proceeds, hence the use of the proceeds for the act of betrothal is null.]

M. 3:1 He who says to his fellow, "Go and betroth Miss So-and-so for me," and he went and betrothed her for himself — she is betrothed [to the agent]. And so: He who says to a woman, "Lo, you are betrothed to me after thirty days [have passed]," and someone else came along and betrothed her during the thirty days — she is betrothed to the second party. [If] it is an Israelite girl betrothed to a priest, she may eat heave-offering. [If he said,] "...as of now and after thirty days," and someone else came along and betrothed her during the thirty days, she is betrothed and not betrothed. [If it is either] an Israelite girl betrothed to a priest, or a priest girl betrothed to an Israelite, she should not eat heave-offering.

T. 4:2 And he who says to his fellow, "Go and betroth for me Miss So-and-so," and he went and betrothed her for himself, she is betrothed [M. Qid. 3:1A-B] to the second man.

T. 4:3 [He who says, "Lo, you are betrothed to me retroactively from now after thirty days," and a second party came along and betrothed her during the thirty days — she is betrothed [M. Qid. 3:1 F-G) to the second party [or: to both of them]. How should they arrange matters? One gives a writ of divorce, and the other marries her. If they were two brothers, she is invalidated from marrying the one or the other

T. 4:4 A creditor and an heir, one of whom went ahead and took over movable goods — lo, this one is prompt and rewarded on that account. He who says to his fellow, "Go and betroth for me Miss So-and-so," [if] he [the fellow] then went and betrothed her for himself — [or if he said to his fellow,] "Go and buy me such-and-such an item," [if] he went and bought it *for* himself, what he has done is done. But he has behaved deceitfully.

Betrothals may be impaired for various reasons. The first is that the token of betrothal must be of adequate value and must be theoretically accessible to the woman (M. 2:8-9), the second, that the woman must be free to marry him, M. 2:7. The agent must carry out the instructions. But if the agent does not but instead acts in his own account, the agent's action is valid (M. 3:1). The interstitial situations further fabricated at M. 3:1 present no surprises.

D.   UNDERLINE STIPULATIONS

M. 3:2 He who says to a woman, "Behold, you are betrothed to me, on condition that I pay you two hundred zuz" — lo, this woman is betrothed, and he must pay [her what he has promised]. "...On condition that I pay you within the next thirty days," and he paid her during the thirty days, she is betrothed. And if not, she is not betrothed. "...On condition that I have two hundred zuz," lo, this woman is betrothed, and [if] he has that sum. "...On condition that I shall show you two hundred zuz," lo, this woman is betrothed, and [if] he will show her that sum. But if he showed her the money on the table of a money changer, she is not betrothed.

T. 3:1 He who says to a woman, "Lo, you are betrothed to me through the bailment which I have in your hand," [if] she went off and found that it had been stolen or had gotten lost if [of that bailment] there was left in her possession something worth a perutah, she is betrothed, and if not, she is not betrothed. But [if it concerned] a loan, even though there was something worth a perutah left in her possession, she is not betrothed.

T. 3:2 [If he said,] "On condition that I speak in your behalf to the government," if he spoke in her behalf as people generally do it, she is betrothed, and if not, she is not betrothed. "... through the value of my speaking in your behalf to the government," if he spoke in her behalf to the value of a perutah, she is betrothed, and if not, she is not betrothed. "...through the act of labor which I shall do in your behalf," if he worked in her behalf to the value of a perutah, she is betrothed, and if not, she is not betrothed. "...on condition that I shall work with you," "...on condition that I shall labor with you tomorrow," if he did work in her behalf value to the extent of a perutah, she is betrothed, and if not she is not betrothed. "... on condition that I have two hundred zuz," lo, this woman is betrothed [M. Qid. 3:2E], for he may have that sum on the other side of the world. "...on condition that I have two hundred zuz in such-and-such a place, ' if he has the money in that place, she is betrothed, and if not, she is not betrothed.

M. 3:3 "...On condition that I have a kor's space of land," lo, this woman is betrothed, and [if] he has it. "...On condition that I have that land in such-and-such a place," if he has it in that place, she is betrothed, and if not, she is not betrothed. "...On condition that I show you a kor's space of land," lo, this woman is betrothed, and [if] he will show it to her. But if he showed her [land] in a plain [which was not his], she is not betrothed.

T. 3:3 "…on condition that I have [money] in the hand of Mr. so-and- so even though [the other party] said, "He has no money in my hand," she is betrothed. For they might have conspired to defraud her. "…until he will say that he has the money in my hand," if he said, "He has money in my hand," she is betrothed, and if not, she is not betrothed. "…on condition that I show you two hundred zuz, '' if he showed her the money on the table [of a money-changer], she is not betrothed. For he stated that he would show her only what in fact belonged to him.

T. 3:4 ".. .on condition that I have a kor of land," lo, this woman is betrothed [M. Qid. 3:3A-B], for he might have such land on the other side of the world. "…on condition that I have it in this place," if he has it in that place she is betrothed, and if not, she is not betrothed. ". . .on condition that I show you a kor of land " if he showed it to her in a plain [of public property], she is not betrothed [M. Qid. 3:3E-G]. For he stated that he would show her only what in fact belonged to him.

M. 3:5 He who betroths a woman and said, "I was thinking that she is a priest, and lo, she is a Levite," "...a Levite, and lo, she is a priest," "A poor girl, and lo, she is a rich girl," "A rich girl, and lo, she is a poor girl," lo, she is betrothed, for she has not deceived him. He who says to a woman, "Lo, you are betrothed to me after I convert to Judaism," or "after you convert," "...after I am freed" or "after you are freed," "...after your husband died," or "...after your sister dies," "after your levir will have performed the rite of removing the shoe with you" — she is not betrothed. And so he who says to his fellow, "If your wife gives birth to a girl-child, lo, [the baby] is betrothed to me" — she is not

betrothed. If the wife of his fellow indeed was pregnant and the foetus was discernible, his statement is confirmed, and if she produced a girl-child, the baby is betrothed.

T. 4:9 He who says to a woman, "Lo, you are betrothed [to me] after I convert, ' "...after you convert," "...after I am freed," "...after you are freed," "...after your husband will die," "...after your sister will die," "...after your Levir will perform the rite of Halisah with you," even though the condition is met, she is not betrothed [M. Qid. 3:5].

M. 3:6 He who says to a woman, "Lo, you are betrothed to me, on condition that I speak in your behalf to the government'" or, "That I work for you as a laborer," [if] he spoke in her behalf to the government or worked for her as a laborer, she is betrothed. And if not, she is not betrothed. "...On condition that father will concur," [if] father concurred, she is betrothed. And if not, she is not betrothed. [If] the father died, lo, this woman is betrothed. [If] the son died, they instruct the father to state that he does not concur.

T. 3:5 "...on condition that So-and-so will concur, "even though he said "I do not concur," she is betrothed. For he may concur a while later. "...unless he will say, 'I concur,'" if he says, "I concur," she is betrothed, and if not she is not betrothed.

T. 3:6 "...on condition that father agrees" [M. Qid. 3:6D], even though his father did not agree, she is betrothed. Perhaps he may agree some other time. [If] the father died, lo, this woman is betrothed. [If] the son died — this was a case, and they came and instructed the father to say, "I do not concur" [so that the woman is exempt from the Levirate connection] [M. Qid. 3:6F-G].

Stipulations in the action of betrothal are enforceable, M. 3:2-3. If the husband claims that his stipulations have not been met and the wife is not responsible for his disappointment, the betrothal remains valid.

E.   UNDERLINE CASES OF DOUBT

M. 3:7 "I have betrothed my daughter, but I don't know to whom I have betrothed her," and someone came along and said, "I have betrothed her," he is believed. [If] this one said, "I betrothed her," and [at the same time], that one said, "I betrothed her," both of them give her a writ of divorce. But if they wanted, one of them gives her a writ of divorce and one of them consummates the marriage.

T. 4:10 "I betrothed my daughter, but I do not know to whom I betrothed her," and someone came along and said, "I betrothed her" — he is believed [M. Qid. 3:7A-C] to consummate the marriage. [If] after he has consummated the marriage, someone else came along and said, "I betrothed her," he has not got the power to prohibit her [from remaining wed to the husband who got there first].

M. 3:8 [If the father said,] "I have betrothed my daughter," "...I have betrothed her and I have accepted her writ of divorce when she was a minor" — and lo, she is yet a minor — he is believed. "I betrothed her and I accepted her writ of divorce when she was a minor," and lo, she is now an adult — he is not believed. "She was taken captive and I redeemed her," whether she is a minor

or whether she is an adult, he is not believed. He who said at the moment of his death, "I have children," is believed. [If he said,] "I have brothers," he is not believed. He who betroths his daughter without specification — the one past girlhood is not taken into account.

T. 4:11 [If a man said], "I betrothed my daughter," the minors are subject to his statement, but the adults are not subject to his statement. "My daughter has been betrothed," — the adults are subject to his statement, but the minors are not subject to his statement. "I received the writ of divorce for my daughters" — the minors are subject to his statement, but the adults are not subject to his statement. "My daughter has been divorced" — the minors are not subject to his statement [cf. M. Qid. 3:8K].

T. 4:12 "She was taken captive and 1 redeemed her" [M. Qid. 3:8G], or, "She was invalidated by one of those who are invalid" [for marriage with a priest] — he has not got the power to prohibit her [from marrying a priest]. [If he said], "I have betrothed my daughter," and he had ten daughters, all of them are prohibited by reason of doubt [from remarrying without a writ of divorce]. If he said, "The oldest one," only the oldest one is deemed to have been betrothed. If he said, "The youngest," only the youngest is deemed to have been betrothed [cf. M. Qid. 3:9]. And so two brothers who betrothed two sisters — this one does not know which one of them he betrothed, and that one does not know which one of them he betrothed — both of them are prohibited by reason of doubt. But if they were engaged in the betrothal of the older girl to the older man, and the younger girl to the younger man [if] the older one says, "I was betrothed only to the older brother," then the younger sister has been betrothed only to the younger brother.

M. 3:10 He who says to a woman, "I have betrothed you," and she says, "You did not betroth me" — he is prohibited to marry her relatives, but she is permitted to marry his relatives. [If] she says, "You betrothed me," and he says, "I did not betroth you" — he is permitted to marry her relatives, and she is prohibited from marrying his relatives. "I betrothed you," and she says, "You betrothed only my daughter," he is prohibited from marrying the relatives of the older woman, and the older woman is permitted to marry his relatives. He is permitted to marry the relatives of the young girl, and the young girl is permitted to marry his relatives.

T. 4:13 "I have betrothed you, but she says, " You have betrothed only my daughter, " he is prohibited to marry the relatives of the older woman, and the older woman is prohibited to marry his relatives. And he Is permitted to marry the relatives of the younger woman, and the younger woman is permitted to marry his relatives.

M. 3:11 "I have betrothed your daughter," and she says, "You betrothed only me," he is prohibited to marry the relatives of the girl, and the girl is permitted to marry his relatives. He is permitted to marry the relatives of the older woman, but the older woman is prohibited from marrying his relatives."

T. 4:14 "I betrothed your daughter," and she says, " You betrothed only me, " he is prohibited from marrying the relatives of the younger girl, and the younger girl is permitted to marry his relatives. And he is permitted to marry the relatives of the older woman, and the older woman is prohibited from marrying his relatives [M. Qid. 3:10].

The Halakhah's facility at inventing and resolving cases of doubt finds ample instantiation here. The first, M. 3:7-8, comes about by the father's action, the second by the man's and the woman's, M. 3:10-11. The principles that govern in the resolution of doubt apply everywhere in the Halakhah.

II.   CASTES FOR THE PURPOSES OF MARRIAGE

A.   THE BASIC PRINCIPLES OF GENEALOGY. THE STATUS OF THE OFFSPRING OF IMPAIRED MARRIAGES 3:12-13

M. 3:12 In any situation in which there is a valid betrothal and no commission of a transgression, the offspring follows the status of the male, What is such a situation? It is [in particular] the situation in which a priest girl, a Levite girl, or an Israelite girl was married to a priest, a Levite, or an Israelite. And any situation in which there is a valid betrothal, but there also is the commission of a transgression, the offspring follows the status of the impaired [inferior] party. And what is such a situation? It is a widow married to a high priest, a divorcée or woman who has undergone the rite of removing the shoe married to an ordinary priest, a mamzer girl, or a Netin girl married to an Israelite, an Israelite girl married to a mamzer or a Netin. And in any situation in which a woman has no right to enter betrothal with this man but has the right to enter into betrothal with others, the offspring is a mamzer. What is such a situation? This is a man who had sexual relations with any of those women prohibited to him by the Torah. But any situation in which a woman has no right to enter into betrothal with this man or with any other man — the offspring is in her status. And what is such a situation? It is the offspring of a slave girl or a gentile girl.
T. 4:15 A priest-girl, a Levite-girl, and an Israelite-girl who were married to a proselyte — the offspring is in the status of a proselyte. [And if they married] a freed slave, the offspring is in the status of a freed slave [cf. M. Qid. 3:12].
T. 4:16 A gentile, or a slave who had sexual relations with an Israelite girl, and she produced a son — the offspring is a mamzer.

The basic principle of intra-Israelite genealogy is, the caste-status of the offspring follows that of the undoubted father. But this is forthwith qualified for a situation in which the betrothal is valid but impaired in some aspect; then the offspring follows the caste status of the inferior party. The key is, what is the status of the offspring of a slave girl or a gentile girl? The answer is, the offspring is in the status of the mother.

B.   CASTES AND MARRIAGE BETWEEN CASTES

M. 4:1 Ten castes came up from Babylonia: (1) priests, (2) Levites, (3) Israelites, (4) impaired priests, (5) converts, and (6) freed slaves, (7) Mamzers, (8) Netins, (9) "silenced ones" [shetuqi], and (10) foundlings. Priests, Levites, and Israelites are permitted to marry among one another. Levites, Israelites,

impaired priests, converts, and freed slaves are permitted to marry among
one another. Converts, freed slaves, Mamzers, Netins, "silenced ones," and
foundlings are permitted to marry among one another.

*Y. 4:1 II:5 He who converts for the sake of love [of a Jew], whether a man because of
a woman, or a woman because of a man, and so too those who converted in order
to enter Israelite royal service, and so too those who converted out of fear of the
lions [that is, the Samaritans], and so too the converts in the time of Mordecai
and Esther [who converted out of fear] — they do not accept them.*

M. 4:2 And what are "silenced ones"? Any who knows the identity of his mother
but does not know the identity of his father. And foundlings? Any who was
discovered in the market and knows neither his father nor his mother.

M. 4:3 All those who are forbidden from entering into the congregation are
permitted to marry one another.

M. 4:4 He who marries a priest girl has to investigate her [genealogy] for four
[generations, via the] mothers, who are eight: (1) Her mother, and (2) the
mother of her mother, and (3) the mother of the father of her mother, and (4)
her mother, and (5) the mother of her father, and (6) her mother, and (7) the
mother of the father of her father, and (8) her mother. And in the case of a
Levite girl and an Israelite girl, they add on to them yet another [generation
for genealogical inquiry].

M. 4:5 They do not carry a genealogical inquiry backward from [proof that one's
priestly ancestor has served] at the altar, nor from [proof that one's Levitical
ancestor has served] on the platform, and from [proof that one's learned
ancestor has served] in the Sanhedrin. [It is taken for granted that at the time
of the appointment, a full inquiry was undertaken.] And all those whose fathers
are known to have held office as public officials or as charity collectors —
they marry them into the priesthood, and it is not necessary to conduct an
inquiry.

M. 4:6 The daughter of a male of impaired priestly stock is invalid for marriage
into the priesthood for all time. An Israelite who married a woman of impaired
priestly stock — his daughter is valid for marriage into the priesthood. A man
of impaired priestly stock who married an Israelite girl — his daughter is
invalid for marriage into the priesthood.

T. 5:3 The daughter of a father of impaired priestly stock is invalid for marrying into
the priesthood for all time [M. Qid. 4:6A, D]. A girl of mixed stock is invalid for
marriage into the priesthood. [If] she was married to an Israelite, her daughter is
valid for marrying into the priesthood. A female convert and a woman of impaired
priestly stock are invalid for marriage into the priesthood. [If] she was married to
an Israelite, her daughter is valid for marriage into the priesthood. A girl taken
captive is invalid for marriage into the priesthood. [If] she was married to an
Israelite, her daughter is valid for marriage into the priesthood. A slave-girl is
invalid for marriage into the priesthood. [If] she was married to an Israelite, her
daughter is valid for marriage into the priesthood. It turns out that Israelites are a
[genealogical] purification-pool for priests, and a slave-girl is a purification-pool
for all those who are invalid.

B. 4:6-7 III.7/77A [IF A HIGH PRIEST HAD SEXUAL RELATIONS WITH] A WIDOW, A WIDOW, A
WIDOW, HE IS LIABLE ON ONLY A SINGLE COUNT; A DIVORCÉE, A DIVORCÉE, A DIVORCÉE, HE

IS LIABLE ON ONLY A SINGLE COUNT. [IF A HIGH PRIEST HAD SEXUAL RELATIONS WITH] A WIDOW, A DIVORCÉE, A WOMAN OF IMPAIRED PRIESTLY STOCK, AND A WHORE, IF IT IS IN RESPECT TO THE SAME WOMAN WHO HAS ENTERED THESE VERY CONDITIONS BY ACTIONS TAKEN IN THAT EXACT ORDER, HE IS LIABLE ON EACH COUNT. IF THE SAME WOMAN FIRST OF ALL COMMITTED AN ACT OF FORNICATION, THEN WAS PROFANED FROM PRIESTLY STOCK, THEN WAS DIVORCED, AND THEN WAS WIDOWED, HE IS LIABLE ON ONLY A SINGLE COUNT.

Israel is divided into ten castes, as specified at M. 4:1. At issue is which castes may intermarry with which others, and this is spelled out. Those "forbidden from entering into the congregation" of Israel are entirely free to intermarry. The critical issue is marriage into the priesthood, M. 4:4-6.

C.   CASES OF DOUBT 4:8-11

M. 4:8 He who says, "This son of mine is a mamzer" is not believed. And even if both parties say concerning the foetus in the mother's womb, "It is a mamzer" — they are not believed.

M. 4:9 He who gave the power to his agent to accept tokens of betrothal for his daughter, but then he himself betrothed her — if his came first, his act of betrothal is valid. And if those of his agent came first, his act of betrothal is valid. And if it is not known [which came first], both parties give a writ of divorce. But if they wanted, one of them gives a writ of divorce, and one consummates the marriage. And so: A woman who gave the power to her agent to accept tokens of betrothal in her behalf, and then she herself went and accepted tokens of betrothal in her own behalf — if hers came first, her act of betrothal is valid. And if those of her agent came first, his act of betrothal is valid. And if it is not known [which of them came first], both parties give a writ of divorce. But if they wanted, one of them gives a writ of divorce and one of them consummates the marriage.

M. 4:10 He who went along with his wife overseas, and he and his wife and children came home, and he said, "The woman who went abroad with me, lo, this is she, and these are her children" — he does not have to bring proof concerning the woman or the children. [If he said,] "She died, and these are her children," he does bring proof about the children, But he does not bring proof about the woman.

M. 4:11 [If he said], "I married a woman overseas. Lo, this is she, and these are her children" — he brings proof concerning the woman, but he does not have to bring proof concerning the children. "...She died, and these are her children," he has to bring proof concerning the woman and the children.

T. 5:6 He who went, along with his wife, overseas, and he came along with his wife and children, and said, "The woman who went overseas with me, lo, this is she, and these are her children, " does not have to bring proof concerning her or concerning the children. [If he said], "She died, and these are her children, " he brings proof concerning the children, but he does not have to bring proof concerning the woman

T. 5:7 [For] a woman is believed to say, "These are my children." And [he who says], "A woman whom I married overseas, lo this is she and these are her children, " has to bring proof concerning the woman, but does not have to bring proof concerning the children [M. Qid. 4:11].

M. 4:12 A man should not remain alone with two women, but a woman may remain alone with two men. A man may stay alone with his mother or with his daughter. And he sleeps with them with flesh touching. But if they [the son who is with the mother, the daughter with the father] grew up, this one sleeps in her garment, and that one sleeps in his garment.

T. 5:9 A woman remains alone with two men [M. Qid. 4:12A], even if both of them are Samaritans even if both of them are slaves even if one of them is a Samaritan and one a slave except for a minor, for she is shameless about having sexual relations in his presence.

T. 5:10 As to his sister and his sister-in-law and all those women in a prohibited relationship to him which are listed in the Torah — he should not be alone with them [M. Qid. 4:12A] except before two [witnesses]. But she should not be alone even with a hundred gentiles.

M. 4:13 An unmarried man may not teach scribes. Nor may a woman teach scribes.

M. 4:14 Whoever has business with women should not be alone with women. And a man should not teach his son a trade which he has to practice among women.

T. 5:14 Whoever has business with women should not be alone with women [M. Qid. 4:14D] — for example, goldsmiths, carders, [hand-mill] cleaners, peddlers, wool-dressers, barbers, launderers, and mill-stone chiselers.

Cases of doubt are resolved in accord with familiar principles, applicable everywhere. Once we speak of doubt, we proceed to the matter treated at M. 4:12. It is assumed that men are virtuous, women, profligate, and family-members meticulous in their sexual conduct with one another. That leads to the rules about proper conduct between unmarried men and women in general, and professions that lead to sinful situations.

IV. DOCUMENTARY TRAITS

A. THE MISHNAH AND THE TOSEFTA

The Tosefta's complements present no surprises; they consistently amplify and clarify matters, but I discern no point at which the Tosefta interprets the present category-formation in terms different from the Mishnah's.

B. THE YERUSHALMI AND THE BAVLI

The two Talmuds take over the Halakhah and accomplish their usual task of refinement and harmonization.

C. THE AGGADAH OF INCARNATE SANCTIFICATION

I have insisted on the actuality of the transaction of sanctification. And that has led to the clear judgment that Israel is holy in not a symbolic or merely taxonomic sense but in a physical, material way. Israel is holy, holiness incarnate in the children of Abraham, Isaac, and Jacob bearing those genealogical consequences that we have identified, the status of priesthood transferred through the father's seed, the status of Israel-ness conveyed through the mother's womb. Up to this point, however, I have not attempted to explain the mechanics of "holy seed," the power of genealogy to define a counterpart category to that of nourishment in the sanctification of Israel. To interpret the Halakhic category-formation that focuses upon genealogy, how it is transmitted, how it is preserved, we have to ask, what corpus of doctrine accounts for the conviction that Israel is Israel by reason of ancestry, not only activity. An Aggadic category, *Zekhut* — "the heritage of virtue and its consequent entitlements" thus, unearned grace — corresponds in theology to the category, genealogy, in the Halakhah. *Zekhut* refers to the empowerment of a supernatural character that derives from the virtue of one's ancestry or from one's own virtuous deeds of a very particular order, with the proviso that one has the power to transmit to his or her descendants that supernatural entitlement of grace that his or her own deeds have gained. When it is the virtue of one's ancestors that have endowed the heir with Heavenly favor, it is called "*zekhut Abot*," the unearned merit deriving from one's forefathers — hence the exact counterpart to the Halakhic category, genealogy (e.g., status as sanctified by reason of parentage, caste-status by reason of one's father's status).

Let us start with the foundation: the source of *zekhut*. What are the deeds that one does, or that one's ancestor has done, to produce *zekhut*? Such remarkable deeds involve actions favored by God but not subject to God's power to compel or command, e.g., love of God, which must be given freely or makes no difference. So too, involved is remarkable abstinence or generosity beyond the expectations of the commandments of the Torah. Whence then the lien on Heaven? It is through deeds of a supererogatory character — to which Heaven responds by deeds of a supererogatory character: acts of grace responding to acts of grace. We deal, then, with supernatural favor to this one, who through deeds done to win the favor of the other or self-abnegation or restraint exhibits the attitude that in Heaven precipitates a counterpart attitude, hence generating *zekhut*, rather than to that one, who does not. So while man cannot coerce Heaven, he can through *zekhut* gain acts of favor from Heaven, and that is by doing what Heaven cannot require: an uncoerced response of divine grace to an attitude and consequent deed of grace. Heaven thus responds to man's attitude in carrying out not his duties but more than his duties.

The character of *zekhut* such as is attained by an individual's actions is best defined by exemplary accounts of the matter, e.g., cases in which ordinary persons are endowed with supernatural power (prayers for rain being answered, for instance), which cannot be attributed to Torah-study. Ordinary folk, not disciples of sages, have access to *zekhut* entirely outside of study of the Torah. In stories not told about rabbis, a single remarkable deed, exemplary for its deep humanity, sufficed to win for an ordinary person the *zekhut* that elicits the same marks of supernatural favor enjoyed by some rabbis on account of their Torah-study. Even though a man was degraded, one action sufficed to win for him that heavenly glory to which rabbis in lives of Torah-study aspired. The mark of the system's integration around *zekhut* lies in its insistence that all Israelites, not only sages, could gain *zekhut* for themselves (and their descendants). A single remarkable deed, exemplary for its deep humanity, sufficed to win for an ordinary person the *zekhut* that elicits supernatural favor enjoyed by some rabbis on account of their Torah-study. The advantages or privileges conferred by *zekhut* may be inherited and also passed on; it stresses "entitlements" because advantages or privileges always, invariably result from receiving *zekhut* from ancestors or acquiring it on one's own; and "virtue" refers to those supererogatory acts that demand a reward because they form matters of choice, the gift of the individual and his or her act of free will, an act that is at the same time (1) uncompelled, e.g., by the obligations imposed by the Torah, but (2) also valued by the Torah one's own volition that also is beyond all requirements of the law.

What about *zekhut Abot*? One's store of *zekhut* may derive from a relationship, that is, from one's forebears. For Israel, in particular, *Zekhut* also derives from the founding saints of Israel, Abraham, Isaac, Jacob, their wives and children, and, by extension, one may acquire *zekhut* via the otherwise-unrequited actions of one's own forebears. God remembers the merit of the ancestors and counts it to the advantage of their heirs, e.g., in the Halakhah, e.g., in the liturgy for praying for rain, at M. Taanit 2:4ff.:

M. 2:4 For the first [ending] he says, "He who answered Abraham on Mount Moriah will answer you and hear the sound of your cry this day. Blessed are you, O Lord, redeemer of Israel."

M. 2:5 For the second he says, "He who answered our fathers at the Red Sea will answer you and hear the sound of your cry this day. Blessed are you, O Lord, who remembers forgotten things."

M. 2:6 For the third he says, "He who answered Joshua at Gilgal will answer you and hear the sound of your cry thus day. Blessed are you, O Lord who hears the sound of the Shofar."

M. 2:7 For the fourth he says, "He who answered Samuel at Mizpeh will answer you and hear the sound of your cry this day. Blessed are you, O Lord, who hears a cry."

M. 2:8 For the fifth he says, "He who answered Elijah at Mount Carmel will answer you and hear the sound of your cry this day. Blessed are you, O Lord, who hears prayer."

M. 2:9 For the sixth he says, "He who answered Jonah in the belly of the fish will answer you and hear the sound of your cry this day. Blessed are

you, O Lord, who answers prayer in a time of trouble." For the seventh
he says, "He who answered David and Solomon, his son, in Jerusalem,
will answer you and hear the sound of your cry this day. Blessed are
you, O Lord, who has mercy on the land."

Here is an explicit appeal to the merit acquired by the fathers in behalf of
their offspring, the genealogy of sanctification fully exposed. Not only so, but when
the sound of the Shofar is heard by God, he is reminded of the readiness of Abraham
and Isaac at Moriah to make the supreme sacrifice, and so God's mercies are aroused.
Zekhut thus extends to the heirs of the saints, and that is in proportion to the actions
of the patriarchs:

IV.6 A.   Said R. Judah said Rab, "Whatever Abraham himself did for the
             ministering angels , the Holy One, blessed be he, himself did for his
             children. Whatever Abraham did for the ministering angels through
             an errand-boy, the Holy One, blessed be he, did for his children
             through an angel.

B.   "'And Abraham ran to the herd' [is matched by] 'And there went
     forth a wind from the Lord' (Ex. 16:4).

C.   "'And he took butter and milk' [is matched by] 'Behold I will rain
     bread from heaven for you' (Ex. 17:6).

D.   "'And he stood by them under the tree' [is matched by] 'Behold, I
     will stand before you there upon the rock' (Ex. 17:6).

E.   "'And Abraham went with them to bring them on the way' [is matched
     by] 'And the Lord went before them by day' (Ex. 13:21).

F.   "'Let a little water, I pray you, be gotten' [is matched by] 'And you
     shall hit the rock, and water will come out of it that the people may
     drink' (Ex. 17:6)."

G.   *But this conflicts with what R. Hama bar. Hanina said, for R. Hama
     bar Hanina said, and so did the household of R. Ishmael teach on
     Tannaite authority,* "As a reward for three things that Abraham did,
     his heirs got three things.

H.   "As a reward for 'and he took butter and milk,' they got the manna.

I.   "As a reward for 'and he stood by them,' they received the pillar of
     cloud.

J.   "As a reward for "let a little water, I pray you, be brought,' they got
     Miriam's well."

Bavli Baba Mesia 7:1 IV.6/86b

The notion of inheriting the entitlements bequeathed by the patriarchs and
matriarchs is spelled out in a specific context. God remembers the deeds of the
patriarchs and credits their descendants with the merit thereby earned, so with
Abraham and Isaac on Mount Moriah. The merit of the patriarchs forms an
inheritance of entitled grace for Israel. *Zekhut* defines the point at which the
supererogatory action takes over, and the commandments no longer govern; then
God's love for Israel's progenitors encompasses their heirs — by reason of that

love. So much for the Aggadic counterpart to the Halakhic category-formation, genealogy. But if the Aggadah supplies an explanation for the concept of holy seed, for the physicalization of sanctification in the process of procreation, only the Halakhah works out the consequences for ordinary everyday life.

v. THE HERMENEUTICS OF QIDDUSHIN

A. WHAT FUSES THE HALAKHIC DATA INTO A CATEGORY-FORMATION?

Much of the category-formation encompasses details of the Halakhah generated by the generic hermeneutics, e.g., cases of interstitiality, mixtures, types of causation, and doubt. But some of the Halakhah, as we have seen, takes up issues particular to the category-formation before us, and that is the sector of the Halakhah for which the hermeneutics of the category-formation at hand accounts. Asking how the data fuse to form a category-formation brings us back to the analogical-contrastive analysis outlined at the outset. For what we have to explain is the union of betrothal and rules of genealogy.

THE TABLE (ALTAR) AND THE BED: What we have seen is that from the altar lines of sanctification radiate outward to encompass the table and the bed; these then form a continuous reality, the paired media for the procreation and maintenance of life. But the relationship is not only generic. Particular points of comparison emerge in the very language commonly used for both animals for the altar and women for men. That is, a woman is consecrated to a particular man, just as an animal is consecrated to the altar for the expiation of a particular inadvertent sin that has been carried out by a particular person. A sin-offering consecrated for a particular person and a specific action he has inadvertently performed proves null if it is used for another offering than the designated class, another person, or another sin by the same person. A woman consecrated for a particular man is subject to exactly the same considerations of sanctification (mutatis mutandis). In both cases the relationship is one of consecration, meaning, differentiation from all secular purposes and designated for a sacred function or task. Just as the Temple altar provides the governing comparison for the formation of the laws about the slaughter of animals for meat for the Israelite table, so the Temple altar provides the pertinent analogy for the transaction that links a selected woman to a given man in a relationship of sanctity. What marks the woman as unique is that, when she is consecrated, she makes a choice of this circumstance, not that, so to effect her sanctification she assents in an act of will responding to the act of will of the counterpart to the sacrifier, the proposed groom. Then she is Isaac at Moriah.

DEGREES OF THE POWER OF INTENTIONALITY: THE WOMAN AND THE SLAVE: Let us broaden the discussion by contrasting the power of the woman to effect an act of intentionality in the transaction of betrothal with the impotence of counterparts in her category, slaves and minors, to effect their will in any way. Along with slaves and minors, women form a classification of Israelites deemed not fully capable of independent will, intentionality, entire responsibility, and action and therefore subject not only to God's will but also to the will of another, the husband or father in the case of the woman, the master in the case of the slave, and the parent in the case of the child, thus M. Ber. 3:3: Women, slaves, and minors are exempt from the recitation of the *Shema'* and from the obligation to wear phylacteries, but are obligated to the recitation of the prayer, and to post a *mezuzah* and to recite the blessing over the meal. But they do not form part of the community of holy Israel that is obligated to recite blessings publicly, thus M. Ber. 7:2: Women, slaves or minors who ate together with adult Israelite males may not invite others to bless on their account. While comparable to slaves and minors in forming a classification of persons of lesser powers of intentionality than the Israelite man, the Israelite woman in the aspect of betrothal stands far above the others of her class.

THE WOMAN AND THE MAN: That comparison and contrast carry us to the main one: how does a woman's intentionality compare with a man's? How does she differ, even with the power to reject an act of sanctification to a particular man, from man? The analogical-contrastive process here reaches the heart of matters, and, not surprisingly, we find ourselves crossing from one category-formation to another. We begin with the one at hand and the explicit comparison of man and woman in the obligation to perform religious duties or commandments. Does the Halakhah of the (written) Torah differentiate explicitly? Indeed it does. When Scripture refers to "man," it may cover both man and woman, but special conditions yield the word-choice, so Sifra CXCV:II.1-2: "Every one Hebrew: man of you shall revere his mother and his father, and you shall keep my Sabbaths": I know only that a man is subject to the instruction. How do I know that a woman is also involved? Scripture says, "...shall revere" using the plural. Lo, both genders are covered. If so, why does Scripture refer to "man"? It is because a man controls what he needs, while a woman does not control what she needs, since others have dominion over her. Here we find in explicit language exactly the point just now registered. The householder (and his male equivalents within other social structures) is possessed of an autonomous will, like God's and in contest with God's. The woman's autonomy is limited by her father's, then her husband's will. The former pertains willy-nilly, the latter with her consent to accept the dominion of that particular man.

In a number of specific contexts, moreover, a man and woman are differentiated not in capacity to effect an act of intentionality but in the functions that they perform or to which they are obligated, e.g., M. Sot. 3:8: What is the difference between a man and a woman? A man goes around with unbound hair and torn garments, but a woman does not go around with unbound hair and torn garments (Lev. 13:44-5). A man imposes a Nazirite vow on his son, and a woman does not impose a Nazirite vow upon her son (M. Naz. 4:6). A man brings the hair offering for the Nazirite vow of his father, and a woman does not bring a hair offering for the Nazirite vow of her father . The man sells his daughter, and the woman does not sell her daughter Ex. 21:6. The man arranges for a betrothal of his daughter, and the woman does not arrange for the betrothal of her daughter (M. Qid. 2:1). A man who incurs the death penalty is stoned naked, but a woman is not stoned naked. A man is hanged after being put to death, and a woman is not hanged (M. San. 6:3-4). A man is sold to make restitution for having stolen something, but a woman is not sold to make restitution for having stolen something (Ex. 22:2). So women are subject to men, daughters to fathers, then wives to husbands; widows are assumed to return to their fathers' households. But man needs woman to complete his existence. Woman is to man as man is to God in the structure of hierarchical classification that is actualized in the Halakhah.

B. THE ACTIVITY OF THE CATEGORY-FORMATION

Now we understand why the category-formation, Qiddushin, encompasses a systematic account of the laws of acquiring various classifications of possessions, from persons to things to real estate. The problematic of the Halakhah of Qiddushin, the sanctification of a particular woman for a particular man, emerges in the intersection of the language of acquisition with the language of sanctification. A householder buys a cow, in acquiring it, he does not sanctify it. Unless he means to offer it on the altar in Jerusalem), a person who utilizes the same cow, e.g., milks it or uses it for ploughing, does not offend God. The issue of sanctification does not enter the transaction. But a householder acquires a woman thereby consecrates the woman as his wife. Another person who utilizes the same woman, e.g., has sexual relations with her and produces children by her, enormously outrages God (not to mention the husband). The category, sanctification and its opposite, applies. Yet in both instances the result is, acquiring title to, rights over the cow or the woman. Indeed, slaves, movables, and real estate prove analogous to the betrothal of a woman. The transaction by which a householder acquires a wife, slave, movables or real estate forms the genus, the language and categories and action-symbols proving constant.

But when it comes to the woman, an enormous point of difference renders the woman an active participant in the transfer of title. It is the now very familiar one: only when the woman consents does her status as person, not merely as property, change; and the change is called not merely acquisition but sanctification. So the opening exposition of the Halakhah serves to establish the genus — money, writ, usucaption for the slave, money, writ, act of sexual relations, comparable to usucaption, for the woman. These are compared and contrasted and firmly situated in a single classification: things that are acquired by the householder through a common repertoire of procedures of transfer of title from owner to owner.

The speciation commences in the comparison as to obligations of the standing before God of the woman to the man, the respective status of each being differentiated by reason of the non-negotiable obligation of a woman at specific times to home and family; that takes priority. The introduction of the exposition that stresses how men and women are equally liable, e.g., to all negative commandments and most positive ones, concludes in a remarkable manner the presentation of the modes of acquisition of women, slaves, cattle, and the like. What is remarkable is that no counterpart discussion is accorded to slaves. The difference, which is implicit, is that while women remain possessed of an autonomous will, not being subject to the unmediated will of their husbands, slaves are deemed in the law to have no autonomous will whatsoever. So the Halakhic unit that commences with the genus, the acquisition of persons and property, concludes with the distinct species, the woman, with the differentiation of the woman from all other classes of things that are acquired by the householder.

The Halakhah of sanctification of a woman to a particular man ("betrothal") pursues a fairly standard agendum of issues: agency, value, and stipulations. When it comes to agency, the point to note is that a woman may designate her own agent, just as a man does, for the transaction; a slave cannot do the same. As to value, the issue of joining together discrete items to form the requisite value for the transaction — comparable to the issue of connection — makes an appearance; the language that effects the transaction comes under discussion; and similar standard analytical questions — the impact of stipulations and conditions, met and unmet — are pursued. Stipulations not met nullify the exchange; deception has the same result. The situation prevailing at the critical turning is deemed decisive: In the case of any condition which is valid at the moment of betrothal, even though it was annulled afterward, lo, this woman is betrothed. And in the case of any condition which is not valid at the moment of betrothal, even though it was validated afterward, lo, this woman is not betrothed.

Stipulations must be met, conditions satisfied, instructions carried out. Where the woman has agreed to the transaction without deceit and bears no responsibility for an unmet stipulation or condition, the transaction takes effect; she is betrothed. How cases of doubt are sorted out receives attention. None of these discussions presents surprises, and the rules that govern are in no way particular to the topic at hand. Indeed, out of the Halakhic principles at hand one could easily construct a handbook of responsibility in ethical transactions. The premise throughout does not require articulation: the woman must consent to the transaction or it is null. But the fact that the woman can appoint an agent and establish conditions and stipulations as much as the man can bears the implication that the woman is an equal partner in the transaction and must consent to it. (That same point will come before us when we deal with the under-age girl whose father marries her off; when she comes of age, she has the right to refuse the arrangement and simply walk out of the marriage.)

God's stake in the transaction of the sanctification of a woman extends beyond individuals to the castes among which the community of Israel is distributed: priests, Levites, Israelites, and others. A man and a woman belong to a particular classification, and that governs whether or not, to begin with, sanctification is possible, sanctity takes effect in their relationship. In this regard the woman is like the crop of the Land of Israel: she is potentially holy, for reasons already spelled out becoming holy by the matched acts of will of the husband and the betrothed and God. That potentiality then accounts for the specification of genealogically-unacceptable unions. The Written Torah defines the classifications of persons who may not intermarry — gentiles do not enter the picture — within the purview of the Torah. A woman's personal status is affected by prior unions, e.g. a marriage to a man to whom the Torah prohibits her, such as a widow to a high priest, a divorcée or equivalent to an ordinary priest, the mamzer (child of parents legally unable ever to marry, such as a brother and a sister, or a married woman and a man other than her husband) to an ordinary Israelite, and so on. These castes are defined in the Halakhah, exquisitely summarized at M. 4:1's catalogue of ten castes.

Here we see how the metaphor of the altar overspreads the formation of the household's family unit. The effect of an act of betrothal is qualified by the caste status of the parties to the betrothal. Just as blemished beasts are not susceptible of sanctification for the altar, so persons of blemished genealogy cannot enter into consecrated relationships with those of unblemished family. The family that forms the foundation of the household then compares with the offering on the altar. What the Halakhah does is extend to the entire community of Israel the Written Torah's intense interest in the eugenics of the priesthood — thus, once more, the now-familiar pattern, at the critical points, of appealing to the altar for a paradigm of the household.

C. THE CONSISTENCY OF THE CATEGORY-FORMATION

The opening exposition accounts for the coherence of the sub-topics of the category-formation, Qiddushin, and shows how they coalesce. But, as we have seen, the category-formation, Qiddushin, works out its interests in the generic hermeneutics of the Halakhah, not so much in the particular hermeneutics of the present category-formation.

D. THE GENERATIVITY OF THE CATEGORY-FORMATION

How does the category-formation extend its reach to encompass a variety of particulars, not encompassed by definition within the category, the sanctification of a woman by a man for the purposes of procreation? Let us start with an obvious point of generativity, the extension of the Halakhah of betrothal to cover all manner of acquisitions. The act of betrothal forms a particular detail of the larger theory of how a man acquires title to, or possession of, persons or property of various classifications. That is the this-worldly side of the Halakhah; the transcendent part emerges with the result: the sanctification of the relationship between a particular woman and a particular man, so that she is consecrated to him and to no other.[1] The upshot is, just as a farmer acquired a slave or an ox or real estate, so he effected possession of, gained title to, a woman. But while the slave or ox or field could never be called "consecrated" to that particular farmer, so that the language of sanctification never operates in such transactions, the act of acquisition of a woman also transformed the relationship of the woman not only to that man who acquired her but to all other men.

But that is only a detail. Where do we encounter the power of the category-formation to make its own a considerable range of topics? We understand the answer when we step back and identify the truly fundamental exercise of analogy and contrast that has nurtured the laws before us. The paramount analogy is the one not made explicit within the Halakhah at all but that is everywhere implicit: Israel as a whole is like the priesthood, "a kingdom of priests and a holy people." If I had to select the generative analogy at the foundation of all else, that is the one I should choose, and it accounts for the generativity of the entire category-formation at hand. As much as food defines a dimension of sanctification, so too, sex and genealogy, the foundations of the Israelite household, invoke the same consideration and accord with the same governing metaphor, that of the Temple and its altar. Within the walls of the Israelite household is recapitulated the basic conception of valid or invalid marital bonds that, to begin with, Scripture legislates for the priesthood. The Written Torah leaves no doubt that God deems a matter of sanctification that Israel conduct its sexual life in the model of the sanctity of its cultic life. The fundamental premise of the Halakhah is that as God oversees the conduct of Temple priests, so God closely watches the conduct of Israel in all that has to do with maintaining life, food and sex above all. But the metaphor of the Temple and priesthood for the household and family is vastly transcended, as we shall see.

Accordingly, when we turn from the sustenance of life to its creation, we move in a straight path from the table to the bed. Both form essential components in sanctifying Israel, and, as we now see, in both matters the same principle governs, just as a single set of conceptions, having to do with the health of the animal and the disposition of its blood, for example, unify the Israelite table and the altar of the Temple in Jerusalem. So the Israelite table and the Temple altar stand on a single continuum, subject to the same rules (where applicable and appropriate). The same is so when we come to the procreation of life, the process of forming, maintaining, and dismantling a family. These prove to be analogous, where applicable and appropriate, to carrying on the sacrificial process. Just as meat for the Israelite's table comparable to meat for the Lord's altar, so that not only the category, sanctification, is the same, but the conceptions that define sanctity in both settings are coherent, so we find in the case of the Israelite's marital bed.

The point of distinction is therefore not to be missed. The difference between the consecrated offering for the altar and the consecrated woman for the marriage canopy, governing the entire process of sanctification of woman to man, lies in what distinguishes the human being, man or woman, from the beast: the freedom of will, the power of intentionality. The man may declare the woman sanctified, but if she objects, the act is null. If of age, she must accept the tokens of betrothal, directly or through her agent. If not of age, when she comes of age, she may reject an act of betrothal, even consummated, taken by others with control over her in her minority, her father if he is alive, her brothers if he is deceased. Then she simply ups and walks out, not requiring even a writ of divorce. No sanctification has ever taken place, the woman not having confirmed what has happened through the exercise of will of others with temporary jurisdiction over her. So the woman consecrated for her husband is like the beast sanctified for the altar, but with the familiar, formidable difference, from which all else in the Halakhah flows, one way or the other.

3

Tractate Abodah Zarah

I. THE DEFINITION OF THE CATEGORY-FORMATION

How, exactly, is the Israelite supposed to live in a world dominated by idolatry, and how is Israel subjugated to pagan nations to conduct its life with God? The question is not one that concerns the morale of Israel, let alone its theological apologetics. Rather, at issue is the conduct of everyday life — a fine instance of how the Halakhah takes up issues of the interiority of Israel's existence, the inner structure and architectonics of its everyday life. In line with the generic hermeneutics of the Halakhah, the problematics finds its definition in differentiating what is absolutely forbidden for all purposes, what is forbidden for Israelite use but permitted for Israelite trade, and what is wholly permitted for both trade and utilization. The problematics of the tractate focuses upon commercial transactions; personal relationships are not at the center of the exposition and do not precipitate the more protracted exegeses of the topic. But the particular hermeneutics, the theory of the category-formation that dictates the selection and interpretation of the data found to pertain — that is another matter altogether.

The category-formation, Abodah Zarah, idolatry, serves as the medium for setting forth the hermeneutical results of the analogical-contrastive analysis of the genus, "humanity," in its two species, "Israel" and "idolaters." The likeness, sustaining the comparison of Israel and the gentiles, is self-evident. Both sectors of humanity are men, in God's image, after God's likeness. Then the category-formation spells out how the Israelite species is unlike the gentile species, and the way in which the former is to sort out relationships with the latter: when the gentile does the deeds that make him — mark him as — gentile, what is the Israelite to do and not to do in context? Within the framework of that analysis, then, the Halakhah will focus on how the Israelite is to relate to the gentile when the gentile is engaged in his act of idolatry. That defines the Halakhic interest in the relationship, that is, the point of comparison yielding the focus of contrast, the Halakhic results then being predictable: the hermeneutical principles that dictate the selection of data and the rulings thereon.

It would be difficult to find a more blatant case in which we work our way back from [3] the details of the Halakhic data — their foci, points of stress and emphasis — to [2] the principles in play, those that are actualized in the concrete Halakhic statements — and thence to [1] the modes of thought — analogy, contrast — that produce those principles, the whole then embodying the hermeneutics that animates, and so accounts for, the selection and interpretation of the pertinent facts. In this project of reconstructing the generative hermeneutics of the Halakhah by its native-categories within the stated theory that the hermeneutics takes shape through a process of analogical-contrastive analysis of a given genus and its species, the case of Abodah Zarah stands out. It does so as a particularly lucid exemplification of what, I attempt to show, characterizes the entire intellectual process that culminates in the Halakhah of Rabbinic Judaism. Comparative hermeneutics then bears a double meaning, first, the comparison of the hermeneutics of one category-formation with that of another, and, second the hermeneutics of comparison that yields (in my estimation) all category-formations.

Now let us turn to the case at hand. The category, "the gentiles" or "the nations," without elaborate differentiation, encompasses all who are not-Israelites. Gentiles by this definition are those who do not belong to Israel and that, also by definition, is because they do not know and serve God. It follows that that category — the nations = not-Israel — takes on meaning only as complement and opposite to Israel, its generative counterpart, having no standing —no autonomous and self-defining characteristics — on its own. What makes the gentile gentile, his act of service to an idol, then encompasses all idolaters without differentiation. "The Canaanites," "the Egyptians," all the more so, "Rome," "Greece," "Media" or "Persia," or "Babylonia," and other distinct nations do not generate Halakhah particular to their respective characters or indicative practices. All gentiles are the same.[1] But, for its part, Israel is heavily differentiated. Laws that apply to one component of "Israel" differ from those that apply to another, and rules of intermarriage govern. Thus Israel is differentiated into priests, Levites, Israelites, and the like, that is, is subjected to hierarchical classification as to sanctification.

So, since Israel encompasses the sector of humanity that knows and serves God by reason of God's self-manifestation in the Torah, analogical-contrastive analysis yields the predictable result: the gentiles are comprised by everybody-else. They are those placed by their own intention and active decision beyond the limits of God's revelation. We shall see in due course how the Bavli's Aggadic complement to the Halakhah of Abodah Zarah makes that point explicit, telling a story that realizes the proposition: they turned it down, and that was because of

---

[1] All gentiles are unclean in an undifferentiated way, bearing uncleanness of the same sort, while when Israelites contract uncleanness, that uncleanness is highly differentiated as to sources, effects, and even modes of removal.

their very essence, what makes them what they are, a decision that expresses their teleology. Since by definition all humanity has the choice of knowing God through the Torah, gentiles bear full responsibility for their actions and the consequences thereof. How then, by this theory, is Israel different? Guided by the Torah Israel submits its will to God's will and worships God. But the Torah contrasted with Israel's nature, its teleology, as well, and so, within this narrative of matters, Israel was coerced until by an act of free will it accepted the Torah. Declining the Torah's illumination left the gentiles to worship idols and so offend God. At the outset, therefore, the main point registers: by "gentiles" sages understand, God's enemies, and by "Israel" sages understand, those who know God as God has made himself known, which is, through the Torah. But this leaves us far from the details of the Halakhah.

To show how the contrast between Israel and the gentiles is made concrete, let us further digress, if briefly, and examine how the Aggadah states explicitly the point I find implicit in the Halakhah. That is in two parts. First, the gentiles, that is, the idolaters, hate God. That forms an act of will. Second, God's response to the gentiles forms part of his engagement with Israel. In this way we see how the Halakhah serves as the means for the translation of theological conviction into social policy. We shall presently examine a Halakhic ruling that presupposes gentiles are ready to murder any Israelite they can get their hands on, rape any Israelite woman, commit bestiality with any Israelite cow. The Oral Torah cites few cases to indicate that that conviction responds to ordinary, everyday events; the hostility to gentiles flows from a theory of idolatry, not the facts of everyday social intercourse, which sages recognize is full of neighborly cordiality. Then why take for granted gentiles routinely commit the mortal sins of not merely idolatry but bestiality, fornication, and murder? That is because the Halakhah takes as its task the realization of the theological principle that those who hate Israel hate God, those who hate God hate Israel, and God will ultimately vanquish Israel's enemies as his own — just as God too was redeemed from Egypt. So the theory of idolatry, involving alienation from God, accounts for the wicked conduct imputed to idolaters, without regard to whether, in fact, that is how idolaters conduct themselves. That matter of logic is stated in so many words:

Sifré to Numbers LXXXIV:IV:

1. A. "...and let them that hate you flee before you:"
   B. And do those who hate [come before] him who spoke and brought the world into being?
   C. The purpose of the verse at hand is to say that whoever hates Israel is as if he hates him who spoke and by his word brought the world into being.

The same proposition is reworked. God can have no adversaries, but gentile enemies of Israel act as though they were his enemies:

> D.   Along these same lines: "In the greatness of your majesty you overthrow your adversaries" (Ex. 15:7).
> E.   And are there really adversaries before him who spoke and by his word brought the world into being? But Scripture thus indicates that whoever rose up against Israel is as if he rose up against the Omnipresent.
> F.   Along these same lines: "Do not forget the clamor of your foes, the uproar of your adversaries, which goes up continually" (Ps. 74:23).
> G.   "For lo, your enemies, O Lord" (Ps. 92:10).
> H.   "For those who are far from you shall perish, you put an end to those who are false to you" (Ps. 73:27)
> I.   "For lo, your enemies are in tumult, those who hate you have raised their heads" (Ps. 83:2). On what account? "They lay crafty plans against your people, they consult together against your protected ones" (Ps. 83:3).

Israel hates God's enemies, and Israel is hated because of its loyalty to God (a matter to which we shall return presently):

> J.   "Do I not hate those who hate you, O Lord? And do I not loathe them that rise up against you? I hate them with perfect hatred, I count them my enemies" (Ps. 139:21-22)
> K.   And so too Scripture says, "For whoever lays hands on you is as if he lays hands on the apple of his eye" (Zech. 2:12).
> L.   R. Judah says, "What is written is not, 'the apple of an eye' but 'the apple of *his* eye,' it is as if Scripture speaks of him above, but Scripture has used an euphemism."

Now the consequences of these propositions are drawn:

> V.   And whoever gives help to Israel is as if he gives help to him who spoke and by his word brought the world into being, as it is said, "Curse Meroz, says the angel of the Lord, curse bitterly its inhabitants, because they came not to the help of the Lord, to the help of the Lord against the mighty" (Judges 5:23)
> W.   R. Simeon b. Eleazar says, "You have no more prized part of the body than the eye and Israel has been compared to it. A further comparison: if a man is hit on his head, only his eyes feel it. Accordingly, you have no more prized part of the body than the eye, and Israel has been compared to it."
> X.   So Scripture says, "What, my son, what, son of my womb? what, son of my vows" (Prov. 31:2).

Y. And it says, "When I was a son with my father, tender, the only one in the sight of my mother, he taught me and said to me, 'Let your heart hold fast my words'" (Prov. 4:3-4).

The proposition announced at the outset is fully articulated — those who hate Israel hate God, those who are enemies of Israel are enemies of God, those who help Israel help God — and then systematically instantiated by facts set forth in Scripture. The systematic proof extends beyond verses of Scripture, with a catalogue of the archetypal enemies assembled: Pharaoh, Sisera, Sennacherib, Nebuchadnezzar, Haman. So the paradigm reinforces the initial allegation and repertoire of texts. The context then of all thought on Israel and the gentiles finds definition in supernatural issues and context in theology. In the Oral Torah sages at no point deem as merely secular the category, the gentiles.

On that basis the analogical-contrastive process yields concrete conclusions. Take the contrast between Israel's and gentiles' respective responses to God's blessings. When God blesses gentile nations, they do not acknowledge him but blaspheme, but when he blesses Israel, they glorify him and bless him; these judgments elaborate the basic principle that the gentiles do not know God, and Israel does. But what emerges here is that even when the gentiles ought to recognize God's hand in their affairs, even when God blesses them, they still deny him, turning ignorance into willfulness. What is striking is the exact balance of three gentiles as against three Israelites, all of the status of world-rulers, the common cluster, Pharaoh, Sennacherib, Nebuchadnezzar, vs. a standard Aggadic-cluster, David, Solomon, and Daniel:

Pesiqta deRab Kahana XXVIII:I.1

A. "On the eighth day you shall have a solemn assembly. [You shall do no laborious work, but you shall offer a burnt-offering, an offering by fire, a pleasing odor to the Lord...These you shall offer to the Lord at your appointed feasts in addition to your votive-offerings and your freewill-offerings, for your burnt-offerings and for your cereal-offerings and for your drink-offerings and for your peace-offerings]" (Numbers 29:35-9):

B. But you have increased the nation, "O Lord, you have increased the nation; [you are glorified; you have enlarged all the borders of the land]" (Is. 17:25):

The proposition having been stated, the composer proceeds to amass evidence for the two contrasting propositions, first gentile rulers:

C. You gave security to the wicked Pharaoh. Did he then call you "Lord"? Was it not with blasphemies and curses that he said, "Who is the Lord, that I should listen to his voice "(Ex. 5:2)!

D. You gave security to the wicked Sennacherib. Did he then call you "Lord"? Was it not with blasphemies and curses that he said, "Who is there among all the gods of the lands.".. (2 Kgs. 18:35).

E. You gave security to the wicked Nebuchadnezzar. Did he then call you "Lord"? Was it not with blasphemies and curses that he said, "And who is God to save you from my power" (Dan. 3:15).

Now, nicely balanced, come Israelite counterparts:

F. "...you have increased the nation; you are glorified:"

G. You gave security to David and so he blessed you: "David blessed the Lord before all the congregation "(1 Chr. 29:10).

H. You gave security to his son, Solomon, and so he blessed you: "Blessed is the Lord who has given rest to his people Israel " (1 Kgs. 8:56).

I. You gave security to Daniel and so he blessed you: "Daniel answered and said, Blessed be the name of God "(Dan. 2:20)

Here is another set of opposites — three enemies, three saints, a fair match. In each case, the Israelite responded to God's favor with blessings, and the gentile with blasphemy. In this way the gentiles show the price they pay for not knowing God but serving no-gods instead. Like philosophers, sages in the documents of the Oral Torah appeal to a single cause to account for diverse phenomena; the same factor that explains Israel has also to account for the opposite, that is, the gentiles; what Israel has, gentiles lack, and that common point has made all the difference. Idolatry is what angers God and turns him against the gentiles, stated in so many words at b. A.Z. 1:1 I.23/4b: "That time at which God gets angry comes when the kings put on their crowns on their heads and prostrate themselves to the sun. Forthwith the Holy One, blessed be He, grows angry." That is why it is absolutely forbidden to conduct any sort of commerce with gentiles in connection with occasions of idolatrous worship, e.g., festivals and the like. So we end up with the opening Halakhic statement, its topic and proposition.

Only within that framework of analogical-contrastive reasoning, then, do we locate the hermeneutics — the principles of selection and interpretation of data deemed pertinent to the category-formation at hand — in which the Halakhah finds its coherence and program. At the foundations of the analogical-contrastive outcome is, Israel stands for life, the gentiles, like their idols, for death. A single concrete law makes that point explicit. An *asherah*-tree, like a corpse, conveys uncleanness to those who pass underneath it, as noted at M. 3:8: "And he should not pass underneath it, but if he passed underneath it, he is unclean." Since corpse-uncleanness is conveyed by overshadowing, that is, an analogous medium (Num. 19), the conclusion is clear. Then the category-formation, Abodah Zarah, sets forth the principles of Israel's relationship with the undifferentiated realm of idolatry.

But one result should not be missed: the comparison is by nature not precise, because one species possesses traits lacking all counterpart traits in the other. Specifically, the species Israel and gentiles contrast in a fundamental way: the one forms a coherent group, the other does not. While "Israel" stands for a group, the category-formation that addresses idolatry treats idolaters as isolated individuals, not part of a differentiated nation, one with a history of its own, or people, such as "Rome" or "Persia." Gentiles' collectivities' histories take on shape and structure solely in relationship to Israel's history, just as the prophets said. It follows that idolaters or gentiles and "Israel" do not form a categorical match. The category, "the gentiles" or "the idolaters," is comprised by "everybody else," the differences among nations making no difference whatsoever. By contrast "Israel" is the one social entity that constitutes a people bearing differentiating qualities, that is, the ones that matter to God. So "Israel" here negotiates with not a counterpart entity, but in exact terms, a non-entity. And that explains why, consequently, in its details the Halakhah addresses the condition of gentiles as individuals, the ordinary life of common folk, both Israelite and gentile, rather than concentrating on the situation of all Israel, viewed as a collective entity. It is only at the Aggadic amplification of the Halakhah that we encounter an explicit theory of idolatry embodied even by a particular nation, e.g., Rome as distinct from Iran, Greece from Persia.

But if they are deemed mere individuals, lacking collectively a non-entity, nonetheless, all individual idolaters are alike, lacking differentiating characteristics that count. All Gentiles, whatever their origin, are persons assumed to conduct themselves in the same unacceptable manner: whenever they can, they will worship their no-gods and anger God. What, within the stated theory, then defines the category-formation's detailed program? It is to regulate relations between Israelites and gentiles when they are acting like gentiles, that is, when they are worshipping their no-gods. And then the details flow. How do they originate, I mean, within what (theoretically-reconstructed) thought-processes? Once the topical program is established within the hermeneutics defined by (a theoretically-reconstructed) analogical-contrastive analysis, the generic hermeneutics of the Halakhah takes over. The generic hermeneutics of the Halakhah, not the particular hermeneutics of the category-formation, guides the articulation of the Halakhic corpus within its own general logic of differentiation, e.g., the systematic refinement of interstitial situations. In articulating the components of its category-formation, "idolatry," the Halakhah moves from the general to the particular, from commercial relationships in commerce and trace to how Israel is to deal with idols in particular, and finally, the matter of that universal medium of godly worship, wine. Here the unspecified genus, wine, yields two species, wine that has served idols, which Israelites may not utilize, and wine that serves God. Throughout, therefore, the focus is not on "Israel" and "the nations" but rather on "the Israelite" and "the gentile." The Halakhic category-formation does not contemplate negotiations between Israel and the nations or relationships between them that require regulation. Only the Aggadic counterpart-category-formation does.

Within the Halakhic hermeneutics, both particular to the category-formation and generic, what are the results? The end-product lies spread out before us. When it comes to individuals and their obligations, the Halakhah identifies three particular foci of legislation. It turns, first, to commercial relationships between Israelites and gentiles, second, to matters pertaining to Israelite disposition of idols, and, finally, to the very urgent issue of the prohibition of wine part of which has served as a libation to an idol. There are a number of unstated principles before us. What a gentile is not likely to use for the worship of an idol is not going to be prohibited. What may serve not as part of idolatry but as an appurtenance thereto is prohibited for Israelite use but permitted for Israelite commerce. What serves for idolatry is prohibited for use and for benefit. Certain further assumptions about gentiles, not pertinent specifically to idolatry, are expressed. Gentiles are assumed routinely to practice bestiality, bloodshed, and fornication, without limit or restriction. This negative image of the gentile finds expression in the laws before us. The outline of the tractate follows.

I.   COMMERCIAL RELATIONSHIPS WITH GENTILES. 1:1-2:7

    A.   Festivals and fairs. 1:1-4
        1:1 For three days before gentile festivals it is forbidden to do business with them.
        1:2 Ishmael: Three days afterward also.
        1:3 These are the festivals of gentiles.
        1:4 A city in which there is an idol – in the area outside of it, it is permitted to do business.
    B.   Objects prohibited even in commerce. 1:5-2:2
        1:5 These are things which it is forbidden to sell to gentiles.
        1:6 In a place in which they are accustomed to sell small cattle to gentiles, they sell them (the consideration being use of the beasts for sacrifices to idols).
        1:7 They do not sell them bears, lions, or anything which is a public danger. They do not help build with them a basilica, scaffold, stadium, or judges' tribunal.
        1:8-9 They do not make ornaments for an idol, sell them produce which is not yet harvested, sell them land in the Holy Land.
        2:1 They do not leave cattle in gentiles' inns, because they are suspect in regard to bestiality.
        2:2 They accept healing for property (e.g., animals) but not for a person.
    C.   Objects prohibited for use but permitted in trade. 2:3-7
        2:3 These things belonging to gentiles are prohibited, and the prohibition concerning them extends to deriving any benefit from them at all: wine, vinegar, earthenware which absorbs wine, and hides pierced at the heart.

2:4 Skins of gentiles and their jars, with Israelite wine collected in them – they are prohibited, the prohibition extends to deriving benefit, so Meir. Sages: Not to deriving benefit.

2:5 On what account did they prohibit cheese made by gentiles?

2:6-7 These are things of gentiles which are prohibited, but the prohibition does not extend to deriving benefit from them. Milk, bread, oil, etc.

2:7 These are things which to begin with are permitted for Israelite consumption.

II.   IDOLS. 3:1-4:7

  A. General Principles. 3:1-7

3:1 All images are prohibited, because they are worshipped once a year, so Meir, Sages: Prohibited is only one which has an emblem of authority.

3:2-3 He who finds the shreds of images – lo, these are permitted.

3:4 Gamaliel: What gentiles treat as a god is prohibited.

3:5 Gentiles who worship hills and valleys – the hills or valleys are permitted, but what is on them is forbidden.

3:6 If one's house-wall served also as the wall of a Temple and it fell down, one may not rebuild it.

3.7 There are three states in regard to idolatry: what is built for idolatrous purposes is forbidden. What is improved is forbidden until the improvement is removed. What merely happens to be used for an idol is permitted once the idol is removed.

  B. The Asherah. 3:7-10

3:7 What is an asherah?

3:8-9 Use of an asherah-tree.

3:10 Desecrating an asherah-tree.

  C. The Merkolis. 4:1-2

4:1-2 Three stones beside a Merkolis (= Hermes) are forbidden, so Ishmael.

  D. Nullifying an idol. 4:3-7

4:3 An idol which had a garden or bathhouse.

4:4-6 An idol belonging to a gentile is prohibited forthwith. One belonging to an Israelite is forbidden only once it has been worshipped. How one nullifies an idol.

4:7 If God does not favor idolatry, why does he not wipe it away?

III.   LIBATION-WINE. 4:8-5:12

4:8 They purchase from gentiles the contents of a winepress which has already been trodden out, for it is not the sort of wine which gentiles use for a libation until it has dripped down into the vat.

4:9 Israelites tread a winepress with a gentile, but they do not gather grapes with him.

4:10 A gentile who is found standing beside a cistern of wine – if he had a lien on the vat, it is prohibited. If he had no lien on it, it is permitted.

4:11 He who prepares the wine belonging to a gentile in a condition of cleanness and leaves it in his domain.

5:1 He who hires an Israelite worker to work with him in the preparation of libation-wine – the Israelite's salary is forbidden.

5:2 Libation-wine which fell on grapes – one may rinse them off, and they are permitted. If the grapes were split and absorbed wine, they are prohibited.

5:3-4 A gentile who with an Israelite was moving jars of wine from place to place – if the wine is assumed to be watched, it is permitted. If the Israelite told the gentile he was going away for any length of time, the wine is prohibited.

5:5 The same point, now in the context of eating at the same table.

5:6 A band of gentile raiders which entered a town peacefully – open jars are forbidden, closed ones permitted.

5:7 Israelite craftsmen, to whom a gentile sent a jar of libation-wine as salary, may ask him to pay in money instead, only if this is before the wine has entered their possession. Afterward it is forbidden.

5:8-9 Libation-wine is forbidden and imparts a prohibition on wine with which it is mixed in any measure at all. If it is wine poured into water, it is forbidden only if it imparts a flavor.

5:10 Libation-wine which fell into a vat – the whole of the vat is forbidden for benefit. Simeon b. Gamaliel: All of it may be sold except the value of the volume of libation-wine which is in it.

5:11-12 A stone winepress which a gentile covered with pitch – one dries it off, and it is clean. One of wood, one of earthenware.

The opening unit unfolds in a fairly orderly way, from a prologue on the special problems of fairs, to the general matter of things Israelites may not even buy or sell, as against things they may not use but may trade, I.B, C. The second unit lays down some general principles about images, then presents special ones on two specific kinds of idols, II.B, C, and at the end asks the logical necessary question about how one nullifies an idol entirely. The third unit is a very long essay about libation-wine and its effect upon Israelite-gentile commerce. I do not see any coherent subdivisions of this sizable discussion, which goes over the same ground time and again. So much for the category-formation and the hermeneutics particular to it, on the one side, and the generic hermeneutics of the Halakhah as applied here, on the other.

Why do sages define a principal category of the Halakhah in this wise? Within my larger theory of the theology of the Oral Torah, stressing its purpose, which is to reveal God's justice (defined by his mercy), it is because sages must devote a considerable account to the challenge to that justice represented by gentile power and prosperity, Israel's subordination and penury. For if the story of the moral order tells about justice that encompasses all creation, the chapter of gentile rule vastly disrupts the account. Gentile rule forms the point of tension, the source of conflict, attracting attention and demanding explanation. For the critical problematic inherent in the category, Israel, is that its anti-category, the gentiles, dominate. So what rationality of a world ordered through justice accounts for the world ruled by gentiles represents the urgent question to which the system must respond. The Halakhah takes up one component of that question, the one that is its task: how is Israel to deal, in everyday detail, with the situation in which it finds itself? And the answer of the Halakhah, as we shall see in rich instantiation, is, while the gentiles dominate, Israel, by an act of will, can still govern those things for which it bears responsibility.

II. THE FOUNDATIONS OF THE HALAKHIC CATEGORY-FORMATIONS

The Halakhic category-formation supplies rules and regulations to carry out the fundamental Scriptural commandments about the destruction of idols and all things having to do with idolatry. It follows that while our tractate deals with facts and relies upon suppositions that Scripture has not supplied, its basic viewpoint and the problem it seeks to solve derive from the Mosaic code, as in the following statements:

Ex. 23:13
> "Take heed to all that I have said to you; and make no mention of the names of other gods, nor let such be heard out of your mouth."

Ex. 23:24
> "When my angel goes before you, and brings you in to the Amorites, and the Hittites, and the Perizzites, and the Canaanites, the Hivites, and the Jebusites, and I blot them out, you shall not bow down into their gods, nor serve them, nor do according to their work, but you shall utterly overthrow them and break their pillars in pieces."

Ex. 23:32-33
> "You shall make no covenant with them or with their gods. They shall not dwell in your land, lest they make you sin against me; for if you serve their gods, it will surely be a snare to you."

Ex. 34:12-16
> The Lord said to Moses, "Come up to me on the mountain, and wait there; and I will give you the tables of stone, with the law and the commandment, which I have written for their instruction." So Moses rose with his servant Joshua, and Moses went up into the mountain of God. And he said to the elders, "Tarry here for us, until we come to you again; and, behold Aaron and Hur are with you; whoever has a cause, let him go to them."
>
> Then Moses went up on the mountain, and the cloud covered the mountain. The glory of the Lord settled on Mount Sinai, and the

cloud covered it six days; and on the seventh day he called to Moses out of the midst of the cloud.

Deut. 7:1-5

"When the Lord your God brings you into the land which you are entering to take possession of it, and clears away many nations before you, the Hittites, the Girgashites, the Amorites, the Canaanites, the Perizzites, the Hivites, and the Jebusites, seven nations greater and mightier than yourselves, and when the Lord your God gives them over to you, and you defeat them; then you must utterly destroy them; show no mercy to them. You shall not make marriages with them, giving your daughters to their sons or taking their daughters for your sons. For they would turn away your sons from following me, to serve other gods; then the anger of the Lord would be kindled against you, and he would destroy you quickly. But thus shall you deal with them: you shall break down their altars, and dash in pieces their pillars, and hew down their Asherim, and burn their graven images with fire."

Deut. 7:25-26

"The graven images of their gods you shall burn with fire; you shall not covet the silver or the gold that is on them, or take it for yourselves, lest you be ensnared by it; for it is an abomination to the Lord your God. And you shall not bring an abominable thing into your house, and become accursed like it; you shall utterly detest and abhor it; for it is an accursed thing."

Deut. 12:2-3

"You shall surely destroy all the places where the nations whom you shall dispossess served their gods, upon the high mountains and upon the hills and under every green tree; you shall tear down their altars, and dash in pieces their pillars, and burn their Asherim with fire; you shall hew down the graven images of their gods, and destroy their name out of that place."

The Written Torah provides instruction on destroying idolatry, in the premise that Israel has the opportunity to do so. The Halakhah explains how to co-exist with idolatry, recognizing that Israel has no choice but to do so. That explains why this repertoire of pertinent verses proves asymmetrical to the topical program of the Halakhic category-formation. Indeed, it is clear, a category-formation resting on Scripture's premises would have taken a course quite different from the one before us. For the Halakhah speaks to a world that is not so simple as that portrayed by Scripture. Scripture takes for granted Israel enjoys total command of the Land of Israel and can with impunity do the deeds that Moses calls for. The Halakhah knows otherwise, its starting point not corresponding to that of Scripture. The Land to be sure belongs to Israel, but now gentiles live there too — and run things. Not only so, but the Halakhah now presupposes that Israel no longer forms a coherent collectivity but a realm made up of households and villages interspersed among gentile counterparts. The Halakhah of the Oral Torah commences its treatment of the same subject with the opposite premise: gentiles live side by side (whether or not in the Land of Israel) with Israelites, and Israelites have to sort out the complex problems of co-existence with idolatry. And that co-existence involves not whole communities, the People, Israel, and the peoples, whoever they may be, but individuals, this Israelite living side by side with that gentile.

III. THE EXPOSITION OF THE COMPONENTS OF THE GIVEN CATEGORY-FORMATION BY THE MISHNAH-TOSEFTA-YERUSHALMI-BAVLI

I. COMMERCIAL RELATIONSHIPS WITH GENTILES

A. FESTIVALS AND FAIRS

M. 1:1 Before the festivals of gentiles for three days it is forbidden to do business with them. (1) To lend anything to them or to borrow anything from them. (2) To lend money to them or to borrow money from them. (3) To repay them or to be repaid by them.

T. 1:1 Under what circumstances [M. A.Z. 1:1A]? In the case of recurrent festivals, but in the case of festivals which do not recur, prohibited is only that day alone. And even though they have said, It is forbidden to do business with them [M. A.Z. 1:1A] — under what circumstances? In the case of something which lasts. But in the case of something which does not last, it is permitted. And even in the case of something which lasts, [if] one bought or sold it, lo, this is permitted.

T. 1:2 A person should not do business with a gentile on the day of his festival, nor should one talk frivolously, nor should one ask after his welfare in a situation which is taken into account. But if one happened to come across him in a routine way, he asks after his welfare with all due respect.

T. 1:3 They ask after the welfare of gentiles on their festivals for the sake of peace. Israelite workmen who were working with a gentile — in the case of an Israelite's household, it is permitted. In the case of a gentile's household, it is prohibited. And even though one has finished work on his utensils before his festival, he should not deliver them to him on the day of his festival, because this increases his rejoicing [on his festival].

M. 1:2 Before their festivals it is prohibited, but after their festivals it is permitted

M. 1:3 (1) On the day on which [a gentile] shaves off his beard and lock of hair, (2) on the day on which he came up safely from an ocean voyage, (3) on the day on which he got out of prison. And a gentile who made a banquet for his son — it is prohibited for only that day, and in regard to only that individual alone [to enter into business relationships of any sort, as listed at M. 1:1].

T. 1:4 [If] one town celebrates, and another town does not celebrate, one people celebrates, and another people does not celebrate, one family celebrates, and another family does not celebrate — those who celebrate are subject to the stated prohibitions, and those who do not celebrate are permitted in regard to them. As to *Calendae,* even though everyone observes the festival, it is permitted only with regard to the actual rite of sacrifice itself. *Saturnalia is* the day on which they took power. *Kratesis is* the day of the anniversary of the emperors [cf. M. A.Z. I:3B-C]. The day of each and every emperor — lo, it is tantamount to a public festival.

M. 1:4 A city in which there is an idol — [in the area] outside of it, it is permitted [to do business]. [If] an idol was outside of it, [in the area] inside it is permitted. What is the rule as to going to that place? When the road is set aside for going to that place only, it is prohibited. But if one is able to take that same road to some other place, it is permitted. A town in which there is an idol, and there were in it shops which were adorned and shops which were not adorned — those which are adorned are prohibited, but those which are not adorned are permitted.

T. 1:6 [If] there is a fair in the town, into the town it is prohibited [to go], but outside of the town it is permitted. And if it is outside of the town, outside of the town it is forbidden [to go], but into the town it is permitted [M. A.Z. 1:4A-C]. And shops which are decorated under any circumstances, lo, these are forbidden [M. A.Z. 1:4I]. [If] a person is passing in a caravan from one place to another, and enters a town in which a fair is going on, he need not scruple that he may appear to be going to the fair [M. A.Z. I:4E-F].

T. 1:7 A fair which the empire held, or which a province held, or which the leaders of a province held, is permitted. Prohibited is only a fair honoring an idol alone.

T. 1:8 They go to a gentiles' fair and accept healing from them — healing involving property, but not healing involving the person. And they do (not) purchase from them fields, vineyards, boy-slaves, and girl-slaves, because he is as one who rescues these from their power. And one writes and deposits [a deed] in an archive. A priest contracts uncleanness [in connection with redemption of land] to give testimony and to engage in a law-suit against them abroad. And just as he contracts uncleanness in connection with affairs abroad, so he surely contracts uncleanness in a graveyard [in the same matter]. And [a priest] contracts uncleanness [if it is] to study Torah or to marry a woman.

T. 1:9 Merchants who pushed up the day of a fair or who pushed back the day of a fair — it is permitted. Prohibited is only the time of the fair alone.

T. 1:15 Israelites who are going to a fair — it is permitted to do business with them. And on [their] return, it is [likewise] permitted. Gentiles who are going to their debauchery — it is forbidden to do business with them. And on [their] return, it is permitted. For [the fair] is tantamount to idolatry, which [on their return trip] its worshippers have abandoned. And as to an Israelite, whether it is on the way there or on the way back, it is prohibited.

T. 1:16 One should not travel with a caravan [en route to an idolatrous fair], even to go out, even to go before it, even to be with it when it gets dark, even if one is fearful because of gentiles, thugs, or an evil spirit, since it is said, "You shall not go after other gods" (Deut. 6:14).

B. 1:4A A-F/12A IF WHILE SOMEONE IS IN FRONT OF AN IDOL, HE GOT A SPLINT IN HIS FOOT, HE SHOULD NOT BEND OVER TO REMOVE IT, BECAUSE HE LOOKS AS THOUGH HE IS BOWING DOWN TO THE IDOL. BUT IF IT DOES NOT LOOK THAT WAY, HE IS PERMITTED TO DO SO. IF HIS MONEY GOT SCATTERED IN FRONT OF AN IDOL, HE SHOULD NOT BOW DOWN TO PICK IT UP, BECAUSE HE LOOKS AS THOUGH HE IS BOWING DOWN TO THE IDOL. BUT IF IT DOES NOT LOOK THAT WAY, HE IS PERMITTED TO DO SO. IF A SPRING FLOWS IN FRONT OF AN IDOL, ONE

SHOULD NOT BEND DOWN TO DRINK, BECAUSE HE LOOKS AS THOUGH HE IS BOWING DOWN
TO THE IDOL. BUT IF IT DOES NOT LOOK THAT WAY, HE IS PERMITTED TO DO SO. ONE
SHOULD NOT PUT HIS MOUTH ON THE MOUTH OF HUMAN FIGURES WHICH SERVE AS FOUNTAINS
IN TOWNS IN ORDER TO DRINK WATER, BECAUSE HE MAY APPEAR TO BE KISSING THE IDOL.

We commence with the broadest generalizations, restrictions on all
commercial intercourse with gentiles for three days prior to their festivals, and, the
Tosefta wisely adds, other forms of social intercourse are equally forbidden. Not
only so, but other occasions on which idolatry figures or is likely to figure, as at M.
1:3, the same prohibitions apply. Here we have the counterpart to the rules, at
Moed Qatan (M. 3:1-2 etc.), on small personal celebrations in the setting of the
intermediate days of a festival. Israel and the idolater are consubstantial, which is
why on occasions comparable to those on which Israel celebrates, intercourse with
the idolater is prohibited. The same prohibitions extend from occasions even to
locations. Israelites may not even enter locations configured for idolatry. But, the
Tosefta clarifies, involved is only a fair or a location devoted solely to idolatry; if
there are other motivations for the fair, e.g., imperial, or other characterizations of
the location, matters are otherwise; then the Israelite intentionality takes over. The
Bavli introduces into the Halakhic repertoire the familiar consideration of what is
forbidden for appearance' sake.

B. OBJECTS PROHIBITED EVEN IN COMMERCE

**M. 1:5 What are the things that are forbidden to sell to gentiles? (1) fir cones, (2)
white figs, (3) and their stalks, (4) frankincense, and (5) a white cock. And as
to everything else, [if] they are left without specification [as to their proposed
use], it is permitted, but [if] they are specified [for use for idolatry], it is
prohibited.**

T. 1:21 One sells [the stated substances] to a merchant, but does not sell [them] to a
householder [M. A.Z. 1:5A]. But if the merchant was suspect [of idolatrous
practices], it is prohibited to sell [them] to him. One sells them pigs and does not
scruple that he might offer them up to an idol. One sells him wine and does not
scruple that he might offer it as a libation to an idol. But if he explicitly stated to
him [that his intent was to make use of what he was buying for idolatry], it is
prohibited to sell him even water, even salt [M. A.Z. 1:5F].

T. 2:1 They purchase a beast from them for a trial and return it to them that entire day.
And just as they purchase from them a beast for a trial and return it to them that
entire day so they purchase from them (a beast) slave-boys and slave-girls for a
trial and return them to them that entire day. So long as you have the right to
return [what is purchased] to an Israelite, you have the right to return [the same
thing] to a gentile. [If] you have not got the right to return [what is purchased] to
an Israelite, you have not got the right to return [the same thing] to a gentile. An
Israelite sells his beast to a gentile on the stipulation that the latter slaughter it,
with an Israelite supervising him while the gentile slaughters the beast [so as to
make sure it is not turned into a sacrifice to an idol]. They purchase from [gentiles]

cattle for an offering, and need not scruple on the count of [the gentile's having practiced] bestiality or suffered bestiality, or having set aside the beast for idolatrous worship, or having actually worshipped [the beast].

M. 1:6 In a place in which they are accustomed to sell small cattle to gentiles, they sell them. In a place in which they are accustomed not to sell [small cattle] to them, they do not sell them. And in every locale they do not sell them large cattle, calves, or foals, whether whole or lame.

T. 2:2 And just as they do not sell them a large domesticated beast, so they do not sell them a large wild beast [M. A.Z. 1:6B]. And also in a situation in which they do not sell them a small domesticated beast, they do not sell them a small wild beast.

Y. 1:6 III.2 [If] one transgressed [the law in a locale in which it is prohibited to sell such beasts to gentiles] and sold [such a beast to a gentile], do they impose a fine upon him [so depriving the Israelite of the use of the proceeds]? Just as the sages impose such a penalty on the Israelite in the case of the violation of a law [e.g., deliberately blemishing a firstling so that the priest has no claim to it], so they impose a penalty on him for the violation of a custom [operative in a given locale].

M. 1:7 They do not sell them (1) bears or (2) lions, or (3) anything which is a public danger. They do not build with them (1) a basilica, (2) scaffold, (3) stadium, or (4) judges' tribunal. But they build with them (5) public bathhouses or (6) private ones. [Once] they reach the vaulting on which they set up an idol, it is forbidden [to help build any longer].

T. 2:3 And just as they do not sell [the listed animals] to them, they also do not exchange them with them, either bad ones for good ones, or good ones for bad ones; either lame ones for healthy ones, or healthy ones for lame ones.

M. 1:8 And they do not make ornaments for an idol: (1) necklaces, (2) earrings, or (3) finger rings. They do not sell them produce as yet unplucked. But one may sell it once it has been harvested.

T. 2:4 They do not sell them either a sword or the paraphernalia for a sword. And they do not polish a sword for them. And they do not sell them stocks, neck-chains, ropes, or iron chains, scrolls, phylacteries, or *mezuzot.* All the same are the gentile and the Samaritan. They sell them fodder which has been cut down, grain which has been harvested, and trees which have been picked

T. 2:7 He who goes up into gentiles' amphitheaters, if he was going about on account of the service of the state's requirements, lo, this is permitted. If one takes account [of what is happening therein], lo, this is for bidden. He who sits in an amphitheater [e.g., where gladiators are fighting], lo, this one is guilty of bloodshed. They may go to stadiums because [an Israelite] will cry out in order to save the life of the loser, and to the performance in a camp on account of the task of preserving order in the province. But if one takes account of what is happening [in the entertainment], lo, this is forbidden.

M. 1:9 Even in the situation concerning which they have ruled [that they may] rent, it is not for use as a residence that they ruled that it is permitted, because he brings an idol into it, as it is said, "You shall not bring an abomination into your house" (Deut. 7:26). And in no place may one rent him a bathhouse, since it would be called by his [the Israelite's] name [and its use on the Sabbath will be attributed to the Israelite].

T. 2:8 They do not rent to them houses, fields, or vineyards. And they do not provide for them fields on the basis of sharecropping [a variable or fixed proportion of the crop, respectively] or of contracting to raise beasts. All the same are a gentile and a Samaritan.

T. 2:9 Here and there an Israelite should not rent out his house to a gentile, because it is certain that the latter will bring an idol into it [M. A.Z. 1:9A-C]. But they may rent out to them stables, storehouses, and inns, even though it is certain that the gentile will bring into it an idol.

M. 2:1 They do not leave cattle in gentiles' inns, because they are suspect in regard to bestiality. And a woman should not be alone with them, because they are suspect in regard to fornication. And a man should not be alone with them, because they are suspect in regard to bloodshed. An Israelite girl should not serve as a midwife to a gentile woman, because she serves to bring forth a child for the service of idolatry. But a gentile woman may serve as a midwife to an Israelite girl. An Israelite girl should not give suck to the child of a gentile woman. But a gentile woman may give suck to the child of an Israelite girl, when it is by permission.

T. 3:1 They leave cattle in Samaritans' inns, even male [cattle] with women, and female [cattle] with men, and female [cattle] with women. And they hand over cattle to their shepherds, and they hand over a child to him to teach him reading and to teach him a craft, and to be alone with him. An Israelite girl serves as a midwife and gives suck to the child of a Samaritan woman. And a Samaritan woman serves as midwife and gives suck to an Israelite child.

T. 3:2 They do not leave cattle in gentiles' inns [M. A.Z. 2:1A], even male cattle with men, and female cattle with women, because a male may bring a male [beast] over him, and a female may do the same with a female beast, and it goes without saying, males with women, and females with men. And they do not hand over cattle to their shepherds. And they do not hand a child over to him to teach him reading, to teach him a craft, or to be alone with him.

T. 3:3 An Israelite girl should not give suck to the child of a gentile woman [M. A.Z. 2:1J], because she raises a child for the service of idolatry [cf. M. A.Z. 2:1H]. But a gentile woman may give suck to the child of an Israelite girl, when it is by permission [M. A.Z. 2:1K]. An Israelite girl should not serve as a midwife to a gentile woman, because she serves to bring forth a child for the service of idolatry [M. A.Z. 2:1G-H].

M. 2:2 They accept from them healing for property, but not healing for the person.

T. 3:4 They accept from them healing as to matters of property, but not healing as to matters of the person [M. A.Z. 2:2A-B]. A gentile woman should not be called upon to cut out the foetus in the womb of an Israelite girl. And she should not give her a cup of bitters to drink, for they are suspect as to the taking of life. And an Israelite should not be alone with a gentile either in a bathhouse or in a urinal. [When] an Israelite goes along with a gentile, he puts him at his right hand, and he does not put him at his left hand.

T. 3:5 An Israelite who is getting a haircut from a gentile watches in the mirror [cf. M. A.Z. 2:2C-E]. [If it is] from a Samaritan, he does not watch in the mirror. They permitted the house of Rabban Gamaliel to look at themselves in the mirror, for they are close to the government.

T. 3:6 An Israelite who is giving a haircut to a gentile, when he has reached the forelock, removes his hands [from the hair and does not cut it off]. They purchase from a gentile scrolls, phylacteries, and mezuzot, so long as they are written properly.

T. 3:16 He who sells his slave to gentiles — [the slave] has gone forth free. And he requires a writ of emancipation from his first master. Whether he sold him to him or gave him to him as a gift, he has gone forth free. And if not, he has not gone forth free, lest he has gone forth to a domain which is not a domain. He borrows money from a gentile on the strength of him. If the gentile did what the law requires [making acquisition], he has gone forth free. And if not, he has not gone forth free. [If] he took him in compensation for his debt, or if he fell to him under the law of the usurper, he has gone forth free. [If] one has inherited slaves from gentiles, before they have actually entered his domain, he is permitted to sell them to gentiles. Once they have actually entered his domain, he is prohibited from selling them to gentiles. And so you say in the case of wine which has served for a libation, which one has inherited: before it has come into one's domain, money received for it is permitted. Once it has come into one's domain, money received for it is prohibited.

T. 3:17 An Israelite and a gentile who made a purchase in partnership and went and made another purchase — he may not say to him, "You take the things which are in such-and-such a place in lieu of the first purchase, and I shall take the things which are in such-and-such a place in lieu of the second purchase." But he says to him, "You take the things which are in such-and-such a place, and I shall take the things which are in such-and-such a place. "In lieu of the first purchase, you take the things which are in such-and-such a place, and I shall take the things which are in such-and-such a place in lieu of the second purchase."

T. 3:18 He who sells his slave abroad — he has gone forth free. And he needs a writ of emancipation from his second master.

T. 3:19 He who sells his slave to a gentile fair — the money received for him is prohibited, and one must take it to the Salt Sea. And they force his master to redeem him, even at a hundred times the price received for him, and then he puts him out to freedom. You turn out to rule: He who does business at a gentile fair — in the case of a beast, it is to be hamstrung. In the case of clothing and utensils, they are left to rot. In the case of money and metal utensils, they are to be taken off to the Salt Sea. As to produce, that which is usually poured out is to be poured out. That which is usually burned is to be burned. That which is usually buried is to be buried.

M. 2:3 These things belonging to gentiles are prohibited, and the prohibition affecting them extends to deriving any benefit from them at all: (1) wine, (2) vinegar of gentiles which to begin with was wine, (3) Hadrianic earthenware, and (4) hides pierced at the heart. With those who are going to an idolatrous pilgrimage — it is prohibited to do business. With those that are coming back it is permitted.

T. 4:7 What are hides pierced at the heart [M. A.Z. 2:3B]? Any which is perforated at the heart [of the beast], and made into a kind of peep-hole. But if it is straight, it is permitted [M. A.Z. 2:3C].

T. 4:8 Pickled and stewed vegetables of gentiles, into which it is customary to put wine and vinegar, and Hadrianic earthenware [cf. M. A.Z. 2:3B, 2:6D] — the prohibition affecting them is a prohibition extending to deriving any benefit from them whatsoever. Sodden olives which are sold at the doors of bathhouses are prohibited for eating, but permitted so far as deriving benefit.

Y. 2:3 I.2Gff. There are three types of wine [so far as the prohibition of gentiles' wine on the count of libation to idolatry is concerned]: [There is wine] that [an Israelite] assuredly saw a gentile offer up as a libation to an idol. This sort of wine imparts uncleanness of a severe sort, like a dead creeping thing. [There is] ordinary wine [of a gentile]. It is prohibited [for Israelite use or benefit]. But it does not impart uncleanness. [If an Israelite] deposited [wine] with [a gentile], sealed by a single seal, it is prohibited for drinking, but permitted for [other sorts of] gain [e.g., sale].

Not only may one not participate in occasions or locations involving idolatry, but even at other times or elsewhere one may not sell gentiles things that serve idolatry in particular. If, however, the gentile announced his intention to use for idolatry any item whatsoever, that changes matters. M. 1:7 crosses the topical boundary and applies the principle of refraining from complicity in idolatry to other matters, e.g., complicity in the licit murder that takes place in gentiles' circuses and courthouses. The given of the law is that gentiles always have idolatry on their mind, and that datum too spills over into a judgment as to their incapacity to refrain from all manner of sexual relations.

C. OBJECTS PROHIBITED FOR USE BUT PERMITTED IN COMMERCE

M. 2:4 Skins of gentiles and their jars, with Israelite wine collected in them — the prohibition affecting them does not extend to deriving benefit from them. Grape pits and grape skins belonging to gentiles if they are moist, they are forbidden. If they are dry, they are permitted. Fish brine and Bithynian cheese belonging to gentiles — the prohibition of them does not extend to deriving benefit from them.

T. 4:9 A water tank on wheels and a leather-bottle belonging to gentiles, with Israelite wine collected in them — [the wine] is prohibited for drinking, but available for other benefit [cf. M. A.Z. 2:4 A, C].

T. 4:10 Skins belonging to gentiles which are scraped are permitted. Those which are sealed or covered with pitch are prohibited. [If] a gentile works it and pitches it, while an Israelite supervises him, one may collect wine or oil in it without scruple. Jars belonging to gentiles — new ones are permitted. Old ones which are old and rubbed are prohibited. And one in which a gentile collected water — [if] an Israelite filled out, an Israelite is permitted also to put wine or oil into it. And if a gentile collected wine in it, an Israelite fills it with water for three whole days, seventy-two hours. [Then] he may collect wine in it without scruple. And in one in which a gentile collected Israelite wine, pickling brine, or brine an Israelite is permitted to collect wine.

Y. 2:4 II:3 [If] a gentile has collected water in [jars], an Israelite [who wishes to make use of the same jars] puts water into them and then goes and puts wine into them and need not scruple. [If] a gentile collected brine or fish-brine in them, an Israelite may then put wine into those same jars. [If] a gentile collected wine in them, an Israelite may put into them brine or fish-brine and then go and put wine into them, and he need not scruple.

M. 2:6 And what are things of gentiles which are prohibited, but the prohibition of which does not extend to deriving benefit from them? (1) milk drawn by a gentile without an Israelite's watching him; (2) their bread; and (3) their oil — (4) stewed and pickled [vegetables] into which it is customary to put wine and vinegar; (5) minced fish; (6) brine without kilkit fish floating in it; (7) hileq fish, (8) drops of asafoetida, and (9) sal-conditum — lo, these are prohibited, but the prohibition affecting them does not extend to deriving benefit from them.

M. 2:7 These are things which [to begin with] are permitted for [Israelite] consumption. (1) milk which a gentile drew, with an Israelite watching him; (2) honey; (3) grape clusters, (even though they drip with moisture, they are not subject to the rule of imparting susceptibility to uncleanness as liquid); (4) pickled vegetables into which it is not customary to put wine or vinegar; (5) unminced fish; (6) brine containing fish; (7) a [whole] leaf of asafoetida, and (8) pickled olive cakes. Locusts which come form [the shopkeeper's] basket are forbidden. Those which come from the stock [of his shop] are permitted. And so is the rule for heave-offering.

T. 4:11 They purchase from gentiles grain, pulse, dried figs, garlic, and onions, under all circumstances, and they do not scruple on account of uncleanness. As to red berry of sumac, under all circumstances it is deemed unclean. As to cedar, under all circumstances it is deemed clean. A hunter is believed to testify, "This bird is unclean," "This bird is clean." An 'am ha'ares is believed to testify, "These pickled vegetables did I pickle in a state of cleanness, and I did not sprinkle liquids [capable of imparting susceptibility to uncleanness] upon them." But he is not believed to testify, "These fish I caught in a state of cleanness, and I did not shake the net over them." Their caper-fruit, leeks, liverwort, boiled water and parched corn [prepared by gentiles] are permitted. An egg roasted by them is prohibited. A loaf of bread which a gentile baked, not in the presence of an Israelite, and cheese which a gentile curdled, not in the presence of an Israelite, are prohibited. A loaf of bread which an Israelite baked, even though the gentile kneaded the dough, and cheese which an Israelite curdled, even though a gentile works it — Lo, this is permitted. An Israelite may sit at the other side of his corral, and a gentile may milk the cows and bring the milk to him, and one does not scruple. What is unminced fish [M. A.Z. 2:7E]? Any in which the backbone and head are discernible. What is brine containing fish [M. A.Z. 2:7F]? Any in which one or two kilbit-fish are floating. A piece of meat on which there is a recognizable sign, whether it is on the whole of it or only part of it, and even if it is on only one out of a hundred — lo, this is permitted. Brine made by an expert, lo, this is permitted.

T. 4:12 Boiled wine and aromatic water — lo, these are prohibited because they begin as wine. Aromatic water in its natural condition — lo, this is permitted. Apple-wine which comes from storage, the storehouse, or a ship — lo, this is permitted. But if it is sold over the counter in the market, lo, this is prohibited, because it may be adulterated [with gentile wine or vinegar]. Locusts and pieces of meat which come from storage or from the storehouse or from a ship — lo, these are permitted. But if they are sold in a basket in front of a store, lo, they are prohibited, because they sprinkle them with wine so as to improve their appearance [M. A.Z. 2:7F-H].

T. 4:13 They purchase Bithynian cheese only from an expert. But seethed [cheese] is purchased from any source. They purchase drops of asafoetida only from an expert. But a leaf is purchased from any source [cf. M. A.Z. 2:6D8, 2:7D7]. They purchase wine in Syria only from an expert. And they purchase brine only from an expert, and a piece of meat lacking any mark only from an expert. But any of these may be eaten in the home of one who is not an expert, and one need not scruple on that account.

Now the generic hermeneutics introduces the issue of interstitiality. In the present case what is involved are classes of things that Israelites may not utilize or exploit, classes of things they may not utilize but may exploit, and classes of things they may utilize. Here the interstitial case involves what Israelites may not themselves utilize, but what they may buy or sell. Israelites may not use or derive benefit from gentiles' wine. But the appurtenances of wine, wine-skins or jars, they may buy or sell, and so throughout. M. 2:6 expands the list of the same set, indicated by the probabilities of contamination, whether by reason of idolatry (wine) or by reason of violation of food rules. Then M. 2:7 completes the account of matters: things a gentile cannot possibly corrupt, whether by reason of the circumstance or the character of the thing itself.

II. IDOLS

A. GENERAL PRINCIPLES

M. 3:1 Images are prohibited that have in its hand a staff, bird, or sphere.

M. 3:2 He who finds the shards of images — lo, these are permitted. [If] one found [a fragment] shaped like a hand or a foot, lo, these are prohibited, because objects similar to them are worshipped.

M. 3:3 He who finds utensils upon which is the figure of the sun, moon, or dragon, should bring them to the Salt Sea. One breaks them into pieces and throws the powder to the wind or drops them into the sea. Also: they may be made into manure, as it is said, "And there will cleave nothing of a devoted thing to your hand" (Dt. 13:18).

T. 5:2 A ring on which there is an idol — when it projects, it is prohibited for benefit. But if it does not project [outward from the ring], it is permitted for benefit. And one way or the other, it is prohibited to make a seal with it. And one on which there is no idol is permitted for benefit and permitted for use as a seal. A ring on which there is a seal is permitted for use as a seal. A ring, the seal of which is incised, is prohibited for use as a seal, because with it an image which projects is made. But it is permitted to put it on one's hand. And one, the seal of which projects, is permitted for use as a seal, because the seal which it makes is embedded [in the clay and does not project]. And it is forbidden to put it on one's hand. A ring on which there is a figure is permitted for use as a seal. The reptile-shaped gem which is made in the figure of a dragon is prohibited, and one on which a dragon is suspended — [if] one takes it off and throws it out, as to the rest [of the object], lo, this is permitted.

M. 3:5 Gentiles who worship hills and valleys — these [hills or valleys] are permitted, but what is on them is forbidden [for Israelite use], as it is said, "You shall not covet the silver or gold that is upon them not take it." On what account is an *asherah* prohibited? Because it has been subject to manual labor, and whatever has been subject to manual labor is prohibited.

T. 6:8 Gentiles who worship hills and valleys [M. A.Z. 3:5A] — even though they [hills and valleys] are permitted, those who worship them are put to death by stoning. A man who is worshipped — even though he is permitted, those who worship him are put to death through stoning

M. 3:6 He [the wall of] whose house was adjacent to [and also served as the wall of the temple of] an idol, and [whose house] fell down — it is forbidden to rebuild it. What should he then do? He pulls back within four cubits inside his own property and then rebuilds his house. [If there was a wall belonging] both to him and to [the temple of an] idol, it is judged to be divided half and half. The stones, wood, and mortar deriving from it impart uncleanness in the status of a dead creeping thing, for it is said, "You will utterly detest it" (Deut. 7:26).

T. 6:2 He who designates his house for an idol — the whole of it imparts uncleanness upon entry [to one who comes in]. And he who stands in it, it is as if he is standing in a temple of idolatry. If the public way cuts through it, however, unclean is only that path alone. He who sets up his house near a temple — the whole of it imparts uncleanness upon entry. [If someone else] set up [a temple] near his house, the whole of it does not impart uncleanness upon entry. But that wall [which is nearest to the idol] is deemed to be divided half and half [M. A.Z. 3:6E]. [If the house] fell down, however, it is permitted to rebuild it [If] one has rebuilt it, it has returned to its original condition. [If other people] rebuilt it, not the whole of it imparts uncleanness upon entry, but only that wall alone. It is deemed to be divided half and half. He who sells his house to an idol — the proceeds received for it are forbidden, and one has to bring them to the Salt Sea. But gentiles who forced someone and took over his house and set up an idol in it — the proceeds received for it are permitted. And one may write a deed in that regard and deposit it in the archives.

Once more we move from the general to the specific, in the present case, images in general to the *asherah* in particular. The important point comes at M. 3:5: the distinction between what nature provides and what man has made, spelled out in connection with the asherah. Now, the particular intentionality of a man has come to expression in the labor carried out for making the object. That is what makes the object prohibited.

B. THE ASHERAH

M. 3:7 There are three sorts of houses [so far as use as a shrine for idolatry is concerned]: (1) a house which was built to begin with for the purposes of idolatry — lo, this is prohibited. (2) [If] one stuccoed and decorated it for idolatry and renovated it, one removes the renovations. (3) [If] one brought an idol into it and took it out — lo, this is permitted. There are three sorts of stones: (1) a stone which one hewed to begin with for a pedestal — lo, this is forbidden. (2) [If] he set up an idol on [an existing] stone and then took it off, lo, this is permitted. There are three kinds of *asherahs*: (1) A tree which one planted to begin with for idolatry — lo, this is prohibited. (2) [If] he chopped it and trimmed it for idolatry, and it sprouted afresh, he may remove that which sprouted afresh. (3) [If] he set up an idol under it and then annulled it, lo, this is permitted.

T. 6:3 He who pokes his head and the greater part of his body into a temple containing an idol is unclean. A clay utensil, the contained airspace of which one has poked into a temple containing an idol, is unclean. Benches and chairs, the greater part of which one has poked into a temple containing an idol, are unclean.

T. 6:8. And what is an asherah [M. A.Z. 3:7N]? It is any tree which gentiles worship and guard, and the produce of which they do not eat. They sow seeds underneath it in the rainy season, but not in the dry season. But as to lettuce. neither in the dry season nor in the rainy season [may one plant it there] [M. A.Z. 3:8C-E].

M. 3:8 One should not sit in [an *asherah's*] shade, but if he sat in its shade, he is clean. And he should not pass underneath it, but if he passed underneath it, he is unclean. If it was overshadowing public domain, taking away property from public use, and one passed beneath it, he is clean. And they sow seeds underneath it in the rainy season, but not in the dry season. But as to lettuce, neither in the dry season nor in the rainy season [may one plant it there].

T. 6:8 He who comes under it is as if he came into a temple of idolatry. But if the public way passed through it, lo, this is permitted [cf. M. A.Z. 3:8C].

M. 3:9 [If] one has taken pieces of wood from [an *asherah*], they are prohibited for benefit. [If] he lit a fire in the oven with them, if it is a new oven, it is to be overturned. If it is an old oven, it must be allowed to cool down. [If] he baked a loaf of bread in [the oven heated by the wood of an *asherah*], it is prohibited for benefit. [If] the loaf of bread was mixed up with other loaves of bread, all of them are prohibited as to benefit. [If] one took a piece of wood for a shuttle, it is forbidden for benefit. [If] he wove a garment with the shuttle, the garment is forbidden for benefit. [If] it was mixed up with other garments, and other garments with still others, all of them are forbidden for benefit.

M. 3:10 How does one desecrate [an *asherah*]? [If] one trimmed it or pruned it, took from it a branch or twig, even a leaf — lo, this constitutes desecration. [If] one has trimmed it for the good of [the tree], it remains forbidden. [If he trimmed it] not for the good of the tree, it is permitted.

T. 6:9 An Israelite who trimmed an asherah, whether it was for the good of the tree, or whether it was for his own good — it is prohibited. A gentile who trimmed an asherah — if it was for the good of the tree, the tree is prohibited, but he is permitted. If it was for his own good, one way or the other, it is prohibited [cf. M. A.Z. 3:10].

The taxonomic power of the Halakhah realized in the Mishnah shows what it can do at M. 3:7. If the intention behind the building of the house was idolatrous, that makes the house forbidden. If one has added to an existing house improvements for idolatrous purposes, the house is permitted, once the improvements have been removed. If the house was fully formed and an idol was brought into it, the idol is removed and that allows the house to be used by Israelites. Nothing has been done to the house to render it a temple of idolatry. We have already noted the analogy, as to contaminating effects, of the idol and the corpse, M.3:8. M. 3:9 undertakes a familiar exercise, showing how mixtures are classified, e.g., the mixture of permitted and forbidden substances. What we have, in all, are fine instances of the workings of the Halakhah's generic hermeneutics.

C. THE MERKOLIS

M. 4:1 Three stones, one beside the other, beside a Merkolis statue, — those which appear to belong to it are forbidden, and those which do not appear to belong to it as permitted.

Y. 4:1 I:1 [If an Israelite] put on the second stone [thus not completing the idol, and also slaughtered a beast before the incomplete idol, and the beast was the dam of an offspring that had been slaughtered on that day, or the offspring of a dam that had been slaughtered on that day, so that there are two transgressions in view, one, building an idol, the other, slaughtering a dam and its offspring on the same day], and they had warned [the Israelite] concerning violation of the law against slaughtering the dam and its offspring on the same day, [the Israelite] is given a flogging [on the count of violating the prohibition against slaughtering the dam and its offspring on the same day], but on the count of idolatry he is not stoned to death.]

M. 4:2 [If] one found on its head coins, clothing, or utensils, lo, these are permitted. [If one found] bunches of grapes, garlands of corn, jugs of wine or oil, or fine flour or anything the like of which is offered on the altar — it is forbidden.

T. 6:10 One should not climb up to the top of a pedestal, even to disfigure it, even to defile it, as it is said, Nothing of what is dedicated shall cleave to your hand" (Deut. 13:18).

T. 6:11 One should not say to his fellow, "Wait for me by the idol of so and so," or, "I'll wait for you by the idol of such-and-such," as it is said, "You will not make mention of the name of any other god" (Ex. 23:13).

T. 6:12 An idol and everything on it — lo, this is forbidden. [If] one found on it jugs of wine, oil, or fine flour, or anything the like of which is offered on the altar [M. A.Z. 4:2C], it is forbidden. [If he found on it] utensils which are used for it and for its body, they are forbidden. [If they are] not [used] for its body, they are permitted. Also as to utensils which are used for them and for its body, [if] priests of idolatry stole and sold them — lo, they are permitted.

T. 6:13 One Scripture says, "You shall not covet the silver or the gold that is on them or take it for yourself" (Deut. 7:25). And one Scripture says, "And you have seen their detestable things, their idols of wood and stone, of silver and gold, which were among them" (Deut. 29:17). How is it possible to carry out both of these verses? On them — whether its body is clothed in them or not clothed in them, they are forbidden. Among them — Those, the body of which is clothed in them, are forbidden, and those, the body of which is not clothed in them, are permitted. And also clothing in which the body [of the idol] is clothed [if] they have sold them, lo, these are permitted. A Merkolis and whatever is on it is forbidden. [If] one found on it jugs of wine, oil, or fine flour, or anything, the like of which is offered on the altar, it is forbidden. [If one found on it] coins or utensils, they are permitted.

T. 6:14 Stones which dropped away from a Merkolis, if they appeared to belong with it, they are forbidden, and if not, they are permitted [M. A.Z. 4:1C]. An Israelite who brought stones from a Merkolis — lo, they are forbidden, for they have been forbidden by the idol. A gentile who brought stones from a Merkolis — lo they are permitted, for they are in the status of an idol where worshippers have abandoned it. And a Merkolis which was ripped up from its place is permitted for benefit [for Israelites].

The Merkolis is, at a minimum, a mound of three stones, constructed as an idol. If one found things not usually offered on such an altar, they are deemed null. We do not take account of an act of intentionality that violates common norms.

D. NULLIFYING AN IDOL

M. 4:3 An idol which had a garden or a bathhouse — they derive benefit from them [when it is] not to the advantage [of the temple], but they do not derive benefit from them [when it is] to the advantage [of the temple]. If it belonged both to the idol and to outsiders, they derive benefit from them whether or not it is to the advantage [of the temple].

T. 6:1 A cow which one fattened using vetches belonging to an idol — [or if such a cow] went down to pasture in a garden which one has manured with a manure belonging to an idol — (. [the field] must be left fallow. A garden which one ploughed with [a plough made of] pieces of wood of an asherah — [the field] must be left fallow. Kelilan-wool which one stamped with wood belonging to an idol — one must burn it. Others say, "One assigns to it the more stringent ruling until its appearance will return to what it was." [If] there were bagpipes belonging to an idol, one is prohibited from making a lamentation with them. If they were rented from the state, even though they were made for the use of an idol, it is permitted to make a lamentation using them. Ships belonging to an idol — it is prohibited to rent [space] in them. But if they were rented from the state, even though they were made for the use of an idol, it is permitted to rent them. Charity collectors for a temple of idolatry — it is prohibited to give anything to them. But if they were paid by the state, even though they are working for the welfare of an idol, it is permitted to give a contribution to them [cf. M. A.Z. 4:3].

T. 6:4 All places which are called by names complimentary to idolatry does one rename with euphemisms insulting to idolatry. A place which they call, "The face of god," do they call, "The face of the dog." "A spring for all" ('YN KL) do they call "A spring of a thorn" ('YN QOS) "Good fortune (GDGYA)" do they call "A mound (GLYA)." He whose coins were scattered in the direction of an idol should not bend over before it to pick them up, because it looks as if he is bowing down to an idol. But he turns his back on the idol and collects the coins [with his behind toward the idol]. And in a place in which he is not seen, it is all right [to do it the other way].

T. 6:5 A spring which flows out of an idol — one should not bend down before it and drink, because he appears to bow down before an idol. But he turns his back and drinks. And in a place in which he is not seen, it is all right.

T. 6:6 Figures which spout out water in towns — one should not place his mouth on the mouth of the figurine and drink, because it appears that he is kissing the idol. But he collects the water in his hand and drinks it.

Y. 4:3 I:1 As to bagpipes belonging to an idol, it is forbidden to sell them [to make a lamentation with them]. If they were rented from the state, even though they were made for use of an idol, it is permitted to make lamentation using them. Shops belonging to an idol's [temple]it is prohibited to rent space in them. But if they provided a rental for the state, even though they were built for the use of an idol['s temple], it is permitted to rent them. Charity collectors for a temple of idolatry — it is prohibited to give anything to them. But if they provided funds to the state, even though they are working for the welfare of an idol — it is permitted to give a contribution to them [as at M. A.Z. 4:3D].

M. 4:4 An idol belonging to a gentile is prohibited forthwith [when it is made]. And one belonging to an Israelite is prohibited only after it will have been worshipped. A gentile has the power to nullify an idol belonging either to himself or his fellow gentile. But an Israelite has not got the power to nullify an idol belonging to a gentile. He who nullifies an idol has nullified its appurtenances. [If] he nullified [only] its appurtenances, its appurtenances are permitted, but the idol itself [remains] prohibited.

T. 5:3 He who purchases metal filings from gentiles and found an idol therein takes it and tosses it away, and the rest — lo, this is permitted. An Israelite who found an idol before it has come into his domain may tell a gentile to nullify it. For a gentile has the power to nullify an idol, whether it belongs to him or to his fellow [M. A.Z. 4:4C], whether it is an idol which has been worshipped or whether it is one which has not been worshipped, whether it is inadvertent or deliberate, whether it is under constraint or willingly. But an Israelite who made an idol — it is prohibited, even though he has not worshipped it [vs. M. A.Z. 4-4B] Therefore he has not got the power to nullify it.

T. 5:4 A gentile who made an idol — it is permitted until it has been worshipped [vs. M. A.Z. 4:4A]. Therefore he has the power to nullify it.

T. 5:5 A gentile who sold an idol to people who worship it — it is prohibited. If he sold it to people who do not worship it, it is permitted. One may lend money on the strength of it [as a pledge]. [If] a wreck fell on it, if a river swept it away, or thugs grabbed it — as in the case of the war of Joshua — if the owner is going to go looking for it, it is forbidden. If not, it is permitted.

T. 5:6 The pedestals which gentiles set up during the persecution [by Hadrian] — even though the time of persecution is over — Lo, these are forbidden. Is it possible that an idol which a gentile nullified — is it possible that it should be deemed prohibited? Scripture says, "The graven images of their gods you shall burn with fire" (Deut. 7:25). That which he treats as a god is prohibited. And that which he does not treat as a god is permitted. Is it then possible that an idol which a gentile nullified should be deemed permitted? Scripture says, The graven images of their gods . . .— Whether he treats it as a god or does not treat it as a god, it is forbidden.

T. 5:7 How does one nullify [an idol]? A gentile nullifies an idol belonging to himself or to an Israelite. But an Israelite does not nullify an idol belonging to a gentile [cf. M. A.Z. 4:4C-D].

T. 5:9 At what point is it called 'set aside [for idolatrous purposes]'? Once some concrete deed has been done to it [for that purpose]

T. 5:10 What is one which has been worshipped? Any one which people worship — whether inadvertently or deliberately. What is one which has been set aside? Any which has been set aside for idolatry. But if one has said, "This ox is for idolatry," "This house is for idolatry," he has said nothing whatsoever. For there is no such thing as an act of consecration for idolatry.

M. 4:5 How does one nullify it? [If] he has cut off the tip of its ear, the tip of its nose, the tip of its finger, [if] he battered it, even though he did not break off [any part of] it, he has nullified it. [If] he spit in its face, urinated in front of it, scraped it, threw shit at it, lo, this does not constitute an act of nullification.

T. 5:8 A pedestal, the greater part of which was damaged — lo, this is permitted. One the whole of which was damaged is prohibited until one will restore it. That belonging to him is permitted, and that belonging to his fellow is prohibited. Before it has been sanctified, it is prohibited. After it has been sanctified, it is permitted.

M. 4:6 An idol, the worshippers of which have abandoned it in time of peace, is permitted. [If they abandoned it] in time of war, it is forbidden. Idol pedestals set up for kings — lo, these are permitted, since they set [images up on them only] at the time kings go by.

If a gentile makes an idol, his intentionality governs, start to finish, and as soon as the idol is complete, it is forbidden. But if an Israelite owns the object, we assume he does not worship it, until by a deed he shows that he does. If an Israelite owns an idol, his intentionality to nullify it is affective; but Israelite will has no affect upon gentile idols. What one does to the principal affects the appurtenance, but not vice versa, M. 4:4, which is another routine, generic exercise, distinguishing primary from subordinate components of a mixture. Nullifying an idol involves an act of disrespect for the object, which then realizes the attitude of nullification.

III.   LIBATION WINE

M. 4:8 They purchase from gentiles [the contents of] a wine press which has already been trodden out, even though [the gentile] takes [the grapes] in hand and

**puts them on the heap ["apple"], for it is not made into wine used for libations
until it drips down into the vat. [And if wine has] dripped into the vat, what
is in the cistern is prohibited, while the rest is permitted.**

T. 7:1 At first they ruled, They do not gather grapes with a gentile. And they do not
press grapes with an Israelite who prepares his wine in a state of uncleanness [cf.
M. A.Z. 4:9C-D]. Truly they gather grapes with a gentile All the same are new and
old ones: they assist him until he passes out of sight. Once he has passed out of
sight, he may turn the wine into libation wine [but Israelites are not responsible
for the fact].

T. 7:3 An Israelite who works with a gentile at the winepress — Lo, this one brings up
the 'bread' [that is, the mass of wine-pulp] to the 'apple' [the heap to be pressed],
and brings down the wine from the 'apple.' Even though the wine flows over his
hands, it is permitted. For it is not their custom to make a libation under such
circumstances [M. A.Z. 4:8A-C]. A gentile who works with an Israelite at the
winepress — Lo, this one brings up the 'bread' to the 'apple,' and brings down
the 'bread' from the 'apple.' Even though the wine flows over his hands, it is
permitted. For it is not their custom to make a libation under such circumstances.

Y. 4:8 I:2 *A winepress that a gentile stopped up [filling in the cracks] — [if he stopped
up the vat from] the inside, [the wine] is forbidden, [and if he stopped up the vat]
from the outside, it is permitted. [The basis for this distinction is that] it is not
possible that there was not there a single moist drop [of wine in one of the cracks],
which the gentile will touch and offer as a libation, thus rendering into libation
wine whatever thereafter flows into the cistern.*

M. 4:9 **[Israelites] tread a wine press with a gentile [in the gentile's vat]. But they
do not gather grapes with him. An Israelite who prepares [his wine] in a state
of uncleanness — they do not trample or cut grapes with him. But they do
take jars with him to the wine press, and they bring them with him from the
wine press. A baker who prepares bread in a state of uncleanness — they do
not knead or cut out dough with him. But they may take bread with him to
the dealer.**

M. 4:10 **A gentile who is found standing beside a cistern of wine — if he had a lien
on the vat, it is prohibited. [If] he had no lien on it, it is permitted. [If] he fell
into the vat and climbed out, or (2) [if gentiles] measured it with a reed — or
(3) [if] he flicked out a hornet with a reed, or [if] (4) he patted down the froth
on the mouth of a jar — in regard to each of these there was a case let it be
sold. [If] (5) he took a jar and threw it in a fit of temper into the vat — this
was a case, and they declared it valid.**

T. 7:4 He who weighs out grapes on a scale — even though the wine flows over his
hands, it is permitted, for it is not their custom to make a libation [under such
circumstances]. He who presses wine into a jar, even though the wine flows over
his hands — it is permitted. For it is not their custom to make a libation under
such circumstances. [If a gentile] fell into the cistern and even a single drop of
wine of any amount touched him, it is forbidden [M. A.Z. 4:10D]. [If] he went
down to draw the grape-skins and the grape pits out of the cistern — this was a
case, and they asked sages. And they ruled, "Let the whole of it be sold to gentiles."

T. 7:5 A gentile who was bringing up grapes in baskets and barrels at the winepress,
even though one has beaten them in the winepress, and the wine has spurted onto

the grapes — it is permitted. For it is not their custom to make a libation under such circumstances. He who bought pressed grapes from a gentile, and found under it little holes [containing wine] — it is prohibited.

M. 4:11 He who in a condition of cleanness prepares the wine belonging to a gentile, and leaves it in his domain, in a house which is open to the public domain, in a town in which there are both gentiles and Israelites — [the wine] is permitted. [If it is] in a town in which all the residents are gentiles, [the wine] is prohibited, unless he sets up a guard. And the guard need not sit there and watch [the room all the time]. Even though he comes in and goes out, [the wine] is permitted.

T. 7:7 An Israelite who put wine into the domain of a gentile — if there is a lock or a seal on [the jug of wine], it is permitted. And if not, it is forbidden [cf. M. A.Z. 4:12A-B]. [If] one borrowed money on the strength of it from a gentile, even though there is on it a lock or a seal, it is forbidden [cf. M. A.Z. 4:12C-D]. But if the storehouse was open to the public domain, it is permitted. In a town, all the residents of which are gentiles, it is forbidden, unless one sits down and guards it [cf. M. A.Z. 4:11].

T. 7:9 An Israelite who prepared the wine of a gentile in a condition of cleanness, and put it in two courtyards or in two towns, even though [the Israelite] comes out and goes in from this courtyard to that courtyard, or from this town to that town — it is permitted. For it is in the assumption of being guarded [cf. M. A.Z. 4:11F-G]. But if it is taken for granted that [the Israelite] spends the night in some one place, it is forbidden [since the gentile may then make a libation of that which he assumes the Israelite will not see].

M. 4:12 He who prepares the wine of a gentile in a condition of cleanness and leaves it in his domain, and the latter wrote for [the Israelite a receipt, saying], "I received its price from you" — it is permitted. But if an Israelite wants then to remove the wine, and [the gentile] would not let him do so unless he paid the price of the wine — this was a case in Bet Shean, and sages declared [the wine] forbidden.

T. 7:8 An Israelite who prepared the wine of a gentile in a condition of cleanness, and the latter wrote for him a quittance, saying, "I received its price from you" [M. A.Z. 4:12A-B]...[if the gentile will not let him remove the wine unless he paid the price of the wine — this was a case, and they came and asked R. Simeon b. Eleazar, who ruled, "Whatever was in the domain of a gentile is subject to the same law" [M. A.Z. 4:11H].

M. 5:1 A [gentile] who hires an [Israelite] worker to work with him in the preparation of libation wine — [the Israelite's] salary is forbidden. [If] he hired him to do some other kind of work, even though he said to him, "Move a jar of libation wine from one place to another," his salary is permitted. He who hires an ass to bring libation wine on it — its fee is forbidden. [If] he hired it to ride on it, even though the gentile [also] put a flagon [of libation wine] on it, its fee is permitted.

T. 7:10 A market into which an Israelite and a gentile bring wine, even though the jars are open, and the gentile is sitting nearby — it is permitted, because it is assumed to be guarded. He who hires a worker to work with him for half a day in that [wine] which was subject to a prohibition, and half a day in that [wine] which was subject to permission, and one put all [the wine which had been prepared] in a single town — Lo, these [both] are forbidden. [If] these are kept by themselves and those are kept by themselves, the first ones are forbidden, and the second ones are permitted. [A gentile] who hires a worker to do work with him toward evening, and said to him, "Bring this flagon to that place," even though an Israelite is not permitted to do so — his wages are permitted. A person may say to his ass drivers and his workers, "Go and get yourselves some food with this denar," "Go and get yourselves some wine with this denar" and he does not scruple because of tithes, violation of the rules governing the seventh year, or the prohibition of wine used for libations. But if he had said to them, "Go and eat a loaf of bread, and you pay for it," lo, this one then must take account of the matter of tithes, produce of the seventh year, and use of libation-wine."

T. 8:1 He who pours out wine from one utensil to another [M.A.Z.5:7H] [if he places] the spout against the lips of the jar and below — Lo, this is prohibited. The vat, ladle, and siphon of gentiles — sages prohibit. And on what account are these prohibited and those permitted? These are made for holding liquid, and those are not made for holding liquid. As to those of wood and of stone, one has to dry them off [M. A.Z. 5:1 A-E]. If they were of pitch, he has to scale them.

M. 5:2 Libation wine which fell on grapes — one may rinse them off, and they are permitted. But if [the grapes] were split, they are prohibited. [If] it fell on figs or dates, if there is sufficient [libation wine absorbed] to impart a flavor [to them], they are forbidden. This is the governing principle: anything which bestows benefit through imparting a flavor is forbidden, and anything which does not bestow benefit through imparting a flavor is permitted — for example, vinegar [from libation wine] which falls on crushed beans.

M. 5:3 A gentile who with an Israelite was moving jars of wine from place to place — if [the wine] was assumed to be watched, it is permitted. If [the Israelite] informed him that he was going away [the wine is prohibited if he was gone] for a time sufficient to bore a hole [in a jug of wine] and stop it up and [for the clay] to dry.

M. 5:4 He who leaves his wine on a wagon or in a boat and went along by a shortcut, entered into a town and bathed — it is permitted. But if he informed [others] that he was going away, [the wine is prohibited if he was gone] for a time sufficient to bore a hole and sop it up and for the clay to dry. He who leaves a gentile in a store, even though he is going out and coming in all the time — it is permitted. But if he informed him that he was going away, [the wine is prohibited if he was gone] for a time sufficient to bore a hole and stop it up and for the clay to dry.

T. 7:12 He who leaves his wine in a store and went into a town, even though he remained there for a considerable time, Lo, this [wine] is permitted. But if he informed him or locked the store, it is forbidden.

T. 7:13 He who leaves his wine on a boat and entered town, even though he remained there for a considerable time, it is permitted. But if he informed him that he was going away, or if the boat cast anchor, Lo, this is forbidden [cf. M. A.Z. 5:4A-C].

M. 5:5 [If an Israelite] was eating with [a gentile] at the same time, and he put a flagon [of wine] on the table and a flagon on a side table, and he left it and went out — what is on the table is forbidden. But what is on the side table is

permitted. And if he had said to him, "You mix and drink [wine]," even that which is on the side table is forbidden. Jars which are open are forbidden. And those which are sealed [are forbidden if he was gone] for a time sufficient to bore a hole and stop it up and for the clay to dry.

T. 7:14 He who sends a jug of wine with a Samaritan, or one of juice, vinegar, brine, oil, or honey, with a gentile — if he recognizes his seal, which stopped it up, it is permitted. And if not, it is forbidden. Wine with a gentile which is sealed is forbidden on the count of libation-wine. But as to juice, brine, oil, and honey, if he saw a gentile who offered them up as a libation, they are forbidden. If not, they are permitted.

T. 7:15 An Israelite who is suspect — they drink from his wine-cellar, but they do not drink from his flask. If he was suspect of [opening the jars and] sealing them, even wine from his wine-cellar is prohibited.

M. 5:6 A band of gentile [raiders] which entered a town in peacetime — open jars are forbidden, closed ones, permitted. [If it was] wartime, these and those are permitted. because there is no time for making a libation.

M. 5:7 Israelite craftsmen, to whom a gentile sent a jar of libation wine as their salary, are permitted to say to him, "Give us its value." But if it has already entered their possession, it is prohibited. He who sells his wine to a gentile [and] agreed on a price before he had measured it out — proceeds paid for it are permitted. [If] he had measured it out before he had fixed its price, proceeds paid for it are prohibited. [If] he took the funnel and measured it out into the flask of the gentile and then went and measured wine into the flask of an Israelite, if there remained [in the funnel] a drop of wine [from what had been poured into the gentile's flask, then what is in the Israelite's flask] is forbidden. He who pours [wine] from one utensil to another — that from which is emptied [the wine] is permitted. But that into which he emptied [the wine] is forbidden.

T. 7:16 A gentile who owed [money] to an Israelite, even though he sold libation-wine and brought him the proceeds, [or sold] an idol and brought him the proceeds, it is permitted [cf. M. A.Z. 5:7A]. But if not [that is, the gentile did not sell the wine or idol, but delivered the wine or idol to him directly], it is forbidden. But if he said to him, "Wait until I sell my libation-wine [or my] idol and 1'11 bring you the proceeds," it is forbidden.

T. 7:17 He who makes an agreement to sell wine to a gentile, and agreed on the price and measured out the wine — even though he is going to dry out the siphons and the measures, it is permitted [cf. M. A.Z. 5:7C-D]. And a storekeeper, one way or the other, is permitted, for each drop as it comes becomes an obligation upon [the gentile] [M. A.Z. 5:7C-D]. A gentile who sent a flagon to an Israelite, and a drop of wine is in it — Lo, this one fills up the flagon and takes from him the value of the whole of it and does not scruple [about libation-wine which may be in it].

M. 5:8 Libation wine is forbidden and imparts a prohibition [to wine with which it is mixed] in any measure at all. [If it is] wine [poured] into wine, or [libation] water [poured] into water, in any quantity whatever [it is forbidden]. [If it is] wine [poured] into water or water [poured] into wine, [it is forbidden] if it imparts flavor. This is the governing principle: [If it is] one species [poured] into its own species [B], [it is forbidden] in any measure at all. [If it is] not [poured] into its own species [C], it is forbidden if it imparts flavor.

M. 5:9 These are forbidden and impose a prohibition in any measure at all: (1) libation wine, (2) an idol, (3) hides with a hole at the heart, (4) an ox which is to be stoned, (5) a heifer, the neck of which is to be broken, (6) birds belonging to a *mesora'*, (7) the hair cut off a Nazir (Num. 6:18), (8) the [unredeemed] firstborn of an ass (Ex. 13:13), (9) meat in milk, (10) the goat which is to be sent forth, (11) unconsecrated beasts which have been slaughtered in the Temple courtyard — lo, these are forbidden and impose a prohibition in any measure at all.

M. 5:10 Libation wine that fell into a vat — the whole of [the vat] is forbidden for benefit.

M. 5:11 A stone wine press which a gentile covered with pitch – one scours it, and it is clean. And one of wood — let him scale off the pitch." And one of earthenware — even though one has scaled off the pitch, lo, this is forbidden.

M. 5:12 He who purchases utensils [for use with food] from a gentile — that which is usually immersed one must immerse. That which is usually scalded one must scald. That which is usually heated to a white-hot flame one must heat to a white-hot flame. A spit or gridiron one must heat to a white-hot flame. A knife one must polish, and it is clean.

T. 8:2 He who purchases utensils from gentiles [M . A.Z. 5:12A] — in the case of things which one knows have not been used, one immerses them and they are clean. In the case of things which one knows have been used, in the instance of cups and flasks, one rinses them in cold water [M. A.Z. 5:12B]. [If they were] pitchers, water-kettles, frying pans, or kettles, one rinses them in boiling water [M. A.Z. 5:12C]. In the case of knives, spits, and grid-irons, one heats them to a white heat, and they are clean [M. A.Z. 5:12D]. In the case of all of them which have been used before they have been polished, if one has scalded, immersed, or heated them to white heat, (and) lo, this is permitted.

T. 8:3 He whose wine-vats and olive-presses were unclean and who wants to clean them — the boards and the two posts supporting the beams of the press and the troughs does he dry, and they are clean. The cylinders of twigs and of hemp does he dry. As to those of bast and of reeds, he leaves them unused.

The basic principle is, if gentiles are subject to supervision, they are not going to spoil wine by using a bit of it for a libation. But if they think they can get away with it, under all circumstances they will make an offering to their idol. The long account of how Israelites deal with wine touched, therefore used as a libation, by idolaters, spins out in detail a few governing principles. The first is, only when wine has reached the state at which it can be used for a libation do the taboos take effect, so if a gentile handles wine before it has dripped into the vat and is deemed wine, the prohibitions do not apply. If the gentile exercises control of wine, e.g., stands by a wine press not under Israelite supervision, and if he thinks he has a right to touch the wine, it is affected. But idolaters know the Halakhah and will not spoil for the Israelite market wine that they control. And their touch must effect their intention; if they touch wine in a fit of temper, we do not assume they have made a libation of a bit of it. Israelites who work for idolaters may not be paid for making wine, since that would be a reward for work done for idolatry. The Halakhah here makes concrete the simple principles that govern throughout.

IV. DOCUMENTARY TRAITS

A. THE MISHNAH AND THE TOSEFTA

The differences between the Mishnah and the Tosefta do not extend to the category-formation and its hermeneutics.

B. THE YERUSHALMI AND THE BAVLI

The two Talmuds conduct their usual exegetical work, undertaking, within the Halakhic framework, no new initiatives.

C. THE AGGADAH AND THE HALAKHAH IN THE BAVLI

Providing a handbook for the conduct of foreign relations between Israel and the gentiles, the Bavli-tractate Abodah-Zarah in its Aggadic complement to the Halakhic category-formation commences with a massive and compelling essay on how Israel and the gentiles relate. There the question is answered of why God has rejected the gentiles in favor of Israel, the Torah supplying the center of the discussion. The Bavli has vastly recast the category-formation, Abodah Zarah, selecting data and interpreting them in response to issues not encompassed within the Halakhic hermeneutics. To see how this is accomplished, to begin with we have to distinguish in the Bavli among the large composites that do not directly address the amplification of the Mishnah between two types. The first is the composite that is tacked on for formal reasons, e.g., more sayings that bear the same attributive formula as the saying that has served the Mishnah, or more information on a subject that the Mishnah treats. The second is the composite that in no way relates to the Mishnah's rules, principles, or authorities. I place the former in parentheses, and catalogue the latter, which then are treated in the proper context: the question of how the intruded composites have affected and drastically changed the re-presentation of the Mishnah-tractate.

Our task is now to survey those large-scale composites that accomplish a task other than that of Mishnah-exegesis. I omit reference to those items that form mere topical appendices or compilations of sayings in the name of an authority who figures in a Mishnah-comment. The remainder are as follows:

I.B: A THEOLOGY OF GENTILE IDOLATRY: ITS ORIGINS AND ITS
        IMPLICATIONS FOR HOLY ISRAEL: Why the gentiles rejected the

Torah. It was offered to each of them, but they were too much
absorbed by their own matters to accept God's will. They did
not even carry out the seven commandments of the children
of Noah.

I.C: THE CRITICAL IMPORTANCE OF TORAH-STUDY FOR THE SALVATION
OF ISRAEL, INDIVIDUALLY AND COLLECTIVELY: Why are human
beings compared to fish of the sea? To tell you, just as fish in
the sea, when they come up on dry land, forthwith begin to
die, so with human beings, when they take their leave of
teachings of the Torah and religious deeds, forthwith they
begin to die.

I.D: GOD FAVORS HOLY ISRAEL OVER THE GENTILES, BECAUSE THE
FORMER ACCEPT, STUDY, AND CARRY OUT THE TORAH AND THE
LATTER DO NOT. THEREFORE AT THE END OF DAYS GOD WILL
SAVE ISRAEL AND DESTROY IDOLATRY: R. Hinena bar Pappa
contrasted verses of Scripture: "It is written, 'As to the
almighty, we do not find him exercising plenteous power'
(Job 37:23), but by contrast, 'Great is our Lord and of abundant
power' (Ps. 147:5), and further, 'Your right hand, Lord, is
glorious in power' (Ex. 15:6). But there is no contradiction
between the first and second and third statements, for the
former speaks of the time of judgment when justice is tempered
with mercy, so God does not do what he could and the latter
two statements refer to a time of war of God against his
enemies."

I.E: GOD'S JUDGMENT AND WRATH, GOD'S MERCY AND FORGIVENESS
FOR ISRAEL: "It is written, 'You only have I known among all
the families of the earth; therefore I will visit upon you all
your iniquities' (Amos 3:2). If one is angry, does he vent it on
someone he loves?" He said to them, "I shall tell you a parable.
To what is the matter comparable? To the case of a man who
lent money to two people, one a friend, the other an enemy.
From the friend he collects the money little by little, from the
enemy he collects all at once."

I.F: BALAAM, THE PROPHET OF THE GENTILES, AND ISRAEL; GOD'S
ANGER WITH THE GENTILES BUT NOT WITH ISRAEL: The prophet
of the gentiles was a fool, but he did have the power to curse;
Israel was saved by God. Said R. Eleazar, "Said the Holy
One, blessed be He, to Israel, 'My people, see how many acts
of righteousness I carried out with you, for I did not grow
angry with you during all those perilous days, for if I had
grown angry with you, there would not have remained from
Israel a remnant or a survivor.'"

I.G: THE TIME OF GOD'S ANGER IN RELATIONSHIP TO THE GENTILES
AND TO ISRAEL; THE ROLE OF IDOLATRY IN GOD'S WRATH AGAINST
THE NATIONS: That time at which God gets angry comes when
the kings put on their crowns on their heads and prostrate

themselves to the sun. Forthwith the Holy One, blessed be He, grows angry.

I.H: THE SINFUL ANCESTOR OF THE MESSIAH AND GOD'S FORGIVENESS OF HIM AND OF ISRAEL: God's forgiveness of David is the archetype of God's forgiveness of Israel. If an individual has sinned, they say to him, 'Go to the individual such as David, and follow his example, and if the community as a whole has sinned, they say to them, 'Go to the community such as Israel. TORAH-STUDY IS THE ANTIDOTE TO SIN: "What is the meaning of the verse of Scripture, 'Happy are you who sow beside all waters, that send forth the feet of the ox and the ass' (Is. 32:20)? 'Happy are you, O Israel, when you are devoted to the Torah and to doing deeds of grace, then their inclination to do evil is handed over to them, and they are not handed over into the power of their inclination to do evil."

III.C: THE DIVISIONS OF ISRAEL'S HISTORY; THE HISTORY OF THE WORLD IN ITS PERIODS: here we deal with the history of Israel by its periods, with special attention to Israel's relationships with Rome, on the one side, and the point at which the Messiah will come, on the other, ca. 468: When four hundred years have passed from the destruction of the Temple, if someone says to you, 'Buy this field that is worth a thousand denars for a single denar, don't buy it.

III.E: COLLECTION OF STORIES ABOUT RABBI AND ANTIGONUS: Rabbi maintained cordial relationships with the Emperor, in which Rabbi gave the sage advice, and the emperor took it.

VIII.C: THE TRIAL OF ELIEZER B. HYRCANUS. IN THE MATTER OF MINUT: Reference to the idolaters' judges' tribunal, scaffold, and stadium, calls to mind the trial of the sage by reason of the charge of Minut, or, in context, Christianity. It is no different in its workings from the state: "the two daughters who cry out from Gehenna, saying to this world, 'Bring, bring.' And who are they? They are Minut and the government."

VIII.D: IDOLATRY AND LEWDNESS: the antidote is Torah-study.

VIII.E: ROMAN JUSTICE, JEWISH MARTYRDOM: Hanina, my brother, don't you know that from Heaven have they endowed this nation Rome with dominion? For Rome has destroyed his house, burned his Temple, slain his pious ones, and annihilated his very best — and yet endures! And yet I have heard about you that you go into session and devote yourself to the Torah and even call assemblies in public, with a scroll lying before you in your bosom.

VIII.F: THE STADIUM, THE CIRCUS, THE THEATER: He who goes to a stadium or to a camp to see the performances of sorcerers and enchanters or of various kinds of clowns, mimics, buffoons, and the like — lo, this is a seat of the scoffers, as it is said, "Happy is the man who has not walked in the counsel of the

wicked...nor sat in the seat of the scoffers. But his delight is
in the Torah of the Lord" (Ps. 1:12). Lo, you thereby learn
that these things cause a man to neglect the study of the Torah.

VIII.G: HAPPY IS THE MAN WHO HAS NOT WALKED IN THE COUNSEL OF THE
          WICKED, NOR STOOD IN THE WAY OF SINNERS, NOR SAT IN THE SEAT
          OF THE SCORNFUL. "'Happy is the man who has not walked' —
          to theaters and circuses of gentiles; 'nor stood in the way of
          sinners' — he does not attend contests of wild beasts..."

IX.B: COMPOSITE ON THE PROHIBITION OF STARING IN A LASCIVIOUS OR
          OTHERWISE IMPROPER MANNER

From its initial insertion of a massive account of gentile idolatry, the Bavli
drastically reframes issues. The Halakhah, beginning with the Mishnah's statement
of it, asks not a single question of history or theology. it deals only with commercial
relationships with gentiles, so far as these are affected by idolatry, idols, and libation
wine. So the topic at hand is treated in a routine and commonplace manner. The
Talmud's Aggadah in the heart of its Halakhic repertoire transforms presentation of
the category-formation — and then transcends it altogether. The Aggadah transforms
it by reframing the issue of idolatry so that at stake is no longer relationships between
Israelites and idolaters but rather, those between idolatrous *nations* and God. It
then transcends the topic by introducing the antidote to idolatry, which is the Torah.
So the Aggadah restores the public dimension, that of collectivity lacking in the
Halakhah. Israel differs from idolatrous nations by reason of the Torah, and that
imparts a special character to all of Israel's everyday conduct, not only its abstinence
from idol-worship. In fact, the Talmud makes this tractate into an occasion for
reflection on the problem of Israel and the nations.

Predictably, the sages in the Aggadic treatment of the category-formation at
hand invoke the one matter that they deem critical to all else: the Torah. Israel
differs from the gentiles not for the merely negative reason that it does not worship
idols but only an invisible God. It differs from them for the positive reason that the
Torah that defines Israel's life was explicitly rejected by the gentiles. Every one of
them had its chance at the Torah, and all of them rejected it. When the gentiles try
to justify themselves to God by appealing to their forthcoming relationships to
Israel, that is dismissed as self-serving. The gentiles could not even observe the
seven commandments assigned to the Noahides. From that point, the composite
that stands at the head of the tractate and imparts its sense to all that will follow
proceeds to the next question, that is, from the downfall of the gentiles by reason of
their idolatry and rejection of the Torah to the salvation of Israel through the Torah.

Lest we miss the point, the reason for God's favor is made explicit: God
favors Israel because Israel keeps the Torah. God therefore is strict with the gentiles
but merciful to Israel. This is forthwith assigned a specific illustration: Balaam, the
gentiles' prophet, presents the occasion to underscore God's anger toward the gentiles
and his mercy to Israel. Bringing us back to the beginning, we then are shown how

God's anger for the gentiles comes to the fore when the gentiles worship idols: when the kings who rule the world worship nature rather than nature's Creator. How God forgives Israel is then shown in respect to David's sin, and Torah-study as the antidote to sin once more is introduced. It is difficult to conclude other than that the framers of the Talmud have added to the presentation of the topic the results of profound thought on idolatry as a force in the history of humanity and of Israel. They thus have re-presented the Halakhah's topic in a far more profound framework of reflection than the Halakhah, with its rather petty interests in details of this and that, would have lead us to anticipate.

The next set of free-standing composites presents episodic portraits of the matters introduced at the outset. The first involves world history and its periods, divided, it goes without saying, in relationship to the history of Israel, which stands at the center of world history. Israel now finds its opposite, and Rome defines that counterpart, so Israel's and Rome's relationships, culminating in the coming of the Messiah, are introduced. The next two collections form a point and counterpoint. On the one side, we have the tale of how Rabbi and the Roman Emperor formed a close relationship, with Rabbi the wise counselor, the ruler behind the throne. So whatever good happens in Rome happens by reason of our sages' wisdom, deriving as it does from the Torah, on which the stories predictably are going to harp. Then comes as explicit a judgment upon Christianity in the framework of world-history as I think we are likely to find in the Talmud. The set of stories involves Eliezer b. Hyrcanus and how he was tried for Minut, which the story leaves no doubt stands for Christianity. Now "Minut" and the Roman government are treated as twin-sources of condemnation. And it is in that very context that the stories of Roman justice and Jewish martyrdom, by reason of Torah-study, are introduced. Not only so, but — should we miss the contrast the compilers wish to draw — the very same setting sets forth the counterpart and opposite: the stadium, circus, and theater, place for scoffers and buffoons, as against the sages' study-center, where people avoid the seat of the scornful but instead study the Torah.

The Talmud's associations with idolatry then compare and contrast these opposites: Israel and Rome; martyrdom and wantonness; Torah and lewdness and other forms of sin; probity and dignity and buffoonery; and on and on. The Mishnah finds no reason to introduce into the consideration of idolatry either the matter of the Torah or the issue of world history. The Talmud cannot deal with the details of conduct with gentiles without asking the profound questions of divine intentionality and human culpability that idolatry in the world provokes. And yet, if we revert to the Mishnah's fabricated debates with the philosophers, we see the issue introduced and explored. What the Mishnah lacks is not a philosophy of monotheism in contrast with polytheism and its idols, but a theology of history and a theodicy of Israel's destiny, a salvific theory. These the Talmud introduces, with enormous effect. And, we note, once these propositions have been inserted, the Talmud allows the systematic exposition of the Mishnah to go forward without theological intrusion of any kind. The point has been made.

Now, we wonder, where have our sages learned to interpret the issue of idolatry in a historical and theological framework, rather than in a merely practical and reasonable one, such as the Mishnah's authorship provides? A glance at the verses of Scripture given earlier answers the question. Idolatry explains the fate of the nations, Israel's covenant through the Torah, Israel's. But the verses of Scripture cited earlier hardly serve as source for the reflections on Israel and Rome, the ages of human history, the power of God to forgive, and, above all, the glory of the Torah as the mediating source of God's love and forgiveness. All of this our sages of blessed memory themselves formulated and contributed. Scripture provided important data, the Mishnah, the occasion, but for the theology of history formed around the center of the Torah, we look to our sages for the occasion and the source. And sages' success in meeting the challenge of the topic at hand explains why no tractate more successfully demonstrates how the Talmud's framers' massive insertions transform the Mishnah's statement into one of considerably enhanced dimensions and depth. None more admirably matched their capacities of deep reflection on the inner structure of Israel's history with the promise and potential of a subject of absolutely primary urgency.

The Aggadah explains, rationalizes as best it can, gentile hegemony such as the Halakhah takes for granted gentiles simply do not exercise. The Halakhah sees that world within Israel's dominion for which Israel bears responsibility; there sages legislate. The Aggadah forms a perspective upon the world subject to gentile rule, that is, the world beyond the limits of Israel's own power. The Halakhah speaks of Israel at the heart of matters, the Aggadah, of Israel within humanity.

V. THE HERMENEUTICS OF ABODAH ZARAH

A. WHAT FUSES THE HALAKHIC DATA INTO A CATEGORY-FORMATION?

While the Written Torah concerns itself with the disposition of idolatry — destroying idols and tearing down altars and the like — the Halakhah takes as its problem the relationship of the Israelite to the gentile, defined through his idolatry. But the category-formation, Abodah Zarah, selects its data and so interprets them within a much more limited and precise framework. It is shaped so as to explain how the Israelite can interact with the idol-worshipping gentile in such a way as to be uncorrupted by his idolatry. All of the Halakhic data fit into that framework, which, then, represents only one component of the larger issue of Abodah Zarah viewed in general terms, as the Aggadic complement of the Bavli has already shown us.

What fuses the Halakhic data into a category-formation is therefore not the topic, idolatry or idolaters, viewed in the abstract nor even the result of an analogical-contrastive analysis of humanity, the Israelite sector being compared and contrasted with the gentile. Many steps past that primary, generative process of thought carry us to the entry-point of the Halakhah, the very particular outcome of the analytical process that captures attention by reason of its immediacy and practicality — the two indicative traits of the Halakhah throughout. As is clear, the Halakhah encompasses a considerable corpus of fundamental conceptions, such as result from the analogical-contrastive process outlined earlier, and finds urgent only one of those conceptions: gentiles cannot be disposed of, as Scripture maintained, but have to be coped with.

In that critical focus, the Halakhic authorities who translated the results of analogical-contrastive analysis into practicalities concur with Scripture: they never concede the autonomous, legitimate existence of idolatry, nor do they make their peace with idolaters. The Halakhah presupposes not gentile hegemony but only gentile power. But the Halakhah also presupposes Israelite power, resting on the legitimacy of Israelite existence, and it further takes for granted that Israelites may make choices. They specifically may refrain from trading in what gentiles value in the service of their gods, and may hold back from gentiles what gentiles require for that service. The Halakhah of Abodah Zarah legislates for a world in which Israelites, while subordinate in some ways, control their own conduct and govern their own destiny — therefore bear responsibility for their own actions, which embody their autocephalic intentions. The Halakhah builds upon Israelites' power of restraint, their valuing the honor of God more than the profit of trading with the enemy in the goods and services indicative of idolatry that make the enemy into what he is. Since that is what is at stake in the Halakhic category-formation, I am on solid ground in insisting that the hermeneutics of analogical-contrastive analysis of the large issue — the genus, humanity, the species, Israel/the gentiles — has generated the details of the law and serves to fuse them into a cogent system for selection and interpretation of data.

The category-formation then yields this result. Israelites may live in a world governed by gentiles, but they form intentions and carry them out. That is what makes Israel responsible for its own deeds even in the confrontation with God's (presently more powerful) enemies. Israel may decide what to sell, but more important, what not to sell, whom to hire for what particular act of labor and to whom not to sell their own labor, and the opposite. Above all, Israelite traders may determine to give up opportunities denied them by the circumstance of gentile idolatry. Restraint is the key.

The Halakhic category-formation is so framed, therefore, as to make a formidable statement of Israel's freedom to make choices, its opportunity within the context of everyday life to preserve a territory free of idolatrous contamination — therefore the range of its responsibility and the true character of its power in the world. This is much as Israel in entering the Land was to create a territory free of the worship of idols and their presence. In the setting of world order Israel may find itself subject to the will of others, but in the house of Israel, Israelites can and should establish a realm for God's rule and presence, free of idolatry. And if to establish a domain for God, Israelites must practice self-abnegation, refrain from actions of considerable weight and consequence, well, much of the Torah concerns itself with what people are not supposed to do, and God's rule comes to realization in acts of restraint: acts of will effected by refraining from action. The quintessential act of will is, after all, represented by refraining from eating the fruit of the forbidden tree.

That fact accounts for the judgment of the Halakhic category-formation on the other sector of humanity, the gentiles. They are prisoners of their impulses, unable to restrain themselves, as much as Israel is transformed by the Torah into masters of their impulses. The basic theory of gentiles, all of them assumed to be idolaters, is, gentiles are represented as thoroughly depraved, not being regenerated by the Torah. Within that datum, the Halakhah will be worked out, and the problematics then precipitates thought on how Israel is to protect itself in a world populated by utterly immoral persons, by their own choice being wholly outside of the framework of the Torah and its government. Basically, the Halakhah embodies the same principle of compromise where possible but rigid conformity to the principles of the Torah under all circumstances, at whatever cost, that governed commercial transactions. Just as Israel must give up all possibility of normal trading relationships with gentiles, depriving itself of the most lucrative transactions, those involving fairs, so Israel must avoid more than routine courtesies and necessary exchanges with idolaters. The very ordering of the Halakhic presentation of the Mishnah-Tosefta-Yerushalmi-Bavli conforms, so that any re-ordering of the topical repertoire will have disrupted the logical unfolding of the Halakhah.

That is why, specifically, the Halakhah of the Oral Torah deals first with commercial relationships, second, with matters pertaining to idols, and finally with the particular prohibition of wine part of which has served as a libation to an idol. The whole is regularized and ordered. Simple principles govern, and these derive from the clarifying thought processes of the Halakhah's generic hermeneutics. There are relationships with gentiles that are absolutely prohibited, particularly occasions of idol-worship; the Halakhah recognizes that these are major commercial events. When it comes to commerce with idolaters Israelites may not sell or in any way benefit from certain things, may sell but may not utilize certain others, and may sell and utilize yet others. Here, we see immediately, the complex and systematic mode of thought that governs the Oral Torah's treatment of the topic vastly transcends the rather simple conception that animates Scripture's discussion of the same matter.[2] The Halakhic category-formation takes shape out of the logic of analogical-

---

[2] It also shows why, in the study of the present category-formation, we err if we start with Scripture and treat the matter as a problem of history. *It is a problem of logic, autonomous of history.* Scripture does not define the category-formation as we have it, though it contributes its absolutes to it. Starting with Scripture predetermines all else, but then begs the question of category-formation and violates the requirements of hermeneutical analysis.

contrastive analysis, which transcends the accidents of temporal or ordinal facts. At no point does Scripture permit us to predict, or account for, the shape and structure of the category-formation, Abodah Zarah — it contributes merely a segment of its contents in detail.

B. THE ACTIVITY OF THE CATEGORY-FORMATION

There are these unstated premises within the Halakhah: [1] what a gentile is not likely to use for the worship of an idol is not prohibited; [2] what may serve not as part of an idol but as an appurtenance thereto is prohibited for Israelite use but permitted for Israelite commerce; [3] what serves idolatry is prohibited for use and for benefit. In reflecting upon relationships with the gentiles, meaning, idolaters, the Oral Torah moreover takes for granted a number of facts. These turn out to yield a single generalization: gentiles are assumed routinely to practice bestiality, murder, and fornication. Further negative stereotypes concerning idolaters occur. The picture of the Halakhah finds its context in the larger theory of idolatry and its ephemeral hegemony that the Aggadah sets forth.

The tractate signals its particular problematics when it opens with rules on how to deal with gentiles before and after festivals. The issue bears heavy consequence, and the presentation of the Halakhah accords the position of prominence to what must be deemed the most fundamental question the Halakhah must address: may Israelites participate in the principal trading occasions of the life of commerce, which are permeated with idolatrous celebrations? Since the festival defined a principal occasion for holding a market, and since it was celebrated with idolatrous rites, the mixture of festival and fair formed a considerable problem for the Israelite merchant. Sages, with their focus upon the householder,[3] by definition an enlandised component of the social order, identified the principal unit of (agricultural) production with the main building block of Israelite society, and they gave nothing to the Israelite traders. Indeed, they so legislated as to close off a major channel of commerce. In connection with gentile festivals, which were celebrated with fairs, Israelites — meaning, traders, commercial players of all kinds — could not enter into business relationships with gentile counterparts (let alone themselves participate); cutting off all contractual ties, lending or borrowing in any form, meant the Israelite traders in no way could participate in a principal medium of trade. That principle is announced at the outset, and, as we see, the Tosefta amplifies and supplies many details to instantiate the main point. The Mishnah's prohibition of all commercial relationships is simply repeated by the Tosefta's "A person should not do business with a gentile on the day of his festival."

---

[3] See my *Soviet Views of Talmudic Judaism. Five Papers by Yu. A. Solodukho.* Leiden, 1973: Brill.

But the Halakhah differentiates between actual commercial relationships on the occasion of festivals and fairs, on the one side, and transactions of a normal, humane character, on the other. The Halakhah does not require Israelites to act out Scripture's commandments utterly to destroy idolatry. Israelites are not commanded by the Halakhah to go out and destroy pagan temples or disfigure idols outside of their own domain. The laws permit them to maintain normal social amenities with their neighbors, within some broad limits. First, while the general prohibition covers all gentiles on the occasion of fairs and festivals, it pertains to individuals' celebrations in a limited way. All gentiles are not subjected to a prohibition for all purposes and at all times, and that is the main principle that the extension and the amplification of the law instantiates in many concrete cases. The effect is to reshape Scripture's implacable and extreme rulings into a construction more fitting for an Israel that cannot complete the task of destroying idolatry but is not free to desist from trying and at any cost must desist from participating, directly or indirectly, in the sin.

In line with the observation that much of the Halakhah prescribes restraint and lists what one must not do, we cannot find surprising the articulation of the law. One must avoid entering into situations of danger, e.g., allowing for opportunities for gentiles to carry out their natural instincts of murder, bestiality, and the like. Cattle are not to be left in their inns, a woman may not be left alone with gentiles, nor a man, the former by reason of probable fornication, the latter, murder, on the part of the gentile. Their physicians are not to be trusted, though when it comes to using them for beasts, that is all right. One also must avoid appearing to conduct oneself as if he were an idolater, even if he is not actually doing so, thus if while someone is in front of an idol, he got a splint in his foot, he should not bend over to remove it, because he looks as though he is bowing down to the idol. If it does not look that way, he is permitted to do so. But there are objects that are assumed to be destined for idolatrous worship, and these under all circumstances are forbidden for Israelite trade. Israelites simply may not sell to gentiles anything that gentiles are likely to use, or that they explicitly say they are intending to use, for idolatry. That includes wine and the like. Whatever gentiles have used for idolatry may not be utilized afterward by Israelites, and that extends to what is left over from an offering, e.g., of meat or wine. Israelites also may not sell to gentiles anything they are going to use in an immoral way, e.g., wild animals for the arena, materials for the construction of places in which gentile immorality or injustice will occur, ornaments for an idol, and the like.

Israelites may, however, derive benefit from, that is, conduct trade in, what has not been directly used for idolatrous purposes. The appurtenances of wine, e.g., skins or tanks, may be traded, but not used for their own needs by Israelites. In the case of jars that have served for water, Israelites may use the jars and put wine into them; gentiles are not assumed to offer water to their idols, so too brine or fish-brine. Gentile milk, bread, oil, and the like, may be traded by Israelites. When it comes to milk Israelites have supervised, or honey, and the like, Israelites may purchase and eat such commodities. When gentiles never use for idolatry is acceptable.

When the Halakhah comes to treat idols themselves, we find no surprises and few problems that require much subtle analysis. Idols are to be destroyed and disposed of — no surprises there. The Written Torah has provided the bulk of the Halakhah, and the Oral Torah contributes only a recapitulation of the main points, with some attention to interstitial problems of merely exegetical interest. When it comes to the *asherah*, the *Merkolis*, and the nullification of an idol, the Halakhah presents no surprises. Here the Oral Torah shows itself derivative of, and dependent upon, the Written, introducing no unfamiliar problems, executing no generative problematics that I can discern. When it comes to libation wine, the issue is equally unremarkable. But the details here show that same concern that we noticed in connection with trade.

That is, how is the Israelite to live side by side with the gentile-idolater in the Land? Here sages find space for the householder-farmer to conduct his enterprise, that is, gentile workers may be employed, gentile produce may be utilized. The contrast with the blanket prohibition against participating in trade-fairs proves striking; here sages find grounds for making possible a kind of joint venture that, when it comes to the trade-fair, they implacably prohibit. Thus they recognize that the gentiles do not deem as wine suitable for libation the grapes in various stages of preparation. Gentile grapes may be purchased, even those that have been trodden. Gentile workers may participate to a certain point as well. Israelite workers may accept employment with gentiles in the winepress. The basic point is not particular to wine-making; the Halakhah recognizes that faithful Israelites may work with other Israelites, meaning, those who do not keep the Halakhah as sages define it, subject to limitations that where there is clear violation of the law, the Israelite may not participate in that part of the venture. The Halakhah generally treats the gentile as likely to perform his rites whenever he can, but also as responsive to Israelite instructions wherever it is to the gentile's advantage or Israelite supervision is firm.

C. THE CONSISTENCY OF THE CATEGORY-FORMATION

The definition of the category-formation by the Mishnah predominates throughout the Halakhah, and no issues emerge in the continuator-documents that do not fit the initial program.

D. THE GENERATIVITY OF THE CATEGORY-FORMATION

What we have seen is how the Halakhah then serves as the means for the translation of theological conviction into social policy. The single point at which the category-formation generates an extension of the Halakhah to an area beyond that set forth by the analogical-contrastive analysis at the foundations should now register. To understand the category-formation's generativity, we note that, despite their unregenerate condition brought on by rejection of the Torah and its possibilities for renewal, gentiles form a category-formation that, like Israel, still bears full responsibility for acts that violate God's will. Even though humanity divides between Israel, those that know God, and gentiles, those that do not, God does not fail to exercise dominion over them. Even in their present condition, idolaters are subject to a number of commandments or religious obligations. God cares for gentiles as for Israel, he wants gentiles as much as Israel to enter the kingdom of Heaven, and he assigns to gentiles opportunities to evince their acceptance of his rule. One of these commandments is not to curse God's name:

> "Any man who curses his God shall bear his sin" (Lev. 24:15)":
> It would have been clear had the text simply said, "A man." Why does
> it specify, "Any"? It serves to encompass idolaters, who are admonished
> not to curse the Name, just as Israelites are so admonished.
> Bavli Sanhedrin 7:5 I.2/56a

Not cursing God, even while worshipping idols, seems a minimal expectation. But, in fact there are seven such religious obligations that apply to the children of Noah. It is not surprising — indeed, it is predictable — that the definition of the matter should find its place in the Halakhah of Abodah Zarah:

T. 8:4 A.   Concerning seven religious requirements were the children of Noah
             admonished:
      B.   setting up courts of justice, idolatry, blasphemy [cursing the Name of
             God], fornication, bloodshed, and thievery.

We now proceed to show how each of these religious obligations is represented as applying to gentiles as much as to Israelites:

      C.   Concerning setting up courts of justice — how so [how does Scripture
             or reason validate the claim that gentiles are to set up courts of justice]?
      D.   Just as Israelites are commanded to call into session in their towns
             courts of justice.
      E.   Concerning idolatry and blasphemy— how so?
      F.   Concerning fornication— how so?
      G.   "On account of any form of prohibited sexual relationship on account
             of which an Israelite court inflicts the death-penalty, the children of
             Noah are subject to warning," the words of R. Meir.
      H.   And sages say, "There are many prohibited relationships, on account
             of which an Israelite court does not inflict the death-penalty and the
             children of Noah are [not] warned. In regard to these forbidden
             relationships the nations are judged in accord with the laws governing
             the nations.

I. "And you have only the prohibitions of sexual relations with a betrothed maiden alone."

The systemization of Scripture's evidence for the stated proposition continues:

T. 8:5 A. For bloodshed— how so?
B. A gentile [who kills] a gentile and a gentile who kills an Israelite are liable. An Israelite [who kills] a gentile is exempt.
C. Concerning thievery?
D. [If] one has stolen, or robbed, and so too in the case of finding a beautiful captive [woman], and in similar cases:
E. a gentile in regard to a gentile, or a gentile in regard to an Israelite— it is prohibited. And an Israelite in regard to a gentile— it is permitted.
T. 8:6 A. Concerning a limb cut from a living beast— how so?
B. A dangling limb on a beast, [which] is not [so connected] as to bring about healing,
C. is forbidden for use by the children of Noah, and, it goes without saying, for Israelites.
D. But if there is [in the connecting flesh] sufficient [blood supply] to bring about healing,
E. it is permitted to Israelites, and, it goes without saying, to the children of Noah.

Tosefta-tractate Abodah Zarah 8:4-6

This exposition complicates our original reconstruction of the process of analogical-contrastive analysis, but not by much. It simply underscores the analogical aspect of matters. And yet another point does as well. As in the case of Israelites, so the death penalty applies to a Noahide:

A. On account of violating three religious duties are children of Noah put to death: on account of adultery, murder, and blasphemy.'"
B. R. Huna, R. Judah, and all the disciples of Rab say, "On account of seven commandments a son of Noah is put to death. The All-Merciful revealed that fact of one of them, and the same rule applies to all of them. But just as Israelites, educated in the Torah, are assumed to exhibit certain uniform virtues, e.g., forbearance, so gentiles, lacking that same education, are assumed to conform to a different model.

Bavli Sanhedrin 7:5 I.4-5/57a

If — in the analogical-contrastive analysis, Israel and the gentiles are deemed comparable, the contrast is all the more stark. The gentiles do not acknowledge or know God, therefore, while they are like Israelites in sharing a common humanity by reason of mythic genealogy — deriving from Noah — the gentiles do not receive in a meritorious manner the blessings that God bestows upon them. The upshot is simple. When it comes to the generative aspect of the Halakhic category-formation,

Abodah Zarah, we see that the category-formation generates its laws when it focuses in particular not upon the gentiles but upon Israel: how does the analogy of the gentiles to Israel yield consequences for the gentiles? And, as we said earlier, what, given the world as it is, can Israel do in the dominion subject to Israel's own will and intention? That is the question that, as we now see, the Halakhah fully answers. For the Halakhah constructs, indeed defines, the interiority of an Israel sustaining God's service in a world of idolatry: life against death in the two concrete and tangible dimensions by which life is sustained: trade and the production of food, the foci of the Halakhah. No wonder Israel must refrain from engaging with idolatry on days of the festivals for idols that the great fairs embody — then especially. The presentation of the Halakhah commences with the single most important, comprehensive point — a signal as to the generative hermeneutics here, as in the opening of Baba Qamma.

Beyond the Torah there not only is no salvation from death, there is not even the possibility of common decency. That is because in the last analysis Israel and the idolaters have nothing in common. What forms them into a common genus, their shared humanity, is what distinguishes them into species: both species die. But that calls into question the very integrity of the genus, humanity, for the Israelite part of humanity rises from the dead, and idolaters do not. The Torah makes all the difference. The upshot may be stated very simply. Israel and the gentiles form the two divisions of humanity. They are alike, because both species die. But they are different, because of the two, the one will , not only die, but then rise from the grave to eternal life with God. When the other dies, it perishes; that is the end. Moses said it very well: Choose life. So, whatever the givens of the moment, when the gentiles sustain comparison and contrast with Israel, the point of ultimate division is, death for the one, eternal life for the other, which, contrary to all logic, demolishes the genus, leaving only the species. Halakhically and Aggadically, Israel is *sui generis* — just as Balaam said.

4

Tractate Keritot

I. THE DEFINITION OF THE CATEGORY-FORMATION

The category-formation, Keritot, works out a single, simple principle. If one has intentionally done a sin or a crime, for the sins or crimes dealt with here he pays the penalty of extirpation, death before age 60, and if he has done it inadvertently, he expiates the sin through a sin-offering, and if he does not know the facts of the matter, then he presents a suspensive guilt-offering. So the state of one's knowledge, critical to an assessment of intentionality, enters in. Predictably, the hermeneutical principle of taxonomic differentiation comes to expression with the Mishnah's usual lapidary clarity:

> "For those [thirty-six classes of transgressions listed at M. 1:1]
> are people liable,
>> "for deliberately doing them, to the punishment of extirpation,
>> "and for accidentally doing them, to the bringing of a sin offering,
>> "and for not being certain of whether or not one has done them,
> to a suspensive guilt offering"
>
> M. 1:2A

We therefore deal with penalties for sins or crimes that are differentiated by the attitude of the person who has done them, with special reference to the sin-offering and the suspensive guilt-offering or extirpation. At issue is whether a sin or crime is expiated through a sin-offering or through extirpation, early death or a suspensive guilt-offering. The category-formation then finds its hermeneutical problem in the differentiation of each of its components, and the hermeneutics once again, predictably, dictates the selection and interpretation of its data through the single variable, intentionality.

The subject-matter of the category-formation, Keritot, is only partially revealed in its title, "sins atoned for by extirpation," so we do best by beginning with an outline of the topical program.

I.   THE SIN-OFFERING: THAT FOR WHICH IT EXPIATES

    A.   Classes of Transgressions that are subject to extirpation or the
        sin-offering, depending on intentionality

II. THE SIN-OFFERING: SPECIAL CASES

    A.   The sin-offering in connection with childbirth
    B.   The single sin-offering and multiple sins

III. THE OFFERING OF VARIABLE VALUE

IV. THE SUSPENSIVE GUILT-OFFERING

    A.   Cases of doubt in which the suspensive guilt-offering is required
    B.   When the animal designated for the suspensive guilt-offering
        may not be required

The topical program reveals little, but that offerings for various sins or crimes are subject to classification.

So much for the species, sins and their penalties, differentiated by intentionality and awareness. Now, to guide our inquiry into the hypothetical thought-processes that yield the species, what about the genus? Obviously, it is comprised by Sanhedrin-Makkot (with Shebuot), on the one side, and Keritot, on the other. What these category-formations bear in common is that they catalogue sins or crimes and the penalties therefor. The sins or crimes penalized by fines, capital punishment inflicted by man, or flogging are listed in the former, those penalized by offerings or extirpation, received by God or inflicted by God, in the latter. Thus man's power to inflict penalties is spelled out in Sanhedrin-Makkot, and those penalties inflicted by, or involving cultic engagement with, God (extirpation, the sin- or guilt-offering, respectively) are worked out in Keritot. The two species for a genus because of an effect in common: they produce the identical result, the reconciliation of the sinner or criminal with God. So much for the genus, now how does the comparison make possible illuminating contrasts?

To answer that question, we must address two others. First, how are we to contrast the comparable species? Instead of fines, capital punishment, or flogging, for the items of Sanhedrin-Makkot, what is required is either a sin-offering or a suspensive guilt offering or extirpation, for the items of Keritot. Second, what explains that contrast?

A negative experiment begins the inquiry. The point of differentiation between Sanhedrin-Makkot and Keritot does not emerge from a comparison of the sins or crimes the deliberate commission of which is penalized through the earthly court's inflicting the death penalty (and comparable penalties) or the Heavenly court's inflicting the death penalty through shortening of life. Here is a sample.

>M. San. 7:4 These are [the felons] who are put to death by stoning: He who has sexual relations with his mother, with the wife of his father, with his daughter-in-law, with a male, and with a cow; and the women who brings an ox on top of herself; and he who blasphemes, he who performs an act of worship for an idol, he who gives of his seed to Moloch, he who is a familiar spirit, and he who is a soothsayer; he who profanes the Sabbath, he who curses his father or his mother. he who has sexual relations with a betrothed maiden, he who beguiles [entices a whole town to idolatry], a sorcerer, and a stubborn and incorrigible son. M. 9:1 And these are those who are put to death through burning: he who has sexual relations with both a woman and her daughter [Lev. 18:17, 20:14], and a priest's daughter who committed adultery [Lev. 21:9]. . And these are those who are put to death through decapitation: the murderer, and the townsfolk of an apostate town. A murderer who hit his neighbor with a stone or a piece of iron [Ex. 21:18], or who pushed him under water or into fire, and [the other party] cannot get out of there and so perished, he is liable. [If] he pushed him into the water or into the fire, and he can get out of there but [nonetheless] he died, he is exempt. [M. 11:1=Bavli 10:1 These are the ones who are to be strangled: he who hits his father and his mother [Ex. 21:15]; he who steals an Israelite [Ex. 21:16, Deut. 24:7]; an elder who defies the decision of a court, a false prophet, a prophet who prophesies in the name of an idol; He who has sexual relations with a married woman, those who bear false witness against a priest's daughter and against one who has sexual relations with her. M. Keritot 1:1 Thirty-six [classes of] transgressions set forth in the Torah are subject to extirpation: he who has sexual relations with (1) his mother, and (2) with his father's wife, and (3) with his daughter-in-law; he who has sexual relations (4) with a male, and (5) with a beast; and (6) the woman who has sexual relations with a beast; he who has sexual relations (7) with a woman and with her daughter, and (8) with a married woman; he who has sexual relations (9) with his sister, and (10) with his father's sister, and (11) with his mother's sister, and (12) with his wife's sister, and (13) with his brother's wife, and (14) with his father's brother's wife, and (15) with a menstruating woman (Lev. 18:6ff .); (16) he who blasphemes (Num. 15:30), and (17) he who performs an act of blasphemous worship (Num. 15:31), and (18) he who gives his seed to Moloch (Lev. 18:21), and (19) one who has a familiar spirit (Lev. 20:6); (20) he who profanes the Sabbath day (Ex. 31:14); and (21) an unclean person who ate a Holy Thing (Lev. 22:3), and (22) he who comes to the sanctuary when unclean (Num. 19:20); he who eats (23) forbidden fat (Lev. 7:25), and (24) blood (Lev. 17:14), and (25) remnant (Lev. 19:6-8), and (26) refuse (Lev. 19:7-8); he who (27) slaughters and who (28) offers up [a sacrifice] outside [the Temple court] (Lev. 17:9); (29) he who eats leaven on Passover (Ex. 12:19); and he who (30) eats and he who (31) works on the Day of Atonement (Lev. 23:29-30); he who (32)

compounds anointing oil [like that made in the Temple (Ex. 30:23-33)], and he who (33) compounds incense [like that made in the Temple], and he who (34) anoints himself with anointing oil (Ex. 30-32); [he who transgresses the laws of] (35) Passover (Num. 9:13) and (36) circumcision (Gen. 17:14), among the positive commandments.

The (abbreviated) lists overlap sufficiently to require a clear point of differentiation as to the same action between the death penalty imposed by man and extirpation imposed by God. The variable — so we now have seen — cannot be the severity or character of the sin or crime, and that is by definition. Nor can it be intentionality, for extirpation at the hands of Heaven, as much as the death penalty inflicted by man depends 8upon the attitude that motivates the action.

Even though the earthly court penalizes some sins or crimes that do not fall into the jurisdiction of the Heavenly court,[1] the point of differentiation between the Heavenly and earthly court can only be procedural. That is for two disparate reasons.

First, it is because some of the same crimes or sins for which the Heavenly court imposes the penalty of extirpation are those for which, under appropriate circumstances (e. g., sufficient evidence admissible in court) the earthly court imposes the death-penalty. That is, the Heavenly court and the earthly court impose precisely the same ultimate sanction — death — for the same crimes or sins. Where man cannot effect the sanction and consequent expiation, Heaven assures that justice will be done so that the sinner or criminal will pay in years of life but thereby retain his share of eternal life.

But, second, procedural considerations do not end there. The medium of expiation is the other, and obvious, point of differentiation between the Heavenly and the earthly court. The contrast sets God's engagement through the Temple sanctions against man's through the earthly penalties. The particular penalties outlined in the lists of Keritot then form the counterpart, in the specified cases of inadvertence, to the death penalty and that of flogging, in the specified counterpart cases in Sanhedrin-Makkot.

So the components of the genus are represented by these three institutions, [1] the altar or [2] the Heavenly court, represented by Keritot, and [3] the earthly court, represented by Sanhedrin-Makkot. All three exercise concrete and material power, utilizing legitimate violence to kill someone, exacting penalties against property, and inflicting pain. Power therefore flows through three distinct but intersecting dominions, each with its own concern, all sharing some interests in common. The Heavenly court attends to deliberate defiance of Heaven, the Temple

---

[1] The earthly court, for its part, penalizes social crimes against the community that the Heavenly court, on the one side, and the Temple rites, on the other, do not take into account at all. These are murder, apostasy, kidnapping, public defiance of the court, and false prophecy. The earthly court further imposes sanctions on matters of particular concern to the Heavenly court, with special reference to taboos of sanctification (e.g., negative commandments).

to inadvertent defiance of Heaven. The earthly court attends to matters subject to man's specific jurisdiction by reason of decisive evidence, proper witnesses, and the like. Then these same matters come under Heavenly jurisdiction when the earthly court finds itself unable to act. Accordingly, we have in our genus, Sanhedrin-Makkot Keritot, a tripartite system of sanctions — Heaven cooperating with the Temple in some matters, with the court in others, and, as noted, each bearing its own distinct media of enforcing the law as well — a complex system of criminal justice aimed at restoring the Israelite sinner or criminal to life in Eden.

Having established the common genus and differentiated principally upon procedural grounds between Sanhedrin-Makkot and Keritot, we turn to Keritot and ask about that category-formation's particular hermeneutics. And here the critical issue is, why does God supervise the process of expiation involving either the sin-offering (and its companions) or extirpation? The answer derives from God's unique knowledge: he knows what is deliberate and what is inadvertent, because he penetrates into the heart of man. That is why the distinction between an offering and extirpation makes a difference in the process of atonement. Offerings expiate those sins that do not are not committed as an act of rebellion against God. These God accepts, graciously, as an appropriate act of atonement for an act for which one bears responsibility but which was not meant as defiance of God. The ones that embody an attitude of rebellion, by contrast, can be expiated not through the surrogate, the blood of the beast, but through that of the sinner himself, who, if he is not put to death by the court here on earth or is not flogged by the court's agents, is cut off in the prime of life. Keritot therefore provides for God's intervention where man's justice fails and so forms a necessary link in the circle of reconciliation of Israel(ites) with God.

So the animating principle that pervades Keritot and rationalizes its formal distinctions into weighty differences is simple: God sees into man's heart. That is why the same act produces diverse consequences, based upon the intentionality with which the act is done. Indeed, in its own way that same conception animates the formal exercises on how many sin-offerings are owing for a single action or how many actions may be subsumed under, and expiated by, a single sin-offering. Beyond Keritot, the matter is expressed best in the Halakhah of Shabbat. There it is made explicit: A sin is atoned for by a sin-offering only when the act is inadvertent. A deliberate action is not covered:

> This is the general principle: All those who may be liable to sin offerings in fact are not liable unless at the beginning and the end, their sin is done inadvertently. But if the beginning of their sin is inadvertent and the end is deliberate, or the beginning deliberate and the end inadvertent, they are exempt — unless at the beginning and at the end their sin is inadvertent.
>
> M. Shab. 11:6J-K

The distinction between deliberate sin and inadvertent law-violation permeates the Halakhah. But when it comes to the specification of the penalty for sin or crime, Keritot remains the principal point at which the Halakhah makes its statement of the prevailing distinction.

II. THE FOUNDATIONS OF THE HALAKHIC CATEGORY-FORMATION

The principal interest then is in animal-offerings that expiate sin committed inadvertently or unknowingly. The Written Torah contributes to the topic the following statement, at Lev. 5:17-19; I underline the key-language for the guilt-offering.

> "If any one sins,_ doing any of the things that the Lord has
> commanded not to be done, though he does not know it, yet he is guilty
> and shall bear his iniquity_. He shall bring to the priest a ram without
> blemish out of the flock, valued by you at the price for a guilt offering,
> and the priest shall make atonement for him for the error that he
> committed unwittingly, and he shall be forgiven. It is a guilt offering;
> he is guilty before the Lord"

Since the generative premise of the Halakhah is the distinction between deliberate and inadvertent sin or crime, with extirpation the penalty for the former, the guilt offering expiating the latter, Scripture has defined the foundations for the articulation and exegesis of the Halakhah. The governing distinction set forth by the Halakhah simply builds upon Scripture's law.

As to expiation of sin through extirpation, the Torah at numerous points states, "that man will be cut off" (e.g., Lev. 17:4, 9; Ex. 30:33, 38, Gen. 17:14, Ex. 12:1`5, 19, 31:14, Num. 15:31), and the like, in many variations.[2]

III. THE EXPOSITION OF THE COMPONENTS OF THE GIVEN CATEGORY-FORMATION BY THE MISHNAH-TOSEFTA-YERUSHALMI-BAVLI

I. THE SIN-OFFERING

A.   CLASSES OF TRANSGRESSIONS THAT ARE SUBJECT TO EXTIRPATION OR THE SIN-OFFERING

M. 1:1 Thirty-six [classes of] transgressions set forth in the Torah are subject to extirpation: he who has sexual relations with (1) his mother, and (2) with his father's wife, and (3) with his daughter-in-law; he who has sexual relations (4) with a male, and (5) with a beast; and (6) the woman who has sexual relations with a beast; he who has sexual relations (7) with a woman and with

---

[2] See H. Albeck, *Shishah Sidré Mishnah.* V. *Seder Qodoshim* (Tel Aviv, 1959), p. 243.

her daughter, and (8) with a married woman; he who has sexual relations (9) with his sister, and (10) with his father's sister, and (11) with his mother's sister, and (12) with his wife's sister, and (13) with his brother's wife, and (14) with his father's brother's wife, and (15) with a menstruating woman (Lev. 18:6ff.); (16) he who blasphemes (Num. 15:30), and (17) he who performs an act of blasphemous worship (Num. 15:31), and (18) he who gives his seed to Moloch (Lev. 18:21), and (19) one who has a familiar spirit (Lev. 20:6); (20) he who profanes the Sabbath day (Ex. 31:14); and (21) an unclean person who ate a Holy Thing (Lev. 22:3), and (22) he who comes to the sanctuary when unclean (Num. 19:20); he who eats (23) forbidden fat (Lev. 7:25), and (24) blood (Lev. 17:14), and (25) remnant (Lev. 19:6-8), and (26) refuse (Lev. 19:7-8); he who (27) slaughters and who (28) offers up [a sacrifice] outside [the Temple court] (Lev. 17:9); (29) he who eats leaven on Passover (Ex. 12:19); and he who (30) eats and he who (31) works on the Day of Atonement (Lev. 23:29-30); he who (32) compounds anointing oil [like that made in the Temple (Ex. 30:23-33)], and he who (33) compounds incense [like that made in the Temple], and he who (34) anoints himself with anointing oil (Ex. 30-32); [he who transgresses the laws of] (35) Passover (Num. 9:13) and (36) circumcision (Gen. 17:14), among the positive commandments.

T. 1: 1 He who anoints [himself] with the oil of anointing [like] that which Moses made in the wilderness, lo, this one is liable to extirpation. Passover and circumcision, even though [people] are liable to extirpation for deliberate transgression thereof [M. Ker. 1:1P], are not subject to an offering, because they are [commandments] which require affirmative action ["they are subject to, 'Arise and do'"].

T. 1:2 An unclean person who ate Holy Things, and he who comes to the sanctuary while unclean [M. Ker. 1:1 K], even though they are liable for deliberately doing so to extirpation and for accidentally doing so to a sin-offering,(. are not subject to a suspensive guilt-offering, because they are subject to a sliding-scale-offering.

T. 1:3 He who curses his father and his mother, he who says to his fellow, "Go and carry out an act of liturgy to idolatry," he who incites and he who leads [Israel] astray, false prophets, and conspiring witnesses, even though they are liable to be put to death at the hands of a court, . are not subject to bring an offering, because their [transgressions] do not contain a concrete action [M. Ker. 1:2F].

T. 1:6 This is the general principle: [For violation of] any negative commandment containing within itself a concrete deed do [violators] receive the penalty of forty stripes. And for the violation of any which does not contain within itself a concrete deed they do not receive the penalty of forty stripes. And as to all other negative commandments in the Torah, lo, these are subject to warning. He who transgresses them violates the decree of the King.

T. 1:19 There are five guilt-offerings: a guilt-offering for theft, a guilt-offering for sacrilege, a guilt-offering brought for having sexual relations with a betrothed handmaiden, a guilt-offering of a Nazirite, and a guilt-offering of a mesora'.

B. 1:1 VI.1/6A HE WHO COMPOUNDS INCENSE IN ORDER TO LEARN ABOUT IT OR IN ORDER TO HAND IT OVER TO THE COMMUNITY IS EXEMPT. BUT IF HE DOES SO IN ORDER TO SNIFF IT, HE IS LIABLE. BUT HE WHO ACTUALLY SNIFFS IT IS EXEMPT FROM LIABILITY, EVEN THOUGH HE HAS COMMITTED AN ACT OF SACRILEGE.

B. 1:1 VII:1/6ʙ Hᴇ ᴡʜᴏ ᴘᴏᴜʀs ᴀɴᴏɪɴᴛɪɴɢ ᴏɪʟ ᴏɴ ᴄᴀᴛᴛʟᴇ ᴏʀ ᴜᴛᴇɴsɪʟs ɪs ᴇxᴇᴍᴘᴛ ꜰʀᴏᴍ
ʟɪᴀʙɪʟɪᴛʏ; ɪꜰ ʜᴇ ᴅᴏᴇs sᴏ ᴏᴠᴇʀ ɢᴇɴᴛɪʟᴇs ᴏʀ ᴄᴏʀᴘsᴇs, ʜᴇ ɪs ᴇxᴇᴍᴘᴛ ꜰʀᴏᴍ ʟɪᴀʙɪʟɪᴛʏ.

**M. 1:2 For those [thirty-six classes of transgressions] are people liable, for
deliberately doing them, to the punishment of extirpation, and for accidentally
doing them, to the bringing of a sin offering, and for not being certain of
whether or not one has done them, to a suspensive guilt offering [Lev. 5:17]
— [except for] the one who blasphemes, as it is said, "You shall have one law
for him that does anything unwittingly" (Num. 15:29) — excluding the
blasphemer, who does no concrete deed.**

T. 1:4 He who hits his father and his mother, he who kidnaps an Israelite, an elder who
rebels against a court ruling, a wicked and incorrigible son, and a murderer, even
though [their transgressions] involve a deed and even though they are subject to
be put to death by a court, are not subject to an offering, because they are punished
by extirpation.

T. 1:5 These are those [transgressions] punishable by death: he who eats untithed food,
a non-priest who ate clean heave-offering, an unclean priest who ate clean heave-
offering, and a non-priest, one who had immersed that self-same day, one who
lacked proper garments, one who lacked proper completion of rites of purification,
one with unkempt hair, one who was drunk, [any of whom] served at the altar —
all of them are subject to the death penalty. But the uncircumcised [priest], the
priest in mourning, and the priest who [performed the rite while he] was sitting
down, lo, these are subject to warning.

T. 1:20 A drunkard is unfit for the sacred service, and [if he carries out an act of service
m the cult] he is liable to the death penalty. What is a drunkard? Any one who has
drunk a quarter-log of wine forty days old or older than that. [If] he drank [wine
fresh] from his press in a volume of more than a quarter-log, he Is exempt. [If] he
drank less than a quarter-log of wine four or five years old, he Whether he mixed
it and drank it, or drank it in little sips, he is liable.

**M. 2:6 In all forbidden sexual relationships, [if] one is an adult and one is a minor,
the minor is exempt. [If] one is awake and one is asleep, the one asleep is
exempt. [If] one does the act inadvertently and one deliberately, the one who
does it inadvertently is liable to bring a sin offering, and the one who does it
deliberately is subject to extirpation [M. 1:2A].**

T. 1:16 These are the points of difference between [intercourse with] the betrothed
bondwoman and all other forbidden sexual relationships: All other forbidden sexual
relationships which are stated in the Torah — lo, these [others] are liable, in the
case of deliberate transgression, to extirpation, and in the case of inadvertent
transgression, to a sin-offering, and in a case of uncertain transgression, to a
suspensive guilt-offering [M. Ker. 1:2], which is not the case for the one who has
intercourse with a betrothed handmaiden [M. Ker. 2:4, M, 2:6D]. All [other]
forbidden sexual relationships in the Torah treat the one who does the act under
constraint as equivalent to the one who does it willingly, the one who does it
unintentionally as equivalent to the one who does it intentionally, [M. Ker. 2:4M],
the one who begins the act only as equivalent to the one who actually completes
it [M. Ker. 2:4K], the one who is sleeping as equivalent to the one who is awake
[M. Ker. 2:6C], the one who does it in the normal way as equivalent to the one
who does it not in the normal way, [and the law] imposes a liability for each and

every act of sexual intercourse [M. Ker. 2:3C/I], which is not the case with the betrothed handmaiden. In the case of all other forbidden sexual relationships, [the law] has treated a minor as equivalent to an adult, to impose the liability solely on the adult [M. Ker. 2:6B]. But in the case of a handmaiden, if he [the male who had sexual relations] was a minor, lo, these are exempt from liability. In the case of all other forbidden sexual relationships, both of the participants receive stripes. But in the case of a handmaiden, she receives stripes but he does not receive stripes. In the case of all other forbidden sexual relationships, both parties bring an offering. But in the case of a handmaiden, he brings, but she does not bring [an offering]. In the case of all other forbidden sexual relationships, the penalty is a sin-offering. But in the case of a handmaiden, the penalty is a guilt-offering. In the case of all other forbidden sexual relationships, one brings a female [sin-offering]. But in the case of a handmaiden, one brings a male [guilt-offering] [M. Ker. 2:4G-H]. In the case of all other forbidden sexual relationships, one is liable for each and every act of sexual intercourse. But in the case of a handmaiden, one brings a single offering for many acts of sexual intercourse [M. Ker. 2:3C/I]. In the case of all other forbidden sexual relationships which are stated in the Torah, a court is liable to give instruction in their regard, which not the case for the betrothed handmaiden. In the case of all other forbidden sexual relationships, an anointed priest who gave instruction and did the deed is liable. In the case of the handmaiden, if he did the deed, even though he did not give instruction, he brings a guilt-offering on account of a confirmed case.

T. 1:18 He who has sexual relations with any one of all those who are prohibited by the Torah — he in a single spell of inadvertence, but she in five spells of inadvertence — he brings a single sin-offering. But she brings five sin-offerings. [If] she does so in a single spell of inadvertence, but he does so in five spells of inadvertence, she brings one sin-offering and he brings five sin-offerings. In respect to all prohibited relationships, [if] one is an adult and one is a minor, the minor is exempt. [If] one is awake and one asleep, the one asleep is exempt. [If] one does it inadvertently and the one does it intentionally: the one who does it inadvertently is liable to bring a sin-offering, and [he one who does it intentionally is subject to extirpation [M. Ker. 2:6].

Once the distinction is made between the sin- or guilt-offering and extirpation, all that remains is to form lists of the various crimes or sins. That is what M. 1:1 does for its stated data. The Tosefta then contributes a massive amplification of the entries. As already noted, M. 1:2 then introduces the operative variables. I move 2:6 to the present rubric because of its strong recapitulation of M. 1:2.

II. THE SIN-OFFERING: SPECIAL CASES

A. THE SIN-OFFERING IN CONNECTION WITH CHILDBIRTH

M. 1:3 (1) There are women who bring a [sin] offering [after childbirth], and it is eaten [by the priests], (2) and there are women who bring an offering, and it is not eaten, (3) and there are women who do not bring [an offering]. These [women after childbirth] bring an offering, and it is eaten: She who aborts (1) a sandal or (2) an afterbirth or (3) a fully fashioned foetus or (4) an offspring which is cut up [during delivery]. And so a slave-girl who gives birth brings an offering, and it is eaten.

M. 1:4 These bring [an offering], but it is not eaten: (1) She who aborts, and it is not known what it is that she has aborted; and so: two women who aborted, one [producing] something which is exempt [from the requirement of bringing an offering], and one [producing] something which is liable [to an offering].

T. 1:7 She who aborts after the completion of the days of purifying and she who aborts an eight-month-old foetus, alive or dead, or a child past term and a proselyte who converted while circumcised, and a deaf-mute, an imbecile, and a minor who lacked the completion of atonement rites bring an offering and it is eaten.

T. 1:8 [If] a woman is subject to doubt whether or not she gave birth to anything at all, or [if] she is subject to doubt that it is viable or not viable or [if] she is in doubt that the foetus does or does not bear human appearance, she brings an offering, but it is not eaten.

T. 1:10 A woman who is liable for the offering for giving birth and for yet another offering for giving birth, or an offering for flux and for yet another offering for flux brings a single offering. [If she is subject to an offering for] giving birth and an offering for suffering flux, she brings two offerings. [If she is subject to an offering] for possibly having given birth and [to an offering for] certainly having given birth, [to an offering for] possibly suffering a flux and [to an offering for] certainly having suffered a flux, she brings an offering for each obligation to which she is certainly subject among them [and] has fulfilled her obligation.

M. 1:5 These are those who do not bring [an offering at all]: She who aborts a foetus (1) filled with water, (2) filled with blood, (3) filled with variegated matter; she who aborts something shaped like (1) fish, (2) locusts, (3) abominable things, or (4) creeping things; she who aborts on the fortieth day. And [she who produces] that which comes forth from the side.

T. 1:12 All those who owe pairs of bird-sacrifices stated in the Torah — half of them [the sacrifices] are a sin-offering, and half of them are burnt-offerings, except for the bird-offering of a proselyte, for even though they are an obligation, both of them were burnt-offerings. [If] he wanted to offer beasts for those which are required, he may offer them [as he wishes]. [If] he offered beasts as burnt-offerings for atonement, he has fulfilled his obligation. [If he did so with] meal-offerings and drink-offerings, he has not fulfilled his obligation. They spoke of a pair of birds only to lighten the burden for him. [If] he brought one sort of offering for his purification from cereal, let him go and bring the same for his atonement-offering. [If he brought one sort of offering] for his Nazirite-offering, let him go and bring the same for his atonement-offering.

M. 2:1 [There are] four whose atonement is not complete [until they bring an offering]. And four bring [an offering] for [a transgression done] deliberately as they do for [one done] inadvertently. These are those whose atonement is not complete [until they bring an offering]: (1) The male-Zab [afflicted with flux in terms of Lev. 15], and (2) the female-Zabah, and (3) the woman who has given birth, and (4) the mesora [afflicted with the skin disease discussed at Lev. 13-14].

B. 2:1 II.2/8B A PROSELYTE IS PREVENTED FROM EATING HOLY THINGS UNTIL HE HAS OFFERED HIS PAIR OF BIRDS. IF HE HAS PRESENTED ONE BIRD IN THE MORNING RITE, HE MAY EAT HOLY THINGS IN THE EVENING [THOUGH HE STILL OWES THE OTHER]. ALL OF THE PAIRS OF BIRDS THAT ARE LISTED IN THE TORAH ARE DESIGNATED, ONE FOR A SIN OFFERING AND ONE FOR A BURNT OFFERING, BUT HERE BOTH OF THEM ARE BURNT OFFERINGS. IF HE HAS BROUGHT HIS OBLIGATORY OFFERING IN THE FORM OF CATTLE [THIS COVERS TWO BIRDS], AND HE HAS CARRIED OUT HIS OBLIGATION. IF HE OFFERED A BURNT OFFERING AND A PEACE OFFERING, HE HAS CARRIED OUT HIS OBLIGATION. IF HE OFFERED A MEAL-OFFERING AND A PEACE-OFFERING, HE HAS NOT CARRIED OUT HIS OBLIGATION. THE PROVISION THAT HE MAY BRING A PAIR OF BIRDS HAS BEEN STATED ONLY AS A LENIENT RULING [TO MAKE THE PROCESS EASIER FOR THE PROSELYTE].

M. 2:2 **These bring [an offering for a transgression done] deliberately as for [one done] inadvertently: (1) He who has sexual relations with a bondwoman; and (2) a Nazirite who was made unclean; and (3) for [him who utters a false] oath of testimony, and (4) for [him who utters a false] deposit oath.**

The composite scarcely acknowledges the particular hermeneutics we have identified. The rules at M. 1:3-5 organize the data introduced at M. 1:3. These then establish a formal match with M. 2:1-2, which makes a point that does respond to the hermeneutical center of this category-formation, the distinction between deliberate and inadvertent action in the liability to an offering for atonement. The second group, joined for formal reasons to the first, then accounts for the inclusion of the entire complex here.

B.   THE SINGLE SIN-OFFERING AND MULTIPLE SINS

M. 1:7 **The woman who is subject to a doubt concerning [the appearance of] five fluxes, or the one who is subject to a doubt concerning five miscarriages brings a single offering. And she [then is deemed clean so that she] eats animal sacrifices. And the remainder [of the offerings] are not an obligation for her. [If she is subject to] five confirmed miscarriages, or five confirmed fluxes, she brings a single offering. And she eats animal sacrifices. But the rest [of the offerings, the other four] remain as an obligation for her [to bring at some later time]**

M. 2:3 **Five bring a single offering for many transgressions. And five bring a sliding scale offering. These bring a single offering for many transgressions: (1) He who has sexual relations with a bondwoman many times, and (2) a Nazirite who is made unclean many times. (3) he who suspects his wife of adultery with many men, and (4) a mesora' who was afflicted by nega'im many times. [If] he brought his birds and [then] was afflicted with a Nega [the skin ailment discussed at Lev. 13-14], they [the birds] do not go to his credit until he brings his sin offering.**

T. 1:13 Four sorts of transgressor bring [an offering] in [the case of deliberate transgression] as in the case of inadvertent [transgression. In the case of all of them, if they are under constraint, they are exempt [from liability] except for the

Nazir. Five bring a sliding-scale-offering [M. Ker. 2:3A]. There are among them poor-and-rich, there are among them the poorest of the poor. A mesora' and one who has given birth [M. Ker. 2:4E4-5] are poor and rich, bringing one for one. One who contaminates the sanctuary [M. Ker. 2:4E3] is the poorest of the poor, bringing two offerings for one infringement.

T. 1:21 He who has sexual relations with his mother is liable on two counts. He who has sexual relations with his father's sister is liable on two counts.

M. 2:4 A woman suffered many miscarriages — (1) she aborted a female during eighty days, and went and aborted another female during eighty days following, and (2) she who bore a multiple of abortions ["twins" — each in the period of purifying of the foregoing].

M. 3:2 [If] he ate [forbidden] fat and [again ate] fat in a single spell of inadvertence, he is liable only for a single sin offering, [If] he ate forbidden fat and blood and remnant and refuse [of an offering] in a single spell of inadvertence, he is liable for each and every one of them. This rule is more strict in the case of many kinds [of forbidden food] than of one kind. And more strict is the rule in [the case of] one kind than in many kinds: For if he ate a half-olive's bulk and went and ate a half-olive's bulk of a single kind, he is liable [since they are deemed to join together to form the requisite volume for incurring guilt]. [But if he ate two half-olive's bulks] of two [different] kinds, he is exempt.

T. 2:1 [If] one witness says, "He ate forbidden fat," and one witness says, "he ate permitted fat," [or if] one witness says, "He ate forbidden fat," and a woman says, "He ate permitted fat," [or if] one woman says, "He ate forbidden fat," and one woman says, "He ate permitted fat," . he brings a suspensive guilt-offering. [If] one witness says to him, "You ate forbidden fat," and he says, "I ate permitted fat," he is exempt.

T. 2:2 All the same are he who eats and he who dissolves [produce into a liquid] and drinks it and one who anoints [with it] — if he ate and went and ate again and went and ate again — if there is from the beginning of the first act of eating to the end of the last act of eating sufficient time for the eating of a half-loaf of bread, the several acts of eating join together. And if not, they do not join together [M. Ker. 3:2E]. [If] he drank and went and drank again and went and drank again, if there i, from the beginning of the first act of drinking to the end of the last act of drinking sufficient time for the drinking of a quarter-log, the several acts of drinking join together [to form the requisite volume to render him unclean or culpable]. And if not, they do not join together.

M. 3:3 And how much should he who eats them tarry? [He is not liable] unless he tarries from beginning to end for sufficient time to eat a half-loaf [of bread]. [If] one ate unclean foods [or] drank unclean liquids, drank a quarter-*log* of wine, and entered the sanctuary and tarried there, [the measure of time between entering the Temple having eaten unclean food or drunk wine is] sufficient time to eat a half-loaf [of bread].

M. 3:4 There is he who carries out a single act of eating and is liable on its account for four sin offerings and one guilt offering: An unclean [lay] person who ate (1) forbidden fat, and it was (2) remnant, (3) of Holy Things, and (4) it was on the Day of Atonement.

M. 3:5 There is he who carries out a single act of sexual intercourse and becomes liable on its account for six sin offerings: He who has intercourse with his daughter is liable on her account because of violating the prohibition against having intercourse with (1) his daughter, and (2) his sister, and (3) his brother's wife, and (4) his brother's father's wife, and (5) a married woman, and (6) a menstruating woman. And who has intercourse with his daughter's daughter is liable on her account because of violating the prohibitions against having intercourse with (1) his daughter's daughter, and (2) his daughter-in-law, and (3) his wife's sister, and (4) his brother's wife, and (5) his brother's father's wife, and (6) a married woman, and (7) a menstruating woman.

M. 3:6 He who has sexual relations with his mother-in-law may turn out to be liable on her account because of the prohibitions against having sexual relations with (1) his mother-in-law, and (2) his daughter-in-law, and (3) his wife's sister, and (4) his brother's wife, and (5) his father's brother's wife, and (6) a married woman and (7) a menstruating woman. And so is the case for him who has sexual relations with the mother of his mother-in-law and with the mother of his father-in-law.

While a sin-offering must be presented to expiate a specifically-designated sin, there are circumstances in which a single offering serves, and these are listed at M. 1:7, 2:3-4, with a fine systematic study of mixtures at M. 3:2, 4-6. The generic hermeneutics does its work here.

III. THE OFFERING OF VARIABLE VALUE

M. 2:4 These bring an offering of variable value: (1) for [oaths such as are involved in] refusing to give evidence ["for hearing the voice" (Lev. 5:1)]; and (2) for an expression of the lips [a rash oath]; and (3) for contaminating the sanctuary and its Holy Things; and (4) the woman who has given birth, and (5) the *mesora*. And what is the difference between the bondwoman and other forbidden sexual relationships (Lev. 18), that they are not alike (1) either in punishment or (2) in the offering [required for the transgression]? For all [other] forbidden sexual relations [are expiated] with a sin offering, but forbidden sexual relations with a bondwoman, with a guilt offering. All other sexual relations [are atoned] with a female animal, but the bondwoman, with a male animal. In respect to all other sexual relations, all the same are the man and the woman. They are equivalent as to flogging and as to an offering. But in respect to the bondwoman, the man is not treated as equivalent to the woman in regard to flogging, and the woman is not regarded as equivalent to the man in respect to an offering. In respect to all other forbidden sexual relations Scripture has treated him who begins the act as culpable as him who completes it, and he is liable for each and every act of sexual relations [which is not the case here, M. 2:3C1]. But this strict rule does the law stringently impose in the case of the bondwoman: that it treats in her regard the man who does the act intentionally as equivalent to the one who does it inadvertently.

B. 2:4D-E I.1/10B There are some who bring the offering that is required both in poverty [bird] and in wealth [lamb], some who bring the offering required only in poverty, some who bring the offering required of the poorest of the poor [a meal offering]. A woman who has given birth presents the offering that is required of the poor and of the rich [a dove, a lamb]; a mesora brings the offering required of the poor [the pair of birds]; and those culpable for refusing to give evidence ["for hearing the voice" (Lev. 5:1)]; and (2) for an expression of the lips [a rash oath]; and (3) for contaminating the sanctuary and its Holy Things bring the offering required in poverty or of the poorest of the poor [a meal offering]. Sometimes one brings one offering in place of one [in the case of poverty], two in place of two, two in place of one, and one in place of two — on this basis you derive the lesson that the tenth ephah must be worth a penny. The woman who has given birth one brings one offering in place of one — the pigeon that she owed anyhow as a sin offering plus one bird in place of a lamb; a *mesora* brings two in place of two — two birds in place of two lambs; those culpable for refusing to give evidence ["for hearing the voice" (Lev. 5:1)]; and (2) for an expression of the lips [a rash oath]; and (3) for contaminating the sanctuary and its Holy Things bring two birds in place of one lamb; and the poorest of the poor bring one tenth of an ephah in place of two birds.

Scripture has distinguished between a sin-offering of fixed value and one of variable value; I see little more here than the systematization of inert data.

IV. The Suspensive Guilt-Offering

A.   CASES OF DOUBT IN WHICH THE SUSPENSIVE GUILT-OFFERING IS REQUIRED

M. 3:1 [If] they said to him, "You have eaten forbidden fat," he brings a sin offering. [If] one witness says, "He ate," and one witness says, "He did not eat" — [of if] a woman says, "He ate," and a woman says, "He did not eat," he brings a suspensive guilt offering. [If] a witness says, "He ate," and he says, "I did not eat" — he is exempt [from bringing an offering]. [If] two say, "He ate," and he says, "I did not eat" — he is exempt.

M. 4:1 It is a matter of doubt whether or not one has eaten forbidden fat, And even if he ate it, it is a matter of doubt whether or not it contains the requisite volume — Forbidden fat and permitted fat are before him, he ate one of them but is not certain which one of them he ate — His wife and his sister are with him in the house — he inadvertently transgressed with one of them and is not certain with which of them he transgressed — The Sabbath and an ordinary day — he did an act of labor on one of them and is not certain on which of them he did it — [in all the foregoing circumstances] he brings a suspensive guilt offering.

M. 4:2 Just as, if he ate forbidden fat and [again ate] forbidden fat in a single spell of inadvertence, he is liable for only a single sin offering [M. 3:2A], so in connection with a situation of uncertainty involving them, he is liable to bring only a single guilt offering. If there was clarification [of the facts of the matter] in the meantime, just as he brings a single sin offering for each and every transgression, so he brings a suspensive guilt offering for each and every [possible] transgression. Just as, if he ate forbidden fat, and blood, and remnant, and refuse, in a single spell of inadvertence, he is liable for each and every one [M. 3:2B], so in connection with a situation of uncertainty involving them, he brings a suspensive guilt offering for each and every one.

T. 2:4 [If] it is a matter of doubt whether or not one has sinned, he brings a suspensive guilt-offering [M. Ker. 4:1, 2A-B]. [If] he has sinned, but is not certain what particular sin he has committed, he brings a sin-offering. [If] he has sinned and is informed of the character of his sin but he as or gotten what sin he has committed, Lo, this one brings a sin-offering [M. Ker. 4:2C-D], and it is slaughtered for the sake of whichever [sin he has committed] and it is eaten. Then he goes and brings a sin-offering for that sin of which he is informed, and It is slaughtered for the sake of whatever [particular sin he has done] and it [too] is eaten.

T. 2:5 He who brings one sin-offering for two distinct sins — it is set out to pasture until it is disfigured, then sold. And [the man] brings with half of its proceeds one for this sin, and with half of its proceeds one for that sin. Two sin-offerings designated for a single sin — let the man offer whichever one of them he prefers. The second then is put out to pasture until it is blemished, and then it is sold, and its proceeds fall [to the Temple-treasury] as a freewill-offering. Two sin-offerings for two sins — this one is slaughtered for one of them, and that one is slaughtered for one of them.

T. 2:10 [If] one forgot the Torah and committed many transgressions, he is liable to bring a sin-offering for each and every one of them. How so? [If] he knew that there is such a thing as forbidden fat but said, "This is not the sort of forbidden fat for which we have been declared liable" — [if] he knew that there is such a thing as [the prohibition of] blood but said, "This is not the sort of blood for which we have been declared liable" — he is liable for each and every violation of the law.

T. 2:11 He who eats an olive's bulk of forbidden fat, an olive's bulk of refuse, an olive's bulk of remnant, and an olive's bulk of that which is unclean in one spell of inadvertence brings [one] sin-offering [M. Ker. 4:2E].

M. 5:1 If one ate the blood of slaughtering in the case of cattle, wild beast, and fowl, whether [said animals are] unclean or clean, the blood [shed in the case of] stabbing, and the blood [shed in the case] of tearing [the windpipe or gullet], and the blood let in bloodletting, by which the lifeblood flows out — they are liable on its account. Blood from the spleen, blood from the heart, the blood from the eggs [or testicles], the blood of fish, the blood of locusts, blood which is squeezed out [that is, blood which oozes out of the arteries after the lifeblood flows out] — they are not liable on their account.

T. 2:18 He who eats an olive's bulk of blood of a clean beast, wild animal or fowl brings a sin-offering. [If] it is a matter of doubt whether or not he ate [it], he brings a suspensive guilt-offering. But he is liable only for the blood of slaughtering alone

T. 2:19 The blood shed in the case of stabbing, blood shed in the case of tearing the windpipe or the gullet, and blood let in blood-letting, by which the life-blood flows out — they are liable on its account [M. Ker. 5:1C]. Blood from the spleen, blood from the heart, blood from the kidneys, blood from the limbs — lo, these are subject to a negative commandment. Blood of those who go on two feet, blood of eggs [testicles], blood of creeping things is prohibited. But they are not liable on their account. Blood of fish and blood of locusts, lo, this is permitted.

T. 2:20 He who mashes forbidden fat and swallowed it, he who coagulates [forbidden] blood and ate it, if it is of the volume of an olive's bulk, is liable. [If] it was mixed up with others, if it is of the volume of an olive's bulk, lo, this one is liable. [If] it was cooked with others, lo, this is prohibited if it is of sufficient quantity to impart a flavor to the whole mixture. [If] one ate a half olive's bulk or drank a half olive's bulk of a single sort [of prohibited fat or blood], lo, this one is liable.

M. 5:3 A woman [after giving birth] who brought a sin offering of fowl in a case of doubt [as to the character or viability of the foetus] , if before the neck was severed, it became known to her that she had certainly brought forth [a viable foetus] — let her make it into an unconditional offering [for certainty]. For the kind of animal that she brings in the case of uncertainty she brings in the case of certainty.

T. 2:22 The woman who brought a sin-offering of fowl in a case of doubt as to whether or not she has given birth to a viable offspring and learns that she has indeed not given birth [M. Ker. 5:3D-G], Lo, this [bird] is unconsecrated. She should give it to her girl-friend [who requires it]. And the one who discovers that she has certainly given birth — let her make it into an unconditional offering [M. Ker. 5:3F]. For the sort of animal which she brings in a case of uncertainty she brings in a case of certainty [M. Ker. 5:3G].

M. 5:4 A piece of meat of unconsecrated food and a piece of meat of Holy Things — [if] one ate one of them, and it is not known which of them he ate — he is exempt. [If] he ate the second, he brings an unconditional guilt offering.

T. 3:1 A piece of meat of forbidden fat of Holy Things and a piece of meat ,of unconsecrated food — [if] one ate one of them and does not know which of them he ate he brings [delete: a sin-offering and] a suspensive guilt-offering. [If] he ate the second, he brings a sin-offering and an unconditional guilt-offering.

T. 3:2 A piece of meat of Holy Things and a piece of meat of unconsecrated food [M. Ker. 5:4A] — [if] one ate the first and then went and ate the second in a single spell of inadvertence he brings a sin-offering and an unconditional guilt-offering. [If] he ate them in two spells of inadvertence, he brings two sin-offerings and one unconditional guilt-offering

. T. 3:3 A piece of meat [of forbidden fat] of refuse and a piece of meat of [if] one ate one of them and does not know which of them he ate, he brings a suspensive guilt-offering.

T. 3:4 A piece of meat of forbidden fat which is refuse and a piece of meat [of forbidden fat which is] of unconsecrated food — [if] one ate one of them and does not know which of them he ate he brings two suspensive guilt-offerings. [If] he ate the second, he brings two sin-offerings.

T. 3:5 A piece of meat of forbidden fat which is refuse and a piece of meat which is remnant — [if] one ate one of them and does not know which of them he ate he brings two suspensive guilt-offerings.

M. 5:5 A piece of meat of unconsecrated food and a piece of meat consisting of forbidden fat — [if] one ate one of them, and it is not known which of them he ate — he brings a suspensive guilt offering. [If] he ate the second, he brings a

sin offering. [If] one person ate the first, and another came along and ate the second, this one brings a suspensive guilt offering and that one brings a suspensive guilt offering.

M. 5:6 A piece of meat consisting of forbidden fat and a piece of meat of Holy Things — [if] one ate one of them, and it is not known which of them he ate-he brings a suspensive guilt offering. [If] he ate the second, he brings a sin offering and an unconditional guilt offering. [If] one person ate the first, and another came along and ate the second, this one brings a suspensive guilt offering, and that one brings a suspensive guilt offering.

M. 5:7 A piece of meat consisting of forbidden fat and a piece of meat consisting of forbidden fat of Holy Things — [if] one ate one of them, and it is not known which of them he ate — he brings a sin offering. [If] he ate the second, he brings two sin offerings and an unconditional guilt offering. If one person ate the first, and another came along and ate the second, this one brings a sin offering and that one brings a sin offering.

M. 5:8 A piece of meat consisting of forbidden fat and a piece of meat consisting of forbidden fat which is remnant — [if] one ate one of them, and it is not known which of them he ate- he brings a sin offering and a suspensive guilt offering. [If] he ate the second, he brings three sin offerings. [If] one person ate the first, and someone else came along and ate the second, this one brings a sin offering and a suspensive guilt offering, and that one brings a sin offering and a suspensive guilt offering.

T. 4:1 He who eats five pieces of meat from a single animal-sacrifice in five dishes in a single spell of inadvertence brings only a single sin-offering. And in a matter of doubt concerning them he brings only a single suspensive guilt-offering. [But if he does so] in five spells of inadvertence, he brings five sin-offerings. And in a matter of doubt concerning them he brings five suspensive guilt-offerings. This is the general principle: Whoever brings a sin-offering for a matter of certainty, brings a suspensive guilt-offering for a matter of uncertainty. And whoever does not bring a sin-offering for a matter of certainty does not bring a guilt-offering for a matter of uncertainty. But if he ate five pieces of meat from a single animal-sacrifice before the sprinkling of the blood, even in a single spell of inadvertence, he brings a sin-offering for each and every piece [which he ate].

The suspensive sin-offering covers a case in which a person is not certain whether or not he actually has committed a sin inadvertently. The cases that exemplify the interstitialities present no surprises and leave no ambiguities.

B.   WHEN THE ANIMAL DESIGNATED FOR THE SUSPENSIVE GUILT OFFERING MAY NOT BE REQUIRED

M. 6:1 He who brings a suspensive guilt offering, and is informed that he did not commit a sin — if this was before it was slaughtered, it [the animal] is set out to pasture until it is blemished, then it is sold, and its proceeds fall [to the Temple treasury] as a freewill offering. If after it was slaughtered he is [so] informed, the blood is to be poured out. And the meat goes forth to the place of burning. [If the man is informed after] the blood is [properly] tossed, the meat is to be eaten.

M. 6:2 An unconditional guilt offering is not subject to the foregoing rule. If [the man is so informed] before it is slaughtered, it goes forth and pastures in the flock. [If the man is so informed] after it has been slaughtered, lo, this is to be buried. [If the man is so informed after] the blood has been tossed, the meat goes out to the place of the burning. The ox which is stoned is not subject to the foregoing rule. If [it turns out that the ox has not killed a man] before it is stoned, it goes forth and pastures in the flock. [If it turns out that the ox has not killed a man] after it is stoned, it is available for benefit. The heifer whose neck is broken is not subject to the foregoing rule. If [the murderer is found] before its neck is broken, it goes forth and pastures in the flock. [If the murderer is found] after its neck is broken, it is buried in its place. For on account of a matter of doubt did it come in the first place. It has made atonement for its matter of doubt and goes its way [having served its purpose].

T. 2:6 Two people whose sin-offerings were mixed up in respect to two sins — it is set out to pasture until it is blemished and then sold. And let him bring with the proceeds of half of it a sin-offering for this one, and with the proceeds of half of it a sin-offering for that one. Two sin-offerings for a single sin — let the man offer whichever one of them he prefers. The second is put out to pasture until it is blemished, then it is sold, and its proceeds fall [to the Temple-treasury] as a freewill-offering. Two sin-offerings for two sins — this one is slaughtered for the sake of one of them, and that one is slaughtered for the sake of one of them.

T. 2:7 Two whose sin-offerings were confused — the sin-offering of an individual and the sin-offering of an individual, [or] the sin-offering of the community and the sin-offering of the community, [or] the sin-offering of an individual and the sin-offering of the community — even if they are two distinct sorts — this one is slaughtered for the sake of one of them, and that one is slaughtered for the sake of one of them.

T. 2:8 He who brings his sin-offering and slaughtered it — it is a matter of doubt whether or not its blood was [properly] tossed —. he has carried out his obligation. If he was lacking the completion of his atonement, it is a matter of doubt whether or not it has gotten dark [so that the blood was tossed by night] — Lo, this one brings the sin-offering of fowl as a matter of doubt.

T. 2:17 The Day of Atonement which coincides with the Sabbath and he did an act of labor, whether before it or afterward, he is exempt from the requirement of bringing a suspensive guilt- For the entire day effects atonement.

T. 2:23 In the case of her the neck of whose bird is broken, and who [then] is informed [that she certainly has given birth] — let its [the bird's] blood be drained out. [Its blood] has effected atonement. It is prohibited as to eating. [If this takes place] after its blood has been drained out [its blood] has effected atonement. is prohibited for enjoyment. For to begin with it is brought on account of doubt. It has effected atonement for its matter of doubt and gone its way [M. Ker. 6:2K].

T. 4:2 He who brings a sin-offering or a guilt-offering for a sin and is informed that he did not commit a sin — [if [this is] before it is slaughtered, it goes forth and pastures in the flock [M. Ker. 6:2B. [If this is] after it is slaughtered, its appearance is allowed to rot, and it is taken forth to the place of burning.

T. 4:3 A beast which is to be stoned, [if] the witnesses against it turn out to be conspirators, is available for benefit. A heifer whose neck is to be broken, [if] the witnesses against it turn out to be conspirators, is available for benefit. Those who owe a heifer whose neck is to be broken, for whom the Day of Atonement passed, are liable to bring it after the Day of Atonement. [If] one found the murderer, one way or the other, they slay him, since it is said, "You shall not thus pollute the land in which you live, for blood pollutes the land, and no expiation can be made for the land, for the blood that is shed in it, except by the blood of him who shed it" (Num. 35:33).

M. 6:4 Those who owe sin offerings and unconditional guilt offerings for whom the Day of Atonement passed [without their making those offerings] are liable to bring [the offerings] after the Day of Atonement. Those who owe suspensive guilt offerings are exempt. [The Day of Atonement has atoned for those transgressions that may or may not have taken place.] He who is subject to a doubt as to whether or not he has committed a transgression on the Day of Atonement, even at twilight, is exempt. For the entire day effects atonement.

M. 6:5 A woman who owes a bird offering as a matter of doubt, for whom the Day of Atonement passed [without her making said bird offering] is liable to bring it after the Day of Atonement. For it renders her fit for eating animal sacrifices [and is not expiatory in character]. A sin offering of fowl which is brought on account of doubt, if after its neck is pinched it is known [that the woman has not actually sinned at all], lo, this is to be buried.

M. 6:6 He who sets aside two selas [Lev. 5:15] for a guilt offering and purchased with them two rams [at one sela each] for a guilt offering — if one of them [went up in value so that it now] is worth two selas, let it be offered for his guilt offering. And the second, [which is no longer required, the proper value having been attained in the first of the two,] is set out to pasture until it is blemished, then sold, and its proceeds fall [to the Temple treasury] as a freewill offering [M. Tem. 3:3: that is, in the class of a guilt offering, the owners of which have effected atonement]. [If] he [who sets aside two selas for a guilt offering] purchased with them two rams for unconsecrated use, one worth two selas and one worth ten zuz — the one worth two selas is offered for his guilt offering [incurred through the act of sacrilege]. And the second is for restitution for his sacrilege. [If] one was for a guilt offering and one was for unconsecrated purposes, if the one for the guilt offering was worth two selas it is offered for his guilt offering. And the second is for restitution for his sacrilege. And let him bring with it a sela and its added fifth.

T. 4:5 A guilt-offering for thievery, a guilt-offering for sacrilege, a guilt-offering for sexual relations with a betrothed handmaiden, which [offering] one brought at an age of less than thirteen months and one day, not worth [two] silver sheqels, are invalid. [If] one brought them at an age of more than thirteen months and one day, even if they are superannuated, they are valid.

T. 4:6 A guilt-offering of a Nazir and a guilt-offering of a mesora' which one brought at an age of more than twelve months are invalid. [If] one brought them at an age of less than twelve months, even on the eighth day [of their life], they are valid. [If] one brought them at the value of a sela, [if] one brought them at the value of a sheqel, [if] one brought them at the value of five denars, they are valid.

T. 4:7 A. He who separates two selas for a guilt-offering land] purchased [M. Ker. 6:6A] with one of them a ram for a guilt-offering — if it was worth two selas, it is to be offered as his guilt-offering. And the [funds for the] second fall to [to the Temple-treasury] as a freewill-offering. If not, let it be put out to pasture until it is blemished and then be and let him bring with its proceeds a guilt-offering. worth two selas And as to the second, let it[s proceeds] fall [to the Temple-treasury] [If] he purchased with them [the two selas] two rams for a guilt-offering. If one of them was worth two selas, it is to be offered as his guilt-offering. And the second is to be put out to pasture until it is blemished then is to be sold, and its proceeds are to fall to the Temple-treasury as a freewill offering [M. Ker. 6:6A-D]. If not, then both of them are to be put out to pasture until they are blemished, then they are to be sold, and let him bring with them a guilt-offering worth two selas. And the rest [of the proceeds] fall [to the Temple-treasury] as a freewill-offering.

T. 4:8 [If] he purchased with them two rams for unconsecrated use, one of them worth two selas and one of them worth ten zuz the one which is worth two selas is to be offered as his guilt-offering. And the second is his restitution for sacrilege. [If] one was for guilt-offering and one for unconsecrated purposes, if the one purchased as a guilt-offering is worth two selas, it is to be offered as his guilt-offering. And the second is for the restitution for sacrilege. Let him [further] bring a sela and its added fifth form his own property [M. Ker. 6:6E-L].

T. 4:9 [If] he purchased one ram for a sela and fattened it up, so that, lo, it is worth two, it is valid. Let him [however] bring a sela from his own property.

T. 4:10 [If] he separated one ram from his flock, worth, at the time of its being separated, a sela, and at the time of its being offered up, two, it is valid. [If] it was worth two selas at the time of its separation and at the time of its being offered up, one sela, it is invalid.

M. 6:7 He who sets aside his sin offering and dies — his son should not bring it after him [for a sin the son has committed (M. Tem. 4:1)]. Nor should one bring for one sin [a beast set aside in expiation] for another — even [a beast set aside as a sin offering] for forbidden fat which he ate last night should he not bring [as a sin offering] for forbidden fat which he ate today, since it is said, "His offering for his sin" (Lev. 4:28) — that his offering should be for the sake of his [particular] sin.

T. 4:11 A. He who brings a suspensive guilt-offering for a matter of doubt concerning forbidden fat or for a matter of doubt concerning blood, and is informed that he did not commit a sin, [if this happened] before it was slaughtered, it goes forth to pasture in the flock. If this happened] after it was slaughtered, its appearance is allowed to rot and it goes forth to the place of burning.

M. 6:8 [With funds] consecrated [for the purchase of] a female lamb [as a sin offering], they purchase a female goat. [With funds] consecrated [for the purchase of] a female goat [as a sin offering], [they bring] a lamb. [With funds] consecrated [for the purchase of] a female lamb and a female goat [they purchase] turtledoves or young pigeons (Lev. 5:7). [With funds] consecrated [for the purchase of]turtle doves or young pigeons [they purchase] a tenth of an ephah [of fine flour, for a meal offering]. How so? [If] one set aside [funds] for the purchase of a female lamb or a female goat and then grew poor, he may bring a bird. [If] he grew still poorer, he may bring a tenth

of an ephah [of flour]. [If] he set aside funds for a tenth of an ephah [of flour] **and got rich, he may bring a bird. [If] he got still richer, he may bring a female lamb or a female goat. [If] he set aside a female lamb or a female goat and they were disfigured, if he wants, he may bring a bird with their proceeds. [If] he set aside a bird and it was disfigured, he should not bring a tenth of an ephah with its proceeds, for a bird is not subject to redemption.**

T. 4:14 [If] he separated coins for the tenth of an ephah or fine flour and got rich — let him add to them [the coins] and purchase with it [the money] turtle-doves or pigeons. [If] he separated turtle-doves or pigeons and got rich, [if they have] not been expressly designated, let them be left to die, for fowl is not subject to redemption [M. Ker. 6:8L]. [If they have been] expressly designated, that which is the sin-offering is left to die. But that which has been designated as a burnt-offering is offered as a burnt-offering. [If] he set aside coins for turtle-doves and pigeons and got rich, let him add and purchase with them [the whole sum] a female lamb and a female goat [M. Ker. 6:8].

We pursue a question of detail: if a suspensive guilt-offering turns out not to be required, how do we dispose of the animal that has been designated for that purpose? How do we deal with the situation of those obligated to sin- and guilt-offerings whose sin is expiated by the Day of Atonement (M. 6:4)? These and associated questions do not respond to the particular hermeneutics of the category-formation but to the considerations of the generic hermeneutics.

IV. DOCUMENTARY TRAITS

A. THE MISHNAH AND THE TOSEFTA

The familiar relationship persists.

B. THE BAVLI

Beyond its exegetical work, not surveyed here, I see little of importance in the Bavli's presentation of the Halakhic category-formation.

C. THE AGGADAH AND THE HALAKHAH IN THE BAVLI

The free-standing composites are to be taken up one by one, each in its context.[3] What we wish to know is, first, why has the free-standing composite in a

---

[3] I summarize briefly the discussion in my *Rationality and Structure: The Bavli's Anomalous Juxtapositions*. Atlanta, 1997: Scholars Press for South Florida Studies in the History of Judaism, which draws upon my *The Talmud of Babylonia. A Complete Outline*. Atlanta, 1995-6: Scholars Press for *USF Academic Commentary Series*. IV.B. *The Division of Holy Things and Tractate Niddah. Bekhorot through Niddah.*

Bavli-construction been inserted where it stands? Second, how has the inclusion of the composition affected our understanding of the topic or proposition that defines the primary framework of discussion — Halakhic exposition of the Mishnah and parts of the Tosefta and *baraita*-corpus?

I.F THE ANOINTING OIL:

The topic is introduced by the immediately-preceding Mishnah-statement. I see no animating proposition in this compilation of topical information.

V.C THE OFFERINGS OF A PROSELYTE:

The reason for the inclusion is obvious: the Mishnah has omitted reference to the proselyte's offerings, and the Talmud has explained why his offerings have been omitted. Then comes a free-standing exposition on the theme. The point is made that the proselyte's offerings really do correspond to the Israelite's. His are different but equivalent, and Scripture is explicit. Just as your forefathers entered the covenant only with circumcision and immersion and sprinkling of blood through the sacrifices, so they [proselytes] will enter the covenant only through circumcision, immersion, and sprinkling of blood on the altar — that is the paramount proposition. The character of the prior list can have left the contrary impression, so a sustained demonstration is required to right matters.

XIII.B A PREGNANT WOMAN OR NURSING MOTHER EATS WHAT OTHERS MAY NOT EAT, BUT ONLY IN LIMITED VOLUME:

The immediately preceding discussion sets forth rules governing the eating, in very small volume, of prohibited food. That may take place over a long period of time, so that the requisite volume of food for which culpability is incurred is not consumed in so brief a period as to warrant being taken into account. We then turn to another case in which forbidden food may be eaten; it is the pregnant woman. To her applies the opposite consideration: she may eat only a limited volume of forbidden food, but there is no restriction that requires her to eat it over a protracted period of time. So she enters the picture in order to give a pertinent, but diametrically opposite, case from the one that has been discussed: now not time but volume matter.

XXVII.B ACQUIRING OWNERSHIP: WHEN DOES THE INITIAL OWNER GIVE UP HOPE OF RECOVERING PROPERTY AND SO RELINQUISH TITLE?

Including this significant discussion makes a profound point. The superficial intersection is topical. In the immediately preceding discussion, we take up the issue of assigning ownership of an abandoned beast. The topic that now comes forward is abandoning ownership of property in general. But the more profound connection is not to be missed. We have been discussing the attitude of a person who dedicates a beast: is it conditional or unconditional? The premise therefore is this: the man's heart is what has moved him, we assume that he has resolved to dedicate the beast unconditionally. That principle calls to mind other ways in which the owner of property gives up his rights of ownership, and, once more, we are reminded, attitude is all. Just as a person may dedicate something to the Temple without condition or qualification, so he may give up ownership of his property through an act of will. That is, he relinquishes ownership of property that he has lost when he gives up hope of recovering it. It goes without saying that that attitude is not subject to qualification or condition. By including what is in fact a free-standing essay, the framer of the large-scale composite has vastly deepened our grasp of the principle operative in his basic Mishnah-commentary, namely, the matter of condition or stipulation as it affects rights of possession and ownership. Seeing the issue of the status of the animal that has been dedicated in this larger context affords us a perspective on what is at stake, and that, is one's attitude towards one's possessions, whether animals given to the Temple or property of which one has lost possession. On the one side, an act of consecration, on the other, an attitude of despair — these form counterparts. Were I a preacher, I would then formulate a sermon based on the contrast between trust in God contained in an act of unconditional consecration, as against the vagaries of trust in property, which we give up by not an act of consecration and hope, but one of despair and renunciation of hope.

XXVIII.D Sins for which the Day of Atonement Effects Atonement:

The context is a reasonable one: the kinds of sin for which the Day of Atonement effects atonement. The principal concern of the thematic composite is precisely the opposite: to specify the matters for which the Day of Atonement does not effect atonement at all. And that comes down to a recurrent point, subject to dispute: is uncleanness a matter of sin at all? This is made explicit in the following language: For all your sins...,' and not 'for all your occasions of uncleanness,' which are not matters of sin in any event, thus eliminating the sin offering brought by the woman after she has given birth, which is a purification rite. That same matter is systematically demonstrated for other categories. The point then is to differentiate sin from uncleanness and to demonstrate that uncleanness concerns access to the Temple and has little bearing on one's moral condition. That too offers an important theological point, and the contrast between the discussion of sins for which the Day of Atonement effects atonement and other considerations altogether — which the composite draws sharply — then sets forward a most fundamental principle.

XXIX.B Attaining Atonement with the Increase in the Value of Consecrated Property:

This theoretical problem is introduced because the Mishnah-passage provides an illustration of how consecrated property may increase in value and the consequence of such an event. But the theoretical issue is quite distinct from the context in which it is discussed. The issue is framed in this language: can a man can attain atonement with the increase in the value of consecrated property? Where his own efforts have led to the increase in value, beyond what is required for the original purpose for which he consecrated a beast, there is a strong case to be made that he may designate that increase in value for some other, also holy purpose, e.g., an offering that he has to make. He has not made secular use of what he consecrated, but he has taken for himself the right to designate, in his own behalf, the particular sacred use to which the increase may be put. The case can also be made that he may not attain atonement with that increase, because the original act of consecration, which has defined the status of the property, e.g., the beast, was not for the purpose that he now has in mind. So, in general terms, the question has been raised: may or may not a person gain atonement through the increase in the value of consecrated property? Introducing the question at just this point is absolutely required, since the Mishnah's case invites precisely this question. But the question is one of theory, and a variety of considerations now enters into the matter: the man's own effort, the conflict between a general act of consecration and an act of consecration for a particular purpose. But the deeper issue circulates throughout: if a person consecrates something, may he make himself a partner with God in the utilization of what he has given to God? Here too, the problem is deepened by what is a theological issue formulated in practical, legal terms of the cult. The problem concerns man's partnership with God in the ownership of the natural world, with special attention to man's right to effect his purposes through what he has donated for God's: is the confluence of interest plausible or inappropriate, sharing or hubris?

XXXII.B Issachar of Kefar Barqai

This singleton has already been dismissed; it is topically relevant but generates no profound thought.

The upshot is simply stated. Most, though not all, of the free-standing topical composites not only make important points of their own but also impart to the context in which they are located a theological dimension that, without them, would be absent. These points emerge.

[1] The proselyte is fully equivalent to the home-born Israelite. The rules of the cult demonstrate that fact.

[2] Food that is prohibited may nonetheless be utilized if it affords no material benefit, e.g., is eaten over a long period of time, or if it is eaten in such small volume as to provide no nourishment of consequence. Prohibitions, then, are set aside when they mark distinctions between the permitted and the prohibited that really make no difference. Only what makes an important difference, e.g., in sustaining life is subject to the prohibitions of the Torah.

[3] Ownership of property depends upon one's attitude toward the property. If one consecrates the property, God through the Temple becomes the owner. An act of will alienates the rights of ownership. If one relinquishes ownership by reason of despairing of recovering possession of the property, he also loses the rights of

ownership. So one may give up property either as a gift to Heaven or as a surrender to bad fortunate. Ownership by itself therefore makes little difference; one's attitude toward one's property, on the one side, and one's disposition of possessions, on the other, govern. One does well, therefore, to hold with open arms; one does better to give up ownership of property to Heaven as an act of donation than relinquish ownership to violence as an act of despair.

[4] Various classifications affect a person, and they are not to be confused with one another. A person finds himself in a variety of grids, each covering a particular territory of life. He may be unclean or clean, with consequences having to do with the Temple. He may do a religious duty or commit a sin, with consequences having to do with the moral life. The rites of the Temple, where they matter, concern not the cultic life of cleanness or uncleanness but the moral life of sin and atonement. The Day of Atonement — the single most consequence exercise of the cult — makes a difference to the moral condition of a human being, not to his cultic classification. The theological statement that morality takes priority over ritual, and that right — forgiveness of sin and atonement — stands above rite will hardly have surprised the prophets.

When we can explain the connections people make, we also can follow the rationality of the conclusions that they draw. The connections between the topic defined in the context of Mishnah-exegesis and that of the free-standing compositions and composites of a topical character yield the conclusions just now set forth. Generalizations about the system that animates the document as a whole will have to await an examination of the entire repertoire of connections between Mishnah-problems and their exegesis and extra-Mishnaic topics and their exposition. The four points we have identified in Bavli tractate Keritot cannot be taken up in isolation from the rest of the document. The demonstration of a single coherent structure imposes its own logic upon the exposition of what may or may not emerge as a cogent and uniform system.

If I had to select a single recurrent problem that attracts the interest of the authors of compositions and compilers of composites, it is the theory of classification, specifically, the subdivision of a genus into species, on the one side, and the way in which Scripture teaches us how to accomplish that generative problem of thought, on the other. This problem is in two parts: how does a given action subdivides into two or more classifications; how do two or more actions coalesce into a single classification. A second problem that occurs wherever relevant concerns the relationship of intentionality and culpability. A third recurrent exercise is to demonstrate the scriptural foundations of Mishnah-propositions. A fourth is the proof that authorities rule in a consistent way, so that their opinions prove harmonious. A fifth is the inquiry into how differences of opinion rest upon reasonable, but conflicting, principles; disputes are not irrational (or personal!) but always involve good reason for each side's ruling. A sixth is the introduction of an abstract, theoretical problem into a concrete case, e.g., may a prohibition apply to what is already prohibited? A sixth is the extension to a variety of concrete problems of a single, encompassing conception, e.g., the sin offering atones for a concrete action, done unwittingly and later found out, and is not generalized but highly particular; the complementary conception that the suspensive guilt offering is governed by the same rule and corresponds, in the case of what may or may not have taken place, to the situation of a sin offering presented when knowledge of what has happened is certain and precise. What we have, in other words, is the application of the generic hermeneutics of the Halakhah.

v. The Hermeneutics of Keritot

a. What fuses the Halakhic data into a category-formation?

How the Halakhic data fuse into a category-formation is now self-evident. It is because of the sanction for inadvertent sin, which is an offering. Hence, in the present context, in the Temple, God's abode, man meets God; here the offering is brought that expiates inadvertent sins or crimes. God is party to the transaction, for reasons already spelled out. And, corresponding to the Temple, it is in the course of the Israelite's life that God uniquely intervenes, shortening the years of the deliberate sinner in response to the offense against life represented by deliberate sin or crime of the specified character. And that brings us back to the classes of transgressions that God punishes and man does not punish: sins involving sex, the Temple, and the violation of negative commandments (e.g., not to eat forbidden fat, not to work on the Day of Atonement and the like). None of these represents a social sin, and none endangers the social order. All involve God and principally God, and none encompasses a victim other than God. So the whole holds together.

Where else, if not in the activities subject to extirpation or the sin-offering (and so too with the other offerings treated here) will God's power to know precisely what man intends be better brought to bear? Sins or crimes that affect the social order, that endanger the health of the commonwealth, come to trial in the court conducted by sages and are penalized in palpable and material ways: death, flogging, and the like. Here God does not intervene, because man bears responsibility for this-worldly transactions. But just as man shortens the life of the criminal or sinner in the matters specified in Sanhedrin and exacts physical penalty in the matters covered by Makkot (not to mention Shebuot, where specified), so God shortens the life of the criminal or sinner in matters of particular concern to God. These are matters that, strictly speaking, concern only God and not the Israelite commonwealth at large: sex, food, the Temple and its cult, the laws of proper conduct on specified occasions. Where the community does not and cannot supervise, God takes over, he who knows what man does in private and what animates and motivates his actions. Israel does Israel's business, God does God's. For both the upshot is the same: sin or crime is not indelible. An act of rebellion is expiated through life's breath, an act of inadvertent transgression through the blood of the sacrificial beast, with the same result: all Israel, however they have conducted themselves in their span of time on earth, will enjoy a portion in the world to come: all but the specified handful, enter to eternal life beyond the grave.

That explains what is unique to Keritot and defines its principle of selection and interpretation of its data, which is its distinguishing the unintentional sin, penalized by a sin- or guilt-offering, from the intentional one, penalized by extirpation. The reason that that critical distinction concerns us in the particular Halakhah at hand is self-evident. Here, at the cult, is where God intervenes. He accepts the blood-offering as an act of expiation of the inadvertent sin — or he rejects it, if improperly motivated; and instead he imposes early death. It is God above all who knows what is in man's heart and can differentiate intentional from unintentional actions. And it also is God who has the heaviest stake in the matter of intentional sin, for intentional sin represents rebellion against the Torah and God's rule through the Torah. So the category-formation finds its most appropriate setting in the division devoted to the altar, and it forms the ideal medium for delivering its particular message.

B. THE ACTIVITY OF THE CATEGORY-FORMATION

Made up mainly of lists of sins or crimes expiated by specified offerings, the tractate carries forward the investigation of sin and the penalty thereof, now with special attention to the use of animal offerings to expiate sins committed inadvertently. At issue to begin with is the penalty of extirpation, inflicted by Heaven for deliberately doing the sins specified above, matched by the sin-offering, required when said sins are inadvertent. These fall into three main categories: incest and other forms of improper sexual relationships, blasphemy, and violations of specified negative commandments (not to impart uncleanness to the Temple, not to eat Holy Things and the like). We note that the earthly court penalizes some of these same actions through flogging, as Chapter Three of Makkot indicates. So what we see here is how God's court not only, or in addition to, the earthly court, takes its part in removing the consequences of sin or crime. The tri-partite system of penalties — in the hands of, respectively, God, what we should call civil authorities (sages, king), and priests — functions to express the interests of the three components of the politics of holy Israel, the three agencies that legitimately inflict violence, God, king through sages, and priests.

The second penalty for inadvertent sin is the offering of variable value, and once more, we list those who are required to present such an offering, and special situations in that regard. The third is the suspensive guilt-offering, presented when one has some reason to suppose that he has carried out a sin but lacks adequate, positive grounds for confessing inadvertent commission of a sin. That once more carries us to address cases of doubt and how these are to be resolved. All of this forms a tight fit.

DESIGNATING AN OFFERING FOR A PARTICULAR ACT OF SINFULNESS: Since we are concerned to match the sin or crime with the correct penalty, we cannot find surprising the Halakhic principle that for an animal to serve in expiation of a given sin, it must be correctly designated for that purpose and only for that purpose. That is a point that we meet many times in the Halakhah, e.g., in the presentation of animal and meal offerings. Not only must the punishment fit the crime or sin, but the particular punishment must match the particular criminal or sinner. What that means is that the beast that the inadvertent sinner or criminal designates for the particular sin or crime that he has committed must be offered by the priest for that particular man and (it goes without saying) that sin or crime and no other. The animal designated as a suspensive guilt offering turns out not to be needed, the man having found out he did not commit the act he thought he might have done. That animal can serve some other purpose, since the designation turns out to have been in error; the proceeds of the beast are available for a freewill offering. A different rule responds to the mis-designation of the unconditional guilt offering. Here there was no doubt, at the moment the beast was designated, that the offering was required. It is, then, an act of sanctification carried out in error and is null.

THE SUSPENSIVE GUILT-OFFERING: The affect of the Day of Atonement comes under consideration. It functions as does a suspensive guilt offering, that is, to make atonement in cases where whether the sin has been committed is in doubt. That accounts for the role of the Day of Atonement in the atonement process; it has no bearing on the requirement of sin- or unconditional guilt-offerings; these must be paid for the specified deed.

THE GENERIC HERMENEUTICS OF THE HALAKHAH: It is one thing to define the hermeneutics of the category-formation, quite another to identify the points at which that hermeneutics engages with the data, or at which the category-formation itself transforms the facts into useful knowledge. What I see, in the main, is a composite of inert information, analyzed through the generic hermeneutics, with much attention to the matter of interstitiality.

C. THE CONSISTENCY OF THE CATEGORY-FORMATION

The category-formation is economical and internally coherent.

D. THE GENERATIVITY OF THE CATEGORY-FORMATION

I see no marks of generativity in the category-formation as I have accounted for it. Once the hypothetical reconstruction of the process of category-formation — comparison of common traits of classifications to constitute a genus, speciation of the classifications by contrasts of where they differ — has done its work, I discern little more than the classification and hierarchization of data. As in the kindred tractates, Sanhedrin-Makkot, so here too, the Halakhah focuses on two matters: the catalogues of sins, the disposition of the offering presented in expiation thereof. The secondary development at unit two — the case of multiple sin offerings, whether a single sin-offering for many sinful actions, or several sin-offerings for a single, complex one — represents the generic hermeneutics, which accounts for the largest part of the category-formation's exegetical activity.

But the failure of the hermeneutics to generate interesting problems and suggestive extensions and amplifications should not surprise us. For the purpose of establishing the category-formations, Keritot and Sanhedrin-Makkot, in the end is to organize data into lists. Once the traits of data for a given list are established, the intellectual task has come to fulfillment, and the scholarly one of data-collection and organization is all that remains. So in Keritot we deal only with crimes or sins that require God's role in the process of saving people from the effects of willful or inadvertent violation of the torah, in Sanhedrin-Makkot with crimes or sins that the expiation of which depends on man's action. The category-formations in both cases lack generativity because they fully respond to their respective hermeneutical programs — selection and interpretation of data — in the construction of their lists. Only where the lists intersect does the hermeneutics come to the fore, and that is only to effect the differentiation of the two category-formations — its sole task.

5

Tractate Parah

The first of three category-formations on media of purification from uncleanness — the others being Miqvaot and Yadayim — Parah draws on Scripture at Numbers 19 to define a distinctive process of purification from corpse-uncleanness in particular. This Scripture does by providing for the preparation of purification-water, a mixture of the ashes of a red cow and water, and for the application of that water upon a person or object that has suffered corpse-uncleanness. The mixture is applied on the third and seventh days after contamination, and on the seventh day the unclean person immerses and regains cleanness with the sunset that marks the beginning of the new week. In that way, death is removed, life is renewed, seven days after uncleanness was contracted.

The Halakhic category-formation, Parah ("the red cow") that deals with the instructions of Numbers 19 addresses preparation of the water for the removal of corpse-uncleanness through application of a mixture of water and the ashes of the red cow. But that statement of facts does not identify or account for the foci and generative issues of the category-formation. For that purpose the familiar exercise of analogy and contrast is required. Parah forms a species of the genus, "removing uncleanness with water," which forthwith identifies for us its companion-species, Miqvaot. How to compare and contrast the two species? Here we are on our own. Scripture says little that pertains to the latter category-formation and nothing that does the work of analogical-contrastive analysis for us in the way that it dictates the results of Negaim in the context of Ohalot. But the work of reconstructing in theory the hermeneutics of comparison and contrast nonetheless produces results that we can test and validate.

What we shall see is that the species, Parah and Miqvaot, of the common genus, "water that purifies," alike in their effect, differ in the role of human intentionality and consequent actual intervention that the respective species provide. Specifically, what the one requires the other prohibits. That fact places the removal of uncleanness in the middle, between susceptibility to uncleanness, where intentionality forms the critical variable, and the formation of sources of uncleanness, where intentionality is explicitly denied any role whatsoever. Here we deal with the interstitial case in which, for one species of the genus, intentionality is essential, for the other, excluded. To spell this out: [1] susceptibility to uncleanness for both utensils and food finds its dynamics in human intentionality, attitude, or will. Objects man regards as useful, foods as edible, are susceptible; objects deemed useless, food deemed inedible, are not susceptible. [2] Sources of uncleanness, as Ohalot and Negaim make explicit, come into being and impart uncleanness in complete isolation from human intentionality. Deliberate action has no bearing upon uncleanness by reason of Nega'-uncleanness, as the Halakhah explicitly states.

What about [3] media for the removal of uncleanness? Among those specified by Scripture, breakage of the unclean object, rendering it useless, fire, and water, in particular, the Halakhah devotes two principal[1] category-formations to purification through water. [1] In the one case, Parah, the highest level of human engagement in the preparation of the water to remove uncleanness is required, while [2] in the other, Miqvaot, the water must collect without human intervention of any kind. Once more the Halakhic category-formations reveal the working of analogical-contrastive analysis, identifying for us the foci and explaining why this, not that. These — Parah, Miqvaot — then form the genus, "water that effects the removal of uncleanness," speciated (in the present context[2]) into "water that depends upon human intervention for proper preparation" (for purification-water for removing corpse-uncleanness) and "water that collects naturally, without man's involvement" (for water for the immersion-pool, miqveh).

The contrast between the two species of the genus now comes to the fore. The principal requirements of engagement of man in collecting the water and the use of a valid utensil in preparing water for purification of corpse-uncleanness find their opposed match in the preparation of the immersion-pool. What man must do to prepare the purification-water (Parah) he may not do to prepare the immersion-pool (Miqvaot). Since the former removes the uncleanness imparted by the corpse and the latter uncleanness of other kinds, the hierarchization of the two kinds of water, that described in Parah and that set forth in Miqvaot, presents no problem. That subject to human intentionality and will — the purification-water of category-formation, Parah, takes priority over that from which the effects of man's attitude are excluded.

Details of the law of Parah convey the full extent to which the particular hermeneutics of intentionality prevails. Acute alertness forms the absolute pre-

---

[1] Yadayim is a spin-off of Parah in its governing principles.
[2] When we turn to Miqvaot, we are given a more elaborate speciation of water. For the present purpose, the speciation given here suffices.

requisites of producing the valid purification-water. The water must be drawn deliberately, for the specific composite of ash alone. One must be constantly occupied with the mixing. There can be no extraneous act of labor along with the drawing or mixing. But an act of labor connected with the drawing or mixing does not invalidate the rite. An individual who drew five jars of water to mix a single mixture, who would take each one out and pour — even though he closed the door behind him, the mixture is fit, because he is occupied with the mixing. And if after he took out the last, he closed the door behind him, it all is unfit, because he did extraneous work with it along with the rite. The closing of the door was no longer intrinsic to the act of mixing and represents a distraction.

In connection with mixing the ash and the water, one may not perform an extrinsic act of labor. Every action that he takes must involve the requirements of the mixing process. One's intentionality plays a role here. If he cuts off olive leaves, if that is done so that it the ash will enter the reed, it is fit. If he does the cutting of the leaves so that it will hold a large quantity of ash, it is unfit. The performance of extrinsic work spoils the drawn water, whether it is for him or for someone else. One must complete his own needs before attending to those of the purification rite. He who draws water for his own use and for the purification-rite draws his own first and ties the jug to the carrying yoke, and afterward he draws the water of the purification-rite. If he was drawing water to drink, and it was not possible to have arrange them other than both on a single yoke whether he drew his own first and afterward drew that of the purification-rite, or whether he drew the water of the purification-rite first and afterward drew his own, he places his own behind him and the purification-water before him. And if he placed the water of the purification-rite behind him, it is unfit. The water is invalidated by someone who, while carrying it, teaches a lesson, shows others the way, kills a snake, or the like.

Intentionality at every point therefore is critical in removing the source of sources of uncleanness, corpse-uncleanness. Most other classifications of uncleanness are overcome by still water, naturally collected, unaffected by the deliberate action of man using a valid utensil; the water that removes corpse-uncleanness must be gathered deliberately, in a useful vessel, the whole subject to a high level of intentionality. These principles are interwoven with the facts supplied by Scripture, and the result, the category-formation at hand, encompasses the usual three components: Scripture's, that of the particular hermeneutics, and that of the generic hermeneutics. Here, as is ordinarily the case, the particular hermeneutics predominates. But Scripture's picture comes first, then the particular hermeneutics, then the combination of the generic hermeneutics and necessary but inert facts — much as at Negaim.

The high degree of concentration on the rite that is required corresponds to the challenge: to create a realm of cleanness in the world outside of the Temple. The generative question that the Halakhah takes as the center of its program is this: how does a rite conducted outside of the Temple courtyard ("the camp") relate to the rules governing rites conducted inside? And, at a still deeper level, the problem awaits attention: how can the mixture of ash and water that purifies derive from a rite that — by Scripture's law — contaminates all of its participants, and how can that same purification-water both purify the person that is made unclean by a corpse and also contaminate the person that applies the water? It should be noted that the condition of uncleanness that the rite and the utilization of its results brings about is not corpse-uncleanness, but that uncleanness that can be removed through immersion and sunset, that is, an uncleanness in the first remove from the Father of uncleanness that contamination by the corpse — the Father of Fathers of uncleanness — imparts.

The rite as set forth in Scripture and amplified in the Halakhah thus encompasses two large paradoxes, involving the creation of cleanness out of uncleanness, and uncleanness out of cleanness. The first paradox is that it is possible to create a realm of cultic cleanness in the unclean world that lies outside the boundaries of the Temple — the world of death. This is expressed in Scripture's proposition that the cow is burned outside of the camp, that is to say, outside of the Temple, in an unclean place. Its blood is tossed not on the altar but in the direction of the altar, toward the front of the tent of meeting. Then the cow is burned outside of the Temple, the ashes are gathered and mixed with water, and the purification-water is then prepared. So the Halakhah underscores that, in the condition of uncleanness, media for achieving cleanness from the most virulent source of uncleanness, the corpse, are to be brought into being. And the Halakhah is explicit in identifying the threat as that of corpse-uncleanness. But through the intense deliberation of man, it is possible to bring into being the medium of purification from that same uncleanness.

In the very realm of death, media for overcoming the contamination of death are brought into being. And, to come back to the main point, that is why the highest level of cleanness is required — higher than that demanded even for eating Holy Things off the Lord's altar in the Temple itself — from all those who are engaged in the rite. That is why the most perfect sentience is demanded from them. Everything they see that can become unclean is deemed (for the present purpose) to be unclean. It would be difficult to state more eloquently the simple proposition that faced with the most extreme challenges to attaining uncleanness, Israel can become cultically clean. Nor does the implicit lesson require articulation: what Israel must do to overcome death is self-evident.

The second paradox is that, even encompassing those who have gained the highest level of purification, uncleanness envelops the world, for all death is ever-present. Thus those who have attained and maintained the extraordinary level of intense concentration required to participate in the rite of burning the cow, collecting the ashes, gathering and transporting water, and mixing the ash and the water, as well as those who propose to utilize the purification-water so brought into being — all by virtue of their very activity in creating media of purification are deemed unclean. They have defied death in the realm of death and overcome — but have contracted uncleanness nonetheless, indeed a paradox. They are decreed to be unclean in the remove that suffices for affecting their clothing as well, therefore requiring immersion and the setting of the sun to return to the ordinary condition of cleanness that they by definition enjoyed prior to entering into the work of the rite itself. So it is not corpse-uncleanness that they suffer, but uncleanness nonetheless. That is Scripture's decree, and it sets forth the paradox that out of cleanness comes the cause of uncleanness. So the upshot is, the high priest, who performs the rite involving the cow, is unclean, so too the one who burns the cow. A clean man (a priest is not specified) gathers the ashes and keeps them in a clean place outside of the Temple; he too is made unclean by participation in the rite.

And all this why? In the paradoxes of the Torah's Halakhah I see two intended statements.

[1] That out of the realm of uncleanness one may produce the medium of purification is to underscore that death is always with us, so too the contamination effected thereby — but the Torah sets forth the provisions by which the effects of death can be removed from the living. The principal medium of removing death is the mixture of ash and living water, flowing or spring-water, which serves only for the corpse and counterpart-uncleanness, those of the Zab and Zabah and the person afflicted with the skin-ailment, three sources of bodily uncleanness in the analogy of corpse-uncleanness, as we saw for Ohalot and Negaim and will in due course observe for Zabim as well. Nature itself supplies the medium, then, for recovering cleanness from death, which is, the kind of water that exhibits the traits of vitality — but only that kind. So nature contains within itself the power of renewal, the source of regeneration.

[2] That the rite that produces purification-water contaminates those that carry it out is to serve as a reminder that the uncleanness that stands for the departing soul is *sui generis;* to contain that uncleanness appropriate consideration is required — and never suffices. Death leaves its mark, which no protracted counting of removes from the original source serves to delimit. But the mixture of living water and ash, prepared with due deliberation beyond death's grasp, may wipe away, may dissolve, the uncleanness of the soul: acute sentience, intentionality beyond all disruption — these produce the Torah's final solution, the mixture of living water and ash of the red cow, applied with hyssop, however sparsely, to the person or object that has come under the shadow of death: the departing soul, en route to its sojourn until the resurrection.

It is at the center of the category-formation that these propositions are set forth through the Halakhic medium: cases and rules. Here is the program of the category-formation:

I.   THE RED COW DEFINED
II.   THE CONDUCT OF THE RITE. A NARRATIVE
III. THE CONDUCT OF THE RITE. LAWS
IV.   UTENSILS USED IN THE RITE

Within this theory of the Halakhic category-formation and its focus, units IV, V, VI form the heart of the matter. Much of the rest, e.g., units II-III, VIII and IX, recapitulate Scripture's facts.

To conclude: out of a contaminating rite comes water for purification, and, still, the one who sprinkles the purification-water also becomes unclean. In this category-formation sages explore the requirements of an offering conducted in a condition of uncleanness, in a place that is unclean by definition, by priests who contract uncleanness (but not corpse-uncleanness) by participating in the rite. Does that mean we impose more stringent purification-rules, to create a circle of cleanness in the unclean world? Or do we impose diminished rules, taking account of the givens of the circumstance? Along these same lines, do we perform the rite exactly as we should in the Temple at the altar, or do we perform the rite in exactly the opposite way, that is, as a mirror-image of how it would be done in the Temple? These parallel questions provoked by the twin-paradoxes of Scripture's and the Halakhah's rules for the rite, respectively, define the problem addressed by the Halakhah, which contains the Halakhah's deepest thinking upon the meaning of sanctifying the secular, ordinary world. These are the issues settled by the Halakhah before us.

II. THE SCRIPTURAL FOUNDATIONS OF THE HALAKHIC CATEGORY-FORMATION

The pertinent verses of Scripture, Numbers 19:1-22, are as follows:

> Now the Lord said to Moses and to Aaron, "This is the statute of the law which the Lord has commanded: tell the people of Israel to bring you a red heifer without defect, in which there is no blemish, and upon which a yoke has never come. And you shall give her to Eleazar the priest, and she shall be taken outside the camp and slaughtered before him; and Eleazar the priest shall take some of her blood with his finger, and sprinkle some of her blood toward the front of the tent of meeting seven times. And the heifer shall be burned in his sight; her skin, her flesh, and her blood, with her dung, shall be burned; and the priest shall take cedar wood and hyssop and scarlet stuff and cast them into the midst of the burning of the heifer. Then the priest shall wash his clothes and bathe his body in water, and afterwards he shall come into the camp and the priest shall be unclean until evening. He who burns the heifer shall wash his clothes in water and bathe his body in water, and shall be unclean until evening. And a man who is clean shall gather

up the ashes of the heifer and deposit them outside the camp in a clean place; and they shall be kept for the congregation of the people of Israel for the water for impurity, for the removal of sin. And he who gathers the ashes of the heifer shall wash his clothes and be unclean until evening. And this shall be to the people of Israel and to the stranger who sojourns among them a perpetual statute. He who touches the dead body of any person shall be unclean seven days; he shall cleanse himself with the water on the third day and on the seventh day and so be clean; but if he does not cleanse himself on the third day and on the seventh day, he will not become clean. Whoever touches a dead person, the body of any man who has died, and does not cleanse himself, defiles the tabernacle of the Lord, and that person shall be cut off from Israel, because the water for impurity was not thrown upon him, he shall be unclean; his uncleanness is still on him. This is the law when a man dies in a tent: every one who comes into the tent, and every one who is in the tent, shall be unclean seven days. And every open vessel, which has no cover fastened upon it, is unclean. Whoever in the open field touches one who is slain with a sword or a dead body or a bone of a man or a grave shall be unclean seven days. For the unclean they shall take some ashes of the burnt sin offering, and running water shall be added in a vessel. Then a clean person shall take hyssop and dip it in the water and sprinkle it on the tent and upon all the furnishings and upon the persons who were there, and upon him who touches the bone or the slain or the dead or the grave; and the clean person shall sprinkle on the unclean on the third day and on the seventh day; thus on the seventh day he shall cleanse him, and he shall wash his clothes and bathe himself in water, and at evening he shall be clean. But the man who is unclean and does not cleanse himself, that person shall be put off from the midst of the assembly; since he has defiled the sanctuary of the Lord, because the water for impurity has not been thrown upon him, he is unclean. And it shall be a perpetual statute for them. He who sprinkles the water for impurity shall wash his clothes; and he who touches the water for impurity shall be unclean until evening. And whatever the unclean person touches shall be unclean; and anyone who touches it shall be unclean until evening."

The Halakhah recapitulates the Torah's account of the purification rite, just as is the case in Negaim. But Scripture says little, and the Halakhah much, about the collection and mixing of water and ash, the protection of both from uncleanness, the role of intentionality in the procedure, and the like.

III. THE EXPOSITION OF THE COMPONENTS OF THE GIVEN CATEGORY-FORMATION BY THE MISHNAH-TOSEFTA

I.   THE RED COW DEFINED

> **M. 1:1 A heifer — two years old, and a cow — three years old, or four years old.**
> **M. 1:3 Lambs — one year old. And rams — two years old. And in all cases, [the year is reckoned] from [birth] day to [birth] day. One thirteen months old is not suitable either for a lamb or for a ram.**
>
> T. 1:1 A bullock twenty-four months and one day old — lo, this is a fully grown bullock. And R. Eleazar says, "They give it thirty days after the twenty-four months. For every place in which, 'A bullock of the herd' is said, [the reference is to one which is] two years old. [But] bullock plain [without further explanation] is three years to five years old." R. Yosé the Galilean says, "Bullocks are two years old, as it is said, 'A (bullock) two [years old] bullock of the herd will you take for purification-offering' [Num. 8:8]." They said to him, "It does not say 'two' [years old], but 'second' [in ordinal relationship] to the first. Just as the first is not eaten, so the second is not eaten." Said R. Simeon, "To what is a purification-[offering] likened? To a paraclete, who enters in to appease [the judge]. Once the paraclete has accomplished appeasement, then the gift is brought in.'"
>
> T. 1:2 Rabbi says, "Why does Scripture say, 'A two [year old] bullock of the herd will you take for a purification-offering' [Num. 8:3]? If it is to teach that they are two [bullocks], lo, it already has been said, 'And he will prepare the one as a purification-offering and the one as a whole-offering' [Num. 8:12]. Might one think that the purification-offering takes precedence over the whole-offering in every aspect of the rite? Scripture says, 'And a second bullock of the herd will you take for the purification-offering.' Or, 'A second bullock of the herd will you take for a purification-offering' — Might one think that the whole-offering should take precedence over the purification-offering in every aspect of the rite? Scripture says, 'And he will prepare the one as a purification-offering and the one as a whole-offering to the Lord' [Num. 8:12]. How so? The blood of the purification-offering takes precedence over the blood of the whole-offering, because it appeases [the Lord]. The limbs of the whole-offering take precedence over the pieces of the purification-offering, because they are wholly burned up in the fire."
>
> T. 1:3 R. Simeon says, "Why does Scripture say, 'And a second bullock of the herd will you take for the purification-offering' [Num. 8:8]? If it is to teach that they are two, lo, it already has been said, 'And he will prepare the one as a purification-offering and the one as a whole offering to the Lord' [Num. 8:12]. If so, why is it said, 'And a second bullock of the herd will you take for a purification-offering' [Num. 8:8]? Might one think, the purification-offering is consumed by the Levites? Scripture says, 'Second.' Second to the whole-offering. Just as the whole-offering is not consumed, so the purification-offering is not consumed."
>
> T. 1:5 R. Simeon says, "In every place in the Torah in which heifer is mentioned without further specification, it means one year old, and a heifer and a lamb [are also to be] one year old [Lev. 9:3]. Of the herd — two years old, as it is said, 'Take for yourself a heifer of the herd for a purification-offering and a ram for a burnt-

offering' [Lev. 9:2].- Perfect — in respect to years. And perfect — free of every sort of blemish." R. Yosé says, "Three atonement-offerings [come] from the bullocks, and three from the rams, and three from the goats. Three [come] from the bullocks: A bullock which comes with the unleavened bread. And the bullock of the Day of Atonement. And the heifer whose neck is broken. Three [come] from the rams: A guilt-offering because of a certain sin, And a suspensive guilt-offering. And a female sheep of the individual. Three [come] from the goats: The goats of the festivals. And the goat of the Day of Atonement. And the goat of the prince."

M. 1:4 (1) The sin offerings of the congregation [Lev. 4:14] and their whole offerings, (2) the sin offering of an individual, (3) and the guilt offering of a Nazir [Num. 6:14], (4) and the guilt offering of a leper [Lev. 14:12], are suitable from [the time that they are] thirty days old and upwards, and even on the thirtieth day. And if they offered them up on the eighth day, they are suitable, (1) Vow and freewill offerings, (2) the firstlings, (3) the tithe [of cattle, Lev. 17:32], (4) and the Passover offering, are suitable from the eighth day and upward, and even on the eighth day.

T. 1:7 A year which is stated with reference to the houses of cities encompassed by a wall, and years said with reference to the field of possession, and the six [years] spoken of with reference to the Hebrew slave, and all other references to years with respect to the son and daughter — all are from [birth] day to [birth] day. Required whole-offerings of the individual are suitable from the thirtieth day and onward, and even on the thirtieth day. And if they offered them up on the eighth day, they are suitable.

T. 1:8 R. Eleazar says, "The Passover is suitable only from the thirtieth day of its birth and onward." This is the general principle which R. Eleazar stated: "Any animal concerning which 'a year old' is said is acceptable from the thirtieth day and onward. But if one offered it up on the eighth day, it is suitable. With reference to a firstling on which, at the moment of birth, a blemish appeared, one may slaughter and eat it even on the very day on which it is born."

M. 2:1 A cow for use in the purification rite which is pregnant is unfit. It is purchased from the gentiles. And not this alone, but: All community and private offerings derive from the Land and from abroad, from what is new and from what is old [produce], except for the offering of the first barley crop [omer] and two bread [loaves, Lev. 23:17], which come only from what is new and from the land.

M. 2:2 A cow whose horns and hoofs are black — let one chop [them] off. The eyeball and the teeth and the tongue [which are blemished] do not render unfit in the [case of the] cow. And the dwarf is suitable. [If] there was on it a wen, and one chopped it off — . R. Judah declares unfit.

T. 2:2 [If] its horns and hoofs were removed and the marrow with them, it is unfit. One [born by Caesarian section] from the side is unfit. The hire [of the harlot] and the price [of a dog] are unfit.

M. 2:3 (1) A [cow born of Caesarian birth] from the side, (2) and the [harlot's] hire and (3) the price [of a dog] — it is unfit. All blemishes which render unfit in the case of Holy Things [sanctified animals] (Num. 19:2) render unfit in the

case of the cow [M. Bekh. 6:1-12]. [If] (1) one rode upon it, (2) leaned upon it, (3) suspended [something] on its tail, (4) crossed the river on it, (5) doubled up its leading rope, (6) placed his cloak upon it — it is unfit. But: [if] (1) one tied it with a rope, (2) made for it a sandal so that it should not slip, (3) spread his cloak over it because of the flies — it is fit. This is the general principle: Whatever [is done] for its need — it is suitable: For some other need — it is unfit.

M. 2:4 (4) [If] a bird rested on it, it is fit. [If] a male [bull] mounted it, it is unfit.

T. 2:3 Any sort of labor on account of which they are liable in connection with Holy Things renders unfit in the case of the cow. [If] one brought it in to the [threshing] team [to suck], and it [accidentally] threshed with its mother, it is fit. And if it is so that it will [both] suck and thresh, it is unfit. This is the general principle: Whatever is for its own necessity is suitable, and for some other necessity [than its own] is unfit.

T. 2:4 And the yoke renders unfit whether it is used for actual work or not for actual work. It may be redeemed for any blemish whatsoever. [If] it died, it may be redeemed. [If] one slaughtered it, it may be redeemed. [If] one found another more beautiful than it, it may be redeemed. [If] one [already] had slaughtered it on its wood-pile. it may not ever be redeemed. If its price comes from the heave-offering [appropriation] of the chamber [of the Temple treasury], [if the beast is redeemed, the funds] go to the heave-offering of the chamber [of the Temple treasury].

T. 2:5 A more strict rule applies to the cow than to Holy Things and to Holy Things which does not apply to the cow. For the cow is suitable only when red, and any sort of labor renders it unfit, which is not the case with Holy Things. And more strict is the rule applying to Holy Things, for Holy Things are redeemed only on account of a permanent blemish, and do not go forth for secular use, [for example] to be sheared and to be worked, and the person who shears them or who does work with them incurs forty stripes, which is not the case with the cow. More strict is the rule concerning the heifer [whose neck is to be broken] than that which applies to Holy Things, and [more strict is the rule applying to] Holy Things than that applying to the heifer. For as to a heifer, age renders [it] unfit, and labor renders it unfit, which is not the case with Holy Things. For Holy Things are redeemed only for a permanent blemish, and never go forth for ordinary use, to be sheared, and to be worked. And the one who shears and the one who works them, lo, this one is smitten with forty stripes, which is not the case with the heifer.

T. 2:6 [More strict is the rule] concerning the cow than applies to the heifer, and [more strict is the rule] concerning the heifer than applies to the cow. For the cow is suitable only if it is red, and blemishes render it unfit, And [if] one did work with it, it is unfit, which is not the case with the heifer. More strict is the rule applying to the heifer. For as to the heifer, age renders it unfit, which is not the case with the cow.

M. 2:5 [If] there were on it two black hairs, or white ones, inside a single follicle, it is unfit. [If] they were in two hollows, and they are opposite [adjacent to] one another — it is unfit. There were on it two hairs — their root is black and their head is red — their root is red and their head is black — [All follows the condition of] the root.

T. 2:7 [If] there were on it two black hairs or white ones in one follicle, it is unfit. In
two follicles — it is fit. R. Judah says, "Even in two follicles, and they are opposite
[adjacent to] one another? it is unfit." [If] there were on it two hairs — their root
is red, and their head black — R. Yosé ben Hameshulam says, "One shaves the
top and does not reckon with the possibility that he is liable on account of shearing."

In a topical unit devoted to the traits as to age that must be met by animals to
be sanctified for various offerings, the opening unit defines the requirements for
the red cow. But we quickly turn to the cow for the purification-rite in particular.
Given the importance of human intervention in the rite, with intentionality the key
to much else, we cannot find surprising that man may help improve the cow for use
in the rite, e.g., by chopping off horns and hoofs that are of the wrong color. But the
cow must be born naturally, and may not be the object of a disreputable transaction.
It can never have been deliberately used for extraneous labor, e.g., for carrying a
weight. The Tosefta's contribution beyond the usual amplification and refinement
lies in its analogical-contrastive exercise, holding together the red cow, the beast
sanctified for the altar, and the heifer that is sacrificed in the case of the discovery
of a neglected corpse (Dt. 22). This set of rules amplifies Scripture's requirements.
I see slight impact of the particular hermeneutics of the category-formation and
only superficial response to the generic hermeneutics of the Halakhah.

II. THE CONDUCT OF THE RITE. A NARRATIVE

M. 3:1 Seven days before the burning of the cow, they separate the priest who
burns the cow from his house, [bringing him] to the chamber which faces the
northeast corner of the Temple building, and it was called the stone house.
And they sprinkle on him all seven days [with a mixture] from all the
purification [waters] which were there.
T. 3:1 What is the difference between the priest who burns the cow and the priest of the
Day of Atonement? The priest of the Day of Atonement — his separation is in a
state [or, for the sake] of sanctity, and his brothers, the priests, touch him. The
priest who burns the cow — his separation is in a state [for the sake] of cleanness,
and his brothers, the priests, do not touch him, except for those who help him,
because he sprinkles.
M. 3:2 There were courtyards in Jerusalem, built on rock, and under them was a
hollow, [which served as a protection] against a grave in the depths. And they
bring pregnant women, who give birth there, and who raise their sons there.
And they bring oxen, and on them are doors, and the youngsters sit on top of
them, with cups of stone in their hands. [When] they reached the Siloam, they
descended and filled them, and mounted and sat on top of them.
T. 3:2 Courtyards were in Jerusalem, built on top of stone, and under them was a
hollow, because of the grave in the depths. They bring pregnant women, who give
birth there and raise their sons there, until they are seven or eight years old. And
they bring oxen, and on top of them are doors. And the children sit on top of them.
R. Judah says, "Oxen with broad bellies, so that the feet of the youngsters should

not protrude and become unclean by reason of the grave in the depths." And all agree that the youngsters require immersion.

T. 3:3 They said before R. Aqiba in the name of R. Ishmael, "Stone cups were suspended from the horns of the oxen. When the oxen kneeled down to drink, the cups were filled up." He said to them, "Do not give the Minim a chance to cavil after you."

M. 3:3 They came to the Temple mount and dismounted. (The Temple mount and the courtyards — under them is a hollow against a grave in the depth.) And at the door of the courtyard was set up a flask of [ashes of] purification [rites done in the past]. And they bring a male sheep, and tie a string between its horns, and they tie a stick or a bushy twig on the head of the rope, and one throws it into the flask. And one hits the male, and it starts backward. And one takes [the ashes spilled onto the stick] and mixes as much of it as could be visible on the surface of the water.

T. 3:4 They came to the gate which opens out from the court of the women to the rampart. And stone flasks were set up along the wall of the stairs of the woman's court, and [with] their covers of stone visible to the rampart, and in them were ashes of every cow which they had burned, as it is said, "And it will be for a testimony of the children of Israel" [Num. 19:9]

T. 3:5 One hits the male and it starts backward. And ash was poured out. He takes and mixes from that which is poured out. "These rites they did when they came up from the exile," the words of R. Judah. R. Simeon says, "Their ashes went down with them to Babylonia and came up with them." They said to him, "Was it not made unclean in the land of the gentiles?" He said to them, "They decreed uncleanness on the land of the gentiles only after they came up from the Exile."

M. 3:4 They did not prepare one purification offering [by virtue of the preparations made] for another purification offering, nor one child for his fellow.

M. 3:5 [If] they did not find [the residue of the ash] from seven [former cows of purification], they did it from six, from five, from four, from three, from two, from one. There were seven from Ezra onward. And who prepared them? Simeon the Righteous and Yohanan the High Priest did two each. Elyehoenai Haqqof and Hanamel the Egyptian, and Ishmael Phiabi did one each.

T. 3:6 Ishmael b. Phiabi — two, one in the status of one who had immersed on the selfsame day, and one in the status of one upon whom the sun has set [and who therefore is completely clean]. About this one which has done in the status of one who had immersed on the selfsame day, they engaged in argument with him. He said to him [them], "Tithe is eaten by one who had immersed on the same day, but heave-offering by one upon whom the sun has set. Tithe, which is eaten by one who had immersed on the same day — all the more so do they add a degree of sanctity to it. Most Holy Things are eaten inside the veils, and lesser Holy Things are eaten outside the veils. Lesser Holy Things, which are eaten outside the veils — all the more so do they add to them a degree of sanctity. Most Holy Things are eaten on one day, and Lesser Holy Things are eaten over a period of two days. Lesser Holy Things, which are eaten over a period of two days — all the more so do they add to them a degree of sanctity." They said to him, "If we preserve them [the ashes prepared by you in perfect cleanness], we give a bad name to the former generations, for they will say that they [who used ashes of the rite done by a tebul yom] are unclean." They decreed concerning it and poured it out, and he went and did another in the status of one who had immersed on the same day."

M. 3:6 And they would make a causeway from the Temple mount to the Mount of Olives, arches upon arches, an arch directly above each pair, because of the grave in the depths, on which the priest who burns the cow, and the cow, and all those that assist it go forth to the Mount of Olives.

T. 3:7 They would make a causeway from the Temple Mount to the Mount of Olives, arches upon arches, an arch directly above each pier, because of the grave in the depths. R. Eliezer says, "There was there no causeway, but pillars of marble were set up there, and planks of cedar on top of them." And the cow did not need to go out on the causeway [being insusceptible anyhow]. And they made the priest who burns the cow unclean, because of the Sadducees, so that they should not say that it is done by someone upon whom the sun has set for the completion of his purification.

M. 3:7 [If] the cow did not want to go forth, they do not bring out with it a black one, so that they should not say, "They slaughtered a black one." Nor a red one, so that they should not say, "Two did they slaughter." And the elders of Israel would precede [them] on foot to the Mount of Olives. And a house for immersion was there. And they would render the priest who burns the cow unclean, because of the Sadducees, so that they should not say, "It is done by one on whom the sun has set."

M. 3:8 They placed their hands on him, and they say to him, "My lord, High Priest, immerse one time." He descended and immersed, emerged and dried off. And wood was laid out there, cedar wood and pine and spruce [or: cypress], and smooth logs of fig [trees]. And they would make it into a kind of tower, and they would open windows in it, and its fore-side was [facing] westward.

M. 3:9 They bound it with a rope of bast and placed it on the pile of wood, with its head southward and its face westward, The priest, standing at the east [side], with his face turned west, slaughtered [it] with his right hand and received the blood with his left hand. R. Judah says, "With his right hand did he receive, and he put into his left hand. And he sprinkled with [the index finger of] his right hand." He dipped and sprinkled seven times toward the house of the Holy of Holies. For every sprinkling is a corresponding dipping. He completed sprinkling. He wiped his hand on the body of the cow. He descended and kindled the fire with chips [of wood].

T. 3:9 [The spaces beneath] the place of its pit and its woodpile and the house of immersion were hollow, because of a grave in the depths. They bound it with a rope of bast and put it onto the wood pile. And some say, "It went up with a contraption." R. Eliezer b. Jacob says, "They made a causeway on which it ascended." Its head was to the south and its face to the west.

T. 3:10 How does he carry out the rite? He slaughters with his right hand and receives the blood with [the palm of] his left hand, And sprinkles with his right finger. And if he changed [hands], it is unfit. R. Judah says, "He would slaughter with his right hand and [then] put the knife [down] before him or [give it] to this one who stands at his side, and he receives the blood with [the palm of] his right hand, and puts it into his left hand, and sprinkles with his right finger, and if he changed [hands], it is unfit." [If] it splashed from his hand when he sprinkles, whether outside its pit or outside its wood-pile, it is unfit. R. Eliezer b. Jacob says, "Outside its pit — it is unfit. Outside its wood-pile — he should not bring it back. And if he brought it back, it is fit. And if he brought the blood which is in his hand outside and [then] put it back, it is fit."

M. 3:10 It burst open. And he [then] stood outside its pit. He took cedar wood and hyssop and scarlet wool. He said to them, "Is this cedar wood? Is this cedar wood? Is this hyssop? Is this hyssop? Is this scarlet wool? Is this scarlet wool?" — three times for each item. And they say to him, "Yes and yes" — three times for each item.

M. 3:11 [When] it was burned up, they beat it with rods and sift it in sieves. A black [cinder] on which is ash they crush. And that on which is none do they leave. The bone, one way or the other, is crushed. And they divide it into three parts. One is placed on the Rampart, and one is placed on the Mount of Olives, and one was divided among all the [priestly] watches.

T. 3:11 [If] some of its skin, its flesh, or its hair burst outside its pit — let him put it back. And if he did not put it back, it is unfit. [If it burst] outside its wood-pile, lo, this one adds wood to it and burns it in its place. R. Eleazar [b. R. Simeon] says, "An olive's bulk [of skin, flesh, or hair] spoils [the rite]; less than an olive's bulk does not spoil [the rite and need not be put back]."

T. 3:12 [If] its horn or its hoof or its excrement burst, one does not have to restore it, for something which does not spoil the cow when it is alive does not spoil it when it is being burned. And R. Eleazar b. R. Simeon adds, "Shall I throw? Shall I throw? And shall I throw?" And they say to him, "Yes, and yes, and yes" — three times for each thing Whether one tore it open by hand, or whether he tore it open with a knife, or whether it was torn by itself, [or] whether one threw [the wool, hyssop, and wool] into its body, or whether one threw [them] into its pyre, (or) whether one threw the three things all at once, or whether one threw the three of them one after the other, it is suitable. [If] one threw them in before the flame had caught most of it, or after it had been made into ashes, it is unfit. '

T. 3:13 [If] one took a bone or a black cinder and mixed [the purification-water] with it, lo, this one has done nothing. If there is on it dirt of any amount from its body, one crushes it and mixes, and it is suitable.

T. 3:14 And they divided it into three parts. One part one places on the Rampart. And one part is placed on the Mount of Olives. And one part is divided among all the watches. [From] this which is divided among all the watches did Israelites sprinkle. [With] this which was put on the Mount of Olives did the priests mix [the purification-water]. And this one which was placed on the Rampart did they keep, as it is said, "And it shall be for a testimony of the children of Israel . It is for water for purification of impurity" [Num. 19:9].

In narrative-form such as characterizes the treatment of Temple rites, the Halakhah underscores two principles. First, the officiating priest is protected from uncleanness in extreme ways, as are all who are to participate; they are transported from the Temple to the Mount of Olives along a causeway that interposes against corpse-matter concealed in the ground. But then, the rite being conducted outside of the Temple, the high priest contracts uncleanness and immerses, conducting the rite in the status of one who awaits sunset for the completion of his purification-rite and his reentry into the status of cleanness. This same general question — the comparison of the conditions governing a rite outside of the Temple with those that pertain inside — requires the orientation of the external rite to the Temple. Is this done exactly as it would be done in the Temple? Or is it done in a mirror-image of the way it would be done in the Temple? That is what is at issue in the positioning of the beast, M. 3:9/T. 3:10.

III. THE CONDUCT OF THE RITE. LAWS

> **M. 4:1 The cow of purification which one slaughtered not for its name, [the blood of which] one received and [or] sprinkled not for its own name, or [which one received] for its own name and [sprinkled] not for its own name, or [which one received] not for its own name and [sprinkled] for its own name, is unfit. And [if the rite was done by one] whose hands and feet were not washed, it is unfit. And [if it was done] not by the high priest, it is unfit. And by one not wearing proper garments — it is unfit. And it was done in the white garments.**
>
> T. 4:1 A cow is not made unsuitable if it is left overnight. And even if one slaughtered it one day and burned it the next day, lo, this is suitable. [If] one sprinkled by night, his sprinkling is unfit. And even if all of them [but one] were by day, and on, was by night, his sprinkling is unfit. [If] one sprinkled with a utensil [instead of with his index finger], his sprinkling is unfit. And even if all of them [but one] were by hand, and one of them was with a utensil, his sprinkling is unfit. [If] one sprinkled with his left hand, his sprinkling ii unfit. And even if all of them [but one] were with the right [index finger], and one was with the left, his sprinkling is unfit.
>
> T. 4:2 [If] seven priests sprinkled at once, their sprinkling is unfit. [If they did so] one after the other, their sprinkling is suitable. Sprinklings with reference to the cow which one sprinkled not for their own name, or which were not properly directed [to the door of the Holy of Holies], or one of which was lacking, or [if] one dipped [his finger] one time and sprinkled twice, [or dipped] two times and sprinkled once, lo, these are unfit.
>
> T. 4:3 Eight from seven — if it is a priest who did [other] work with it, it is unfit. But if another priest [did it], it is fit. [If] a mourner before the kin's burial [or] one who was lacking in atonement burned it, it is suitable. Joseph the Babylonian says, "A mourner before the kin's burial is suitable. One who lacks atonement is unsuitable."
>
> T. 4:4 [If] one whose hands and feet were not washed burned it, it is unsuitable, as it is said, "When they come to the Tent of Meeting, they will wash in water and not die" [Ex. 30:20] — lo, the washing of the hands applies only inside [the Temple court, and not on the Mount of Olives].
>
> T. 4:5 R. Yosé the Galilean says, "The sacrifices that our fathers offered on Mount Sinai did not require flaying and cutting up, for flaying and cutting up apply only from the time of the giving of the Torah and thereafter."

T. 4:6 The burning of the cow and its sprinklings [are done] by the high priest, and all of the other aspects of its rite [are done] by an ordinary priest. "It is said, 'And you will give it to Eleazar the Priest' [Num. 19:3] — it [is burned by] Eleazar, who is prefect, but all other cows [in the future are burned] by an ordinary priest,'" the words of R. Meir. R. Yosé b. R. Judah and R. Simeon and R. Eliezer b. Jacob say, "It [is done] by Eleazar, who is prefect, and all other cows [are offered up] even by the high priest." Its requirement is with the four white garments of a n ordinary priest [even if the high priest does it]. [If] one did it in the golden garments or in the secular garments, it is unfit.

T. 4:7 His disciples asked Rabban Yohanan b. Zakkai, "A cow — in [what garments] is the rite carried out?" He said to them, "In the golden garments [of the high priest]." They said to him, "You have taught us, 'In white garments.'" He said to them, "Well have you spoken. And a deed which my own hands did, and my own eyes witnessed — and I forgot [the rule] — when my ears hear [the rule], all the more so [should I remember i]." Not that he did not know, but he wanted to stimulate the disciples. And there are those who say they asked Hillel the Elder. Not that he did not know, but that he wanted to stimulate the disciples. For R. Joshua says, "He who repeats but does not work [at remembering the tradition] is like a man who sows and does not harvest. "And one who learns Torah and forgets is like a woman who bears and buries."

M. 4:2 (1) [If] one burned it outside of its pit, (2) or [divided it and burned it] in two pits, (3) or [if] one burned two [cows] in one pit — it is unfit. [If] one sprinkled and did not aim at the door [of the Holy of Holies], it is unfit. [If] one sprinkled from the sixth for the seventh, and went and sprinkled the seventh time, it is unfit. [If one did so] from the seventh for the eighth and went back and sprinkled for the eighth, it is fit.

T. 4:8 They do not burn two cows in one pit. After the ashes are formed, one may bring another and burn on top of it and need not be concerned. [If] one burned it in two halves, one after the other — said Rabbi, "I say in this case that it is suitable."

M. 4:3 If one burned it without wood, or with any sort of wood, even with straw or with stubble, it is fit.

M. 4:4 All those who are engaged in the work of the cow from the beginning to the end [of the process]: (1) render clothing [or other utensils which they touch] unclean, and (2) render it [the rite] unfit through [other] work. If an invalidity happened to it in its slaughter, it does not render clothing unclean. If it happened to it in its sprinkling, all who participate in the work involving it before its unfitness — . it renders clothing unclean. And [those who do so] after its unfitness it does not render clothing unclean. It turns out that its strict rule is its lenient rule. And the elders of Israel would precede [them] on foot to the Mount of Olives. And a house for immersion was there. And they would render the priest who burns the cow unclean, because of the Sadducees, so that they should not say, "It is done by one on whom the sun has set." At all times: (1) do they commit sacrilege against it; (2) and do they add wood to it. (1) And its rites are done by day; (2) and by a priest. (1) And [other) work [done by those involved in the rite] renders it unfit, (2) until it is made into ashes. (1) And [other) work [done by those involved in the rite] renders the water unfit, (2) until they will put the ashes into it.

T. 4:9 A cow to which an invalidity happened, before it was made invalid, renders clothing unclean. After it was made invalid, it does not make clothing unclean. R. Simeon says, "Whether before or after it was made unsuitable, it does not render T. 4:10 At all times do they add wood to it. Said R. Judah, "Even when they would add [wood], they would add only bundles of hyssop, whose ashes are good and abundant."

T. 4:11 Every aspect of the rite of the cow is by day, except for the gathering of the ashes and the drawing [of water] and the mixing [of the ashes and the water]. Every aspect of the rite is done by priests [or: by men], except for gathering the ashes and drawing [of water] and mixing. The sprinkling is done by day only. They do not draw [water] and do not mix and do not sprinkle from it before the ashes are formed [or: except with a utensil]. All aspects of its rite does work [for some other purpose] render unclean except for gathering its ashes and sprinkling its water.

We recall that the officiating priest must perform the critical actions of the sacrificial rite — slaughtering the animal, collecting the blood, conveying the blood to the altar, tossing the blood on the altar — with the proper intentionality, meaning, his act must be for the sake of the purpose for which the beast was originally set aside and consecrated. But if that is not the case, in most instances the rite is not disqualified, though the sacrifier must still perform the obligation that he originally undertook. This, predictably, is not one of those instances. Every detail must conform to the highest expectations of the Halakhah. We note, M. 4:2, that the blood when it is tossed must be aimed at the door of the Holy of Holies. All who are engaged in the rite, start to finish, convey uncleanness as Fathers of uncleanness to what they touch. They must be engaged solely in the present task and must not commit an act of extraneous labor. Both rules heighten the concentration on this rite alone.

IV. UTENSILS USED IN THE RITE

M. 5:1 He who brings a clay utensil for the purification [rite] immerses and spends the night [watching over] at the furnace. For all are believed [to preserve cleanness) concerning the purification [rite]. And [for one used in connection with] heave offering: he opens the oven and takes [out the needed utensil].

T. 4:12 There are six distinctive traits [which apply] to the purification [water]. They fill and mix the purification-water anywhere [with any sort of utensil. They sprinkle purification-water and purification-ashes anywhere [with any sort of utensil]. An 'am ha'ares who said, "I am clean so far as purification-water is concerned" — they accept [that statement] from him. [If he said], "These utensils are clean for purification-water" — they accept [that statement] from him. [If] one immersed in order to sprinkle but did not sprinkle, he eats heave-offering in the evening [after sunset]. [If] they saw in his hands purification-water and purification-ashes [not mixed], they prepare clean things with him [or] (on) his garments or (on) his sandals.

T. 4:13 An 'am ha'ares who brought utensils for his purification — a haber may take [purchase these same utensils] from him for his purification and for his heave-offering. [If] he brought them for his heave-offering, a haber does not take [purchase] them from him for his purification- and for his heave-offering. [If] a haber said to an 'am ha'ares, "Bring utensils for my purification" — the haber accepts them from him for his purification- and for his heave-offering. [If] he brought them for his heave-offering, the haber does not accept them from him for his purification- and for his heave-offering. [If] he brought them for the purification- and for the heave-offering [of a haber], for the purification-offering of a haber one takes them from him, whether they are for him or for someone else, on condition that he not practice deception [needing only the one [or heave-offering]. But if he practices deception, lo, these are unclean. And as to utensils for heave-offering, a haber does not take them from him for his purification or for his heave-offering.

T. 4:14 An 'am ha'ares who said, "These utensils have I brought for my purification, and I changed my mind concerning them and decided to use them for my heave-offering" — since they were designated [for a base purpose] in the possession of the 'am ha'ares [even] for one moment, lo, these are unclean.

T. 5:1 He who brings a clay utensil for the purification [rite] immersed and spent the night with the oven. [If] he spent the night before immersing — Rabbi declares unclean. R. Yosé b. R. Judah says, "[If] he spent the night and afterward immersed, if it was not in the presumption of being guarded, it is unclean." As to heave-offering, one opens the oven and takes [the utensil]. [If] one found it open or one of them opened it — R. Simeon says, "From the second row." R. Yosé says, "From the third row." R. Simeon ben Judah says in the name of R. Simeon, 'The House of Shammai say, 'From the third row.' And the House of Hillel say, 'From the second row.' And this is the first Mishnah. Our rabbis have said, "One [an 'am ha'ares] opens and takes and is not held back. And the haber comes even after three days and takes [a pot out]."

T. 5:2 [If] one ['am ha'ares] removed the cover and [a haber] found dirt on the utensils, lo, this one [the haber] takes [a utensil]. [If however] one of them was [already] taken out, they all are in the possession [domain] of an 'am ha'ares. [In] a place in which they plaster over the half-burned [utensils] with white mud, the haber stands and supervises their plastering. The column [of pots] which he supervises is not unclean — but that row only [is clean].

T. 5:3 The haber stands above and the 'am ha'ares stands below. He pulls [out a utensil with something insusceptible lo uncleanness, but does not touch the utensil himself] and gives [it] to him. The 'am ha'ares is believed to say, "I did not make it unclean," because [in any event] he is in the presumption of being guarded.

M. 5:2 He who immerses a utensil for the purification [rite] in water which is not suitable for mixing must dry [it] off. [If he does so] in water which is suitable for mixing, he need not dry [it] off. If [he does so] in order to collect in it water which has been mixed, one way or the other, he does need to dry [it] off.

T. 5:4 [If] one filled the bucket to drink [from it] and changed his mind concerning it, [if he changed his mind] before it [the bucket] touched the water and he emptied it out, he needs to wipe it off. [And if] after it touched the water he changed his mind concerning it, he empties it and does not have to dry it off. Rabban Simeon b. Gamaliel says, "He does not even have to pour it out.

T. 5:5 [If] one let down the bucket to draw water with it, and the rope slipped from his hand, if before it touched the water he changed his mind concerning it, he empties it out and needs to dry it off. [If] it is still in the water and he changed his mind concerning it, he empties it out and does not have to dry it off. Rabban Simeon says, "He does not even have to empty it out."

M. 5:3 A pumpkin which they immersed in water which is not suitable for mixing — they mix with it before it is made unclean. [If however] it is made unclean, they do not mix with it. One way or the other he should not collect in it water which has been mixed [with ashes].

M. 5:4 A reed which one cut off [for use as a container] for [ashes of] the purification [rite] — he makes it unclean and [then] immerses it. All are suitable for mixing, except for a deaf mute, an idiot, and a child.

T. 5:6 A reed which one cut off for [use in collecting the ashes of] the purification [rite] — R. Eliezer says, "He immerses it and does not have to make it unclean . " And R. Joshua says, "He makes it unclean and immerses it." [If] one gathered into it purification-water and purification-ashes — [if he did so] before he immersed it, they are unclean. And R. Simeon declares clean.

T. 5: 7 All are suitable for mixing, except for a deaf-mute, idiot, and child. And R. Judah declares fit in the case of the child. R. Ishmael b. R. Yohanan b. Beroqah says, "A deaf-mute, idiot, and child who mixed, and others are supervising them — their mixing is valid." A tumtom [one whose sex is not known] — his mixing is unfit, because he is in the status of one who might need to be circumcised, and the uncircumcised person is unfit for mixing. An androgyne — his mixing is valid. R. Judah declares unfit, because it is a matter of doubt whether he might be a woman, and the woman is unfit for mixing.

M. 5:5 With all utensils do they mix, even with utensils of dung, and with utensils of stone, and utensils of clod. And as to [a utensil shaped like] a ship, they mix with it. They do not mix either with the sides of utensils, or with the flanks of the pot, or with the bung of the pitcher, and not with his cupped hands, because they do not draw, and they do not mix, and they do not sprinkle purification water except with a [whole] utensil. They do not afford protection with a tightly sealed stopper except utensils, for they do not afford protection from the power of clay utensils except utensils.

M. 5:6 An egg of the potters is suitable. An egg of hens — sages declare unfit.

M. 5:7 The trough which is [hewn] in the rock — (1) they do not draw with it, (2) they do not mix with it, (3) they do not sprinkle from it, (4) it does not require a tightly sealed stopper, and (5) it does not render an immersion pool unfit. [If] it was a [movable] utensil, and one [then] joined it with plaster [to the ground] — (1) they do draw with it, (2) they do mix with it, (3) they do sprinkle from it, (4) it does require a tightly sealed stopper, and (5) it renders unfit in the case of the immersion pool. [If) it was perforated on the bottom and one stopped it up with a rag — the water which is in it is unfit, because it is not wholly enclosed by the utensil. [If it was perforated] on the side and one stopped it up with a rag, the water in it is suitable, because it is wholly enclosed by the utensil. [If] they made for it a brim of mud, and the water rose to that spot, it is unfit. [If] it was firm so that it [the utensil] may be moved with it [while grasping the brim], it is fit.

T. 5:8 The [broken] sides of wooden utensils, bone utensils, and glass utensils — they do not mix in them. [If] one planed and smoothed them and made them into utensils, they do mix in them. A stopper which one shaped into a utensil is suitable for mixing. The egg of the ostrich is suitable for mixing. Whether one hews [a hole] in the water channel or whether [he hews a] receptacle, even though the water uprooted it and attached it — they do not draw with it, and they do not mix in it, and they do not sprinkle from it, and it does not require a tightly sealed stopper, and it does not render the immersion-ritual pool unclean. [If] one [deliberately] uprooted it and then affixed it to the ground and gave thought to it after its being uprooted — they do draw with it and mix with it and sprinkle from it, and it requires a tightly sealed stopper, and it renders the immersion-ritual pool unfit.

M. 5:8 Two [movable] troughs which are in a single [movable] stone — one mixed [in] one of them — the water in the second is not mixed. [If] they were perforated from one to the other [through a hole the size of] the spout of a water-skin — or [if] the water overflowed on top of them, even [a film of water of] the thickness of a garlic peel, and one mixed [the water which is] in one of them, the water in the second is mixed.

T. 5:9 A spring which flows down to a basin, and one wishes to mix in it [the basin] — one stops it [the water] up, and lets it [the basin] dry off, and goes and then leads the water channel [to it] and mixes in it. A trough which is encompassed by holes, if they were mixed [by a connecting channel as wide as] the stopper of a leather skin, one mixing serves all of them, and if not, they require mixing for each one separately. R. Judah says in the name of R. Eleazar, "[If] one made for it a brim of mud to lead the water, whether it may be moved with it, or whether it may not be moved with it, it is suitable." The trough which is in the mud, if it is moved with it, it [the water in the mud trough] is suitable, and if not, it [the water in the mud trough] is unsuitable.

M. 5:9 Two stones which one placed close to one another and made into a trough, and so two kneading troughs, and so the trough which was divided, the water between them [in the gaps] is not mixed. [If] one repaired them with plaster or gypsum and they can move about as one, the water between them is mixed.

T. 5:10 Two stones which one placed near one another and made into a trough, and so two kneading troughs, and so the trough which was divided — Said R. Yosé, "In this case, I besought the law before R. Aqiba. I said in his presence, 'The two of them are not mixed, for the water which is in the crack is not gathered together in a utensil.'"

The water must be collected in a valid utensil, one that is whole and susceptible to uncleanness but preserved from contamination. The utensil in which the water and ash are mixed must form a receptacle and must be used in the ordinary fashion. The utensil must be distinct from its natural setting, e.g., a trough hewn in a rock is not suitable. A movable one is.

v.   MIXING THE ASH AND WATER

M. 6:1 He who mixes [ash and water in a trough], and the ash fell on his hand, or on the side [of the trough], and afterward it fell on the trough, it [the act of mixing] is unfit. [If] it [ash] fell from the reed to the trough, it is unfit. [If] he

took [ash] from the reed and [then, before mixing] covered [the reed], or shut the door, the ash is fit, but the water is unfit. . [If before mixing] he put it [the reed] in the ground, it [the water] is unfit. [If he put the reed] into his hand, it is fit, because it is possible [to do so without distraction].

T. 6:1 He who goes to mix [ashes and water], lo, this one takes a key and opens [a door, if need be], or a spade and digs, or a ladder and moves it from one place to another, and it [the mixing] is acceptable, because he is occupied with the mixing. But if, after he took the ash out, he closed the door behind him, it [the water] is unfit, because he is thus carrying out an [extrinsic] act of labor along with it [the mixing process]. [If] he cuts off olive leaves, if so that it [the ash] will enter the reed, it is fit. If [he does so] so that it will hold a large quantity of ash, it is unfit. [If] he stuck it into the ground or gave it to those standing by his side, if there are there watchmen, it is suitable. If there are no watchmen there, it is unfit.

T. 6:4 [If] one was standing and mixing and trembled or got tired, or his fellow pushed him, or the wind pushed him, or another came and mixed [in his place] — lo, this is unfit, as it is said, "And for the unclean they take of the ashes" [Num. 19: 1 7]. until they [explicitly] intend [to do the work] for drawing and for mixing and for sprinkling.

M. 6:2 **[If] the ash was floating on the surface of the water — whatever [ash] has touched the water — they do not mix [another preparation] with it. [If] he emptied out the water, and ash was found below, on the bottom — whatever has touched the water — they do not mix with it.**

T. 6:2 [If] one took the ash and saw that it is excessive and put it back [in the reed], it is suitable. [If] he put the ash [into the water] and saw that it is excessive, he takes part of it out and goes and mixes [it] in some other place [another quantity of water]. [If] the wind blew the ash and thereby put it on to the water, he dries it off and mixes with it, and it is suitable. [If] one put it into the mixture — R. Simeon and R. Meir say, "He dries it off and mixes therewith." And sages say, "Whatever has touched the water — they do not mix with it [in some other mixture]."

M. 6:3 **He who mixes in the trough, and the flask is in it — even though its mouth is ever so narrow [in any amount at all] — the water which is in it is mixed. [If] there was a sponge [in the trough], the water which is in it [the sponge] is unfit.**

T. 5:10 And if one touched the sponge which is outside the water, it is unfit. And if it fell into water which was mixed, one takes it and rings it out, and the water is suitable.

An extrinsic act of labor performed in the mixing process invalidates the mixture. That is assumed to have distracted attention from the work.

VI. DRAWING THE WATER FOR MIXING WITH THE ASHES

M. 6:4 **[If] he placed [under running water] his hand or his foot or vegetable greens so that the water should flow into the jar, it [the water] is unfit. [If for this purpose he made use of] leaves of reeds or nuts, it is fit. This is the principle: Something which is susceptible to uncleanness — it is unfit. And something which is not susceptible to uncleanness — it is fit.**

M. 6:5 He who diverts the spring into the wine vat or into the cistern — it [the water] is unfit for Zabs [Lev, 15:13] and for lepers [Lev. 14:5] and to mix therein purification water, because they have not been filled up by means of a utensil.

T. 6:3 [If] one splashed water with his hand and with his feet and with the clay shards, not with a trough [a utensil] — it is unsuitable, because the water was not drawn with a utensil. But if the jar broke and one splashed it out with his hands, feet, and clay shards, not with a trough, it is suitable, because it was [originally] drawn with a utensil. [If] he put in the ash and afterward put in the water, it is unfit. And R. Simeon declares fit. R. Simeon agrees that if he put in the water and afterward put in the ash and saw it, that it is excessive, and then added other water to it, that it needs a second mixing [of ashes]. For purification-water does not produce purification-water. But only the putting in of the ashes produces purification-water.

M. 7:1 Five who drew five jars [of water] to mix [with them] five mixtures [of ash and water] and changed their minds [and decided] to [empty all the water into one jar and] mix them in a single mixture — or [five who filled five jars to mix with them] a single mixture, and changed their minds [decided] to mix [with them] five mixtures — lo, all [the water] is suitable. An individual who drew five jars [of water] to mix [with them] five mixtures and changed his mind [and decided] to mix [with them] single mixture — suitable is only the last [such mixture, in which no drawing preceded a mixing). [An individual who filled five jars to mix with them] one mixture and [after drawing the five] changed his mind and decided to mix [with them] five mixtures [in succession, drawing, then mixing five times] — suitable is only this one which he mixed first. [If] one said to someone, "Mix these [each one separately] for yourself " — suitable is only the first. [If he said], "Mix these for me" — lo, all of them are suitable.

T. 7:1 An individual who drew five jars of water to mix a single mixture he would take each one out and pour — even though he closed the door behind him, it is fit, because he is occupied with the mixing. And if after he took out the last, he closed the door behind him, it [all] is unfit, because he did [extraneous] work with it [along with the rite]. And if there are guards there, he has rendered unfit only that which is in his hand alone [but not what is already mixed].

T. 7:2 [An individual who drew five jars of water] to mix [with them] five mixtures — he would bring out each one and pour it — if there are guards there, this one with [the exit of] which he closed the door is fit. This one with [the exit of] which he did not close the door is unfit. [If] his jar was lying before him, and his fellow said to him, "Give it to me," and he gave it to him, they are both unfit. And if he said to him, "Take it for yourself"— his own is unfit, and that of the other is fit. Id there were two jars before him, and his fellow said to him, "Give them to me," and he gave them to him — his own is unfit, and that of his fellow is fit. If he said to him, "Take it for yourself" — they are both fit.

M. 7:2 He who draws with one hand and does [other, extrinsic] work with the other hand — he who draws for himself and for someone else — or who drew for two [jars] at once — they both are unfit. For the [performance of extrinsic] work spoils the drawn [water], whether it is for him or for someone else.

M. 7:3 He who mixed — with one hand and does work [extrinsic to the rite] with the other hand — if it is for himself, it is unfit. And if it is for someone else, it is fit. He who mixes [simultaneously] for himself and for someone else — [that which he mixed] for himself is unfit, and [that which he mixed] for another person is fit. He who mixes for two [other people] at once — they both are fit.

T. 6:4 If one [simultaneously] drew for himself with one hand and did work with the other hand and mixed for himself with one and [simultaneously] did work with the other hand — and mixed for himself with one hand and did work with the other hand — drew and mixed — mixed and drew — for himself with both hands as one [simultaneously] — in all cases it is unfit. If one drew for another person with one hand and did work with the other hand — mixed for another person with one hand and did work with the other hand — drew and mixed — mixed and drew — for another person with both hands at once — if it is for himself, it is fit. And if it is for someone else, it is unfit.

T. 6:5 Said R. Simeon, "When [does this rule apply]? When there are guards there. [If] there are no guards there, [if] he mixed for others, it is as if he mixed for himself." [If] he drew for himself with his two hands at once, for a single mixture, it is unfit. In the case of two mixtures, it is fit. [If] one mixed for himself with his two hands at once, in a single mixture, it is suitable; in two mixtures, it is unfit. [If] one drew and mixed, mixed and drew, with his two hands at once — they are both unfit. [If] one drew for another person with his two hands at once in respect to a single mixture, it is fit. In respect to two mixtures, it is unfit. [If] one mixed for someone else with his two hands at once, whether this is in connection with a single mixture or whether it involves two mixtures, it is fit. [If] one drew and mixed — mixed and drew — with his two hands at once — the mixture is fit [the owner has done no work], and the drawing [of water] is unfit. This is the principle: Any sort of work with which there is drawing whether it is for oneself or for someone else, — it [the water] is unfit. And any sort of work with which there is no drawing of water — work done for himself — [the water] is unfit; and for someone else — it is fit.

T. 6:6 Whatever is in one's hand and one did work, whether there are guards there or there are no guards there — it is unfit. Anything which is in one's hand and one did not work — if there are guards there — it is unfit. [If] there are no guards there, it is unfit. [If] one drew for himself and for someone else with his two hands at once — they all are unfit. [If] one mixed for himself and mixed for someone else with his two hands at once — that for himself is unfit, and that [mixture done] for someone else is fit. [If] one drew for himself and mixed for someone else — with his two hands at once — they both are unfit.

T. 6:7 [If] one drew for himself with his two hands, one after the other [in succession], the first [mixing] is unfit, and the second is fit. [If] one mixed for himself with his two hands, one after the other, the first is fit, and the second is unfit. [If] one drew and mixed for himself with his two hands, one after the other, they both are unfit. [If] one mixed and drew for himself with his two hands one after the other, they are both fit. [If] one drew for someone else with his two hands, one after the other [if] one mixed for someone else with his two hands, one after the other — [if] he drew and mixed — mixed and drew — for someone else with his two hands, one after the other — they all are fit.

T. 6:8 [If] one drew for himself and for someone else with his two hands one after the other, his own is unfit, and his fellow's is fit. [If] one mixed for himself and for someone else with his two hands, one after the other, his own is fit, and that of the other is unfit. [If] one drew for himself and mixed for another with his two hands, one after the other, both are unfit. [If] one mixed for himself and drew for someone else with his two hands, one after the other — they both are fit. [If someone said], "Draw for me, and [then] draw for yourself," "Mix for me, and mix for yourself" — they are all suitable. "Draw them for me and mix them for me, and I shall draw them for you and I shall mix them for you" — they are all unfit. "Draw for me and draw for yourself, mix for me and mix for yourself" — the first and the last are unfit, and the one in the middle is fit. "Draw for me and I shall draw for you, mix for me and I shall mix for you" — the first and the last are fit and the middle ones are unfit. And if there are guards there, they are all fit.

M. 7:4 [If someone, having drawn water with a second party, said], "Mix for me, and [then] I shall mix for you," — the first is suitable. [If someone said], "Draw for me, and [then] I shall draw for you," — the last is suitable. [If someone said], "Mix for me, and [then] I shall draw for you," — they both are suitable. [If someone said], "Draw for me, and [then] I shall mix for you" — they both are unsuitable.

M. 7:5 He who draws [water both] for himself and for a purification rite draws for himself first and ties it [the bucket] to the carrying yoke, and afterward he draws the water for the purification rite. And if he drew [water] for the purification rite first, and afterward drew for himself, it is unfit. He places his own [bucket of water] behind him, and that of the purification rite before him. And if he put that of the purification rite behind him, it is unfit. [If] both of them are for the purification rite, [if] he places one before him and one behind him, it is fit, because it is not possible [to do otherwise].

T. 7:3 He who draws water for his own use and for the purification-rite draws his own first and ties it to the carrying yoke, and afterward he draws the water of the purification-rite. [If] he was drawing water to drink, and it was not possible to have [arrange] them other than both on a single yoke whether he drew his own first and afterward drew that of the purification-rite, or whether he drew the water of the purification-rite first and afterward drew his own, he places his own behind him and the purification-water before him. And if he placed the water of the purification-rite behind him, it is unfit.

M. 7:6 He who brings the [borrowed] rope in his hand — if it is on his way [to the rite], it is suitable. And if it is not on his way, it is unfit. On [this issue, concerning the rope,] one went to Yabneh three festival seasons, and at the third festival season they declared it fit for him — as a special dispensation.

M. 7:7 He who [when raising the bucket] wraps the rope hand by hand [little by little] — [the water] is suitable. And if he arranged it [wrapping it around his hand] at the end, it is unfit.

T. 7:4 He who brings the rope to the owner — [if] it is on his way, it is fit. [If] it is not on his way, it is unfit. [For] this law did the men of Asya come up on three festivals to Yabneh . On the third festival they declared it fit for them, as a special dispensation [an instruction of the interim]. Said R. Yosé, "Not [concerning] this did they give [a dispensation], but concerning one who brings up the rope and goes and arranges it at the end of the process. They taught him [who asked] that it is suitable in the past and unfit in the future."

M. 7:8 He who puts away the bucket [in connection with drawing water] so that it should not be broken, or who turned it upside down so as to dry it off, [if he did so] so as to draw with it — it is suitable. [If he did so] in order to convey the mixture [of water and ashes already prepared] with it — it is unsuitable. He who clears out shards from the trough so that it may hold a larger quantity of water — it is suitable. And if [he did so] so that they should not hinder him when he empties out the [mixed] water [into flasks for sprinkling], it is unfit.

M. 7:9 He whose water was on his shoulder, and he taught a lesson, and showed others the way, and killed a snake or a scorpion, took foodstuffs to put them aside [for storage] — it [the water] is unfit. [If he took] food in order to eat it — it is suitable. [If he killed] the snake and the scorpion who were standing in his way — it is suitable. Said R. Judah, "This is the principle: Anything which is done on account of work, whether he stood still [to do it] or did not stand [to do it] — it is unfit. And anything which is not on account of work — if he stood still [interrupting his journey to do it], it is unfit. And if he did not stand still, it is suitable."

T. 7:6 He whose water was on his shoulder — and a minor declared her unwillingness to remain wed, in his presence, and [another] performed the rite of Halisah, in his presence, and he put aside a stone for someone, and he showed the way to someone, if he stood still [in order to do so], it [the water] is unfit, and if he did not stand still [in order to do so], it is fit. Said R. Judah, "This is the principle: something which is on account of work, whether he stood still or did not stand still — it is unfit. Something which is not on account of work, if he stood still — it is unfit; and if he did not stand still — it is fit."

M. 7:10 He who gave his water over to someone who was unclean — it is unfit. [If he gave it over to] someone who was clean — it is fit.

T. 7:7 R. Eliezer says, "He who gives his water over to one who is unclean, and the owner did work — it is unfit." R. Judah says in his name, "[If] the unclean person did work, the water is fit, since it remains in the possession of the owner. [If] the owner did work, it is unfit, since it is in the possession of the unclean person." R. Yosé says, "He who breaks down in order to make a fence and one made a condition with him — even though he made a fence, it is fit." And so did R. Yosé say, "He who eats on condition of storing up [dates in the harvest], and one made a condition with him — even though he actually did store [dates], it is fit."

M. 7:11 Two who were drawing water for the purification rite and they raised [the bucket] with one another — or one took out the thorn from the other, in connection with a single mixing, it is suitable. And in connection with two mixings, it is unfit.

M. 7:12 He who [while carrying water] breaks down [a fence] on condition of putting up a fence [afterward] — it is suitable. But if [before mixing] he [actually] built a fence — it [the water] is unfit. He who eats on condition of storing [up dates or figs, that is, if someone gave him figs on condition of his doing some work to earn them] — it is suitable. But if he [actually] stored [some of them], it is unfit. If he was eating and left over some food and threw what he left in his hand under the fig tree or among drying figs, so that it should not be wasted — it is unfit.

M. 8:1 Two who were guarding the trough [containing water drawn for mixing with the ashes of the red cow] — and one of them was made unclean — it [the water] is suitable, because it is in the domain of the second. [If the first guard] became clean, and the second became unclean — it is suitable, because it is in the domain of the first. [If] both of them became unclean simultaneously — it is unfit. [If] one of them did work [extraneous to the rite] — it is suitable because it is in the domain of the second. [If the one who did the work extraneous to the rite] arose [and ceased to labor], and the second did work — it is suitable, because it is in the domain of the first. [If] both of them did work simultaneously, it is unfit.

M. 8:2 He who mixes purification water should not wear the sandal, for if the liquid fell on the sandal, it [the sandal] is made unclean, and they [the sandals] make him [the man himself] unclean, Lo, he [the man) says, Those things which made you [clothing] unclean could not have made me unclean, but you made me unclean. [If] the liquids fell on his skin, he is clean. [If] they fell on his garment, it is made unclean and makes him unclean. Lo, this one [man] says [to the clothing], Those things which made you unclean could not have made me unclean, but you made me unclean.

M. 8:3 He who burns the red cow, and [he who burns] bullocks, and the one who sends the goat away render clothing unclean [which they touch at the time of the rite. But they do not render men and clay utensils unclean]. A red cow and bullocks and the goat which is sent away themselves do not render clothing unclean. Lo, this one [= clothing] says [to the man], The things which made you unclean could not have made me unclean, but you made me unclean.

T. 7:8 He who burns the cow and [he who burns] bullocks and the one who sends out the goat render clothing unclean. "A cow and bullocks and the goat which is sent forth themselves do not render clothing unclean. But they render food and liquid unclean," the words of R. Meir. And sages say, "A cow and bullocks which are burned render food and liquid unclean. A goat which is sent forth does not render food and liquid unclean, because it is alive, and that which is alive does not render food and liquid unclean."

T. 7:9 R. Simeon says, "A cow which was fit for one moment [at the very least] renders food and liquid unclean. Bullocks which are burned and goats which are burned which were not fit a single moment [at the very least] do not render food and liquid unclean." R. Judah says, "A cow, once it has been slaughtered, renders unclean through carriage, as do its ashes."

M. 8:4 He who eats from the carrion of the clean bird, and it [that which he ate] is in his gullet, renders clothing unclean. The carrion itself does not render clothing unclean. Lo, this one [= clothing] says [to the man], The things which made you unclean could not have made me unclean, but you made me unclean.

M. 8:5 No Offspring of Uncleanness renders utensils unclean, but [it does render] liquid [unclean]. [If] liquid [which is on a utensil] is made unclean, it makes them [utensils] unclean. Lo, this one [= utensil] says [to the liquid], The things which made you unclean could not have made me unclean, but you made me unclean.

M. 8:6 A clay utensil does not make its fellow [clay utensil] unclean, but [it does make] liquid [unclean]. [If] the liquid is made unclean, it makes it [a clay utensil] unclean. Lo, this one says, The things which made you unclean could not have made me unclean, but you have made me unclean.

T. 8:1 There is thus that which says, "Those things which made you unclean could not have made me unclean, but you [delete: did not] made me unclean . " How so? A defective vessel which is full of clean liquid, with an unclean defective vessel overturned on its mouth — the liquid flowed from the lower one and was made unclean in the airspace of the upper one and went back, rendering the lower one unclean. Lo, this one says, "That which made you unclean did not make me unclean, but you made me unclean."

M. 8:7 Whatever spoils heave offering renders the liquid unclean, to be in the first [remove], to render something unclean at one [further] remove and to render [heave offering] unfit at one [still further, namely, a third] remove (except for a tebul-yom.) Lo, this one [food] says [to liquid], The things which made you unclean could not have made me unclean, but you made me unclean.

T. 8:2 A Zab who sat on an immovable stone — the food and liquid which are under it are clean. Something on which to lie or on which to sit which is under it is unclean . Lo, this [food, liquid] says, "That which made you [something for lying etc.] unclean could not have made me unclean, but you made me unclean." R. Judah says, "There is thus that which says, 'The things which make the things unclean which make you unclean cannot make me unclean, but you made me unclean.' How so? A bowl which is full of clean liquid, and its outer side is unclean. And it is placed on top of a table, and a loaf of [bread of] heave-offering, wrapped up, is on top of the table. [If] the liquid flowed from inside it [the bowl] and touched its outer part, it [the liquid] is made unclean and renders the table unclean, and the table goes and renders the loaf unclean. Lo, this says, 'That which could make the things unclean which made you unclean could not have made me unclean, but you made me unclean.'"

T. 8:3 There is thus that which says, "He made me unclean, and I made him unclean." How so? A tebul yom who had in his hand flour of heave-offering and unconsecrated liquid which is clean, and he mixed this with that — they are unclean. Lo, this one says, "He made me unclean, and I made him unclean." A pot which is full of clean liquid, and unclean lupines of a size smaller than an egg are placed inside it. [If] they swell up and so are made into the size of an egg, they are unclean. Lo, this one says, "He made me unclean, and I made him unclean." A clean person on the head and greater part of whom fell three logs of drawn water, even if he is clean, and they are clean, is made unclean and makes them unclean. Lo, this one says, "He made me unclean, and I made him unclean."

T. 8:4 There is thus that which says, "He made me unclean, and I made him clean." How so? An [unclean] patch which one patched on the basket renders unclean at one remove and renders unfit at one remove. [If] one separated it from the basket, the basket renders unclean at one remove and renders unfit at one remove, and the patch is clean. Lo, this one says, "He made me unclean, and I made him clean."

T. 8:5 There is thus that which says, "I made him clean, and I made him unclean" [Better: he made me]. How so? A pool which contains exactly forty seahs of water — one went down and immersed in it — he is clean. And the pool is unclean [= unfit]. Lo, this one says, "I made him clean, and he made me unclean."

T. 8:6 There is thus a case in which he says, "He made me clean, and I made him clean." How so? A box which is unclean with corpse uncleanness, and one brought a nail which is unclean and fastened it [the box] with it [the nail, onto a wall] The box is clean, and the nail is clean. Lo, this one says, "He made me clean, and I made him clean." A clean person who sprinkled the unclean person — the one who sprinkles is clean, and the unclean person is clean. Lo, this one says, "He made me clean, and I made him clean." Three pools — in this one are twenty [seahs of water], and in this one are twenty [of valid water], and in this one are twenty seahs of drawn water — and that holding drawn water was at the side — [if] three people went down and immersed in them, and they [the three pools] were mixed together — the pools are clean, and those that immerse in them are clean. Lo, this one says, "I purified him, and he purified me."

The running water is to be gathered only using a utensil. One may not guide the flow of water into the utensil, as one may guide the flow of naturally-collected rain water into an immersion pool. The whole must be done through deliberate action, using a utensil, for the collection of running water. The act of drawing must immediately precede the act of mixing. One who drew five jars of water in sequence, planning to use each for a mixture on its own, and then poured all five into a single mixture, has spoiled the rite; only the jar drawn immediately preceding the act of mixing can be used. If one draws water with one hand and does an extrinsic act of labor with the other, the water cannot serve. Nor may he draw two jars at once, for the reason given: performance of extrinsic work, whether for oneself or for another, spoils the drawn water. M. 7:9 shows the full extent to which the Halakhah excludes the performance of labor extraneous to the rite — all with the result of acutely focusing attention upon the rite alone. We note the inclusion of a variety of problems of mixtures, e.g., M. 8:1, which indicate the presence of the generic hermeneutics, even where the particular hermeneutics predominate. The paradoxes set forth at M. 8:2ff. contain nothing new, except the principle of category-formation that operates, which is uncommon in the Halakhah from the Mishnah forward.

VII. THE KIND OF WATER THAT IS USED FOR THE RITE

M. 8:9 Smitten [harmful] water is unfit. What is smitten [water]? That which is salty and [or] that which is lukewarm. Intermittent water is unfit. What is intermittent water? [Water] that fails once in seven years. The [water] that fails in wartime or in years of drought is suitable.

M. 8:10 Water of Qarmyon and water of Pugah are unfit, because they are swamp [miry] water. Water of the Jordan and water of the Yarmuk are unfit, because they are mixed water. What is mixed water? One suitable [for mixing with ashes] and one unsuitable that were mixed together. [If] both [sources of water] are fit and they are mixed together, they are fit.

M. 8:11 The well of Ahab and the cave of Pamyas — it [water therefrom] is suitable. Water which changed [in color], and its change is on account of itself [comes about by itself] — it is fit. A water channel that comes from a distance — it [

= its water] is fit, and on condition that one guarded it so that no man interrupt it[s flow]. A well into which clay or earth fell — one waits until it becomes clear.

T. 9:1 [Water from] all rivers is unfit for mixing the purification-water. R. Judah agrees concerning a spring which wells forth from two separate locations and goes back and is mixed together in a single place, [that it is] suitable. And so did R. Judah say, "A man draws a jar from this spring and a jar from that spring and pours them into a single trough and mixes."

T. 9:2 And so did R. Judah say, "A man draws a flask from this jar and a flask [of water] from that jar and puts them into a single trough and mixes." And so did R. Judah say, "The sources of Salmon are prohibited because it ceases to flow in time of war." They said to him, "And were not all the waters of Creation interrupted in the time of war? Siloam — an ant would walk in it [in time of war]." But a spring which emerges on one side in one year and on the other side in the next year, or which flows abundantly during the rainy season and diminishes in the dry season is fit.

T. 9:3 All agree concerning a well into which a freshet of rain ran down, that one has to wait until the water returns to its former condition. "A spring which emerges for the first time — one has to investigate [its status]," the words of R. Judah. And sages say, "One does not have [to examine it]" [If] his jug was lying before him, and into it flowed a freshet of rainwater — it is unfit. [If] dew descended into it, it is unfit. [If] dew descended into it by night — R. Eliezer says, "Let him leave it in the sun, and the dew will evaporate." And sages say, "Dew evaporates only upon [the surface of] fruit alone."

T. 9:7 Purification-water, the color of which changed on account of itself [naturally], is suitable. [If] it changed on account of soot, or there fell into it a plant producing blue dye, dyer's madder — it is unfit. This is the general rule: Whatever renders unfit through a change of color in a spring renders unfit in the case of purification-water in a flask.

T. 9:8 The ash of purification, the color of which changed on account of itself [naturally] and on account of soot, is fit. [If] it changed on account of stove-ash, or there fell into it lime or gypsum, it is unfit. Purification-water which froze over and then went and melted is fit. [If] one made them melt in [by the] fire, it is unfit. [But if he did so] in the sun, it is fit. Said R. Eleazar b. R. Sadoq, "[If it is] something in which one keeps something warm on the Sabbath, it is fit. And [if it is] something in which one does not keep something warm on the Sabbath, it is unfit for the purification-rite." The water which is drained off and which is drawn off is unfit.

M. 9:1 A flask [of purification water] into which any amount of [unmixed] water fell — sages declare unfit. Dew fell into it — sages declare unfit. Liquid or fruit juice fell into it — let him empty [it), and he needs to dry it off. [If there fell into the flask of purification water] ink, gum, and copperas, and anything which leaves a mark — let him empty it out, and he does not need to dry it off.

T. 9:5 Said Rabbi, "If [the law is in accord with the words of R. Eliezer, [then] sprinkling of any amount at all [of purification-water] is acceptable." [If] half of it is from suitable water and half of it is from unsuitable water, then sprinkling renders clean in any amount at all.

M. 9:2 [If there] fall into it [a flask of purification water] insects or creeping things, and they burst, or its [the water's] color changed — it is unfit. A beetle, one way or the other, renders [water] unfit, because it is like a reed [tube].

M. 9:3 Cattle or a wild animal drank from it — it is unfit. All the fowl render unfit, except for the dove, because it sucks up [the water, not drooling into it]. All the creeping things do not render unfit, except for the weasel, because it laps up [the water].

T. 9:6 [If] there fell into it a kind of spider, an [other sort of] spider, an [other sort of] spider, a fish, a frog — and they burst open, and its color [that of the water] changed — it is unfit. [If] they did not burst open and [if] its color did not change, it is fit. R. Judah says, "Even though they did not burst and its color did not change, it is unfit, because they run." And all agree concerning the locust [which falls into the purification-water] that it [the water] is unfit, because it runs. And all agree that [if] it bursts, it does not render unfit [since it is dry]. R. Eliezer and R. Simeon say, "The opinion of Rabban Gamaliel appears [to us to be correct] in the case of the snake, and with his opinion do we agree." Said R. Yosé, "And is it not so that the rulings of R. Eliezer in matters concerning the cow are entirely directed toward leniency? For R. Eliezer says, 'When he will [actually] turn it up [to drink, but not merely think about doing so].' And R. Joshua says, 'When he will [actually] drink, 'on account of the liquid of his mouth. And if he poured it directly into his throat, it is suitable.'"

M. 9:4 He who forms the intention concerning purification water, [saying he plans] to drink it — R. Eliezer says, "He has rendered it unfit [by mere intent]." R. Joshua says, "[He only renders it unfit] when he will turn it up [in order actually to drink. But mere intent does not spoil the water]." Said R. Yosé, "Under what circumstances? In the case of water which is not mixed. But in the case of water which is [in fact] mixed — R. Eliezer says, 'When he will turn it up.' R. Joshua says, 'When he will drink it. And if he poured it into his throat [without actually touching the flask with his mouth], it is fit.'"

M. 9:5 Purification water which has been made unfit — one should not trample it into the mud, so that one does not make it into a snare for others. A cow which drank purification water — its flesh is unclean for twenty-four hours.

M. 9:6 Purification water and purification ash — one should not take them across the river in a boat, nor should he float them on the water, nor should he stand on one side and throw them across to the other side. But he himself crosses in the water up to his neck. He who is clean for the purification rite crosses with an empty vessel which is clean for purification rite and with water which has not yet been mixed.

T. 9:9 A man should not take purification-water and purification-ash and ride on a cow or on his fellow in a situation in which his feet do not touch the ground. But he brings them over on a bridge. All the same is the Jordan and all other rivers. R. Hananiah b. Aqabya says, "They spoke only concerning the Jordan alone."

M. 9:7 Suitable ash which became mixed with ash of a stove — they follow the majority [of the ash in the mixture], so far as rendering [a person] unclean. And they do not mix with it.

T. 9:4 Purification-water into which fell spring-water and pool-water and fruit-juice — if the greater part is purification-water, it renders unclean through carriage. And if the greater part is fruit-juice, it does not render unclean through carriage. Half and half [if the mixture is exactly half purification-water and half fruit-juice] — it renders unclean in carriage. One way or the other, it is unfit for sprinkling.

The definition of water that is mixed with the ashes is Scripture's: running or living water. If it flows in a water channel, the water is fit, so long as no human action intervene in the flow. The generic hermeneutics accounts for M. 9:1ff. The relationship of action to intentionality, M. 9:4, introduces a larger issue of principle: does intention unconfirmed by deed affect that which is subject to the improper intention? That issue will predominate in Makhshirin. Here it comes as part of a miscellany.

VIII. UNCLEANNESS AND THE PURIFICATION RITE

M. 9:8 Purification water which was made unfit renders unclean the person who is clean for heave offering, both [if it touched] his hands and [if it touched] his body; and as to the one who is clean for the purification rite, neither [by contact with] his hands nor [by contact with] his body. [If] it was made unclean, it renders unclean the one who is clean for heave offering [if it touches] his hands and his body, and [renders unclean] the one who is clean for the purification rite [if it touches] his hands, but not [if it touches] his body.

M. 9:9 Suitable ash which one put in the water which is not appropriate for mixing renders unclean the person who is clean for heave offering [if it touches] his hands and [if it touches] his body. [Suitable ash which one put on the water which is not appropriate for mixing does] not [render unclean] the person who is clean for the purification rite [if it touches] his hands or his body.

T. 10:1 Purification-water and purification-ash which are mixed, whether they are unclean or whether they are clean, render the person who is clean for heave-offering unclean through contact and through carrying. R. Yohanan b. Nuri says, "Purification-water which has been made unclean — lo, it is like the ash of the hearth." Ash which is unfit which one placed in the water, whether it [the water] is suitable for mixing, or whether it is not suitable for mixing, renders the hands of the person who is clean for heave-offering unclean through contact and through carrying. R. Yohanan b. Nuri says, "Ash of the purification-rite which was made unclean, lo, it is like the ash of the hearth."

M. 10:1 Whatever is appropriate to be made unclean with Midras uncleanness is regarded as [actually] unclean with Maddaf uncleanness so far as the purification rite is concerned, whether it is [actually] unclean or whether it is [actually] clean. And man [clean in all respects but not clean for the purification rite] follows suit. Whatever is appropriate to be made unclean with corpse uncleanness, whether it is [actually] unclean or whether it is [actually] clean — that which is [actually] unclean [because of the corpse] is [regarded as] unclean with Maddaf uncleanness. And that which is [actually] clean is not [regarded as] unclean with Maddaf uncleanness.

T. 10:2 "Whatever is suitable to become unclean through corpse-uncleanness, even if it is [in fact] unclean, is not regarded as [unclean with] Maddaf-uncleanness, and whatever is not [unclean with] Maddaf-uncleanness in respect to heave-offering is not [regarded as unclean with] Maddaf-uncleanness with respect to the purification-rite. And they did not innovate uncleanness in respect to the purification-rite," the words of R. Eliezer.

T. 10:3 R. Ishmael was following after R. Joshua. He [Ishmael] said to him, "He who is clean for the purification-rite who moved the key which is clean for the heave-offering — what is the rule? Is he unclean or clean?" Said he [Joshua] to him, "He is unclean." He said to him, "And why?" He said to him, "Perhaps there was in its [the key's] hand [power] a former uncleanness. Or perhaps [if permitted to move something clean] he may forget and move the unclean thing." He said to him, "But even if not, [he is not unclean even if] he most certainly moved it, [for the key does not convey uncleanness if it is moved]." But your words appear correct in a matter which is susceptible to become unclean with Midras-uncleanness [in which case:] Or perhaps there was in its hand a former uncleanness. Or perhaps he may forget and move the unclean thing."

T. 10:4 Rabbi says, "One who is clean for the purification-rite who moved the spittle or the urine of one who is clean for the heave-offering rite is unclean. "[If] he moved his blood, lo, he is clean." [If] he moved the insect and the carrion and semen — R. Eliezer declares clean. And R. Joshua declares unclean.

M. 10:2 He who is clean for the purification rite who touched that which is unclean with Maddaf uncleanness is unclean. A flagon of purification water which touched something [regarded as] unclean with Maddaf uncleanness is unclean. He who is clean for the purification rite who touched foods and liquids — [if he did so] with his hand, he is unclean. And with his foot — he is clean. [If] he moved them with his hand — R. Joshua declares unclean. And sages declare clean.

M. 10:3 A jar of purification water which touched an insect — it is clean. [If] one put it on top of it — sages declare [the ash] unclean. [If] it touched foods and liquids and holy scrolls — it is clean. [If] one put it on top of them — sages declare unclean.

T. 10:5 A jar of purification-water which one placed on top of a dead creeping thing — R. Eliezer declares clean. And sages declare unclean. Under what circumstances? In a situation in which, if one removed the dead creeping thing, the jar would move. But in a situation in which, if one removed the dead creeping thing, the jar would stand [unmoved], and even if a corpse or carrion were touching it on its outer side, it is clean. [If] one set it on top of something on which one sits or lies, or on top of an unclean clay utensil, it is unclean. [If] one placed it on top of food and liquid and on top of a scroll of the Torah — R. Yosé declares clean. And sages declare unclean. If one passed it over a clay utensil or over] carrion or over a dead creeping thing — R. Aqiba declares unclean.

M. 10:4 The person who is clean for the purification rite who touched a [clean] oven [of clay] — [if he touched it] with his hand, he is unclean. And [if he touched it] with his foot, he is clean. [If] he was standing on top of an oven and stretched his hand beyond the oven, and the [clay] flagon of purification water is inside it [his hand] — and so the yoke which is placed on top of the oven, and on it are two jars, one on one side, and one on the other side — sages declare unclean.

M. 10:5 If one was standing outside of an oven and stretched his hand to the window and took the flagon and passed it over the oven — sages declare clean. But: he who was clean for the purification rite stands on top of the oven, and in his hand is an empty utensil which is clean for the purification rite, and with water which is not mixed.

T. 10:6 R. Aqiba agrees that if one passed it, in a case of sprinkling, on top of something on which one lies and sits, and on top of an unclean clay utensil, that it is clean. For nothing renders unclean above and below except an olive's bulk of corpse-matter and things which defile through overshadowing.

M. 10:6 A pitcher of purification water which touched a [utensil] which [contains] holy food and heave offering — that which [contains] the purification water is unclean. And those which [contain] holy food and heave offering are clean. Two of them are in his two hands — they both are unclean. Both of them [are wrapped] in two [pieces of] paper — they are both clean. That which [contains] purification water is [wrapped up] in paper, and that which [contains] heave offering [or holy things] is in his hand [without wrapping] — they are both unclean. That [containing] heave offering [or holy things] is [wrapped in paper] and that [containing] the purification water is in his hand [without wrapping] — they are both clean. [If] they are placed on the ground and one touched them [simultaneously] — that [containing] the purification water is unclean, and [those containing] holy food and heave offering are clean. [If] he moved them — sages declare clean.

T. 10:7 A jar of purification-water and a jar of heave-offering which touched one another — they are both clean. [If he carries them] with his two hands [simultaneously], they are both unclean. [If they were wrapped] in two pieces of paper, they are both clean. R. Joshua says, "That containing the purification-water is unclean." A jar of purification-water and a pitcher of heave-offering which touched one another — they are both clean. [If one wrapped them up] in two pieces of paper, they are clean. R. Joshua says, "That containing the purification-water is unclean." Under what circumstances? When it is of stone. But if it is of clay all agree that the jar of purification-water is clean.

T. 10:8 A pitcher of purification-water and a pitcher of heave-offering which touched one another — they are both clean. [If they were wrapped in] two pieces of paper, they are both clean. R. Joshua says, "That containing the purification-water is unclean." This is the general principle which R. Joshua laid down: "Whatever renders purification-water unclean in contact renders it unclean in carrying, and whatever does not render purification-water unclean [supply: in contact] does not render it unclean in carrying."

M. 11:1 A jar [of purification water] which one left uncovered, and which one came and found covered — it [the water] is unfit. [If] one left it covered and came and found it uncovered — if the weasel can drink from it, or a snake, according to the opinion of Rabban Gamaliel [M. 9:3], or dew fell into it by night — it is unfit. The purification [jar containing mixed ashes and water] is not afforded protection by a tightly sealed cover. And [but] water which is not mixed is afforded protection by a tightly sealed cover.

T. 7:5 He who was, he and his water, in the Tent of a corpse, and his water was in a jar which was tightly sealed with a stopper — just as he is unclean, so it is unclean.

[If] he is inside and the water is outside, just as he is unclean, so his water is unclean. [If] he is outside and his water is inside, just as he is clean, so his water is clean. Said R. Simeon, "To such a one as this they say, 'Keep yourself [clean] so that your water should be clean as well.'"

M. 11:2 Any matter of doubt [which is regarded as] clean for heave offering is [regarded as] clean for the purification rite. Any matter of a suspended [decision] in respect to heave offering — in regard to the purification water rite, it [the water] is poured out. [If] they prepared clean things on account of it — they are left in suspense. Lattice-work is insusceptible to uncleanness in respect to holy things and in respect to heave offering and in respect to purification water.

T. 11:1 Hyssop which is susceptible to uncleanness and utensils which are clean for the purification-rite are afforded protection by a tightly sealed cover. Any matter of doubt which is clean for heave-offering is clean for the purification-rite — except for the hands, since they are a matter of doubt which pertains to the body. A matter of doubt concerning QWPSYN [?] is clean for heave-offering [and] unclean for the purification-rite, since it is a matter of doubt about that which is unfit. Lattice work is clean for holy things and for heave-offering and for purification-rite. And R. Eleazar says, "The lattice work is unclean for the purification-rite and clean for holy things and heave-offering."

M. 11:3 A ring of pressed figs of heave offering which fell into purification water and which one removed and ate — if there is in it an egg's bulk, whether it is unclean or whether it is clean, the water is unclean. And the one who eats it is liable to the death penalty. [If] there is not in it an egg's bulk — the water is clean. And the person who eats it is liable to the death penalty. A person clean for the purification rite who put his head and the larger part of his body into purification water is made unclean.

T. 11:3 A ring of pressed figs of heave-offering which fell into purification-water, which one removed and ate, even though it is the size of an egg's bulk, whether it is unclean or clean — if so, cleanness does not apply to the purification-rite, for I say, "The one who sprinkles is made unclean, and the one who sprinkles goes and makes the water unclean: the hyssop is made unclean by the water, and the hyssop goes and makes the water unclean."

T. 11:4 Said R. Meir, "Under what circumstances? When he drew it out with a spindle or with a chip. But if he removed it with his hand, he is made unclean and makes the purification-water unclean." R. Yosé and R. Simeon say, "The person who is clean for heave-offering does not make the purification-water unclean."

M. 11:4 Whoever requires immersion in water according to the rules of the Torah renders unclean (1) holy things, (2) heave offering, (3) unconsecrated food, (4) tithe, and (5) such a one is forbidden to enter the sanctuary. After his immersion, He spoils (1) the holy things and (2) the heave offering. And he is permitted to eat unconsecrated food and tithe. And if he came to the sanctuary, whether before or after his immersion, he is liable.

M. 11:5 Whoever requires immersion in water according to the rules of the scribes (1) renders the holy things unclean and (2) spoils the heave offering. And he is permitted in respect to unconsecrated food. After he has immersed, he is

permitted for all of them. And if he came to the sanctuary, whether before his immersion or after his immersion, he is free.

M. 11:6 Whoever requires immersion in water, whether according to the rules of the Torah or according to the rules of the scribes renders unclean (1) purification water, (2) purification ash, and (3) the one who sprinkles purification water — in contact and in carrying, and (4) the hyssop that has been made susceptible to uncleanness, (5) the water which has not been mixed, and (6) an empty utensil which is clean for the purification rite — in contact, but not in carrying.

T. 11:5 Whoever requires immersion in water, whether on account of the rulings of the Torah or on account of the rules of the scribes, before his immersion in water renders purification-water and purification-ash and the one who sprinkles purification-water unclean through contact and through carriage. R. Eleazar says in the name of R. Tarfon, "The one who is unclean on account of corpse-uncleanness takes utensils which are clean for the purification-rite on a yoke on his shoulder and does not fear [that he renders them unclean]."

Scripture's provision that the purification water imparts uncleanness to those who handle it is extended to such water that cannot serve its purpose. But that is not the case with suitable ash. The rules of uncleanness governing the rite are vastly augmented by M. 10:1ff., to the results of which we have made reference several times already. If something can be made unclean with Midras uncleanness, e.g., a chair or a rug or a blanket, it is regarded as unclean with Maddaf-uncleanness, a lesser classification of uncleanness, whatever the facts of the matter. That uncleanness represents a status is indicated by the rule that a man who is cultically clean except for the purification rite is classified as unclean for the purification rite. Whatever is subject to corpse uncleanness, without regard to actuality, is deemed unclean with Maddaf-uncleanness too. On that basis, we realize, the person engaged in the rite, e.g., going to collect the water, cannot touch anything or sit anywhere or come into contact with anybody, except for what has been readied for utilization in connection with the rite. These rules, which express the principles of the particular hermeneutics, then at M. 11:1ff. are amplified in accord with the generic hermeneutics of doubt. It is a clear pattern in the Halakhah that the particular hermeneutics will take priority, with the results subjected to the clarification effected by the generic hermeneutics, e.g., cases of doubt, problems of hierarchization (M. 11:4ff.).

IX. THE RULES FOR SPRINKLING PURIFICATION-WATER

M. 11:7 Every hyssop which has a special name is unfit. "This hyssop" — it is fit. Greek hyssop, stibium hyssop, Roman hyssop, and wild hyssop are unfit. And that of unclean heave offering is unfit. And that of [heave offering] clean [for the purification rite] — one should not sprinkle [with it]. But if he sprinkled with it, it is fit. They do not sprinkle either with young shoots or with berries. They are not liable on account of young shoots for entering the sanctuary. What are the young shoots? Stalks before the buds have ripened.

T. 11:6 A hyssop taken from an asherah and from an idol and an apostate city is unfit. And that which is taken from clean [heave-offering] — he should not sprinkle with it. But if he sprinkled with it, it is suitable. They do not sprinkle either with the young shoots or with the berries. And if one sprinkled with the young shoots and entered the sanctuary, he is free. With young shoots [better: berries], and he entered the sanctuary, he is free. With the young shoots and he entered the sanctuary, he is liable.

T. 11:7 What are the young shoots? "Calyxes which have not ripened, whereas leafage refers to what has not sprouted," the words of R. Meir. Sages say, "Leafage refers to calyxes which have not ripened, whereas sprigs designate what has not sprouted at all."

T. 11:8 They did not disagree about law but about language, for: R. Eliezer says, "They burn heave-offering on their account, but they are not liable on their account for rendering the sanctuary and its holy things unclean." "That which is gathered for purification-water is as if it were gathered for food," the words of R. Meir. R. Judah and R. Yosé and R. Simeon say, "It is as if it were gathered for wood."

M. 11:8 A hyssop with which one sprinkled is fit for use in purifying the leper. [If] one gathered it for firewood, and liquid fell on it, one dries it, and it is fit. [If] one gathered it for food, and liquid fell on it, even though one dried it, it is unfit. [If] one gathered it for the purification rite, it is as if one gathered it for firewood.

M. 11:9 The commandment concerning the hyssop: three [separate] stalks, and on them three buds. Hyssop on which are three stalks — one cuts it up and binds them together. If one cut it up and did not bind it, bound it and did not cut it up, did not cut it up and did not bind it, it is fit.

T. 12:1 Hyssop — when is it suitable for sprinkling? When it has begun to sprout. [If] one sprinkled with it before it has begun to sprout — Rabbi declares unfit. R. Eleazar b. R. Simeon declares fit. R. Yosé agrees concerning hyssop that, if in the first instance it has two [stalks], and its remnant one, (that) it is unfit.

T. 12:2 The remnants of hyssop are suitable, and the remnants of *Sisit* are suitable. One descended and immersed and came up — if there is on him a rivulet of rain water, and he sprinkled, his sprinkling is unfit. And if there is on him dripping moisture, and he sprinkled, his sprinkling is fit. And R. Judah says, "If there are on him liquid-pearls, and he sprinkled, his sprinkling is unfit."

M. 12:1 Hyssop which is [too] short — one makes it suffice with a thread and with a spindle and immerses it and brings it up and holds on to the hyssop [itself] and sprinkles.

T. 12:3 A hyssop, the wood of which one dipped with the young shoots, even though he sprinkles and the water drips from the wood of the young shoot, it is fit. He sprinkles in the normal way and does not scruple lest it [the water] goes forth from the wood.

M. 12:2 One sprinkled — it is in doubt whether the sprinkling was done from the thread, or from the spindle, or from the bud — his sprinkling is unfit. One sprinkled on two utensils — it is in doubt whether he sprinkled on both of them, [or] it is in doubt whether from its fellow it dripped on to it — his sprinkling is unfit. A needle which is fixed in the earthenware utensil, and one sprinkled on one is in doubt whether he sprinkled on the needle or whether

from the clay utensil it [water] dripped on it [the needle] — his sprinkling is unfit. A flask the mouth of which is narrow — one immerses it and brings it up in the usual way. Purification water which was diminished — one dips even the tips of the buds and sprinkles, and on condition that the hyssop does not absorb [moisture on the sides of the flask as it is pulled out] — If one intended to sprinkle before him, and sprinkled behind him — behind him and sprinkled before him — his sprinkling is unfit. Before him and he sprinkled to the sides which are before him — his sprinkling is suitable. They sprinkle on a man when he knows about it and when he does no know about it. They sprinkle [simultaneously] on the man and on the utensils, and even if they are a hundred.

T. 12:4 A hyssop only part of which one dipped — R. Judah declares fit. For R. Judah says, "One dips part of it and goes back and adds to it until he dips the whole thing." [If] one dipped the whole thing, he should not sprinkle a second sprinkling from it, except after he dries it off.

T. 12:5 "A flask the mouth of which is narrow — they sprinkle from it a second sprinkling, but not the first sprinkling, because the water is wrung out," the words of R. Judah.

T. 12:6 Three rules did R. Simeon b. Gamaliel state in the name of R. Simeon b. Kahana: "In the times of the priests they did not refrain from sprinkling with a hyssop that was immersed in a flask with a narrow mouth. And they crack nuts of heave-offering with unclean hands and did not scruple on account of uncleanness."

T. 12:9 [If] one intended to sprinkle before him and sprinkled behind him behind him, and the sprinkling went before him — his sprinkling is unfit. [If one intended to sprinkle] before him, and he sprinkled to the sides behind him, and he sprinkled to the sides behind him — his sprinkling is fit.

T. 12:10 They sprinkle on a man and upon things connected to him, whether he is awake or asleep, and on utensils, whether on the inside or on the outside, except for the fender of the kettle of those that boil olives, for it renders the sprinkling unclean in its airspace opposite the fender, in which case they sprinkle on its outer parts [first].

M. 12:3 [If] one intended to sprinkle on something which is susceptible to uncleanness and sprinkled on something which is not susceptible to uncleanness, if there is [purification water] on the hyssop, he should not repeat [the dipping of the hyssop in the water] — [If one intended to sprinkle] on something which does not receive uncleanness and sprinkled on something which receives uncleanness, if there is [more purification water] on the hyssop, he should repeat [the dipping]. [If he intended to sprinkle] on the man, and he sprinkled on the cow, if there is [more purification water] on the hyssop, he should not repeat. [If he intended to sprinkle] on the cow, and he sprinkled on the man, if there is [more purification water] on the hyssop, he should repeat. The water that drips off is fit. Therefore it renders unclean as [does] the usual water of the purification rite.

T. 12:11 If one dipped the hyssop for the sake of [sprinkling] something which is suitable for sprinkling and then sprinkled something which is suitable for sprinkling, water which drips is unclean, and suitable for sprinkling [something else]. And if there is [more water] on the hyssop, one may repeat [the sprinkling].

[If one immersed the hyssop] for the sake of something which is suitable for sprinkling, and sprinkled on something which is not suitable for sprinkling — 1. (and) on the gentile, 2. and on the cow, 3. on a trough of stone, the water which drips is clean, and unfit for sprinkling. And if there is [more water] on the hyssop, he should not repeat [the sprinkling, since the water is unfit]. [If one dipped the hyssop] for the sake of something which is not fit for sprinkling, since at the beginning of its dipping it was unfit, so its sprinkling is unfit.

M. 12:4 He that sprinkles from the window in the public domain, [and a man so sprinkled] entered the sanctuary, and the water turned out to be unfit — he is free. [If one sprinkled] from a window [wall niche] in the private domain, [and a man so sprinkled] entered the sanctuary, and the water turned out to be unfit — he is liable. But as to a high priest, [sprinkled] whether from a window of the private domain or from a window of the public domain — he is free, for the high priest is not liable for coming to the sanctuary. They would slip [on water] before a window of the public domain and trample [there] and did not refrain [from entering the sanctuary]. For they said, "Purification water which has carried out its purpose does not render unclean."

M. 12:5 The clean person holds an unclean ax in his skirt, and one sprinkles on Even though there is on it sufficient water for a sprinkling, he is clean. How much must be in the water for it to be sufficient for sprinkling? Enough so that one may dip the tips of the buds and sprinkle.

T. 12:12 And so did Rabban Simeon b. Gamaliel say to one who sprinkles, "Step back, lest you be made unclean." They said to him, "And did they not slip in front of a window in the public place, trampling there, and they did not refrain, because they said, 'Purification-water which has carried out its purpose does not render unclean.'"

T. 12:13 And how much must be in the water['s volume] so that there should be enough for sprinkling? Enough for him to dip the tips of the buds and sprinkle, except for that which the hyssop absorbs. R. Judah says, "They regard them as if they were on a hyssop of brass, which does not absorb [water]."

M. 12:6 He who sprinkles with an unclean hyssop — if there is in it an egg's bulk, the water is unfit, and his sprinkling is unfit. If there is not in it the bulk of an egg — the water is fit, and his sprinkling is unfit. And it [the hyssop] renders its fellow [other hyssop] unclean, and its fellow [hyssop], its fellow [hyssop], even if they are a hundred.

M. 12:7 The person who is clean for the purification rite whose hands become unclean, his body is made unclean. And he makes his fellow unclean, and his fellow, his fellow, even a hundred.

T. 12:14 One who is clean for the purification-rite, the hands of whom were made unclean — his body is made unclean. He makes his fellow unclean, and his fellow, his fellow. And as to the outer part of a pitcher: A pitcher of purification-water, the outer side of which is made unclean — its inside is made unclean. It renders its fellow unclean, and its fellow, its fellow, and also the one who sprinkles.

T. 12:15 They do not say in connection with the purification-rite, "This is first and this is last." But they are all [in the] first [remove of uncleanness]. For they do not count [removes of uncleanness] with reference to sprinkling the purification-water. A piece of dough which is prepared in connection with the purification-rite, and the dead creeping thing touched one of them even if they are a hundred, they are all first. For they do not count [removes of uncleanness] with reference to the purification-rite.

M. 12:8 A pitcher of purification water, the outer side of which is made unclean — its inside is made unclean. And it makes its fellow [pitcher] unclean, and its fellow, its fellow, even if they area hundred. A bell and a clapper are regarded as connected. A spindle used for coarse material — one should not sprinkle on the spindle [alone] and not on the ring [alone]. And if one sprinkled, it is regarded as sprinkled. And [in a spindle used for spinning] flax — it is connected. A hide of a cot which is attached to knobs [of the cot] — [both are] connected. The base is not connected [to the bed] either for uncleanness or for cleanness. All handles of utensils which are drilled [with a hole to fasten them to utensils] are connected.

M. 12:9 The baskets of a packsaddle, and the bed of the barrow, and the [iron] corner of the bier, and the horns of travelers, and the key chain, and the loose stitches of washermen, and the garment which is stitched together with mixed fabrics — it is a connector for uncleanness, and it is not a connector for sprinkling.

T. 12:16 An Arbelite spindle is a connector for uncleanness and for sprinkling. And one used for spinning flax and of a wick — lo, one should not sprinkle on it. And if one sprinkled, it is sprinkled.

M. 12:10 The cover of a kettle which is joined [to the kettle] by the chain — If one sprinkled the kettle, he has sprinkled on the cover. If he has sprinkled on the cover, he has not sprinkled on the kettle. All are fit to sprinkle, except for one of doubtful sex, an androgyne, and a woman, and a child who is without understanding. The woman helps him [a child who possesses understanding] and he sprinkles, and holds the water for him, and he dips and sprinkles. If she held him by the hand, even in the moment of the sprinkling, it is unfit.

T. 12:17 All handles of utensils which come from [are attached at] the factory, for example, the handle of the sickle and the handle of the knife, are connected for uncleanness and for sprinkling. All handles of the utensils which are drilled are connected. And R. Yohanan b. Nuri says, "Even that which is wedged." "Excrement which is on the toilet-seat is connected for sprinkling, but it is not connected for uncleanness," the words of R. Yosé the Galilean. R. Aqiba says, "Whatever is connected for sprinkling is connected for uncleanness, but there is something which is connected for uncleanness and not connected for sprinkling."

T. 12:18 The [small] kettle is connected for uncleanness and for sprinkling. The cover of the kettle which is connected by a chain — The House of Shammai say, "It is all one connector." And the House of Hillel say, "If one sprinkled on the kettle, he has sprinkled on the cover. If one has sprinkled on the cover, he has not sprinkled on the kettle." Said R. Yosé, "These are the words of the House of Shammai. The House of Hillel say, 'It is all one connector.'"

T. 12:7 He who says to his fellow, "Sprinkle on me and I shall sprinkle on you" — R. Aqiba declares unclean. And sages declare clean. He who watches over purification-water, even for ten days, lo, he is confirmed in his assumed status [of cleanness] and does not require immersion.

T. 12:8 All are fit to sprinkle, except for a deaf-mute, an idiot, and a minor. R. Judah declares fit in the case of a minor. R. Ishmael b. R. Yohanan b. Beroqah says, "A deaf-mute, an idiot, and a minor who sprinkled, and others oversee them — their sprinkling is fit."

M. 12:11 He dipped the hyssop during the day and sprinkled on the same day — it is fit. He dipped during the day and sprinkled at night — dipped at night and sprinkled during the day — it is unfit. But he immerses himself at night and is sprinkled during the [next] day. For they do not sprinkle before the sun has risen. And in all cases in which they did so once the morning star had come up — it is fit.

T. 12:19 [If] one dipped the hyssop at night — [it is unfit]. Not that the water is unfit. But one has to dip a second time. [If] one dipped [the hyssop] at night, his sprinkling is unfit. And the water is unclean because of [being suitable] purification-water

The rules for the utilization of the purification-water in removing corpse-uncleanness amplify the basic facts supplied by Scripture, M. 11:7ff., then work out problems of the generic hermeneutics, M. 12:2ff.: doubt, confusion, mixture and connection, and the like.

IV. THE HERMENEUTICS OF PARAH

A. WHAT FUSES THE HALAKHIC DATA INTO A CATEGORY-FORMATION?

It was by an act of will that Man brought about death: violating God's will through his own intentional willfulness. So it is by an act of will that Man's counterpart, Israel, removes the effects of death.

> When I violated his instructions, I brought about my own death,
> for it is written, 'On the day on which you eat it, you will surely die
> '(Gen. 2:17)."
>
> Pesiqta deRab Kahana XIV:V.1

What fuses the Halakhic data into a category-formation is the joining of Scripture's facts to the result of the analogical-contrastive analysis, which has identified as the critical variable of the species, Parah, of the common genus, Parah-Miqvaot, the consideration of human deliberation, the actualization of man's will. That defines the particular hermeneutics of Parah. Since the critical principle of speciation — how Parah contrasts with Miqvaot — is the role accorded to intentionality, we see that what fuses the data into a coherent category-formation is that same matter. The focus and stress of the shank of the Halakhah therefore identify as critical the acute state of alertness — an effect of intentionality — that is required for the preparation of the purification-water. That is how the Halakhah decisively answers the generative question, how to create a realm of cleanness outside of the Temple? The highest level of alertness, the keenest exercise of caution against uncleanness — these alone will create that circle of cleanness in the world beyond the Temple courtyard that, by definition, is unclean. That accounts for the bizarre arrangements for transporting the youngsters with the stone cups from the Temple, where they have been born and brought up, to the Siloam pool and thence to the Mount of Olives — all to avoid corpse-matter buried at great depths. And still more to the point, the Halakhah sets aside the strict purity-rules protecting from contamination not only common food or priestly rations but even Holy Things and imposes much more stringent ones.

This it does in a variety of ways, three of which represent the rest. First, while hand-washing suffices for eating in a state of cleanness food in the familiar classifications, to purify oneself for participating in preparing the purification-water, total immersion is required; the familiar distinction between hands and body falls away. Second and more decisive, purification-water contracts uncleanness (and so is rendered useless) at any number of removes from the original source of uncleanness, even one hundred; that is to say, we do not count removes. Everything is unclean by reason of its history — a history of which we may well be ignorant. So the realm of death is everywhere, constantly to be guarded against. Third, persons involved in preparing the mixture — collecting the ashes, gathering the water, mixing the two — must remain not only constantly alert but perpetually active. From the beginning to the end of their work, they may do only what concerns the task. If they sit down on a chair or lie down on a bed, they *automatically* contract uncleanness, for what can contract uncleanness is deemed unclean for them. And intentionality enters in at critical points in the classification of actions, e.g., whether or not they are extrinsic to the rite. We need hardly review the details of the law to reach the Halakhah's obvious proposition: perfect concentration on the task, uninterrupted by any extrinsic action or even consideration, alone suffices. Do not stand, do not sit, do not stop, do only the job, until the job is done — and then go immerse from the uncleanness that under ordinary circumstances you cannot have contracted.

The paradox of the Halakhic category-formation is fully exposed in yet another component: the rules governing the priesthood's participation. The rite enjoys distinctions comparable to those distinguishing the offerings on the Day of Atonement. It is performed by the high priest, wearing white garments, with feet and hands sanctified. But we take account of the location of the rite, outside the holy place. Having prepared the priest and the water and transported them in such a way as to avoid corpse-uncleanness, we want the priest to be in a diminished condition of cleanness, as a tebul yom; that status accords recognition to the location of the rite, conducted with remarkable punctiliousness to the requirements of cleanness, but at the same time differentiated, as to cleanness, from rites conducted in the Temple itself.

The priest who performs the rite is to be free of all uncleanness, so he is subjected to a seven-day purification-rite to remove the corpse-uncleanness that may have affected him. The water is collected by youngsters who have been born and raised in a condition of cultic cleanness, that is, in rock cells, immune to corpse-uncleanness that may be buried in the ground. They fill stone cups, being carried on doors borne by oxen, which interpose against buried uncleanness. So the officiating priest and the required assistants are protected from corpse-uncleanness that may be buried in the depths and unknown. The priest, the cow, and all assistants cross from the Temple Mount to the Mount of Olives on a causeway over arches, once more to protect against graves in the depths. The upshot is, the conditions of cultic cleanness pertaining in the Temple courtyard are replicated outside of the Temple, so far as this is possible, for transport to, and labor on, the Mount of Olives opposite the Temple mount. But then, on the mount of Olives, the officiating priest would be rendered unclean by the hands of others, and he would then immerse. He would slaughter the beast in the status of one unclean as a Tebul Yom. Thus the rite in the world outside of the cult was carried on by a person in the condition of uncleanness — but on the cusp of cleanness, when sunsets; but that is after the rite is over. That preserves the distinction between the Temple and the world.

We find no difficulty in understanding the extreme character of the rules governing the activity and intentionality of those involved in the rite. These rules form the paradigm of what it means, of what is required, to attain cultic cleanness: the most intense, best focussed, concentration on the matter at hand. But what lessons does the Halakhah set forth in its context through those rules? The key to the entire construction, so remarkably cogent as it is, presents itself in the paradoxes noted just now. Scripture is clear that those who participate in preparing the water or in using it in a purification-process later on contract uncleanness through their activity. So, as the medieval commentaries, e.g., Bammidbar Rabbah, to Numbers 19 underscore, we have the paradox of uncleanness produced by what is clean, matching that of cleanness produced from a rite involving uncleanness. Now in the setting of a system that concerns itself with establishing a domain of cleanness in the world beyond the Temple, matching the situation of holy Israel among the gentiles, what message may we discern from the stringent Halakhah at hand, and what is the household to learn in particular?

The lesson is in two parts: cleanness is possible, but death lurks round about and is omnipresent. The first is that even on the Mount of Olives, outside of the Temple, proper effort, sufficient energy, appropriate intentionality serve to establish a domain of cultic cleanness. In the world outside the holy place, there killing and burning the red cow will produce ashes for mixing with properly-gathered water, the mixture then serving to remove the most virulent uncleanness that the Torah knows, the uncleanness of the corpse. The second is that that domain of cleanness that man creates beyond the Temple retains its essential character as the realm of death. And that is why (so the Halakhah might propose) all parties to the preparation and use of purification-water, from the high priest who kills the red cow to the person who tosses the water on an unclean person or object, are classified as unclean, must immerse and await sunset to return to a condition of cleanness. The encounter with death overcomes even the most pure level of intentionality and its realization — but Israel can overcome death and its effects.

So cultic cleanness beyond the cult is possible, only through the exercise of enormous resources of will and concentration. But however devotedly Israel undertakes the work, the perpetual prevalence of uncleanness persists: the person who has attained an astonishing level of cleanness to participate in the rite and who has concentrated all his energies and attention upon the rite and succeeded — that person, Scripture itself decrees, emerges unclean from his labor in perfect cleanness to prepare purification-water. The one proposition — to participate, the highest, most extraordinary level of cleanness is required — requires the other — one emerges unclean from the labor. Thus cultic cleanness beyond the cult is possible, but the world beyond the Temple remains what it is — no matter what. Having created the instruments for removing corpse-uncleanness, the parties to the rite immerse just as they ordinarily would, wait for sunset, and only then eat their evening meal in the condition of cultic purity that the Halakhah makes possible: the ordinary immersion-pool, the quotidian sunset suffice, but only provisionally. Tomorrow is another day, and it already has begun, if in the state of cleanness that is, or ought to be, the norm for Israel.

Accordingly, if Israel wishes to attain that status of cleanness that marks the way station to sanctification, enormous efforts alone will make possible the realization of such an aspiration. Perfect concentration on the task at hand, pure intentionality to accomplish the goal to the exclusion of all extrinsic considerations and activities — these alone will make attainable the accomplishment of such purity as is possible, that transient kind that is all for now. To accomplish the extraordinary deed of preparing purification-water to overcome death, the Halakhah prohibits participants in the rite from sitting or lying or even touching receptacles of any kind, other than actions of sitting or lying intrinsic to the labor at hand and utensils required therefor.

B. THE ACTIVITY OF THE CATEGORY-FORMATION

THE COW ACCEPTABLE FOR THE PURIFICATION-ASH: The cow must be unblemished; it must never have been used, e.g., for labor, for bearing burdens, or for mating. It may never have been ridden or leaned upon, it may never have carried weight or been used even for crossing a river or holding a cloak. It must be born naturally, it may never have served in commerce (e.g., in exchange for personal services). Ambiguous actions, e.g., tying it up to a rope, are classified by intent: if they are done for the sake of the cow, they do not invalidate it; if for the convenience of the owner, they do. If one brought it in to the threshing team to suck, and it accidentally threshed with its mother, it is fit.

CONDITIONS OF SLAUGHTERING THE COW AND BURNING THE CARCASS: The wood for burning the cow was laid out so that its fore-side faced westward, that is to say, the Temple. The head of the beast was faced toward the Temple, that is, to the west. The priest slaughtered the beast facing the Temple. The blood is tossed toward the door of the Holy of Holies. The priest slaughtered with the right hand and received the blood in his left hand, as he would in the Temple. Judah has him receive the blood in the right hand and put it into the left hand, a mirror image of what he would do in the Temple: He would slaughter with his right hand and then put the knife down before him or give it to this one who stands at his side, and he receives the blood with the palm of his right hand, and puts it into his left hand, and sprinkles with his right finger. So the issue is clear: having created a realm of reduced uncleanness, do we conduct the rite exactly as we would in the Temple or, facing the Temple, in the opposite way? Here the issue is a familiar one: do we invoke the analogy or the contrast, when the two intersect in an interstitial circumstance such as this one? The particular hermeneutics of Parah here develops a subordinate problem.

THE CHARACTER OF THE WATER: The water for mixing with the ash of the red cow must be spring-, or living-water. Only flowing water serves to remove corpse-uncleanness and the other types of uncleanness of the same classification, that is, *Zob*-uncleanness and *nega‘*-uncleanness. This is made explicit, also, at M. Miq. 1:8: "Above them: Living water — in which [take place] immersion for Zabim, and sprinkling for lepers; and which is suitable to mix the purification water." It must derive from a source that flows reliably and that is pure and clear, not turbid. Water from rivers is unfit for mixing the purification-water. It may come from a distance, so long as it is watched over the length of its flow.

The water must be drawn only by a utensil, not by human intervention in any other wise. If one splashed water with his hand and with his feet and with the clay shards, not with a trough a utensil — it is unsuitable, because the water was not drawn with a utensil. But if the jar broke and one splashed it out with his hands, feet, and clay shards, not with a trough, it is suitable, because it was originally drawn with a utensil.

CONDITIONS OF GATHERING THE WATER AND MIXING THE WATER AND THE ASHES: I already have emphasized that the water must be collected by sentient man, and it must be constantly subject to the intentionality of man that it serve for the specified purpose. It must be collected in valid utensils, recognized by man as useful, for that purpose. The water and ashes must be mixed in valid utensils. All utensils serve, of whatever material they are made. But the utensils must be made subject to human will and purpose. They cannot take shape by nature, e.g., a trough hewn from a rock cannot be used for drawing water or mixing ashes with the water and so on. If it was originally movable and then attached to a rock, it may be used. Broken utensils cannot be used, but if they are planed and repaired and made useful, they can.

UNCLEANNESS AND THE PURIFICATION-RITE: We assume that because the rite involves the Temple, even though it is performed outside of the Temple, the entire population observes the cleanness rules in connection with the preparation of purification-ash and water. Everyone, even lay folk, is assumed to take precautions to preserve the cleanness of the rite, including all utensils to be used in the rite. The utensils that are to be used are constantly watched as they are fired. If people do not ordinarily keep the laws of cultic cleanness outside of the Temple, they nonetheless are assumed to do so for this rite, and people who do keep those laws take for granted that utensils kept pure by outsiders for the purification-rite are valid also for use in connection with priestly rations. But the outsider is not assumed to observe the same rules when it comes to utensils for use with priestly rations alone.

Those involved in the work of burning the cow — e.g., carrying the water — impart uncleanness to their clothing or other utensils that they touch at the time of the rite. They do not contaminate persons or clay utensils. While the activity imparts uncleanness, the cow itself does not. The clothing cannot be made unclean by the activity, but it is made unclean by the made who has engaged therein. If the rite is unfit, then the persons involved to not render clothing unclean.

To protect the purification water, the highest standard of alertness for preserving cultic cleanness is required. A higher standard of cleanness applies to preserve the purity of purification-water and ash as these are prepared and mixed than even to the preservation of the cleanness of Holy Things. That is expressed at Mishnah-tractate Hagigah 2:5, 7, as follows:

A. For purposes of cultic purification, it is sufficient if they wash the hands for eating unconsecrated food, tithe, and heave offering;

B. and for eating food in the status of Holy Things it is sufficient only if they immerse;

C. and as to the preparation of purification water through the burning of the red cowl, if one's hands are made unclean, his entire body is deemed to be unclean as well.

Mishnah-tractate Hagigah 2:5

A. The clothing of ordinary folk is in the status of Midras uncleanness for abstainers who eat unconsecrated food in a state of cultic cleanness.

B. The clothing of abstainers is in the status of Midras uncleanness for those who eat heave offering priests.

C. The clothing of those who eat heave offering is in the status of Midras uncleanness for those who eat Holy Things officiating priests.

D. The clothing of those who eat Holy Things is in the status of Midras uncleanness for those engaged in the preparation of purification water.

Mishnah-tractate Hagigah 2:7

Not only so, but in connection with preparation of the mixture, anything that is susceptible to Midras-uncleanness, e.g., chairs and beds, is deemed actually unclean with Maddaf-uncleanness, and that is without regard to the facts of the matter. The same considerations govern in connection with corpse-uncleanness.

The distinction between the hands and the body, important in Yadayim, does not pertain. The hands are always active, so form a distinct domain for uncleanness; but in the present case, what they touch affects all else. This extreme conception is expressed in this language: One who is clean for the purification-rite, the hands of whom were made unclean — his body is made unclean. He makes his fellow unclean, and his fellow, his fellow. And as to the outer part of a pitcher: A pitcher of purification-water, the outer side of which is made unclean — its inside is made unclean. It renders its fellow unclean, and its fellow, its fellow, and also the one who sprinkles. Removes of uncleanness do not pertain — even to a hundred removes. They do not say in connection with the purification-rite, "This is first and this is last." But they are all in the first remove of uncleanness. For they do not count removes of uncleanness with reference to sprinkling the purification-water. A piece of dough which is prepared in connection with the purification-rite, and the dead creeping thing touched one of them even if they are a hundred, they are all first. For they do not count removes of uncleanness with reference to the purification-rite

The upshot is, those involved in preparing the water cannot relax in any way; they cannot touch chairs or beds, which are afflicted by definition — by their own unknown "history," — with pressure-uncleanness. They must assume that everything that forms a receptacle is unclean with Maddaf-uncleanness. In cases of doubt, any matter of a suspended decision in respect to heave offering — in regard to the purification water rite, the water is poured out. A person who requires immersion, whether by the rules of the Torah or of the scribes, imparts uncleanness in the context of the purification-rite.

THE ROLE OF INTENTIONALITY: We have already stressed that the rules of uncleanness guarantee the highest level of alertness beginning to end, and that means, an intense focus of intentionality to prepare the purification-water in a proper manner must define the entire process, start to finish. So far as assessing whether or not an act of labor has been done with the cow, we differentiate the intention that has brought about the action. If the owner utilized the cow for his own convenience, it is invalidated; if for the cow's own benefit, it remains valid. So the particular hermeneutics does its work: intentionality forms the taxonomic criterion. One's intention in slaughtering the beast, receiving and sprinkling the blood, and the like, must focus on the purification-rite in particular. That is to say, the beast having been designated for the purification-rite, the priest must offer the beast for that purpose and for no other purpose, and so with the other activities connected to the sacrifice. Improper intentionality invalidates the rite, just as it does the sin- and guilt-offering; the animal must be used for the purpose for which it was originally designated. It is improper to form the intention to drink purification-water, but the water is rendered unfit not by mere intent but only by an action confirming the intentionality.

C. THE CONSISTENCY OF THE CATEGORY-FORMATION

The survey of the Halakhah in detail has shown that the category-formation encompasses components that cohere with its points of generative tension and takes up nothing that would divert attention from its main concerns.

D. THE GENERATIVITY OF THE CATEGORY-FORMATION

The full extent of the generativity of the category-formation, the genus, "water that removes uncleanness," will become clear only when we reach Makhshirin and find the key to the centrality of water (prepared in a particular way). Then we see why the very working of the system of cleanness and uncleanness, so far as food is concerned, is precipitated by water, which imparts susceptibility to uncleanness to dry, hence insusceptible, grain or other foodstuffs; and why the results of the system, the cultic contamination of food, are removed by water as well. Any answer to the question of the generativity of Parah attempted outside of the context of Makhshirin (therefore, also, Hallah) and Miqvaot would be, if necessary, only insufficient and partial.

6

Tractate Miqvaot

I. THE DEFINITION OF THE CATEGORY-FORMATION

As usual, the category-formation — in this case, immersion-pools — announces its own hermeneutics, both the particular and the generic. As always, the category-formation takes up the former at the outset, the latter afterward. An outline of the category-formation leaves no doubt about the regnant theory of the selection and interpretation of data concerning the immersion-pool, a species of the genus, water that removes uncleanness:

I.   THE PARTICULAR HERMENEUTICS OF ANALOGY AND CON-TRAST: THE SIX GRADES OF GATHERINGS OF WATER

II. THE GENERIC HERMENEUTICS: DOUBTS. RESOLVING DOUBTS ABOUT IMMERSION AND IMMERSION-POOLS

III. THE GENERIC HERMENEUTICS. MIXTURES. DIVERSE VOL-UME AND MIXTURES OF WATER OF IMMERSION-POOLS

IV. THE GENERIC HERMENEUTICS. MIXTURES. THE UNION OF POOLS TO FORM THE REQUISITE VOLUME OF WATER

V.   THE GENERIC HERMENEUTICS. MIXTURES. WATER AND WINE, WATER AND MUD, WATER IN VARIOUS LOCALES

VI. THE GENERIC HERMENEUTICS: CONNECTION. USING THE IMMERSION POOL. THE MATTER OF INTERPOSITION

Units ii-vi, self-evidently, go over the familiar program of the generic hermeneutics, doubts, mixtures, connections, so the entire hermeneutics particular to Miqvaot is engaged in the opening unit. And there, a theory that Rabbinic Judaism forms its Halakhic hermeneutics in a process of analogical-contrastive analysis finds explicit validation. There, as my theory of matters leads us to expect, we deal with an exercise of hierarchical classification, making possible analogical-contrastive analysis, as the outline indicates. The opening unit sets explicitly forth the genus, water that serves to remove uncleanness, and six species thereof. Then it systematically conducts the work of comparison and contrast that, in other category-formations, I have hypothetically recapitulated on my own. Here the Halakhah not only identifies its particular hermeneutics but also makes explicit the process of analogical-contrastive analysis that has generated that hermeneutics.

The key-contrast, as we shall see, of the two like classifications of water — water that removes uncleanness — is between the third and the sixth of the six classifications, still water against running water. Here is where the generative hermeneutics enters. The former — the immersion-pool of forty seahs of still water — defines the problematic of the Halakhah, in these aspects:

[1] it must not be subjected to human intervention or intentionality,

[2] it must not be collected in utensils;

[3] but it must flow naturally (with the flow permissibly directed by man) to its collection-point in the pool.

And, conversely, drawn water imparts uncleanness and if poured into a collection of rain-water of a volume insufficient to constitute a valid immersion pool spoils the water into which it is poured. We recall, Parah requires exactly the opposite traits for the water that will mix with the ash of the red cow and remove corpse-uncleanness:

[1] it must be subjected to human intervention or intentionality at the most acute level,

[2] it must be collected in utensils;

[3] and it must not flow naturally but only as directed by human decision to its collection-point in the utensil.

By itself still water that has accumulated through rainfall bears one message, and in comparison with living water, the category-formation yields a still more eloquent one. The lesson of the classification, still water, seen on its own is that still water does not purify, only sunset does. That lesson is important at Tebul Yom but immaterial here. The latter — the contrast between still and living water — governs the Halakhic exposition before us, which can be understood only in the context of analogical-contrastive analysis. The companion species of the shared genus, Parah, then supplies the key to Miqvaot, living water for the one, still water for the other. Of the six kinds of water that the Halakhah differentiates for purposes of removing uncleanness, these two take priority, still water that in the requisite volume has collected from rain-drippings, which is to say, water that accumulates naturally from heaven, and living or spring or flowing water, from deep in the earth, which removes corpse-uncleanness and that of the Zab and of *nega'*-uncleanness.

What is it that turns still water from a source of uncleanness (if drawn) or a facilitator for the transmission of uncleanness (if poured upon seed through an act of will, in line with Lev. 11:34, 37=the category-formation, Makhshirin) to the medium for removing uncleanness of a certain classification? The matter may be expressed positively and negatively. It is the negative fact that the water has not served human purposes or been subjected to human activity. Water left in its natural condition, in sufficient volume, pouring down from heaven in the form of rain and collecting on its own upon the earth — that is Heaven's medium for removing uncleanness imparted by dead creeping things and certain other kinds of uncleanness. Living water, subjected to human intentionality and activity, drawn by man in a utensil, removes corpse-uncleanness and comparable types of uncleanness. The contrast between Parah's insistence on use of a valid utensil and Miqvaot's exclusion of the same is expressed in the following, among many cases:

> A potsherd which is sunk down into the ground of a cistern of a
> press — and rain fell, and it was filled up — lo, it [the water] is unfit,
> because it has been guided by means of a utensil.
>
> T. 3:1

Required to preserve passivity, man may only dig a hole into which rain-water will naturally flow. But that is how uncleanness takes place, by nature, rarely by an act of human intentionality.

And that match underscores the positive message in response to the particular hermeneutics. Just as uncleanness comes about by nature — nature's failing to realize its teleology, and not by human activity or intentionality, so nature serves to remove uncleanness and naturally to restore the normal condition of persons and objects, which is cleanness. Nature restores what nature has disrupted, the celestial removing the chthonic, so to speak. That is in two stages, still water marks the cessation of uncleanness, sunset the beginning of the new cycle of Israel in conformity with the purposive character of nature, as we shall note in connection with the status of Tebul Yom. Just as human intentionality cannot create sources of uncleanness, so, in the context of the immersion-pool and the kinds of uncleanness it removes, human intentionality cannot directly bring about the sources of purification. But the opposite rule pertains to purification water, which can be brought into being only through unremitting and intense intentionality on the part of all participants in the rite.

Now when we come to interpret the opposed rules of water for immersion pools and water for mixing with ash to form purification-water for removal of corpse-uncleanness, the question is simply stated. It is, why does still water unaffected by human agency restore the natural condition disrupted by uncleanness other than that of the corpse and its analogues, while by contrast purification-water systematically subjected to human intervention — constant attention, deliberate action, start to finish — alone removes corpse-uncleanness? We have then to account for the exclusion of man from the one process, the radical insistence upon his inclusion, in full deliberation, within the other. The contrastive process then produces the reason. We deal with two essentially distinct types of uncleanness, one ordinary and natural, the other extraordinary and in violation of nature. And in this matter we find the explanation for how the category-formation fuses its facts into a coherent statement. The dead creeping and counterpart sources of uncleanness are part of nature; death and media of uncleanness that are analogous thereto violate the natural course that God intended at creation.

The facts must carry their own message. Uncleanness that comes about by reason of any cause but death and its analogues is removed by the Heaven's own dispensation, not by man's intervention: rain-fall and the sunset marking the new creation suffice. To explain: ordinary purification is done by nature, resulting from natural processes. Water that falls from heaven and, unimpeded by man, collects in sufficient volume restores the natural condition of persons and objects that have contracted uncleanness at second hand or by reason of minor sources of contamination. Still water serves for the moment, until sunset marks the new now-clean spell in the story of the person or the object. But as to persons and objects that have contracted uncleanness from death, nature on its own cannot produce the kind of water that bears the power to remove that uncleanness and restore the condition of nature. Only man can. And man can do this, as Parah has shown us, only by the highest level of concentration, the most deliberate and focussed action. The water is not still, but flowing water: living water overcoming death. And the water is kept alive, in constant motion until it is stirred with the ash. Any extrinsic action spoils the water; stopping to rest on a bench, doing any deed other than required for the rite itself — these disrupt the circle of sanctification within the world of uncleanness that the burning of the cow has required.

So the facts lead us to the critical question at the heart of matters: why does the state of human intentionality govern in the confrontation with corpse-uncleanness? To that matter we turn at the end, for it is a question generated by the category-formation, but not limited to the framework thereof: a mark of the generativity of the hermeneutics that has governed the category-formation but that transcends it.

II. THE SCRIPTURAL FOUNDATIONS OF THE HALAKHIC CATEGORY-FORMATION

Of all this Scripture knows nothing, though to such a taxonomy of types of water, Scripture makes its contribution. When Scripture speaks of "putting into water" — immersing — an unclean person or garment, it further specifies, "and it shall be unclean until evening, then it will be clean." So immersion does not purify, but in a measure removes uncleanness. Scripture proves remarkably reticent to deal with questions involving how the "putting into water" is carried out, not defining the sort of water that works, as the pertinent verses show:

Lev. 11:31-2: "Any anything upon which any of them [dead creeping things] falls when they are dead shall be unclean...it must be put into water and it shall be unclean until evening, then it shall be clean."

Lev. 15:13: "And when he who has a discharge is cleansed of his discharge, then he shall count for himself seven clean days for his cleansing and wash his clothes and he shall bathe his body in running water and shall be clean."

Lev. 11:32: "What is touched by a dead creeping thing must be put in water and it shall be unclean until evening; then it shall be clean."

Lev. 11:40: "He also who carries the carcass shall wash his clothes and be unclean until evening."

Lev. 14:8: "And he who is to be cleansed shall wash his clothes and shave off all his hair and bathe himself in water and he shall be clean."

Lev. 15:5: "And any one who touches the Zab's bed shall wash his clothes and bathe himself in water, and he shall be unclean until evening."

Lev. 15:16: "And if a man has a discharge of semen, he shall bathe his whole body in water and be unclean until evening."

Lev. 15:21: "And whoever touches her bed shall wash his clothes and bathe himself in water and be unclean until evening.:"

"Lev. 15:27: "And whoever touches these things shall be unclean and shall wash his clothes and bathe himself in water and be unclean until evening."

Lev. 16:28: "And he who burns them shall wash his clothes and bathe his body and afterward he may come into the camp."

Lev.17:15: "And every person that eats what dies of itself...shall wash his clothes in water and be unclean until evening. Then he shall be clean."

Lev. 22:6-7: "The person who touches any such shall be unclean until evening and shall not eat of the holy things unless he has bathed his body in water. When the sun is down, he shall be clean."

Num. 10:7: "Then the priest shall wash his clothes and bathe his body in water and afterwards he shall come into the camp. And the priest shall be unclean until evening."

Num. 17:17: "And the clean person shall sprinkle upon the unclean...and he shall wash his clothes and bathe himself in water and at evening he shall be clean."

Dt. 23:11:12: "If there is among you any man who is not clean, but when evening comes, he shall bathe himself in water, and when the sun is down, he may come into the camp."

Scripture supplies no information about the character of the water into which the unclean object is to be put, how such water is collected, how much is required, and the like. Here is a case in which Scripture supplies facts, but the Halakhah, the context in which those facts are formed into a category-formation particular to the Halakhah.

III. The exposition of the components of the given category-formation
by the Mishnah-Tosefta

I.   Six grades of Gatherings of Water

> M. 1:1 Six grades in gatherings [of water], this above that, and this above that: Water
> in ponds — (1) An unclean person drank, and a clean person drank — he is
> unclean. (2) An unclean person drank and drew water with a clean utensil — it is
> unclean. (3) An unclean person drank, and a loaf of heave offering fell — if he
> rinsed, it is unclean. And if he did not rinse, it is clean.
>
> T. 1:1 Said R. Nehemiah, "Why have they said, 'If he did not rinse, it is clean?' For the
> water which is in the pond is not going to receive uncleanness until it is detached.
> [Even when] one has lifted it up, the clean predominates over the unclean.
>
> T. 1:2 "And why have they said, 'If he rinsed, [it is unclean]?' The water which is on
> his hands is rendered susceptible to uncleanness and made unclean, and it makes
> the loaf unclean."
>
> **M. 1:2 (4) [If] one drew with an unclean utensil, and a clean person drank — he is
> unclean. (5) [If] one drew [water] with an unclean utensil and drew [water]
> with a clean utensil — it is unclean. (6) [If] one drew with an unclean utensil,
> and a loaf of heave offering fell [into the water], if he rinsed [it off], it is
> unclean, and if he did not rinse it, it is clean.**
>
> **M. 1:3 (7) Unclean water fell, and a clean person drank — he is unclean. (8) [If]
> unclean water fell into it, and one drew with a clean utensil — it is unclean.
> (9) [If] unclean water fell, and a loaf of heave offering fell [into it], if he
> rinsed, it is unclean, and if he did not rinse, it is clean.**
>
> **M. 1:4 [If] a corpse fell into it, or the unclean person walked in it, and a clean
> person drank — he is clean. All the same are (1) water of ponds, (2) water of
> cisterns, (3) water of ditches, (4) water of caverns, (5) water of rain drippings
> which have stopped, and (6) immersion pools which do not contain forty seahs:
> during the rainy season, all are clean. [When] the rain ends, those that are
> near the village and the road are unclean. And those that are far are clean,
> until the larger numbers of people have passed by.**
>
> T. 1:3 A pond into which wine, honey, or milk has fallen — they follow the majority.
> [If] olive-oil fell into it, even though it congealed, lo, this [pool] is unclean, because
> it is not possible for it to be freed from the particles of oil.
>
> T. 1:4 Wine of heave-offering which fell on fruit — one should rinse them off, and they
> are permitted. And so olive-oil of heave-offering which fell into pieces of fruit —
> one should rinse them off, and they are permitted. Olive-oil of heave-offering
> which fell on wine — one should skim it off, and the wine is permitted. That
> which fell on brine — one should skim it off so that he annuls the taste of the
> olive-oil which is in it.
>
> **M. 1:5 When is the [the water's] purification? [If] they formed the greater part,
> even though they did not overflow. [When purified], they are suitable for
> dough-offering and for the washing of hands therefrom.**
>
> T. 1:5 The assumption concerning mud and puddles which are by the doors of shops in
> the public domain during the rainy-season — all are clean. [When] the rain ceased,

lo, they are like dirty water which is in the market-places — they follow the majority.

T. 1:6 Dirty water and rain-water which got mixed together — whether in utensils or on the ground — it is unclean. [When] the rain ceased, those which are near the village and the road are unclean. Those which pools of water that are distant are clean until the larger number of people will walk there. Under what circumstances? In the case of a pool from which it is not possible to drink without one's footprints being discerned. But a pool from which it is possible to drink without one's footprints being discerned — [if] one found there the footprints of man [or] footprints of large cattle, it is unclean. [If one found there] footprints of small cattle, it is clean.

T. 1:7 A pool which does not contain forty *seahs* of water, and into which less than three *logs* of drawn water fell — it is suitable for unconsecrated food, for dough offering, and for heave offering, and for washing the hands therewith. And it is fit to be added to. [If] rain fell — [if] they formed the greater part and overflowed, — [if] they formed the greater part, even though they did not overflow — they are suitable for *dough offering* and for heave-offering and for washing the hands therewith. And it is fit to be added to. And how [is a case in which] they formed the greater part, even though they did not overflow?

T. 1:8 An immersion-pool which holds forty *seahs* and in it are nineteen *seahs,* and less than three *logs* of drawn water fell therein — once twenty-one *seahs* of rain-water have fallen in it is clean because they [rain-water] have formed the greater part.

T. 1:9 An immersion-pool which holds twenty *seahs,* and in it are nineteen *seahs,* and less than three *logs* of drawn water fell therein — it is unclean. Once one *se'ah* of rain-water has fallen therein, it is clean, because [now] it has overflowed. And how much must it overflow. Any amount at all. [If] there fell into three *logs* of unclean drawn water — it is unfit for *dough offering* and for heave-offering and for washing the hands therewith. And it is unfit to be added to. [If] the rain fell — until there will go forth from it its fullness and a bit more.

T. 1:10 [If] rain fell — [if] it formed the greater part, even though it did not overflow — it is suitable for *dough offering* and for heave-offering and for washing the hands therewith. And it is unfit to be added to, until there will go forth from it its fullness and a bit more.

T. 1:11 And how much is *and more?* Its fullness and more. An immersion-pool which holds twenty *seahs,* and in it are nineteen *seahs* — three *logs* of unclean water fell into it — and rain fell, and it was filled up — it [the water] always remains in [its] unfitness, until there will go forth from it its fullness and a bit more — some small amount more to remove the three *logs.*

T. 1:12 An immersion-pool which contains forty *seahs* less a *qortob* and three *logs* of unclean drawn water fell therein — they are unfit for dough offering and for heave-offering and for washing the hands therewith. And unfit to be added to. [If] less than three *logs* [fell in], even if they are all unfit [or: unclean], once a single *qortob* of rain-water fell therein — they are clean.

M. 1:6 Above them: Water of rain drippings which have not ceased. (1) [If] an unclean person drank [from it], and [afterward] a clean person drank — he is clean. (2) [If] an unclean person drank and drew [water] with a clean utensil — it is clean. (3) [If] an unclean person drank, and a loaf of heave offering

fell, even though he rinsed — it is clean. (4) [If] one drew with an unclean utensil, and a clean person drank — he is clean. (5) [If] one drew with an unclean utensil and drew with a clean utensil — it is clean. (6) [If] one drew with an unclean utensil, and a loaf of heave offering fell, even though he rinsed — it is clean. (7) [If] unclean water fell, and a clean person drank — he is clean, (8) [If] unclean water fell, and one drew with a clean utensil — it is clean. (9) [If] unclean water fell, and a loaf of heave offering fell, even though he rinsed — it is clean. They are suitable for heave offering and for rinsing the hands therefrom.

T. 1:13 And just as they are clean for immersion, so they are clean for everything. Above them: Rain-drippings which have not ceased — For they immerse [unclean] water in them. And they do not immerse in them man and hands and utensils. This is the general rule: Any place in which man immerses, hands and utensils immerse. [If] a man does not immerse, hands and utensils do not immerse. And what are rain-drippings? So long as the rains fall, and the mountains trickle [with water] lo, they are like the water of a spring. [If] they ceased to trickle, *lo,* they are like the water of pools.

M. 1:7 Above them: A pool of water which has forty seahs, in which they immerse and dunk. Above them: A spring, whose waters are sparse, and in which drawn water forms the greater part: it is equivalent (1) to the pool, to render clean by standing water; and (2) to a fountain, to dunk in it in any amount [of water] at all.

M. 1:8 Above them: Smitten [spring] water — which render clean when they are flowing. Above them: Living water — in which [take place] immersion for Zabim, and sprinkling for lepers; and which is suitable to mix the purification water.

T. 1:14 He who digs at the side of the ocean and at the side of the river, in a swampy place — lo, it [the water] counts as water in rain ponds. He who digs at the side of the spring — for so long as it [water] comes on account of the spring — even though it stops and starts seeping again, lo, it is like spring-water. [If] it again ceases to flow, lo, it is like the water of pools.

T. 1:15 A spring, the waters of which are sparse, and it [drawn water] formed the greater part and expanded — it cleanses when it is standing water. And it does not cleanse when it is flowing, except to the place to which it can reach in the first place.

The one point of interest at M. 1:1ff., on the water that when raised out of the pond (T. 1:1) is susceptible to uncleanness, comes third: if the loaf fell in and the person rinsed it, that means the loaf was wet down intentionally, and it is made susceptible and contracts uncleanness forthwith. If he did not rinse it, it means he did not want the loaf to be wet down, so, whatever the actual condition of the loaf, it is as if it were dry and insusceptible. The contrast between the classification of water at M. 1:1-5 and that at M. 1:6 is neatly drawn, and the continuation, which omits the generic hermeneutics operative at M. 1:1-6, is self-explanatory in its contrasts.

II. RESOLVING DOUBTS ABOUT IMMERSION AND IMMERSION-POOLS

M. 2:1 The unclean person who went down to immerse — it is a doubt whether he immersed or whether he did not immerse — [and] even if he did immerse — it is a doubt whether there are forty seahs in it, or whether there are not — two immersion pools, in one of which there are forty seahs, and in one of which there are not forty seahs — he immersed in one of them and does not know in which one of them he immersed — his matter of doubt is deemed unclean.

M. 2:2 An immersion pool which was measured and found lacking [forty seahs] — all things requiring cleanness which were made depending on it — retroactively — whether in private domain or whether in public domain. are unclean. Under what circumstances? With reference to a major uncleanness. But with reference to a minor uncleanness: for example, (1) [if] one ate [a half-loaf of] unclean foods, (2) drank [a quarter-qab of] unclean liquids, (3) one's head and the greater part of one's body came into drawn water, (4) or three logs of drawn water fell on one's head and the greater part of one's body and he went down to immerse — it is a matter of doubt whether he immersed or did not immerse — and even if he immersed, it is a matter of doubt whether there are forty seahs [of rainwater] in it or there are not [forty seahs] in it — two immersion pools, in one of which there are forty seahs, and in one of which there are not — one immersed in one of them and does not know in which one of them he immersed — his matter of doubt is deemed clean.

T. 1:16 An immersion-pool which was measured and found lacking — all the acts requiring cleanness which were carried out depending upon it whether this immersion-pool is in the private domain, or whether this immersion-pool is in the public domain — are unclean.

M. 2:3 A doubt about drawn water that sages have declared clean — it is a matter of doubt whether they [three logs of drawn water] fell or did not fall. [And] even if they did fall, it is a matter of doubt whether there are forty seahs in it or whether there are not — two immersion pools, in one of which there are forty seahs and in one of which there are not — it fell into one of them, and one does not know into which one of them it fell — its [the pool's] matter of doubt is deemed clean, because it has something upon which to depend. [If] both of them were less than forty seahs, and if [drawn water] fell into one of them and one does not know into which of them it fell — its matter of doubt is deemed unclean, for it has nothing upon which to depend. Whether in the first place or at the end, its measure is three logs of drawn water [to invalidate the immersion pool].

T. 2:1 An immersion-pool which one left empty and came and found full fit, because it involves a matter of doubt concerning drawn waters in an immersion-pool, and the assumption concerning immersion-pools is that they are fit.

T. 2:2 A water-duct which is pouring water into an immersion-pool, and a mortar is set at its [the duct's] side — and it is a matter of doubt whether it [water] is [pouring] from the water-duct to the immersion-pool, or whether it is [pouring] from the mortar into the immersion-pool — it is unfit, because the matter of unfitness is demonstrable. And if the greater part [of water] in the immersion-pool is fit,

[Supply: it is fit] because this is a matter of doubt concerning drawn water in connection with an immersion-pool.

T. 2:3 Two immersion-pools which do not contain forty *seahs* [of rainwater], and three *logs* of drawn water fell [into one of them], and it is known into which of them it has fallen, and afterward, a second [volume, three further *logs* of drawn water] fell, but it is not known into which of them they have fallen — lo, I am able to attribute [the matter], saying, "To the place into which the first [three *logs* of drawn water] have fallen, there have the second ones fallen [as well]."

T. 2:4 Three *logs* [of drawn water] fell into one of them, and it is not known into which of them they fell, and afterward a second [volume of *logs* of drawn water] fell, and it is known into which of them they fell — one cannot attribute [the matter], saying, "Into the place into which the second ones have fallen, there did the first ones fall [as well]." In one [of the immersion-pools] there are forty *seahs* [of rain-water], and in one of them there are not [forty *seahs* of rain-water] — lo, I declare, "Into the one containing forty *seahs* of rain-water have they fallen." [If] one is drawn water and one is fit water — lo, I declare, "They have fallen into the drawn water."

T. 2:5 Two immersion-pools which do not contain forty *seahs* [of rainwater], and three *logs* [of drawn water] have fallen into one of them, and it is not known into which of them they have fallen — and afterward rain came, and they [the two pools] were filled up [with suitable water] — R. Yosé says, "They say to him that he should not immerse in [either] one of them. But if he did immerse in one of them and prepared things requiring cleanness, because this is a matter of doubt concerning drawn water in respect to an immersion-pool [supply: they are deemed clean]. To what is the matter likened? To a person, one of whose hands has been made unclean, and it is not known which of them [is unclean]. They say to him that he should not prepare things requiring cleanness with either one of them. But if he did prepare things requiring cleanness with one of them, they are clean, because it is a matter of doubt involving the hands.'"

T. 2:6 Two immersion-pools — one containing forty *seahs* [of rain-water] and one not containing [forty *seahs* of rain-water] — one immersed in one of them on account of a condition of uncleanness deriving from a major source of uncleanness and prepared clean things, [he immersed] in the first and prepared [things requiring cleanness], [he immersed] in the second and prepared [things requiring cleanness], [if] these and those are lying [before him] — the first are held in a state of suspense, and the second are clean. Under what circumstances? When [we deal with] a condition of uncleanness deriving from a major source of uncleanness. But [if we deal with] a condition of uncleanness deriving from a minor source of uncleanness, these and those are clean.

T. 2:7 [If] he immersed in one of them on account of a condition of uncleanness deriving from a minor source of uncleanness and prepared things requiring cleanness — they are clean. [If] between times he was made unclean by a major source of uncleanness, and he immersed in the second [pool] and prepared [things requiring conditions of cleanness] — these and those are lying [before him] — lo, these prove [the condition of one another and both are kept in a state of suspense]. [If] the first were eaten, and [or] made [definitely] unclean, or perished before the second were prepared — the second are deemed clean. [If this took place] after the second were prepared, the second are held in a state of suspense.

T. 2:8 [If] he immersed in one of them on account of a condition of uncleanness deriving from a major source of uncleanness and prepared things requiring cleanness, they are suspended. [If] he was made unclean in the meantime by a minor source of uncleanness, and he immersed in the second [pool] and prepared things requiring cleanness — they are deemed clean. [And if] these touched the others, the first are held in a state of suspense, and the second are burned. [If] he immersed in one of them on account of a condition of uncleanness deriving from a minor source of uncleanness, and prepared clean things, they are deemed clean. [If] he was made unclean in the meantime by a major source of uncleanness and immersed and prepared things requiring cleanness, they are held in a state of suspense, [And if] these touched those, the second are held in a state of suspense and the first are burned.

T. 2:9 Two immersion-pools of forty *seahs* each, one containing drawn [water], and one containing suitable [water] — and one immersed in one of them on account of a condition of uncleanness deriving from a major source of uncleanness and prepared things requiring cleanness — they are held in a state of suspense. [If he immersed] in the second and prepared things requiring cleanness — they are clean. [If he immersed] in the first and did not prepare things requiring cleanness, then immersed in the second and prepared things requiring cleanness — they are clean. [If he immersed] in the first and prepared [things requiring cleanness], [then immersed] in the second and prepared [things requiring cleanness] — [if] these and those are lying [before him] — the first are suspended, and the second are clean. Under what circumstances? In the case of a condition of uncleanness deriving from a major source of uncleanness. But in the case of a condition of uncleanness deriving from a minor source of uncleanness, these and those are held in a state of suspense.

T. 2:10 [If] two people went down and immersed in the two of them, one unclean with a condition of uncleanness deriving from a major source of uncleanness, and one unclean on account of a minor source of uncleanness — he who immerses on account of a major source of uncleanness is unclean. And the one who immerses on account of uncleanness deriving from a minor source of uncleanness is clean. One who is unclean with uncleanness deriving from a major source of uncleanness and one who immerses to cool himself — he who immerses on account of uncleanness deriving from a major source of uncleanness is unclean, and the one who immerses to cool himself is clean. One is unclean with uncleanness deriving from a minor source of uncleanness, and one immerses to cool himself — both of them are kept in a state of suspense. To what is the matter likened? To two paths, one unclean and one clean, and there were two who went in the two of them and prepared things requiring cleanness. In the case of one there is sufficient intelligence for interrogation, and in the case of the other there is not sufficient intelligence for interrogation — in the case of the private domain, both of them are kept in a state of suspense. In the case of public domain, the one who has intelligence for interrogation in a matter of doubt is deemed to be unclean. And the one who does not have intelligence for interrogation in a matter of doubt is deemed clean.

T. 2:11 Two immersion-pools, each containing twenty *seahs*. one with drawn water, and one with suitable water — one immersed to cool himself in one of them and prepared things requiring cleanness — they are clean. [If he then immersed] in the second, and prepared things requiring cleanness — they are burned. [If one immersed] in the first and did not prepare [things requiring cleanness], [and then immersed] in the second and prepared [things requiring cleanness] — they are burned. [If one immersed] in the first and prepared things requiring cleanness, and [then immersed] in the second [and prepared things requiring cleanness] — if these and those are lying before him — the first are deemed clean, and the second are to be burned.

T. 2:12 Two women who engaged in preparing a bird which is suitable to produce [only] one] *sela'* of blood, after a while, on this one a *sela'* of blood is found, and a *sela'* of blood is found on the other — both of them are in disarray.

Because we confirm the status quo, M. 2:1's rule follows, and that is made explicit in the case of M. 2:2. If, however, we can find reason to declare clean, M. 2:3, we take that into account.

III. DIVERSE VOLUME AND MIXTURES OF WATER OF IMMERSION-POOLS

M. 2:5 An [empty] ritual pool which has in it three holes of drawn water, each one [containing] a log [of drawn water] — if it is known that forty seahs of suitable water have fallen into it, before the water spread to the third hole, it is fit. And if not, it is unfit.

M. 2:6 He who scrapes up mud [from the pool containing less than forty seahs, and heaps it] by the sides, and three logs [of water] drained from it — it is fit. [If] he was removing [the mud away from the pool] and three logs [of water] drained [down] into the pool, it is unfit.

T. 3:1 A potsherd which is sunk down into the ground of a cistern of a press — and rain fell, and it was filled up — lo, it [the water] is unfit, because it has been guided by means of a utensil.

T. 3:2 [If] there were [poured] on one's head three *logs* of drawn water, and one went down and immersed in an immersion-pool which contains [exactly] forty *seahs* — it is fit. [If] one squeezed it out into it, it is unfit. [If] one dunked a thick [wet] blanket into it, and three *logs* [of drawn water] exuded from it into the immersion-pool, it is fit. [If] one squeezed it [water] from it [the blanket], it is unfit.

T. 3:3 A legion which is passing from place to place, and so a caravan [or: a cow] which is passing from place to place and they splashed with their hands or their feet (and) three *logs* into the immersion-pool — it is fit. And not only so, but even if they made an immersion-pool in the first place, it is fit.

T. 3:4 And what is mud which is measured with the water? R. Yohanan b. Beroqah says, "That which is measured in a *log*." R. Yosé says, "That which goes forth in a funnel." And what is the measuring rod? This is the shuttle containing the spool. The mud which is on the sides counts in the measure of forty *seahs*. but they do not immerse in it. Three holes [containing water] in a gulch — the lowest and the uppermost are of twenty *seahs* each, and the middle one is of forty *seahs* — the rivulet of rain-water enters into them and goes out of them — One way or the other, they immerse only in the middle one, in which forty *seahs* have come to a standstill.

M. 2:7 He who leaves [empty] wine jars on the top of the roof to dry them, and they filled with water — he breaks them, or turns them upside down. But he does not empty them out [into a cistern].

M. 2:8 The plasterer who forgot a lime pot in the cistern, and it filled with water if there was any amount of water flowing on top of it [the pot], one way or the other, he does break it.

M. 2:9 He who arranges [empty] wine jars inside the cistern, and they filled with water, even though the cistern soaked up [all] its water, lo, this one breaks [them].

M. 2:10 A ritual pool which contains forty seahs of water and mud — they dunk [objects] in the water, and [them] in the mud. In what sort of mud do they immerse [objects]? In mud on the surface of which the water flows. [If] there was water on one side [only], they immerse in water, and they do not immerse in mud. Of what sort of mud did they speak? In mud in which a reed will sink on its own.

M. 3:1 Two immersion pools which [respectively] do not contain forty seahs — and into this one fell a log and a half [of drawn water], and into that one [fell] a log and a half and [then] they were mingled together are fit, since the category of unfitness never applied to them. But: an immersion pool which does not contain forty seahs [of fit water] — and three logs of drawn water fell into it — and it was divided into two [parts] — is unfit, since the category of unfitness applied to it. It always remains in its unfitness, until there will go forth from it its fullness and more.

M. 3:2 How so? The cistern which is in the courtyard — and three logs [of drawn water] fell into it — it always remains in its state of unfitness, until there will go forth from it its fullness and more. Or: until one will set up in the courtyard [another pool containing] forty seahs, and the upper [water] will be cleaned by the lower one.

M. 3:3 A cistern which is full of drawn water, and the water channel enters it and leaves from it — always is in its state of unfitness, until it will be reckoned that there do not remain of the first [unfit water] three logs. Two who were pouring [drawn water] into the immersion pool, this one [pours in] a log and a half — and this one pours in a log and a half — he who wrings out his garment and puts in [drawn water] from many places — and he who empties out the water cooler and puts in [water] from many places — sages declare unfit.

T. 3:5 Two pools of [exactly] forty *seahs* [of fit water] in each — this one on top of that one — and three *logs* fell into the upper one, and they were diverted and came into the lower one — it is suitable, for I say, "The forty *seahs* were complete before three *logs* came down."

T. 3:6 Two immersion-pools, each containing twenty *seahs* — and this is beside that one — and three *logs* of drawn water fell into one of them, and they were diverted and came into its fellow — it is suitable.

M. 3:4 [If three logs of drawn water fell or are poured into a pool] from one utensil, from two, and from three, they join together. [If three logs of drawn water fell into a pool] from four utensils, they do not join together. A person who had an emission of semen who was sick, upon whom nine qabs of water fell — and a clean person on whose head and the greater part of whose body three logs of drawn water fell — from one utensil, from two, and from three — they join together. From four — they do not join together. Under what circumstances? When the second began before the first ceased. And under what circumstances? When he did not intend to add more [drawn water]. But if he intended to add more, even one qortob in the entire year they join together to form three logs [of drawn water].

T. 3:8 Three *logs* [which fell] into an immersion-pool — and one who had an emission of semen who was ill, upon whom nine *qabs* of water have fallen — a clean person on whose head and the greater part of whose body three *logs* of drawn water have fallen — if it is from one utensil, two or three, they join together; if from four, they do not join together.

T. 3:9 He who enters drawn water except for his finger-tips — even if only his head and the greater part of his body entered into drawn water, he is unclean. [If] there entered drawn water on his head but not the greater part of his body, or the greater part of his body but not his head, or his head and the greater part of his body, whether from the top or from the side came [into drawn water] — he is clean, until his head [and greater part of his body] will enter into drawn water in accord with the normal way [of doing so].

T. 3:10 [If] part of it [the water] is drawn water and part of it is not drawn water — [or if it is drawn water] into which wine, honey, or milk has fallen — he is clean — until it will be wholly drawn water. Even if he is clean, and it [the drawn water] is clean, he is made unclean and renders it unclean. Lo, this one says, "He made me unclean, and I made him unclean."

T. 3:11 A clean person on whose head and the greater part of whose body three *logs* of drawn water have fallen is unclean. [If] they fell on his head but not on the greater part of his body, on the greater part of his body but not on his head [if] they fell on his head and on the greater part of his body whether from above or whether from the side — he is clean — until they fall on his head and the greater part of his body in the usual way.

T. 3:12 [If] part of it was drawn water and part of it was not drawn water [if] there fell into it wine, honey, or milk — he is clean, until it will be entirely drawn water. And even if he is clean, and it is clean, he is made unclean, and renders it unclean. Lo, this one says, "He made me unclean, and I made him unclean."

T. 3:13 R. Ishmael says, "[If] they [the three *logs* of drawn water] are clean, he remains clean, on account of the following argument a *fortiori*. And if when the rule concerning other liquids mixed with water is that they render the body unfit if one drinks a quarter-qab, the rule is not that the clean is like the unclean, in a situation in which liquids mixed with water do not render the body unfit, when three *logs* fall, is it not logical that we should not regard the clean as equivalent to the unclean?"

T. 3:14 An immersion-pool will prove the matter: For it is not the rule that other liquids which fall into it are treated as water. And [here the law] treats the clean as equivalent to the unclean.

M. 4:1 **He who leaves utensils under the waterspout — all the same are large utensils and small utensils — and even utensils made of dung, of stone, and of dirt — it [the water] renders the immersion pool unfit in the case of the one who leaves or forgets.**

M. 4:2 **He who leaves a tray under the waterspout if it has a rim, it [water gathered in it] renders the immersion pool unfit. And if not, it does not render the immersion pool unfit. [If] he set it upright to rinse [it], one way or the other, it does not render the immersion pool unfit.**

T. 4:1 A tray which one put beneath the water-spout to rinse [it]. and so too: utensils which one placed under the water-spout to rinse them — the first drops of water [as they fall onto the tray or utensil] are susceptible to receive uncleanness. [If] the requisite volume of forty *seahs* of rain water is completed, lo, these are fit. A water-spout which one hewed out and afterward affixed spoils the immersion-pool.

M. 4:3 **He who makes a cavity in the waterspout to catch the pebbles [in the rainwater] — [if it is] of wood, [it renders the immersion pool invalid as a receptacle to catch rainwater if it holds] any amount at all. [And if it is] of earthenware, [it renders the immersion pool invalid if it holds] a quarter-log. [If] pebbles were rolling about inside it [the hole], they render the immersion pool unfit. [If] dirt fell into it and it was pressed tight, it is fit. A water pipe which is narrow on one side and the other and wide in the middle does not spoil [the immersion pool], since it is not made as a receptacle.**

M. 4:4 **Drawn water and rainwater which mingled in the courtyard, or in a hollow, or on the steps of a cave — if the greater part is formed by fit [water], it is fit, and if the greater part is [formed by] unfit [water], it is unfit. Half and half — it is unfit. When? At the time that they mingled together before they reached the immersion pool. [If] they [each] were flowing in an unbroken stream into the water — if it is known that forty seahs of fit water fell into it before three logs of drawn water fell into it, it is fit. And if not, it is unfit.**

T. 4:2 Water which is drawn on its own in buckets from the ocean and from the river, and that which goes up on the water-pump spoil the immersion-pool.

T. 4:3 A roof on top of which there are twenty-one *seahs* of rain-water — one draws water and carries it on the shoulder and puts in it nineteen *seahs,* opens [a sluice], and mingles them in the courtyard.

T. 4:4 [If] there were forty *seahs* [on the roof], and it [the roof] was broken through, and they [the forty *seahs* of rain-water] came [flowed] into the house it [the water] is ft. But [as they are flowing into the house] they do not dunk [utensils] in them, for they do not dunk in air. [If] one of its ends [the water-stream from the roof] reaches the ground, they do immerse in it. But they do not immerse in air.

M. 4:5 **The trough which is [hewn] in the rock — (1) they do not draw water from it, (2) they do not mix [ashes of the red cow and water] in it, (3) they do not sprinkle from it, (4) it does not require a tightly stopped-up cover, and (5) it does not spoil the immersion pool. [If] it was a [movable] utensil, and one [then] attached it [to the rock] with plaster — (1) they do draw in it, (2) they**

do mix in it, (3) they do sprinkle from it, (4) it does require a tightly stopped-up cover, and (5) it does spoil the immersion pool. [If] it was perforated below or on the side, and it cannot hold any amount of water — it is suitable. And how large a hole must there be [so it is no longer a utensil with a receptacle]? As large as the spout of a water-skin.

T. 4:6 A reservoir which distributes water [in pipes] among the villages, if it was perforated by a hole the size of the stopper of a water-skin, does not spoil the immersion-pool, and if not, it spoils the immersion-pool. This law did the people of Assya bring up three festival seasons to Yabneh, and at the third season, they declared it fit — even if it was perforated by a hole the size of a needle.

T. 4:7 Under what circumstances? When [it is perforated] from the side. But [if it is perforated] from the bottom, it does not spoil the immersion-pool [even at less than the requisite hole of a stopper]. And if it was able to serve as a receptacle from the perforation and downward, [holding] any amount at all [of water], it spoils the immersion-pool. [If] one stopped it up with plaster or with building materials, it does not spoil the immersion-pool. [If one stopped it up] with plaster and with gypsum, it does spoil the immersion-pool. [If one put it] on the ground [thereby stuffing up the hole] or on plaster and gypsum, or [if] one plastered it with mud on the sides, it does not spoil the immersion-pool.

M. 5:1 [The water of] a spring which one passed over [into] the trough is unfit. [If] one passed it over the edge in any amount — valid is what is outside [of the trough], for the [water of] a spring renders clean in any quantity at all. [If] one passed it over [into] a pond, and one [then] stopped it up, lo, it [the pond] is like an immersion pool. [If one then] went and made it continue to flow, it is [still] unfit for Zabs and for lepers and for mixing purification water therewith, until one knows that the first [water] has flowed away.

T. 4:8 A spring which flows to the bidet, and from the bidet to the pool — the first drops, as they flow — lo, they are unfit, because they are drawn water. What should one do? One should perforate it at the "eye of the beard" in any amount at all. And it will come out that the small part of the water cleans the larger part. One stops up the flow by a corpse. Water which flows over the furrows and the indentation — one dunks [utensils] in them [if the waters are] at a height of the thickness of a garlic peel and the breadth of the stopper of the water-skin.

M. 5:3 A spring which is drawn like a centipede — [if] one added to it [drawn water] and it was made to flow further — lo, it is as it was. [If] it [the spring] was standing [still] and one added to it [drawn water], and made it flow further — it is equivalent to an immersion pool, to purify in standing water, and to a spring, to immerse therein in any amount. [It is subject to polythetic classification, being an interstitial case.]

T. 4:9 A spring which is drawn out like a centipede — and it [drawn water] formed the greater part over it [spring-water] — and made it [the channel] wider — it renders clean in a hollow [like an immersion-pool]. And it does not purify when it is flowing, except up to the place to which it was able to reach in the first place.

M. 5:5 Flowing water is like a spring. And that which drips is like an immersion pool. Testified R. Sadoq concerning flowing water which was more than dripping water [with which it was mixed] that it is fit. And dripping water

which one made into flowing water, one sticks in even a staff, even a reed, even a Zab and a Zabah, one goes down and dips.

Mixtures of valid and invalid water form the focus of this sizable composite, e.g., M. 4:4's standard case, where we resolve a case of mixture by assigning the status of the whole to that of the predominant part. The contrast between M. 4:5's treatment of water in a trough for use in an immersion pool and the same for use in purification-water realizes the particular hermeneutics. Once an immersion-pool lacks the requisite volume, it falls into the category of a pool that is susceptible to uncleanness. But if it is lacking and valid water is mingled with the water in the pool, it recovers its status as an effective immersion pool. M. 3:1-3 go over this ground.

IV. THE UNION OF POOLS TO FORM THE REQUISITE VOLUME OF WATER

M. 5:6 A wave which broke off, and in it are forty seahs — and it fell on man and on utensils — they are clean. Any place in which are forty seahs. they dip and dunk: They dunk (1) in trenches, (2) in ditches, and (3) in the tracks of an ass which are mixed in the valley. They do not dunk in the rain-stream. One dams it with utensils and dips in it. And utensils with which one dammed — they are not deemed to have been dunked thereby.

T. 4:5 A wave [of water] which was detached from the sea or from the river — they do not immerse in it, for they do not immerse in air. If the two ends [of the wave] touched the ground, they do immerse in it, but they do not immerse in the crest [of the wave].

T. 4:10 What is the rain-stream? Rain-water which comes down an incline. they do not dunk in it unless there will be before it a circle containing forty *seahs.*

M. 6:1 Any [pool of water] which is mingled with [water of] an immersion pool is [deemed to be as valid] as the immersion pool. Holes of the cave and clefts of the cave — one dunks in them as they are. A pit of the cavern — they do not dunk in it unless it [the hole between the pit and the immersion pool] is as large as the spout of a water-skin. Said R. Judah, "When is that the case? At the time that it stands by itself. But if it does not stand by itself, they dunk in it just as it is."

T. 5:1 Holes on the rim of the immersion-pool, and so tracks of the hooves of cattle — if [the water in these] is joined together [with water in an immersion-pool] by a hole the size of the stopper of the water-skin — they dunk therein. And if not, they do not dunk therein. The projections which are in the immersion-pool — they dunk therein, and on condition that they are mingled together through a hole the size of the stopper of the water-skin.

T. 5:2 A trough which is full of utensils — and one brought it[s water] into touch with an immersion-pool — it requires [mingling of water through] a hole the size of the spout of the water-skin. But a spring [suffices] with [an intermingling] of any amount at all. In regard to a large utensil [we require a hole the size of] four handbreadths." [And in the case of a small one], its greater part.

M. 6:2 A bucket which is full of utensils, which one dunked — lo, they [the utensils] are clean. And if it did not immerse, the water is not mingled [with that of the immersion pool], until it [the water in the bucket] is mingled [with the water of the pool] by [a stream) the size of the spout of a water-skin.

T. 5:3 A kettle which is full of utensils, and one brought it into touch with [the water of] an immersion-pool even though its mouth is narrow, in any amount at all, the utensils which are in it are clean. [If] one tipped it on its side, [the water in the kettle and that in the immersion-pool are not intermingled] until there will be a hole in its mouth the size of the spout of a water-skin.

M. 6:3 Three immersion pools — in this one are twenty seahs [of fit water], and in this one are twenty seahs [of fit water], and in this one are twenty seahs of drawn water — and [the one containing] drawn [water] is at the side — and three people went down and dipped in them, and it [the water in the three pools] was mingled together — the immersion pools are clean. And the people who immersed are clean. [If] the one containing drawn [water] was in the middle, and three people went down and immersed in them, and they were mingled together — the immersion pools are as they were. And those who immersed are as they were.

T. 3:7 Two immersion-pools, each containing twenty *seahs,* one with drawn water, and one with fit water — two went down and brought the two into contact and immersed in them — even if it [water] was red and turned white, or white and turned red — the immersion-pools remain as they were, and the ones who immersed remain as they were.

M. 6:4 The sponge and the bucket which contained three logs of water, and they fell into the immersion pool — they have not rendered it unfit. For they said only, "Three logs which fell."

M. 6:5 The box and the chest which are in the sea — they do not dunk in them, unless they were pierced to the size of the stopper of the water-skin. R. Judah says, "In the case of a large utensil, four handbreadths. And in the case of a small one, its greater part [must be broken down]." If it was a sack or a basket — they dunk in them as they are, since the water is mixed together. [If] they were set under the water pipe, they do not spoil the immersion pool. But they dunk them and bring [them] out in the ordinary way.

M. 6:6 A defective earthenware vessel which is in the immersion pool, and one dunked the utensils in it — they are clean from their uncleanness. But they are unclean because of the clay utensil. If the water flowed over the top of it in any amount at all, they are clean. A spring which comes up out of an oven, and one went down and immersed in it — he is clean. And his hands are unclean. And if it was higher than it by the height of his hands, even his hands are clean.

T. 5:4 A spring which emerges through the oven, and one immersed in it a radish and a gourd [in order to rinse them off] — if the water overflowed on top of it to their full [bulk], lo, they are clean. The two fingers of which they have spoken — [they are in accord with the] average man. And not [in accord with] the four which are in the handbreadth. An olive's bulk of carrion, a lentil's bulk of the insect — [if] there is a doubt whether they form the requisite bulk or do not form the requisite bulk — it is unclean. For any matter the principle [of contamination] of which derives from the Torah, but the requisite measure of which derives from the words of Scribes — its matter of doubt is deemed unclean.

M. 6:7 The intermingling of immersion pools is through a hole the size of the spout of a water-skin, in the thickness and capacity — two fingers turned around in full. [If there is] doubt whether it is the size of the spout of a water-skin or not the size of the spout of a water-skin, it is unfit, because it derives from the Torah. And so: the olive's bulk of a corpse, and the olive's bulk of carrion, and the lentil's bulk of a [dead] creeping thing. Whatever stops up the spout of the water-skin diminishes it.

M. 6:8 They clean immersion pools: a higher pool by the lower pool, and a distant by a nearby [pool]. How so? One brings a pipe of earthenware or lead, and puts his hand under it until it is filled with water, and draws it along and makes it touch. Even by as much as a hair's breadth suffices. [If] the upper one contains forty seahs [of fit water], and in the lower pool there is nothing — one draws [water and carries it] on the shoulder and puts it into the upper one, until there will descend into the lower one forty seahs.

T. 5:5 They clean the immersion-pools, the upper by the lower, and the distant by that which is near — how so? One brings a pipe of wood or of bone or of glass and places his hand(s) [under] the lower [end of the pipe] until it will be filled with water, and conveys it, and touches it [the water of the pool to the water of the pipe]. Even if it is [touching] by as little as a hair's breadth, it suffices. And if the pipe is bent in any measure at all, it is unfit. Under what circumstances? When they were on top of the other. But if they were side by side, he brings a knee-shaped pipe on one side, and a knee-shaped pipe on the other side, and a pipe in the middle — and he touches [the water of the one to that of the other] and descends and immerses.

M. 6:9 A wall which is between two immersion pools which was cracked perpendicularly — it joins together. [If the crack is] horizontal, it does not join together, until there will be in one place a hole the size of the spout of a water-skin. [If] they flow together into one another through a hole [in the top of the dividing wall, they can be included together] if the height [of the connecting stream] is [only] the thickness of a garlic peel and the breadth, the size of the spout of a water-skin.

T. 5:6 A wall is between two immersion-pools which was cracked horizontally — it joins together. And [if it was cracked] perpendicularly, it does not join together. [If] they flow together into one another, a full handbreadth over the whole breadth of the split is required for intermingling of water.

M. 6:10 The outlet of a bath — if the bath holds a quarter-log before the water reaches the outlet, it is valid, and if not, it is invalid.

T. 5:7 [If] the corpse is in the bath house, the furnace-room is unclean. [If] the corpse is in the furnace-room, the bath house is unclean, because of the outlet. He who touches the outlet is unclean, but he is clean when he ascends [from the water].

M. 6:11 The filter of the bath — the lower [pipe] is full of drawn water, and the upper [pipe] is full of fit water — if [the space] in front of the hole [holds] three logs [of drawn water] — it is unfit [as an immersion pool].

T. 5:8 The filter which is in the bath — the lower one is full of drawn water — and the upper one is full of fit water — and on condition that it be opposite the hole — and it contributes to the measure of forty seahs.

Once one mingles the valid water of an immersion pool with another body of water, the whole is deemed completely mixed, with the result that the entire volume is valid. How this is done is spelled out in the present composite.

v. WATER AND WINE, WATER AND MUD, WATER IN VARIOUS LOCALES

M. 7:1 There are things which raise the immersion pool and do not invalidate [it], invalidate and do not raise, do not raise and do not invalidate. These raise and do not invalidate: (1) the snow, (2) hail, (3) hoarfrost, (4) ice, (5) salt, and (6) thin mud. How do they raise and not invalidate? An immersion pool which has forty seahs, but one — a seah of one of them fell into it and raised it — they thus turn out raising and not invalidating [the immersion pool].

M. 7:2 These invalidate and do not raise: (1) [Drawn] water, whether unclean or clean,(2) and water in which food has been pressed or (3) seethed, (4) and grape skin wine before it has fermented. How do they spoil and not raise [the immersion pool]? An immersion pool which has forty seahs [of fit water], less a qortob and a qortob of one of them fell into it — they have not raised it[s volume]. It spoils it at three logs. But (1) other liquids, and (2) fruit juice, and (3) brine, and (4) fish brine, and (5) grape skin wine which has fermented — sometimes they raise, and sometimes they do not raise. How so? An immersion pool which contains forty seahs, lacking one — a seah of one of them fell into it — it does not raise it. [If] it contained forty seahs, and one put in a seah and took out a seah — lo, this is fit.

T. 5:8 Snowballs which are sunk down into an immersion-pool — lo, they raise the level of the water.

T. 5:9 Water in which food has been pressed or seethed, and olive-water they immerse in it, and on condition that it does not contain sediment of oil. And the grape-skin wine before it has fermented — they do not immerse in it.

M. 7:3 [If] one rinsed in it [an immersion pool] baskets of olives and baskets of grapes, and they changed its color, it is valid. [If] wine and olive sap fell into it and changed its color, it is unfit. What should one do? He should wait on it until rain falls and its color returns to the color of water. [If] there were forty seahs [of fit water] in it, one may draw [water in buckets and carry it] on his shoulder and pour it into it, until its [the pool's] color returns to the color of water.

M. 7:4 [If] wine or olive sap fell into it and changed the color of part of it [the water], and forty seahs of [fit] water are not in it — lo, this one should not immerse in it.

T. 5:10 An immersion-pool which does not have forty *seahs* [of fit water], and one puts into it wine, and its color changes — it is not made unfit in the measure of three *logs*. And not only so, but even if its color returned to what it had been, [the pool] is fit [to be added to]. [If] there were in it forty *seahs* [of fit water], and wine fell in and its color changed in part, he who immerses, whether in the place of the water or in the place of the wine, is as if he did not immerse. [If] three *logs* of wine fell in, it is as if they did not fall in. [If] it was drawn water and one made it touch — [if] he made it touch at the place of the wine, this and this have not become clean. [If] one touched [them together] at the place where the water is located, it is clean. [If he touched it] at the place [at which] the wine [is located], it is not clean.

T. 5:11 A jar which broke in the Great Sea and the color of that place is like the color of that wine — he who immerses in that place is as if he did not immerse. And not only so, but even if a loaf of heave-offering fell there, it is unclean.

M. 7:5 Three logs of [drawn] water — and into them fell a qortob of wine — and lo, their color is the color of wine — and they fell into the immersion pool — they have not rendered it unfit. Three logs of water, lacking a qortob — and a qortob of milk fell into them, and lo, their color is the color of the water — and they fell into the immersion pool — they have not rendered it unfit.

M. 7:6 An immersion pool which contains exactly forty seahs — two people went down and immersed in it, one after the other — the first is clean, and the second is unclean. [If] one immersed the thick mantle in it and brought it up, and part of it is touching the water, it [the pool still] is clean. The cushion or mattress of leather once one has lifted their lips out of the water, the water in them is deemed drawn water. What should he do? He should immerse them and raise them by their bottoms.

T. 5:12 An immersion-pool which contains exactly forty *seahs,* and two people went down and immersed one after the other — the first is clean, and the second is unclean. What should one do? While the first still is in the water, one should draw [water in utensils and carry it] on the shoulder and put it into it, and it is clean.

T. 5:13 [If] one immersed in it a large kettle. lo, this is unclean, because the water gushes forth. What should one do? He puts it in with its mouth downward and turns it over and immerses it, and raises it up by its bottom.

M. 7:7 [If] one immersed the bed therein, even though its legs sink down into thick mud — it is clean, because the water touched them before [the mud did]. An immersion pool, the water of which is [tool shallow [to cover the body] — one presses down, even with bundles of wood, even with bundles of reeds, so that the [level of the] water may rise,. and he goes down and immerses. An [unclean] needle which is located on the steps of the cavern — [if] one stirred the water to and fro — after a wave has broken over it, it is clean.

T. 5:14 He who jumps into an immersion-pool, lo, such a one is blameworthy. He who immerses twice in an immersion-pool, lo, this one is blameworthy. This one says to his fellow, "Press your hand down on me in the immersion-pool" — lo, this one is blameworthy.

M. 8:1 The Land of Israel is clean, and its immersion pools are clean. The immersion pools of the peoples which are [located] outside of the Land are fit for those who have had a seminal issue, even though they have been filled with water from a swape well. Those which are in the Land of Israel which are outside the town gate are fit even for menstruating women. Those which are inside the town gate are fit for those who have had a seminal issue. And they are unfit for all [other] unclean people.

T. 6:1 Samaritan territory [in the Land of Israel] is clean, [and] its immersion-pools and its dwellings and its paths are clean. The land of the gentiles [in the Land of Israel] is unclean, [and] its immersion-pools and its dwellings and its paths are unclean. The immersion-pools of the gentiles which are outside of the Land are fit for those who have suffered a pollution, and unfit for all [other] unclean Israelites. Those in the Land of Israel which are outside the town gate are fit for all unclean people, and it does not need saying, for an Israelite who has had a seminal emission. And those which are inside the gate are unfit for those who have had a seminal issue, and, it does not require saying, for all unclean people.

T. 6:4 A bath whose bath-attendants are gentiles, when its filters are open to the private domain, is unclean. [When they are open] to the public domain, it is clean [fit]. A bath whose bath-attendants are gentiles, and which an Israelite entered in the morning and touched [the waters of which to a fit immersion- pool] — even though this [gentile] goes in and the other comes out, is clean. [If] it was locked or if it was designated as private property, it is unclean.]

M. 8:2 These are those who have had a seminal emission who require immersion: [if] one noticed urine [issuing] in drops or turbid — at the outset, he is clean. [If these occur] in the middle or at the end [of urinating], he is unclean. [If he notices them] from beginning to end of urination, he is clean. [If they are] white and viscous, he is unclean. He who dreams erotic dreams by night and arose and found his flesh [penis] heated is [assumed to be] unclean.

M. 8:4 A gentile woman who discharged semen from an Israelite is unclean, An Israelite woman who discharged semen from a gentile is clean. The woman who had sexual relations and went down and immersed but did not clean the house is as if she did not immerse. A person who has had an emission who immersed and did not first urinate when he does urinate is unclean.

T. 6:5 He who dreams erotic dreams by night and arose and found his flesh hot is unclean. [If] he dreamt erotic dreams but was not heated, or [if] he was heated but did not dream erotic dreams, he is clean.

T. 6:7 The semen of an Israelite under all circumstances, lo, this is unclean. And that of a gentile, under all circumstances, is clean, except for the urine in which it is located. All those concerning which they have said that they are clean [are clean] for unconsecrated food and unclean for heave-offering, except for the woman who discharges semen, who is unclean for unconsecrated food.

The opening exposition, M. 7:1ff. classifies various liquids in solid form or in mixtures in relationship to the immersion pool. The criteria for classifying the mixtures are standard, not particular to the category-formation at hand, e.g., which component of the mixture imparts its traits to the entire mixture?

VI. Using the Immersion Pool. The Matter of Interposition

M. 8:5 A menstruating woman who placed coins in her mouth and went down and immersed is clean on account of her uncleanness [as a menstruant], but she is unclean because of her spit. If she put her hair in her mouth, closed her hand, pressed her lips together — it is as if she did not immerse. He who kept hold on a man or on utensils and immersed them — they are unclean. And if he rinsed his hand in the water, they are clean. The private parts, [and] the wrinkles — it is not necessary that water should come into them.

M. 9:1 These interpose on man: 1. threads of wool, 2. and threads of flax, 3. and the ribbons which are on the heads of girls. R. Judah says, "Those of wool and those of hair do not interpose, because the water enters into them."

M. 9:2 4. the matted hair over the heart, 5. and [on] the beard, 6. and the woman's privy parts, 7. the pus outside the eye, 8. and the hardened pus outside the wound, 9. and the bandage which is on it, 10. and dried juice, 11. and dried clots of excrement which are on his flesh, 12. and dough which is under the fingernail, 13. and sweat crumbs, 14. and miry clay, 15. and potter's clay, 16. and road clay. What is miry clay? This is clay of pits, as it is written, And he brought me up out of a horrible pit, out of the miry clay (Ps. 40:3). Potter's clay is in accord with its literal sense. And road clay? The pegs by the roadsides in which they do not dip and in which they do not dunk. And all other mud — they dunk in it when it is wet. And one should not dip with the dust which is [still] on his feet. And one should not dunk the kettle with soot, unless one scrapes.

M. 9:3 These are [things] which do not interpose: 1. matted hair of the head, 2. and of the armpits, 3. and of the privy parts of a man. Whatever one takes note of interposes, and whatever one does not take note of does not interpose.

M. 9:4 4. Pus in the eye, 5. and hardened pus in the wound, 6. and moist fruit juice, 7. and moist excrement which is on his flesh, 8. and excrement which is under the fingernail, 9. and a fingernail which is dangling: 10. downy hair of the child is not unclean and does not convey uncleanness. The membrane that grows over a sore is susceptible to uncleanness and conveys uncleanness.

T. 6:8 And as [to the things about which] they have said, "They interpose," and as [to the things about which] they have said, "They do not interpose" they do not convey uncleanness and do not receive cleanness, except for the membrane on the sore. And the bandage which is on the sore, and the splints which are on the fracture, and the chains, and the ear-rings, and the beads, and the rings, when they are tightly-bound, interpose, and when they are loosely bound, they do not interpose.

T. 6:9 A dry poultice which is on the sore, and the eye-paint which is in the eye — lo, these do not interpose. The blood, and the ink, and the honey, and the milk, and mulberry juice, and fig juice, and sycamore juice, and carob juice — when they are dry, interpose, and when they are moist, they do not interpose. And all other juices, whether wet or dry — lo, these interpose for they are gummy. Stains of fruit juice, and the eye-paint which is outside the eye — lo, these interpose.

T. 6:10 And excrement under the fingernail which is not opposite the flesh, the mud, and the dough under the fingernail even opposite the flesh do [not] interpose. The downy hair of an adult, about which he is not fastidious, and the limb and flesh which are dangling in the case of a man, lo, these do interpose.

T. 6:14 And what are the pegs by the road-sides? Those on which people walk in the rainy season, and they are rubbed against [and stick to the garments].Ss As to clothing: [mud] on one side does not interpose. On both sides, it interposes.

T. 7:1 [If] one tied his hands and feet together and sat down in a stream of water — if the water covered his whole [body], he is clean. And if not, he is unclean. [If] his hands and feet were covered with dust, and he went down and immersed in an immersion-pool which contains forty *seahs,* he is clean. [If] he rubbed [his hands or feet], or [if] he immersed in hot water, he is unclean. A kettle which is full of soot and which one immersed is unclean. [If] one polished it or immersed it in hot water, it is clean.

T. 7:10 [If] there was a single hair outside of the sore, and its head cleaves to the sore, or [if] there were on him two hairs, and their tops cleaved to the knots surrounding the anus or excrement, lo, these interpose. [If] there were on him two hairs on his eyelids below, and they pierce a way through to the eyelids above — this was a case, and five sages in Lud took a vote concerning it and declared it unclean.

M. 9:5 These interpose in utensils: (1) pitch, (2) and the gum of myrrh. On glass utensils — whether inside or outside. On the table, and on the tray, and on the couch — on the clean ones, they interpose, and on the dirty ones, they do not interpose. On the beds belonging to the householder it interposes, and on those be — longing to the poor man, it does not interpose. On the saddle of the householder it interposes, and on that of the water-skin carriers, it does not interpose. On a packsaddle it interposes.

M. 9:6 On garments: On one side, it does not interpose. On both sides, it interposes.

M. 9:7 [As to] the aprons of pitch workers or potters or tree trimmers — they do not interpose. This is the general rule: Whatever one takes note of interposes, and whatever one does not take note of does not interpose.

T. 6:11 Whatever [substances] interpose in utensils, interpose in the case of the menstruating woman and in the case of the convert at the time of immersion. And in connection with [immersion for eating] unconsecrated food, they do not interpose.

T. 6:12 A ring which one put into a brick of wet mud, and which one immersed, is clean. If it was miry clay and [mud] like it, it is as if one did not immerse it.

T. 6:13 A flagon which is full of unclean water, and moist mud is placed on its mouth — if the water reaches down into the mud, and one dunked it, it is clean. If it was miry clay and its equivalents, it is as if one did not immerse it.

T. 6:15 Pitch which is on the cup and which is on the flask — [if] it is on its inside, it interposes; and [if] it is on the outside, it does not interpose. Under what circumstances? At the factory. But [if it belongs to] the householder, whether it is inside it or on its outer parts, lo, this interposes. In the case of a tray and dish, whether it is on the inside or whether it is on the outside, whether at the factory or at home, lo, this interposes.

T. 6:16 Gum of myrrh and resin, whether in the case of a cup or in the case of a flask, or whether in the case of the tray or whether in the case of the dish, whether on the inside, or on the outside whether at the factory or at home — lo, these interpose. [Mud] on the sandal: — [if it is] on its inside and above, it interposes and [if it is] on the lower part [of the inside], it does not interpose. And [mud] on the bench: [if it is] on top [or] on the sides, it interposes, and if it is below, it does not interpose.

T. 6:17 [As to] pieces of excrement which are on the toilet and on the chairs [or: pots] — those which are pressed down — whether on the inside or on the outside, whether below or on the sides, lo, these interpose. Those which are on the bed of the householder — if it is on the outer frame it interposes, and if it is on the inner, it does not interpose.

T. 6:18 Moist wine lees which are in the cup and the flask, and the fluff on a chain or a bell, and the mud and the dough which are on the handle of the ax and on the handle of a shovel — lo, these do not interpose. [If] they turned solid, lo, they interpose.

M. 10:1 **All handles of utensils (1) which one affixed not in their usual fashion, or (2) which one affixed in their usual fashion but did not fix firmly, or (3) which one did fix firmly but which broke — lo, these interpose. A utensil which one immersed downward — it is as if it did not immerse. [If] one immersed it in its usual way, without [immersing] the handle, [it is not deemed immersed] until he will turn it on its side. A utensil which is narrow on both ends and broad in the middle is not clean until one will turn it on its side. A flask the mouth of which is turned downward is not clean until one will make a hole on its side. The ink-pot of an ordinary person is not clean until one will make a hole in its side. The ink-pot of Joseph the Priest was perforated on its side.**

T. 6:19 All handles of utensils which are affixed in the ordinary way, lo, these do not interpose. [If] one put pitch or wax, whether in the place of the hollow [of the handle] or whether in the place of the spout, lo, these do not interpose. [If] one put them in not in the normal way, lo, these interpose. [If] one put pitch or wax, whether in the place of the hole or in the place of the spout, lo, these interpose.

T. 6:20 All handles of utensils which broke, for example, the handle of the sickle, and the handle of the knife, if they serve their original function, interpose, and if not, they do not interpose.

T. 6:21 The sickle, the handle of which was broken within that part of the handle which is indispensable in using the tool, does not interpose, because it is equivalent to the private parts. [If it is broken] beyond the indispensable part of the handle, if it serves its original function, it does not interpose; and if not, lo, this interposes. [If] one joined it with reed grass or with rope, lo, this interposes. [If] one affixed it with resin, lo, this does not interpose.

T. 6:22 A utensil which is narrow on both ends and broad in the middle, for example a quarter-measure and a half-quarter measure — can never have purification, until one will turn it on its side. A flask, the rim of which is flattened downwards into its midst, and the shoulders of which are high, and so a flagon, the rim of which is flattened downwards into its midst and the shoulders of which are high — can never have purification until one will turn it [on its side].

T. 6:23 A flask the lip of which is turned outward — one immerses it and raises it by its bottom.

M. 10:2 **(1) The mattress and (2) the pillow of leather — lo, these require that the water come into them. (1) The round pillow, and (2) the ball, and (3) the shoemaker's last, and (4) the amulet, and (5) the phylactery do not require that the water come into them. This is the general principle: Whatever it is not the way to put in and take out — they immerse sealed up.**

M. 10:3 **These [are objects] which do not require that the water enter into them: 1. the knots of the poor man, 2. and the tassels, 3. and the knotted thong of the sandal, 4. and the phylactery of the head when it is fastened tightly, 5. and**

that of the arm when it does not move up and down, 6. and the hand-grip of a
water-skin, 7. and the hand-grip of a shepherd's wallet.

**M. 10:4 These are [objects] which require that the water enter into them: 1. the
knot of undergarments which [is tied to] the shoulder, 2. and the hem of sheets
(-it is necessary to unstitch-) 3. and the phylactery of the head when it is not
fastened tightly, 4. and that of the arm when it moves up and down, 5. and the
straps of a sandal. And clothing which one immersed washed — [they must
remain in the water merely] until they bulge. If one immersed them dry, [they
must remain in the water] until they will bulge and cease from bulging.**

T. 7:2 Baskets of the wine-press and of the olive-press — [when] they [the holes
therein] are tightly packed [by grapes or olives] — one needs [to clean them by]
picking. And [when] they are loose, one needs to shake [them loose, so water will
permeate the basket]. The knots of the money-bag and of the bands, and the knots
of the shoe and sandal, and the knots of the hole of a shirt [of a woman] — these
interpose. The knots of the fringes of a money-bag, and bands, and the knots of
the thongs of the shoe, and the sandal, and the knot of the undergarment which is
on the shoulder, and the sheet the fringes of which one tied up, lo, these interpose.
[If] they were knotted on their own, lo, these do not interpose.

T. 7:3 The knots of the poor person about which he is fastidious and [those] of the
householder — lo, these interpose. And the knots of the householder about which
he is not fastidious and those of the poor man — lo, these do not interpose.

**M. 10:5 All handles of utensils which are too long and which one is going to cut off
— one immerses them up to the place of [their proper] measure. The chain of
a large bucket [is immersed to a length of] four handbreadths [from the bucket],
and that of a small [bucket] is [immersed to a length of] ten [handbreadths
from the bucket]. They immerse them up to the place of [their proper] measure.
The rope which is tied to the basket is not connected, unless one has sewed [it
on to the bucket].**

T. 7:3B And R. Judah says, "One has to immerse the whole thing on account of [the
place where the handle is intended to be] lopped off." And so did R. Judah say in
the name of R. Tarfon, "One has to immerse the entire ring."

**M. 10:6 They do immerse [unclean] hot water in cold [immersion pool water], and
not cold in hot, and not fresh water in foul, and not foul water in fresh. An
[unclean] utensil which is full of liquid and which one immersed is as if it did
not immerse. [If it is] full of urine, they regard it as if it were water. [If it is]
full of purification water, [it is not clean] until the water [of the immersion
pool that enters the utensil] exceeds the purification water.**

T. 7:4 A utensil which is full of wine and which one immersed, if its [the wine's] color
is [so diluted as to be] annulled, it is clean, and if not, it is unclean. [If] it was
filled with white wine or milk, if it [the water of the immersion-pool that enters
the utensil] exceeds it [the wine or milk], it is clean. If not it is unclean.

**M. 10:7 All [unclean] foods join together to render the body unfit [for eating heave
offering] at the measure of a half a loaf. All [unclean] liquids join together to
render the body unfit at the measure of a quarter-log. This [rule] is more
strict in the case of one who drinks unclean liquids than in the case of an
immersion pool, for [in the present case] they treat other liquids as equivalent
to water.**

T. 7:5 All foods join together to render the body invalid in the measure of a half a loaf
— in the time that it takes to eat a loaf. [If] one ate and went back and ate again
and went back and ate again, if from the beginning of the first act of eating to the
end of the last act of eating, [the time has elapsed which is] sufficient for eating a
loaf, they join together, and if not, they do not join together. And they do not
require him who eats less than the required measure to go down and immerse. But
one who eats in accord with the established measure goes down and immerses.
[If] one ate less than the established measure and goes down and immerses in the
middle, he is unclean.

T. 7:6 They permitted a woman who is pregnant to taste a small quantity [of unclean
food], because of the danger to life.

T. 7:7 All liquids join together to render the body invalid for eating heave-offering —
in [the case of one who] drinks a quarter-log in the time it takes to eat a loaf [or:
to drink a quarter-log]. [If] one drank and went and drank again and went and
drank again, if [the time elapsed] from the beginning of the first act of drinking to
the end of the last act of drinking is sufficient for the drinking of a quarter-log [or:
to eat a loaf], they join together, and if not, they do not join together. They do not
make him liable who drinks less than the established measure to go down and
immerse. But he drinks in the established measure and goes down and immerses.
[If] one drank ¹ess than the established measure and went down and immersed in
the middle, he is clean. They permitted a woman who touches something which
has touched an object unclean with corpse-uncleanness to suckle her child, and
he is clean.

**M. 10:8 [If] one ate unclean food or drank unclean liquids, immersed, the n vomited
them up — they are unclean, because they are not cleaned with the body. [If]
he drank unclean water, immersed, and vomited it up — it is clean, because it
is cleaned with the body. If one swallowed a clean ring, entered the Tent of the
corpse, was sprinkled and repeated the sprinkling and immersed and then
vomited it up — lo, it is as it was [clean]. If one swallowed an unclean ring, he
immerses, eats heave offering, then vomited it up — it is unclean and renders
him unclean. An arrow which is stuck in a man — when it is apparent to the
eye, it interposes, and if it is not apparent to the eye, he immerses and eats his
heave offering.**

T. 7:8 [If] one swallowed an olive's bulk of corpse-matter and entered a house, it is
clean, for whatever is swallowed by man or cattle or beast or fowl is clean. [If] it
decomposed or emerged from below [the rectum], it is clean. [If] one drank unclean
water and vomited it up, it is unclean, because it was made unclean when it went
out. [If] one immersed, or [if] it decomposed or it came out below, it is clean. [If]
one drank other [unclean] liquids even though he immersed and vomited them
out, they are unclean, because they are not made clean in the body. [If] they
decomposed or went forth, they are clean.

T. 7:9 A cow which drank unclean water and vomited it up — it is unclean, because it
is not made clean in the body. [If] it decomposed or went out below, it is clean. He
into whose knee an arrow penetrated — lo, this interposes. Under what
circumstances? In the case of one made of metal. But in the case of one made of
wood, lo, this interposes. And if the flesh formed a membrane over it, all agree
that it does not interpose, for whatever is swallowed up in man, cattle, beast, and

fowl is clean [If] pieces of gravel or splinters went into the cracks beneath his feet, it does not interpose, because it is like the privy parts.

What interposes between man and the water of the immersion pool and so impedes the process of purification through contact with the water is what man takes into account, and what does not interpose is that of which he does not take cognizance. So attitude governs: Whatever one takes note of interposes, and whatever one does not take note of does not interpose. The rule for handles carries us to the matter of connection and is familiar in its principle from Kelim.

IV. THE HERMENEUTICS OF MIQVAOT

A. WHAT FUSES THE HALAKHIC DATA INTO A CATEGORY-FORMATION?

While dealing with the hierarchization of six classifications of water, at its center the Halakhah contrasts the immersion pool of forty seahs of still water with the flowing water of the spring, which, in any volume at all, purifies. Here is where the analogical-contrastive analysis takes place, and so far as the Halakhic data fuse into a coherent category-formation, here is where the particular hermeneutics is realized. All the rest of the category-formation in detail responds to the program of the generic kind, which depends upon the particular hermeneutics for everything but its problematics. The two classifications of water that purifies are alike in that both accomplish purification through water (excluding fire, breakage, and other media Scripture identifies); they are different solely in the obvious fact that spring-water flows, and the immersion-pool is a gathering of still water. Spring water, deriving from the earth, and immersion-pool-water, deriving from heaven, are equivalent in their purificatory power, so long as they are preserved in their natural form. Then living water removes corpse-uncleanness, and still water, uncleanness of other classifications, in general, of much less virulence.

The principal interest of the Halakhah is in the definition of that water that serves for removing uncleanness through immersion in a valid immersion-pool, and nearly the entire repertoire of detailed, analytical exercises concerns the collection and utilization of that pool's water. That is what fuses the Halakhic data into the category-formation, Miqvaot, and to that matter, all else is subordinate. Essentially, the Halakhah makes two points, one concerning the character of the water, which carries the entire particular hermeneutics of the category-formation, the other, its required volume, which precipitates many of the problems raised by the generic hermeneutics. In this context, we note, it is the generic hermeneutics that predominates, so to claim that the particular hermeneutics fuses the Halakhic data into the present category-formation is to overstate matters. The Halakhic tractate does not fuse so much as it holds together nicely by reason of its topic, not because of the cogency of the twin-hermeneutics, particular and generic, that yields the exegetical program for the topical exposition. In this respect, the paramount position of the particular hermeneutics in Kelim and Ohalot forms a striking contrast. Take away the generic hermeneutics and we still have formidable category-formations in both cases. Remove the generic hermeneutics from Miqvaot and we scarcely have a category-formation worthy of the name, substantive and encompassing.

The particular hermeneutics nonetheless is exquisitely realized, and, situated at the outset, the beautifully articulated composite makes the statement that is unique to the category-formation. The opening unit could not state matters more lucidly or expose its generative method more clearly than it does in its taxonomy of types of water and their hierarchization.[1] Water that has flowed and collected naturally or that flows on its own removes uncleanness; drawn water will not. Stagnant pool water serves for cleanness for dough-offering and for washing hands; rain water that still flows is suitable for washing for heave-offering and hand-washing; immersion pool water in the correct volume is suitable for removing uncleanness from men and utensils; and living or flowing spring water serves for removing corpse-uncleanness and that which is analogous to it.

Let me spell out this hierarchical classification-scheme, fully exposed in the Halakhah.

[1] Water in insufficient volume or of inappropriate character both receives and transmits uncleanness. Such water is called "water in ponds." But it encompasses a variety of types of water; what all have in common is that they are of insufficient volume: All the same are (1) water of ponds, (2) water of cisterns, (3) water of ditches, (4) water of caverns, (5) water of rain drippings which have stopped, and (6) immersion pools which do not contain forty seahs. During the rainy season, all such collections of water are clean. When the rain ends, those that are near the village and the road are unclean. And those that are far are clean, until the larger numbers of people have passed by. That is the kind of water that fully participates in the system of uncleanness.

[2] Then we come to water that serves for immersion-pools, meaning, water that, in requisite volume, removes uncleanness. At this next level we deal with bodies of water that are still receiving the run-off of rain. Such bodies of water do not contract uncleanness but remove uncleanness. These serve for immersion. The suitable type of water — rain-drippings — is defined as follows: "And what are rain-drippings? So long as the rains fall, and the mountains trickle with water lo, they are like the water of a spring. If they ceased to trickle, *lo*, they are like the water of pools."

---

[1] For the microbiological bases for these same distinctions among types of water, see Aloys Hüttermann, "Water and Purity: Microbiology and the Precepts of the Torah, Mishnah, and Talmud," in *Annual of Rabbinic Judaism, Ancient, Medieval, and Modern* (Leiden, 1999: E. J. Brill), ed. by Alan J. Avery-Peck, Volume I. Hütterman explains why flowing water or water in cisterns differs from the other types of water listed here.

[3] The third level of water is constituted by a pool of water, collected rain-drippings, that has the requisite volume, forty seahs, to cover the body of a person who immerses therein. Such a pool of water is suitable for immersion for removal of uncleanness or for dunking utensils for the same purpose.

[4] The fourth level is flowing, or spring-water, mixed with drawn water that forms the larger part of the volume. That is interstitial, bearing traits of the immersion-pool and of the spring. It removes uncleanness, like standing water, and it may serve in any small volume at all to clean utensils. The full measure of forty seahs required for still water is not required for spring water.

[5] The fifth sort is spring water that is "smitten," or turbid at times; when that water flows, it serves.

[6] Sixth, at the apex is flowing, or living water, which serves for the purification rites for removing corpse-uncleanness and its counterparts, the uncleanness of the Zab and of the *nega'*.

That, some and substance, sets forth the category-formation in all of its particularity: cogent and orderly and proportionate and compelling. All the rest of the category-formation serves to ask the conventional exegetical questions of clarification that the generic hermeneutics precipitates.

B. THE ACTIVITY OF THE CATEGORY-FORMATION

WATER FOR THE IMMERSION-POOL, ITS CHARACTER AND VOLUME. The water of type three, collected rain-drippings, for the immersion-pool must accumulate naturally, deriving from the run-off of rain and equivalent natural sources, e.g., sea-water. It may not be drawn by human action. But by the indirect action of man it may be led into the pool on its own, e.g., in a duct. So the main point is that it must not be drawn water or in any way collected through human intentionality and intervention. In volume, the immersion pool must be comprised of sufficient water to cover the entire body of a human being. Insufficient pools may be intermingled through a whole of a given size. One may further pipe valid water, e.g., a higher pool may be emptied into a lower pool to form the requisite volume. But one may not carry or draw the water. As we noted, what validates water for the purification-rite invalidates it for the immersion-pool. Drawn water may be used to augment the volume of a valid pool, meaning, a small quantity of drawn water is neutralized by, and fully integrated with, valid water. If water collects in jugs, one may break the jugs or turn them outside down, with the water flowing naturally into the cistern. But he may not pick up the jugs and empty them into the cistern. Mud of an appropriate character may serve.

If an immersion pool is of insufficient volume, the addition of water in solid form, e.g., snow, hail, ice, and the like, may raise the volume to the required level. Drawn water, by contrast, invalidates the insufficient volume of rain-water and does not raise it to the requisite volume. If wine or olive sap change the color of the pool, the pool is unfit until the color of water is restored. If two people descend into an immersion pool that contains exactly forty seahs of water, the first is clean by the immersion, but the second is not, because the first party has removed enough water to reduce the volume to less than is required.

DRAWN WATER, HUMAN INTERVENTION. CASES. Any sort of man-made utensil serving as a catchment for gathering rain-water is ruled out. He who makes a cavity in the waterspout to catch the pebbles in the rainwater — if it is of wood, it renders the immersion pool invalid as a receptacle to catch rainwater if it holds any amount at all. And if it is of earthenware, it renders the immersion pool invalid if it holds a quarter-log. While a man-made utensil may not be used, a trough hewn in rock is permitted, but one that was free-standing and then attached to the rock is forbidden. And, conversely, a trough hewn in the rock may not be used for drawing water for use with the ashes of the red cow or mixing the ashes or sprinkling said water. Spring water that one passed into a trough is unfit, but what flows over the edge remains in its status as free-flowing water. Spring water may be drawn forward, and it also may be augmented by drawn water. If spring water was standing still and augmented with drawn water and made to flow further, it is deemed an immersion pool, that is, it purifies in still water, but also is equivalent to spring for immersion in even less than forty seahs.

Drawn water absolutely may not be used for the immersion pool; a person on the greater part of whose body drawn water is poured in the volume of three logs is unclean. The Tosefta's formulation is clear: A clean person on whose head and the greater part of whose body three *logs* of drawn water have fallen is unclean. If they fell on his head but not on the greater part of his body, on the greater part of his body but not on his head if they fell on his head and on the greater part of his body whether from above or whether from the side — he is clean — until they fall on his head and the greater part of his body in the usual way. Accordingly, water that is subject to human action and intent not only does not purify but contaminates.

THE USE OF THE IMMERSION POOL: The person must immerse fully, even to the fingertips, and the pool must contain forty seahs of water to make that immersion possible. Cases of doubt in instances of major uncleanness are generally resolved in favor of the status quo; the unclean person is assumed to remain unclean who has not definitively immersed in a valid pool. In instances of minor uncleanness, they are resolved in favor of cleanness.

Issues of interposition carry us to the generic hermeneutics of connection and mixture. The water must be able to reach all parts of the body-surface; what interposes between the water and the person invalidates the immersion. The same is so for utensils; pitch and the like interpose. This is expressed very simply: A menstruating woman who placed coins in her mouth and went down and immersed is clean on account of her uncleanness as a menstruant, but she is unclean because of her spit. If she put her hair in her mouth, closed her hand, pressed her lips together — it is as if she did not immerse. He who kept hold on a man or on utensils and immersed them — they are unclean. And if he rinsed his hand in the water, they are clean. As to handles, if they are tightly affixed in the ordinary way, they are integral to the utensil and do not interpose.

Here is a point at which intentionality enters in. Whatever one takes note of interposes, and whatever one does not take note of does not interpose. If one is going to cut off part of a handle, the part that he is not going to cut off is part of the utensil and affected by its immersion. All of these rulings express in context the principles of the Halakhah of Kelim and Uqsin.

C. THE CONSISTENCY OF THE CATEGORY-FORMATION

The particular hermeneutics cannot be said to pervade the category-formation. The topical exposition responds to the generic hermeneutics described in Chapter Seven.

D. THE GENERATIVITY OF THE CATEGORY-FORMATION

The paradox of water is that it both contracts and also removes uncleanness. It imparts susceptibility to uncleanness, when deliberately put onto seed for example, and among other liquids water also receives uncleanness when touched by a source of uncleanness. But under some conditions, in correct volume, deriving from the appropriate source, water also has the power to diminish or even remove uncleanness, still water the former, flowing water the latter. So, it is clear, the Halakhic structure deals with diverse classifications of water, on the one side, and with rules governing those classifications of water that bear the power to remove uncleanness but then do not themselves receive uncleanness, on the other. But within the present category-formation, only one component of the entire structure is represented, the particular type of water that Heaven provides and man must not affect. Once that point is made, nothing follows, so far as I can see. That component does not lead to conceptions that, by reason of the principle that is contained in a given case, transcend the topic under discussion. By that criterion, we cannot point to how generative power of the particular hermeneutics vastly extends the limits of present category-formative.

But when we take a step back and see Miqvaot and Parah as they should be seen — species of a common genus — then matters change considerably. Parah insists that man intervene in the preparation of the water for the purification-mixture that will remove corpse uncleanness, Miqvaot forbids man from intervening in the preparation of the water for the purification of uncleanness of other sorts. Why is the uncleanness of the soul treated differently?

The contrast points to a judgment that leads us beyond the limits of the category-formation, Miqvaot, the point of its generativity. Man's supreme act of will, embodying intentionality in highly-purposive activity, can overcome even the effects of death. If the Halakhah wished to say, man can overcome death through the correct and deliberate attitude, it could not have embodied that message in more powerful language than the activities required for the formulation of purification-water. *Man's act of will overcomes the uncleanness of death, just as man's willful act of deliberate rebellion brought about death to begin with.* Man restores what man has disrupted. As to the rest, man refrains from deliberate action, and nature, providing purifying water from heaven, accomplishes the restoration. That is because the other forms of uncleanness come about by nature's own failure to realize itself, so nature provides the medium of the removal of the consequence: water that Heaven supplies naturally matches nature's condition. But since death comes about by reason of Adam's and Eve's original act of will, their heirs' supreme act of concentration and deliberation upon doing things as God wants them done is required to bring about the preparation of the medium of purification. That view of matters is made explicit in the Aggadic account, part of which we have already noted, of how Adam acknowledged that he bore full responsibility for his own fate, and built into the human condition, therefore, is that same recognition:

A. It is written, "Thus said the Lord, What wrong did your fathers find in me that they went far from me and went after worthlessness and became worthless?" (Jer. 2:5)

B. Said R. Isaac, "This refers to one who leaves the scroll of the Torah and departs. Concerning him, Scripture says, 'What wrong did your fathers find in me that they went far from me.'

C. "Said the Holy One, blessed be He, to the Israelites, 'My children, your fathers found no wrong with me, but you have found wrong with me.

Now a case — the archetypal one, man himself — will illustrate the generalization contained within the statement of Isaac. People who violate the Torah do so on their own volition, not by reason of a tradition of rebellion. They therefore bear responsibility for their own sins. Man is the archetype; he brings upon himself his own death:

J. "So too all the generations came to the first Man, saying to him, 'Is it possible that the Holy One, blessed be He, is imposing the attribute of justice on you?'

K. He said to them, 'God forbid. I am the one who has brought about my own death. Thus did he command me, saying to me, 'Of all the trees of the garden you may eat, but of the tree of the knowledge of good and evil you may not eat' (Gen. 2:17). When I violated his instructions, I brought about my own death, for it is written, 'On the day on which you eat it, you will surely die '(Gen. 2:17)."

Pesiqta deRab Kahana XIV:V.1

God is not at fault for Adam's fall; Adam brought about his own death. It was through an act of deliberation and will. So let an act of deliberation and will remove the consequence corpse-uncleanness. Had the Halakhah wished in its terms and categories to accomplish a reprise of the story of man's fall, it could not have made a more eloquent statement than it does in the contrast between the Halakhah of Miqvaot and that of Parah. To what man has caused man must pay full mind, and nature restoring itself to its own purposive condition takes care of the rest.

7

The Generic Hermeneutics
of the Halakhah

Now that we have identified the particular hermeneutics of six Halakhic category-formations, it is time to ask, can we define traits of the generic hermeneutics of the Halakhah? By "generic hermeneutics" I mean, principles of interpretation of Halakhic category-formations that pertain everywhere, not being specific to a given topic? What are analytical procedures that apply throughout?

The category-formations of the Halakhah, the hermeneutics of which we seek (hypothetically) to reconstruct and to describe through a process of analogical-contrastive analysis, come to full realization in the Mishnah, ca. 200 C.E. That is clear from the sample now surveyed. The successive compilations, the Tosefta, Yerushalmi, and Bavli, recapitulate the received hermeneutics. In Chapters One through Six, for each category-formation, we have seen a striking fact. It is that the outline of the Mishnah's presentation of the details of the law, yielding its exegetical program, defines the structure of the Halakhah for the Tosefta-Yerushalmi-Bavli as well.

The Tosefta contains some free-standing, autonomous compositions and even composites; I found little in the Yerushalmi or the Bavli; and none of the successor-documents radically revised the received category-formations and their hermeneutics. The Tosefta, the Talmud of the Land of Israel and Talmud of Babylonia take up the tasks of exegesis, along lines defined to begin with by the Mishnah's category-formations and the hermeneutics that animates them. Occasionally in the Tosefta, and still less commonly in the two Talmuds, we find composites that respond to the logic of a different theory of category-formation and, consequently, can have generated a hermeneutics and a detailed exegetics of a quite different character from the governing one that is laid down by the Mishnah.

II. THE MISHNAH AS THE SOURCE OF THE HALAKHAH'S GENERIC HERMENEUTICS

That is so not only in form — the later documents depend for order and structure on the Mishnah — but in substance. For the topical logic inherent in the Mishnah's presentation of the category-formation frames that category-formation's particular hermeneutics. That fact has been established in Chapters One through Six. The particular hermeneutics framed by the Mishnah further dictates the character of the exegetical program embodied in the actualities as amplified and extended by the Mishnah-Tosefta-Yerushalmi-Bavli. So the Mishnah sets forth not only the starting point in temporal order, it defines also the matrix of the whole. The continuator-documents refine, clarify, augment, extend, improve upon — but they rarely innovate in fundamental ways and they never radically revise the received category-formations and their particular hermeneutics.

Since the Mishnah's program predominates, it follows that any account of the particular hermeneutics of the Halakhic category-formations will focus upon the Mishnah's presentation of matters, that is to say, the Mishnah's framers' decision to organize data by particular topics and their indicative traits. The hypothetical reconstruction of the thought-processes of analogical-contrastive analysis that — I allege — yielded the hermeneutics of the category-formations in our hands has already shown us the result. The Mishnah therefore accomplishes not only the first but also the definitive realization of the generic hermeneutics.

When we come to the generic hermeneutics of the Halakhah, therefore, we find ourselves in a familiar situation. What applies to the particular hermeneutics of the category-formations equally pertains to the generic hermeneutics that transcend the bounds of the category-formations. The generic hermeneutics set forth by the Mishnah plays itself out through the Tosefta's contribution to the same category-formation (though not to the entirety of the Tosefta's part), and thereafter through the two Talmuds' contributions (to the extent that they contribute at all). We have already noted how the Halakhic category-formations respond not only to a hermeneutics particular to the topics thereof, but also to a generic hermeneutics that diverse topics serve to realize. Much of the Halakhah, we now realize, undertakes the exegesis of problems precipitated by generic and not particular hermeneutics, thus a hermeneutics that transcends the topical category-formations and extends to them all. The Halakhah, for instance, builds upon the hierarchical classification of data, so issues of interstitiality — rules of how we classify and hierarchize data responsive to distinctive taxonomic considerations — demand attention. Here the large and general question is, can we through cases produce rules for sorting out issues of interstitiality? So too, issues of connection and mixtures, the resolution of doubts, and the one in which one thing produces many and many things return to one — these issues arise in many contexts and take many forms. But the hermeneutics that governs remains constant.

To grasp the generic hermeneutics in its broader, encompassing context, in the remainder of this chapter we examine the fundamental and generative modes of thought that characterize the Halakhic enterprise, whether articulated in response to the generic or the particular hermeneutics that have now been fully exposed. These begin with and are defined by the Mishnah, so I focus my entire discussion on the Mishnah's realization of them.[1] Set forth in this chapter in the framework of the Mishnah, these analytical initiatives that pervade the entire corpus of hermeneutics of the Halakhah are, first, the principles of classification (unit iii), yielding, second, modes of polythetic and hierarchical classification (unit iv) , producing, third, the modes of definition of the genus and its species and the principles of speciation (units v and vi). These principles I implicitly invoked in my hypothetical reconstruction of the thought-processes that yielded the hermeneutics particular to the Halakhic category-formations. Then, in the shank of the book, I define the parts of the generic hermeneutics that I have been able to identify. Colleagues, examining the same data, may discern still others.

III. MAIN PRINCIPLES OF CLASSIFICATION

The Mishnah, in this context therefore the Halakhah viewed whole, forms a massive quest for order, an exercise of classification and then hierarchization of the data of nature and society as mediated by the Torah of Moses. The first six chapters of this study have shown how the quest accomplishes its goals, once the category-formations that classify data have come to definition. But what traits prevail throughout?

In the Mishnah the fundamental purpose of intellectual inquiry is to secure for each thing its correct place in the natural order of the world. If we know the category to which what appears to be an apparent singleton belongs, then we define the rule that governs that item too. In that way we secure for what appears abnormal a normal status. Doing so, we accomplish rational explanation, in this context meaning the task of finding a genus for what appears to be *sui generis,* so beyond rationality. Classification therefore represents the medium by which we explain. By definition, a single rationality pertains to the givens of all being, natural and supernatural, here and above too. The power of intellect, obeying the laws of correct classification or organization of things, holds the whole together in perfect balance, sense, and consequence. At stake in identifying the principles of classification therefore is the correct understanding of the dynamic of the Mishnah.

---

[1] In this presentation I have gone over, making revisions, the results of several of the chapters of *Judaism as Philosophy*, which, while using exactly the same data, aims at establishing, for the Mishnah, not the Halakhah viewed whole, a different thesis from the one set forth in this book. I refer to *Judaism as Philosophy. The Method and Message of the Mishnah.* Columbia, 1991: University of South Carolina Press. Paperback edition: Baltimore, 1999: The Johns Hopkins Uriversity Press.

I see three basic principles that the system repeatedly invokes.

The first is teleological: to identify the correct definition or character of something, its purpose and its essence, and to preserve that essence. So we begin with the thing itself. Our premise is that we can identify the intrinsic or true or inherent traits of a thing, once more, the thing seen by itself, but in teleological context.

But, having our answer, second, we then ask in what way something is like something else, and in what way it differs. Our premise is that in some ways things are like other things, traits may be shared. So we proceed to the comparison of things. That requires us to identify the important traits that impart the definitive character or classification to a variety of distinct things. So we proceed to a labor of comparison and contrast.

The third principle is that like things fall into a single classification, with its rule, and unlike things into a different classification, with the opposite rule. That conception, simple on the surface, defines the prevailing logic throughout the entire philosophy and forms the foundation for the hermeneutics as I reconstruct that process. At no point do we find any other logic in play.

The system of ordering all things in proper place and under the proper rule maintains that like belongs with the like and conforms to the rule governing the like, the unlike goes over to the opposite and conforms to the opposite rule. When we make lists of the like, we also know the rule governing all the items on that list. We know that and one other thing, namely, the opposite rule, governing all items sufficiently like to belong on those lists, but sufficiently unlike to be placed on other lists. That rigorously philosophical logic of analysis, comparison and contrast, served because — so it would seem — in that context it was the only logic deemed able to sustain a system that proposed to make the statement concerning the social order.

The mode of thought is that of natural philosophy, out of which natural science has evolved. That is to say, faced with a mass of facts, we are able [1] to bring order — that is to say, to determine the nature of things — by finding out which items resemble others and, [2] determining the taxic indicator that forms of the lot a single classification, and then [3] determining the single rule to which all cases conform. That method of bringing structure and order out of the chaos of indeterminate facts pertains, on the very surface, to persons, places, things; to actions and attitudes; to the natural world of animals, minerals, vegetables, the social world of castes and peoples, actions and functions, and the supernatural world of the holy and the unclean, the possession of Heaven and the possession of earth, the sanctified and the common.

To understand the conception that everything had that intrinsic character to which I referred, that assured and correct place in the order of things, we move out of these abstractions. First of all, we must ask, is the emphasis on the taxonomic priority of the intrinsic traits of things self-evident or deliberate? If it is merely how things are ordinarily to be done, then my claim that we deal with a coherent mode of analytical thought that derives from intellection competes with the alternative. That is, that we address the mere traits of a received culture, a tradition in other-than-traditional garb. But if I can show that the stress on the taxic priority of the inherent qualities of things forms a choice as against alternatives, then my insistence upon the crafted, not merely the received, character of the writing and its modes of thought finds ample justification. My task then is to demonstrate that people recognized what was at issue and responded in precisely the terms I have outlined to that issue. For that purpose, I turn directly to a sustained critique of the Mishnah's philosophers' insistence that classifications derive from the inherent traits of things. When we realize that some sages rejected the Mishnah's traits, we may recognize that the Mishnah's framers made choices among alternatives, for good reason, with reasonable intent, and others took different views of these same matters: not tradition, but selection on the basis of rationality.

In Sifra,[2] a cogent and sustained discourse about the book of Leviticus, we find a powerful critique of the Mishnah's view of the principles of category-formation. That critique is so specific and pointed as to leave no doubt of the state of affairs. It shows beyond doubt that, in the view of the successors and critics of the Mishnah's framers, we deal with results of intellection, decisions people made to do things in one manner and not in some other: philosophy, not merely tradition. The specificity of that judgment is clear, for the authorship of Sifra cited verbatim passages of the Mishnah and repeatedly criticized the Mishnah's mode of classification by appeal to the traits of things. In that authorship's view the correct classification of things is dictated only by Scripture. Logic that appeals to intrinsic traits, ignoring the classifications dictated by Scripture, is flawed and unreliable. This other principle of the logical classification of things shows a deep affinity for the logic of fixed association, because it appeals to a received and not an intrinsic mode of classification. Specifically, it is *Scripture's* classifications, and not those inherent in things by their very nature and teleology, that alone serves to dictate how we make our lists and so derive our general principles.[3]

How does the Sifra's authorship's critique of the logic of cogent discourse of the Mishnah come to expression? Time and again, — so Sifra's writers claim to show — we can easily demonstrate things have so many and such diverse and contradictory indicative traits that, comparing one thing to something else, we can

---

[2]I refer to my argument in my *Uniting the Dual Torah: Sifra and the Problem of the Mishnah* (Cambridge, 1990: Cambridge University Press), some of the points of which I summarize here.

[3]That fact of logic explains the complementary fact of literary character. It is that Sifra's authorship organizes its propositions through the logic of fixed association, that is, as a commentary, rather than in propositional and even syllogistic form, as do the Mishnah's writers. Scripture dictates not only the correct medium of classification but also the correct representation of propositions: coherent only as Scripture imparts coherence.

always distinguish one species from another. Then there are species but no genus; or — *tant pis!* — there is no species, there are only cases. Even though we find something in common, we also can discern some other trait characteristic of one thing but not the other. Polythetic taxonomy (to which we turn presently) is by itself no solution; it too leads to contradictory results. Consequently, we also can show that the hierarchical logic on which we rely, the argument *a fortiori* or *qol vehomer*, will not serve. For if on the basis of one set of traits which yield a given classification, we place into hierarchical order two or more items, on the basis of a different set of traits, we have either a different classification altogether, or, much more commonly, simply a different hierarchy.[4]

How does the critique of the practical reason of the Mishnah take shape? Time and again Sifra's authorship demonstrates that the formation of classifications based on monothetic taxonomy, that is to say, traits that are not only common to both items but that are shared throughout both items subject to comparison and contrast, simply will not serve. For at every point at which someone alleges uniform, that is to say, monothetic likeness, Sifra's authorship will demonstrate difference. Then how to proceed? Will it be appeal to some shared traits as a basis for classification: this is not like that, and that is not like this, but the indicative trait that both exhibit is such and so, that is to say, polythetic taxonomy? No, that is not a reliable solution. For the self-evident problem in accepting differences among things and insisting, nonetheless, on their monomorphic character for purposes of comparison and contrast, cannot be set aside: *who says*? That is, if I can adduce in evidence for a shared classification of things only a few traits among many characteristic of each thing, then what stops me from treating all things alike? Polythetic taxonomy opens the way to an unlimited exercise in finding what diverse things have in common and imposing, for that reason, one rule on everything. Then the very working of *Listenwissenschaft* as a tool of analysis, differentiation, comparison, contrast, and the descriptive determination of rules yields the opposite of what is desired.

Let us consider one example of how Sifra's authorship rejects the principles of the logic of hierarchical classification precisely as these are worked out by the framers of the Mishnah. I emphasize that the critique applies to the way in which a shared logic is worked out by the other authorship. For it is not the principle that like things follow the same rule, unlike things, the opposite rule, that is at stake. Everyone had known that for millennia. Nor is the principle of hierarchical

---

[4]The attack on the way in which the Mishnah's authorship has done its work appeals to not merely the limitations of classification solely on the basis of traits of things. The more telling argument addresses what is, to *Listenwissenschaft*, the true source of power and compelling consequence: hierarchization. Things are not merely like or unlike, therefore following one rule or its opposite. Things also are weightier or less weighty, and that particular point of likeness of difference generates the logical force of *Listenwissenschaft*.

classification as it is embodied in particular in the argument *a fortiori* at issue. What our authorship disputes is that we can classify things on our own by appeal to the traits or indicative characteristics, that is, utterly without reference to Scripture.

Sifra's argument now is simple. On our own, unaided by the Torah, we cannot classify species into genera. In some way everything is different from everything else. But Scripture tells us what things are like what other things for what purposes, hence Scripture imposes on things the definitive classifications, that and not traits we discern in the things themselves. When we see the nature of the critique, we shall have a clear picture of what is at stake when we examine, in some detail, precisely how the Mishnah's logic does its work. That is why at the outset I present a complete composition in which Sifra's authorship tests the modes of classification characteristic of the Mishnah, resting as they do on the traits of things viewed out of the context of Scripture's categories of things.

5. PARASHAT VAYYIQRA DIBURA DENEDABAH PARASHAH 3

V:I.1 A. "[If his offering is] a burnt offering [from the herd, he shall offer a male without blemish; he shall offer it at the door of the tent of meeting, that he may be accepted before the Lord; he shall lay his hand upon the head of the burnt offering, and it shall be accepted for him to make atonement for him]" (Lev. 1:2):

B. Why does Scripture refer to a burnt offering in particular?

C. For one might have taken the view that all of the specified grounds for the invalidation of an offering should apply only to the burnt-offering that is brought as a freewill offering.

D. But how should we know that the same grounds for invalidation apply also to a burnt offering that is brought in fulfillment of an obligation [for instance, the burnt offering that is brought for a leper who is going through a rite of purification, or the bird brought by a woman who has given birth as part of her purification rite, Lev. 14, 12, respectively]?

E. It is a matter of logic.

F. Bringing a burnt offering as a free will offering and bringing a burnt offering in fulfillment of an obligation [are parallel to one another and fall into the same classification].

G. Just as a burnt offering that is brought as a free will offering is subject to all of the specified grounds for invalidation, so to a burnt offering brought in fulfillment of an obligation, all the same grounds for invalidation should apply.

H. No, [that reasoning is not compelling. For the two species of the genus, burnt offering, are not wholly identical and can be distinguished, on which basis we may also maintain that the grounds for invalidation that pertain to the one do not necessarily apply to the other. Specifically:] if you have taken that position with respect to the burnt offering brought as a free will offering, for which there is no equivalent, will you take the same position with regard to the burnt offering brought in fulfillment of an obligation, for which there is an equivalent? [For if one is obligated to bring a burnt offering by reason of obligation and cannot afford a beast, one may bring birds, as at Lev. 14:22, but if one is bringing a free will offering, a less expensive form of the offering may not serve.]

I.   Accordingly, since there is the possibility in the case of the burnt offering brought in fulfillment of an obligation, in which case there is an acceptable equivalent [to the more expensive beast, through the less expensive birds], all of the specified grounds for invalidation [which apply to the in any case more expensive burnt offering brought as a free will offering] should not apply at all.

J.   That is why in the present passage, Scripture refers simply to "burnt offering," [and without further specification, the meaning is then simple:] all the same are the burnt offering brought in fulfillment of an obligation and a burnt offering brought as a free will offering in that all of the same grounds for invalidation of the beast that pertain to the one pertain also to the other.

2. A.   And how do we know that the same rules of invalidation of a blemished beast apply also in the case of a beast that is designated in substitution of a beast sanctified for an offering [in line with Lev. 27:10, so that, if one states that a given, unconsecrated beast is to take the place of a beast that has already been consecrated, the already-consecrated beast remains in its holy status, and the beast to which reference is made also becomes consecrated]?

B.   The matter of bringing a burnt offering and the matter of bringing a substituted beast fall into the same classification [since both are offerings that in the present instance will be consumed upon the altar, and, consequently, they fall under the same rule as to invalidating blemishes].

C.   Just as the entire protocol of blemishes apply to the one, so in the case of the beast that is designated as a substitute, the same invalidating blemishes pertain.

D.   No, if you have invoked that rule in the case of the burnt offering, in which case no status of sanctification applies should the beast that is designated as a burnt offering be blemished in some permanent way, will you make the same statement in the case of a beast that is designated as a substitute? For in the case of a substituted beast, the status of sanctification applies even though the beast bears a permanent blemish! [So the two do not fall into the same classification after all, since to begin with one cannot sanctify a permanently blemished beast, which beast can never enter the status of sanctification, but through an act of substitution, a permanent blemished beast can be placed into the status of sanctification.]

E.   Since the status of sanctification applies [to a substituted beast] even though the beast bears a permanent blemish, all of the specified grounds for invalidation as a matter of logic should not apply to it.

F. That is why in the present passage, Scripture refers simply to "burnt offering," [and without further specification, the meaning is then simple:] all the same are the burnt offering brought in fulfillment of an obligation and a burnt offering brought as a substitute for an animal designated as holy, in that all of the same grounds for invalidation of the beast that pertain to the one pertain also to the other.

3. A. And how do we know [that the protocol of blemishes that apply to the burnt offering brought as a free will offering apply also to] animals that are subject to the rule of a sacrifice as a peace offering?

B. It is a matter of logic. The matter of bringing a burnt offering and the matter of bringing animals that are subject to the rule of a sacrifice as a peace offering fall into the same classification [since both are offerings and, consequently under the same rule as to invalidating blemishes].

C. Just as the entire protocol of blemishes apply to the one, so in the case of animals that are subject to the rule of a sacrifice as a peace offering, the same invalidating blemishes pertain.

D. And it is furthermore a matter of an argument *a fortiori,* as follows:

E. If to a burnt offering, which is valid when in the form of a bird, [which is inexpensive], the protocol of invalidating blemishes apply, to peace offerings, which are not valid when brought in the form of a bird, surely the same protocol of invalidating blemishes should also apply!

F. No, if you have applied that rule to a burnt offering, in which case females are not valid for the offering as male beasts are, will you say the same of peace offerings? For female beasts as much as male beasts may be brought for sacrifice in the status of the peace offering. [The two species may be distinguished from one another].

G. Since it is the case that female beasts as much as male beasts may be brought for sacrifice in the status of the peace offering, the protocol of invalidating blemishes should not apply to a beast designated for use as peace offerings.

H. That is why in the present passage, Scripture refers simply to "burnt offering," [and without further specification, the meaning is then simple:] all the same are the burnt offering brought in fulfillment of an obligation and an animal designated under the rule of peace offerings, in that all of the same grounds for invalidation of the beast that pertain to the one pertain also to the other.

The difference between burnt offerings and peace offerings is simple. According to Sifra's view, the distinction between them is not that one does not yield meat to the sacrificer or sacrifier [the one who benefits from the offering, e.g., whose sins are atoned for] and the other does. Rather, it is, first, that burnt offerings may be brought only from particular species among beasts and birds, while peace offerings may not be brought from all of them; also, burnt offerings may be brought only from the males of those species, and peace offerings may be brought from both genders.

The systematic exercise proves for beasts that serve in three classifications of offerings, burnt offerings, substitutes, and peace offerings, that the same rules of invalidation apply throughout. The comparison of the two kinds of burnt offerings, voluntary and obligatory, shows that they are sufficiently different from one another so that as a matter of logic, what pertains to the one need not apply to the other. Then come the differences between an animal that is consecrated and one that is designated as a substitute for one that is consecrated. Finally we distinguish between the applicable rules of the sacrifice; a burnt offering yields no meat for the person in behalf of whom the offering is made, while one sacrificed under the rule of peace offerings does. What is satisfying, therefore, is that we run the changes on three fundamentally different differences and show that in each case, the differences between like things are greater than the similarities. I cannot imagine a more perfect exercise in the applied and practical logic of comparison and contrast.

The upshot is very simple. The authorship of Sifra concurs in the fundamental principle that right thinking requires discovering the classification of things and determining the rule that governs diverse things. That authorship differs from the view of the Mishnah's concerns — I again emphasize — about *the origins of taxa.* Precisely how do we know what diverse things form a single classification of things? The answer of this discourse in the form of a commentary is, taxa originate in Scripture. They are not discovered by inherent traits but are revealed from above. Accordingly, at stake in the critique of the Mishnah are the principles of logic necessary for understanding the construction and inner structure of creation.[5]

Now that we recognize the first premise represented by the Mishnah's mode of *Listenwissenschaft,* the indicative significance imputed to the intrinsic traits of things, we move to the second of its principles of classification. It is that things are always what they are, never anything else. It comes second in logical order because, once we maintain that taxic indicators are inherent and intrinsic, only then the complementary principle emerges. One way of expressing that conception of the *Ding an Sich* is the notion of intrinsic classification. Something bears intrinsic and inherent traits, which are not relative to the traits of other things and furthermore are not imputed by function or extrinsic considerations of any other kind.

---

[5]Once more we notice that appeal to Scripture forms the counterpart, in analytical logic, to the principle of cogent discourse that rests upon the dictated order of verses of Scripture, that is, the logic of fixed association. The authorship of the Mishnah appeals to philosophical logic of classification and philosophical logic of cogent discourse, and in doing so, we now realize, it made choices others recognized and rejected.

The conception of true value, hence intrinsic character, emerges, among other components of the Mishnaic system, within the economics of the Mishnah.[6] Sages proposed to effect the vision of a steady-state economy, engaged in always-equal exchanges of fixed wealth and intrinsic value. Therein lies the conception of true value or of characteristics inherent in a given thing. In the interchanges of buying and selling, giving and taking, borrowing and lending, transactions of the market and exchanges with artisans and craftsmen and laborers, it is important to preserve the essential equality, not merely equity, of exchange. Fairness alone does not suffice. *Status quo ante* forms the criterion of the true market, reflecting as it does the exchange of value for value, in perfect balance. No party in the end may have more than what he had at the outset, and none may emerge as the victim of a sizable shift in fortune and circumstance. All parties' rights to and in the stable and unchanging political economy are preserved. When, therefore, the condition of a person is violated, the law will secure the restoration of the antecedent status. This entire conception rested on the notion of true value: not relative, but intrinsic. And the idea of an intrinsic or true value depended upon the prior conception that things have a single, fixed, and determinate character or definition, quality or "name," and that character or definition dictates all questions of worth (for economics) or classification (for philosophical metaphysics).

Before proceeding to the metaphysical expression of the principle that all things belong within the classification that their intrinsic traits dictate, let me show how the concrete notion works. Just how does true value intervene to effect the exchange of goods and services outside of the market-mechanism? That intervention expresses in a practical way the notion of inherent value or true worth.[7] In the following dispute, we see what is at issue:

Mishnah-tractate Baba Batra 5:1

A.   If one sold the wagon, he has not sold the mules. If he sold the mules, he has not sold the wagon. If he sold the yoke, he has not sold the oxen. If he sold the oxen, he has not sold the yoke.

B.   R. Judah says, "The price tells all."

C.   How so? If he said to him, "Sell me your yoke for two hundred zuz," the facts are perfectly clear, for there is no yoke worth two hundred zuz.

D.   And sages say, "Price proves nothing."

---

[6] I briefly review the findings of my *Economics of Judaism* (Chicago, 1989: University of Chicago Press).

[7] We note that prices must accord with something akin to true value, and the market simply facilitates the reasonable exchange of goods and services by bringing people together. The market provides no price setting mechanism that operates on its own, nor is the market conceived as an economic instrument, but rather, as one of (mere) social utility in facilitating barter, encompassing, of course, barter effected through specie or money.

Judah's view is that there is an intrinsic value, against which the market does not operate. This notion of true value,[8] though in the minority in the case at hand, in fact dominates in Mishnaic thought about the market-mechanism. The notion that true value inheres in all transactions, so that each party remains exactly as he was prior to the engagement, comes to concrete expression in a variety of circumstances.

How then do we actually conduct a classification of diverse facts in accord with intrinsic indicative traits? Let us consider a simple case of how those principles operate and what they accomplish. Every tractate of the Mishnah can supply us with examples of hierarchical classification based on intrinsic taxic indicators; the one I have chosen derives from Mishnah-tractate Bikkurim, which deals with firstfruits and their presentation in the temple in Jerusalem. The problem addressed, the solution proposed, the medium of logic by which the one is identified and the other accorded the status of self-evident truth — these emerge in the case that follows.

The facts are not complicated. Mishnah-tractate Bikkurim deals with the disposition of firstfruits, in line with Dt. 26:1-11. There are two principal issues. First, there is the concern for bringing firstfruits, second, for making the required declaration specified in Scripture. So the facts are entirely scriptural. But a considerable program concerning classification and connection comes into play. The concern of M. Bikkurim 1:1-2 is to set up a taxonomic grid to cover three possibilities as specified, [1] do not bring first fruits at all, [2] bring but do not recite, [3] bring and recite. The criterion is ownership of the land on which the firstfruits have grown. Status and circumstance are held together. The farmer must own the land, and those who do not bring firstfruits do not own the land. If someone owns the land but is not entitled to inherit a portion of the land, if someone buys trees without buying the ground on which they grow, and the like, they do not recite. All of these amplifications of the base-verse of Scripture in fact hold together diverse indicators in a single well-crafted taxic construction — therefore also proposition. I give only excerpts of the complete discussion.

MISHNAH-TRACTATE BIKKURIM 1:1-2, 4, 10-11

1:1   A.   There are [those who] bring [the] firstfruits [of the produce of their land] and recite [the confession, "I declare this day. . ." (Dt. 26:3-10)].

B.   those who bring [firstfruits] but do not recite,

C.   and there are [those] who do not bring [firstfruits at all].

D.   These are the [people] who do not bring [firstfruits]:

---

[8]I cannot explain what is meant by "value," e.g., the value of the worker's work, which clearly is taken into account, as against the "true value" inherent in an object up for sale in the marketplace.

E. (1) he who plants [a tree] on his own [property] and bends [a branch of the tree and sinks it into the ground so that it grows on private [property] or on public [property, as an independent plant];

F. (2) [as well as] he who bends [a branch of a tree which is growing] on private [property] or on public [property, and sinks the branch into the ground so that it grows] on his own [property];

G. (3) he who plants [a tree] on his own [property] and bends [a branch of the tree and sinks it in the ground so that it still grows) on his own [property], but a private road or a public road [runs] in between [the tree and its offshoot],

H. lo, this one does not bring [firstfruits from the offshoot]—

I. R. Judah says: "Such a one does bring [them] ."

1:2 A. For what reason does he not bring [them]?

B. Because it is written, "[You shall bring] the first of the firstfruits of your land" (Dt. 26:2).

C. [You may not bring firstfruits] unless all of their growth [takes place] on your land.

D. (1) Sharecroppers, (2) tenant farmers, (3) a holder of confiscated property, and (4) a robber

E do not bring firstfruits,

F. for the same reason:

G because it is written, "the first of the firstfruits of your land."

1:4 A. These [people] bring [firstfruits] but do not recite:

B. a proselyte brings but does not recite,

C. because he is not able to say, "[I have come into the land] which the Lord swore to our fathers to give us," (Dt. 26:3).

D. But if his mother was an Israelite, he brings and recites.

E. And when he [the proselyte] prays in private, he says, "God of the fathers of Israel."

F. And when he prays in the synagogue, he says, "God of your fathers."

G [But] if his mother was an Israelite, he says, "God of our fathers."

1:10 A. And these [people] bring [firstfruits] and recite:

B. [Those who bring firstfruits] (1) from Pentecost until the Festival [of Sukkot], (2) from the seven kinds [of produce native to the Land of Israel], (3) from fruit of the hill country, (4) from dates of the valley, [and] (5) from olives [used] for oil [that grow] in Transjordan.

C. R. Yosé the Galilean says, "They do not bring firstfruits from [produce grown in] Transjordan, for [Transjordan] is not a land flowing with milk and honey [Dt. 26:15]."

1:11 A. He who buys three trees [that are growing] on [the property] of his fellow brings [firstfruits from those trees] and recites.

B. R. Meir says, "Even if [he buys only] two [trees, he brings and recites]."

C. [If] he bought a tree and the ground [on which it grows], he brings and recites.

D. R. Judah says, "Even sharecroppers and tenant farmers, [who do not own the land on which their produce grows], bring [firstfruits] and recite."

The composition does more than assemble a mass of information in a simple arrangement, though that is our first impression of what is at hand. In fact, the authorship has generated a problem — how different classes of persons fall under a single rule, that is to say, the relationship of species to genus. The information that is adduced rests upon premises that each class of persons has its indicative traits, which afford the possibility of comparison and contrast with other classes of persons subject to the rule at hand. In this way the law concerning firstfruits, which Scripture has supplied, forms the foundation for the organization of a taxonomic grid. The concern of M. Bik. 1:1-2 then is to set up a taxonomic grid to cover four possibilities as specified, do not bring first fruits at all, bring but do not recite, bring and recite. M. Bik. 1:10-11 complete the program.

I may now generalize on the foregoing to answer the question, precisely what are the principles of classification? To state the obvious: the answer is, first identify the pertinent taxic indicators, then apply those indicators to the relevant data, seeking out interstitial cases in which two or more contradictory indicators are present.[9] In such cases they determine either which of the indicators takes priority or how a case in the excluded middle is to be disposed of. Here in a very simple case we see that the taxic indicators derive from the facts of the case, which Scripture (in the reading of the philosophers) has defined. The criterion is ownership of the land on which the firstfruits have grown. Status and circumstance are held together. The farmer must own the land, and those who do not bring firstfruits do not own the land. If someone owns the land but is not entitled to inherit a portion of the land, if someone buys trees without buying the ground on which they grow, and the like, they do not recite. On that basis the diverse cases are formed into a few simple classes, and the rule governing each is firmly set.

Since the traits of a thing, which are intrinsic, indicate the classification to which the thing belongs, we must ask, are these traits always concrete? Can we now show that traits also may refer to an abstract, intangible aspect of the thing? Mishnah-tractate Besah sets forth the now-familiar conception that something has an intrinsic character, and our task is to identify, or define, that character. We do so when we can identify the correct taxic indicators, which dictate the classification to which the thing is to be assigned. What is fresh is the abstract nature of the taxic indicator. It concerns what is actual as against what is potential. Do I take account of the traits of a thing as they presently are or as they will inevitably evolve? That conception, clearly an advance over the simple notion that things bear intrinsic traits, is set forth in a debate on the classification of the egg that is in a chicken. Is

---

[9]This simple case appeals to palpable and material traits, characteristics of things that we may readily identify on the surface. But while, it is clear. persons, places, things are deemed to bear indicative traits, which dictate the classes into which things are to be placed, and to the rule of which they conform, precisely what these indicative traits are is not always determined at the surface of matters. As a matter of fact, that intrinsic character that tells us the classification to which something belongs is both inherent and abstract.

it part of the chicken, hence within its classification? Or is it distinct from the chicken, hence within a classification of its own?

A.   An egg that is born on the festival-day —

B.   the House of Shammai say, "It may be eaten [on that day]."

C.   And the House of Hillel say, "It may not be eaten."

D.   The House of Shammai say, "[A minimum of] leaven in the volume of an olive's bulk, and [a minimum of] what is leavened in the volume of a date's bulk [are prohibited on Passover (Ex. 13:7)]."

E.   And the House of Hillel say, "This and that are [prohibited in the volume of] an olive's bulk."

Now what is the inside issue at hand? In classifying the egg, we identify the principal taxic indicator: is it distinct from the chicken or part of it? And the variable derives from our assessment of the relationship between the potential and the actual. At stake in the matter of the chicken, M. Bes. 1:1, is whether we regard what is going to happen as though it already has happened, or whether we interpret a potentiality as tantamount to an actuality. The House of Shammai take the latter position, the House of Hillel, the former.

What is at stake will be concrete, even while the conceptions are highly abstract. But that is characteristic of the discourse of the philosophy, as distinct from its issues, methods, results, and general principles and propositions. For this mode of thought based on classification works out its conceptions through practical reason and applied logic. The problem is simple. It is permitted on the festival-day to slaughter a chicken and to prepare it for eating on that same day. What is the law having to do with an egg born on the festival-day? The House of Shammai classify the egg under the rule governing the dam. The dam is deemed ready, so is the egg. The House of Hillel regard the egg as distinct from the dam. When it is born, it follows its own rule. The egg was not available prior to the festival, so, it is not permitted on the festival itself. There was no prior act of designation or preparation of the egg for use on the holy day. These secondary concerns do not obscure the primary philosophical method at hand, but they show us how, in a case of applied logic, we sort out our issues.

Identifying taxic indicators forms only the initial step, for matters never are simple. A given person or object may possess a variety of traits, and, moreover, may fall into more than a single class. Accordingly, as soon as we ask about the traits of things or persons, we also have to identify the ones that for a given purpose, in a given context, or in connection with a determinate issue prove indicative by their paramount and definitive status. We have also to notice those that are subsidiary and not determinative. And we have to explain the difference. So the process of classification proves altogether too abstract in theory; but in the concrete expression of material cases, the theory becomes useful and serves to afford solutions to real problems. When I speak of practical reason and applied logic, I mean a reason that gains force in concrete cases, a logic that bears consequence in the everyday.

Then what captures the attention of the exegetes behind the system and excites their imagination? It is the confusion of categories, which requires rectification. Let me give a single case of the chaos brought about — as a matter of fact — by conflicting requirements of Scripture itself! But these are now solved by the right reason of the theory of classification. The confusion derives from Scripture's law that [1] a man may not wed his brother's ex-wife (e.g., divorced by the brother, or his widow), but [2] a man must marry his childless brother's ex-wife (widow). So the woman falls into two distinct categories: [1] forbidden by reason of having been married to the brother; but [2] permitted, by reason of the brother's having died childless.

That explains why a project in classification is demanded by Scripture, which establishes categories that intersect. Dt. 25:5-10 states that when a man dies childless, his wife must marry a surviving brother or undergo the rite of removing the shoe (Halisah). This law sets aside the prohibition of Lev. 18:16 against marriage with a brother's wife (that is, the brother has divorced the wife, in which case another brother may not marry her). The entire composition of Mishnah-tractate Yebamot Chapters One through Five consists of a sustained and encompassing work of classification, with each set of taxic indicators invoked the tell us whether a union is wholly permitted, partially recognized, or impermissible.

MISHNAH-TRACTATE YEBAMOT 1:1FF.

1:1   A.   Fifteen women [who are near of kin to their deceased, childless husband's brother] exempt their co-wives, and the co-wives, from Halisah and from levirate marriage, without limit. [This means that if a man dies childless, and one of his widows has to marry the surviving brother, but the widow or co-wife is the daughter of the surviving brother or in some other specified relationship, then none of the widows of the deceased has to enter into levirate marriage at all. All of them are exempt from the obligation because of the prohibited status of one of them. Why is this the case? Dt. 25:5-10 states that when a man dies childless, his wife must marry a surviving brother or undergo the rite of removing the shoe (Halisah). This law sets aside the prohibition of Lev. 18:16 against marriage with a brother's wife (that is, the brother has divorced the wife, in which case another brother may not marry her).]

      B.   And these are they:

      C.   (1) His daughter, and (2) the daughter of his daughter, and (3) the daughter of his son;

      D.   (4) the daughter [by a former marriage] of his wife, and (5) the daughter of her son [by a former marriage], and (6) the daughter of her daughter [by a former marriage];

E. (7) his mother-in-law, and (8) the mother of his mother-in-law, and (9) the mother of his father-in-law [married to his brother by the same father];

F. (10) his sister by the same mother, and (11) the sister of his mother, and (12) the sister of his wife;

G. (13) and the wife of his brother by the same mother, and (14) the wife of his brother who was not [alive] at the same time as he [but who died before he was born, in which case the surviving brother has no claim];

H. and (15) his [former] daughter-in-law [who then married his brother] —

I. lo, these exempt their co-wives and the co-wives of their co-wives, from Halisah and from levirate marriage, without limit [= A].

J. And in the case of all of them, if they died [before the husband], or exercised the right of refusal, were divorced [by the childless husband], or turned out to be barren —

K. their co-wives are permitted [to enter into levirate marriage, since they are not deemed co-wives].

L. But you cannot rule in the case of his mother-in-law and in the case of the mother of his mother-in-law, or in the case of the mother of his father-in-law [E], "Who turned out to be barren," or "Who exercised the right of refusal."

2:3 A. A general rule did they lay down in regard to the levirate woman [widow of a deceased childless brother]:

B. (1) Any [sister-in-law] who is prohibited as one of the forbidden degrees [of Leviticus Chapter Eighteen] neither executes the rite of Halisah nor is taken in levirate marriage [and exempts her co-wife (M. 1:1A)].

C. (2) [If] she is prohibited [to her brother-in-law] by reason of a prohibition on account of a commandment or a prohibition on account of sanctity, she executes the rite of Halisah but is not taken in levirate marriage [nor does her co-wife (M. 1:1A)].

D. (3) [If] her sister is [also] her sister-in-law [widow of her childless brother-in-law], she either executes the rite of Halisah or is taken into levirate marriage.

3:8 A. And in every case [of M. 1:11 in which the betrothal or divorce [of the deceased brother] is subject to doubt,

B. lo, these co-wives perform the rite of Halisah but [of course] do not enter into levirate marriage.

C. What is a case of doubt concerning betrothal?

D. [If] he threw her a token of betrothal —

E. it is a matter of doubt whether it landed nearer to him or nearer to her —

F this is a case in which there is doubt concerning betrothal.

G And a case of doubt concerning a writ of divorce?

H. [If] one wrote the writ of divorce in his own hand, but there are no witnesses to attest the document —

I.   [if] there are witnesses to attest the document, but it is not dated —
J.   [if] it is dated, but it [contains the attestation of] only a single
       witness—
K.   this is a case in which the divorce is subject to doubt.

The entire composition of Mishnah-tractate Yebamot Chapters One through Five, of which I have given only a small part, consists of a sustained and encompassing work of classification of persons who exhibit confused or contradictory traits, with each set of taxic indicators invoked the tell us whether a union is wholly permitted, partially recognized, or impermissible. We sort out or data — our cases — by appeal to three distinct taxic indicators, which then define three classifications. [1] There is a consanguineous relationship that will result from the levirate union, e.g., the deceased childless husband's brother is himself married to a sister of the widow. Then we invoke Lev. 18:16 (and, for the other items listed, parallel verses or considerations). Then there is no levirate connection at all, by reason of consanguinity. The upshot is we permit neither levirate marriage nor impose the rite of Halisah. That matter is worked out in Chapters One and Two. [2] A second classification of persons will undergo the rite of Halisah but not enter into levirate marriage, set forth in Chapter Three. [3] A third classification of persons does enter into Levirate marriage, so Chapter Four. Then Chapter Five provides a reprise of rules governing these classes of marital relationship: marriage, divorce, levirate marriage, the rite of Halisah.

What we have through these remarkably coherent chapters is a complete system of classifying the severing of marital relationships. In theory no distinction as to subject matter or intrinsic traits of things can form an obstacle to the same successful ordering of relationships, whether concrete or abstract. We see here an example among an unlimited number of possible cases for the demonstration of a single proposition, which is that things are orderly, and that we can identify the order that inheres in them. What is accomplished by this work of classification? An abstract answer, already given, is that it brings order out of chaos. But in concrete terms alone is the urgency of such an intellectual enterprise shown in full clarity. Then the meaning of practical reason is shown to bear high stakes indeed, at least, in a world of the everyday subjected to the rationality of philosophical order.

To show how applied reason and practical logic accomplish the abstract goals of the system, finally, we address the issue of saying blessings for the benefits of this world. As to the facts, when someone derives a benefit from this world, eating a given species of produce, for instance, then that person is supposed to acknowledge the benefit by saying a blessing. There is no limit to the kinds of produce. But this approach wishes to show how many things are really one thing, and, in this case, it does so by demonstrating that, among all the varieties of nourishing food, only a few blessings pertain. Then the labor of intellect is to classify within a given genus the species that fall therein; the upshot is that a given formulation of the blessing will apply to all the species of produce within a common genus. As a matter of fact, the whole of Mishnah-tractate Berakhot forms an essay on the principles of classification as these apply to, and are illustrated by, issues of liturgy. The working of speciation in matters involving everyday liturgy is shown in the following:

MISHNAH-TRACTATE BERAKHOT 6:1-5

6:1   A.   What blessing does one recite over produce?

     B .   Over fruit of a tree he says, "[Blessed are you, 0 Lord, our God, King of the Universe] Creator of the fruit of the tree,"

     C.   except for wine.

     D.   For over wine he says, "Creator of the fruit of the vine."

     E.   And over produce of the earth [vegetables] he says, "Creator of fruit of the ground,"

     F.   except for loaves [of bread].

     G.   For over the loaf he says, "Who brings forth bread from the earth,"

     H.   And over greens he says, "Creator of the fruit of the ground."

     I.   R. Judah says, "Creator of kinds of herbs."

6:2   A.   If one recited over fruit of trees the blessing "Creator of the fruit of the ground"' he has [anyway] fulfilled his obligation.

     B.   But [if one said] over produce of the ground, "Creator of the fruit of the tree," he did not fulfill his obligation.

     C.   [As regards] any [kinds of produce] if one says, "[Blessed are you, Lord, our God, King of the Universe] for all was created according to his word," he fulfilled his obligation.

6:3   A.   Over something which does not grow from the earth one says, "For all [was created according to his word]."

     B.   Over vinegar, unripe fruit, and edible locusts one says "For all [was created at his word] ."

     C.   Over milk, cheese, and eggs one says, "For all...."

     D.   R. Judah says, "Over anything which is a curse, one does not recite a blessing."

6:4   A.   If one had before him many different types [of food] —

     B.   R. Judah says, "If there are among them [foodstuffs] of the seven types [of foods of the Land of Israel], he recites a blessing over that [particular foodstuff]."

     C.   But sages say, "[He recites a blessing] over whichever type he desires."

6:5   A.   If one recited a blessing over the wine before the meal, he exempted the wine after the meal [he need not bless again].

     B.   If one recited a blessing over the appetizer before the meal, he exempted the appetizer after the meal.

     C.   If one recited a blessing over the loaf [of bread], he exempted the appetizer.

     D.   [If one recited a blessing] over the appetizer, he did not exempt the loaf.

E.   The House of Shammai say, "[A blessing over the appetizer exempts]
      not even that [cooked food] made in a pot."

The protracted account at M. Berakhot 6:1-5 goes over the classification of
foods. A blessing appropriate to each classification is prescribed, which means that
we have to determine the correct category of various types of edibles. The taxonomy
involves produce of trees and of the ground, fruit and vegetables, respectively.
Bread and wine are treated as unique. Other foods, milk, cheese, eggs, fall into a
third, more general category. So the principal categories are fruit and vegetables,
distinguished by the locus of their cultivation, and then each yields a distinctive
item of its own. The practical reason makes the theoretical point in yet another way,
as the system endlessly returns to the same problem and solves it in the same way:
many varieties form only a few species, and these comprise the common genus:
subject to the recitation of a blessing.

Without giving the details, let me show how the taxonomy recognizes further,
and more abstract, problems. At stake at M. Berakhot 6:6 is when individuals who
are eating in the same place constitute a group, that is, the issue of connection.
When do many individuals form a single group? They do so when a formal indicator
shows that the constitute a group and not just isolated individuals. M. Berakhot 6:7
concerns the genus and the species. What is a species is covered by a blessing
recited for a genus, thus: "Any primary [food] accompanied by a secondary [food]
— one recites the blessing over the primary and [thereby] exempts the secondary."
The issue of M. Berakhot 6:8A-D is whether figs, grapes, and pomegranates
constitute a complete meal. If so, sages want the entire Grace after Meals to be
recited. Aqiba restates that principle in more general terms, so providing a definition
of the correct indicator. If food serves or functions as a complete meal, then the
Grace after Meals is to be recited. So the criterion for classifying food vis à vis the
Grace after Meals is entirely functional, and, at that point, the differentiation among
species and a genus is no longer pertinent; that consideration applies prior to, but
not after, the meal. At M. Berakhot 7:1, once more we reckon with the identification
of those in the class of obligation, and those excluded from that class, M.
Berakhot7:2. If one is in the class of obligation, then he may form a quorum with
others of that class for the public recitation of Grace after Meals; if not, not. So a
principal taxic indicator for persons is one's status as to obligatory deeds or rites.
Clearly, the matter may go on indefinitely — and does. I maintain that that defines
the power and dynamic of the mode of thought: its endless accessibility to concrete
exegesis, the solution of problems.

The final question addressed by the main principles of classification then
concerns the dynamic of rationality. What exactly is the process of thought that
accounts for my determination of the class into which a given thing falls? Self-
evidently, we deal with a process of systematic search for either analogy or contrast:
analogical-contrastive thinking. Specifically, what bears the same taxic indicator
as something else — therefore is analogous to that other thing in a consequential

aspect — falls into the same class as that other thing and accordingly conforms to the rule that applies. In that way we are able to move from the known to the unknown, by finding in the unknown, that is, the thing we must clarify, the pertinent taxic trait that joins that unknown to an already-known thing. Then deep speculation on the nature of analogical and metaphorical thinking is going to take place.

The process of classification is shown in Mishnah-tractate Besah to appeal to analogy in classifying permitted or forbidden things, in this case, acts of labor. The generative rule is that on a festival day, one is permitted to prepare food, but to do no other act of labor. Then the issue is, to what extent is cooking deemed an analogy for a variety of acts of labor? The answers to that question will involve either inclusion within what is deemed a metaphor or exclusion in what is deemed not a case but a self-contained rule: thus, acts like cooking, seen as a metaphor, or cooking only, read as a self-contained rule?

To spell out how I discern the philosophical issue and proposition in remarkably humble discussions, let me explain the facts. It is forbidden to work on festival days, but cooking is permitted. Do we then regard the act of cooking as broadly analogous such that all acts connected with cooking are permitted as well? Or do we regard cooking as narrowly analogous, so that only acts that are directly connected with cooking are acceptable on the festival day? At M. Besah 1:5-6, M. Besah 1:7-9+10, 2:4-5, 2:6-7, the House of Hillel take an inclusionary view, permitting all actions that fall within the basic classification of cooking; the House of Shammai take an exclusionary view, permitted only actions connected with cooking itself. So the interpretation of a metaphor is at stake: broadly classificatory or not taxonomic at all. The House of Shammai do not regard the reference to cooking as taxonomic but specific to itself, and the House of Hillel regard "cooking" as a taxon, covering everything that falls into a single class of actions, connected with food preparation. The debate as to whether a scriptural reference is exclusionary or inclusionary — a particular case or an example of a larger classification of actions — is at M. Bes. 1:2 as well.

MISHNAH-TRACTATE BESAH 1:5-6

1:5 A. The House of Shammai say, "They do not remove cupboard doors on the festival."

B. (1) And the House of Hillel permit (2) even putting them back.

C. The House of Shammai say, "They do not take up a pestle to hack meat on it."

D. And the House of Hillel permit [doing so].

E. The House of Shammai say, "They do not place a hide before the tread [as a doormat],

F. "nor may one lift it up,

G. "unless there is an olive's bulk of meat on it."

H. And the House of Hillel permit.

I. The House of Shammai say, "They do not take out into public domain a minor, a *lulab,* or a scroll of the Torah."

J.   And the House of Hillel permit.

1:6   A.   The House of Shammai say, "They do not bring dough offering and priestly gifts to the priest on the festival-day,

B.   "whether they were raised up the preceding day or on that same day."

C.   And the House of Hillel permit.

D.   The House of Shammai said to them, "It is an argument by way of analogy:

E.   "The dough offering and the priestly gifts [Dt. 18:3] are a gift to the priest, and heave-offering is a gift to the priest.

F.   "Just as [on the festival-day] they do not bring heave-offering [to a priest], so they do not bring these other gifts [to a priest]."

G.   Said to them the House of Hillel, "No. If you have stated that rule in the case of heave-offering, which one [on the festival] may not designate to begin with, will you apply that same rule concerning the priestly gifts, which [on the festival] one may designate to begin with?"

We take up secondary actions connected with the preparation of food. The House of Hillel regard such actions as permissible, and the House of Shammai impose a narrow interpretation on what is permitted. The issue is the power of intentionality. If the purpose is to get at food in the cupboard, we may take off and even replace the doors. The point of each dispute is the same, only the details shift. The same reasoning as at M. 1:5E-H applies to M. 1:6. If there is food on the hide, then the hide may be handled by reason of that food. The Hillelites permit handling the hide and stretching it, even if there is no food connected with it, to encourage the people to slaughter beasts for festival use without risk of the hide. So the basic action, which is permitted, of cooking, extends to a range of actions quite unconnected with cooking.

MISHNAH-TRACTATE BESAH 1:7-9

1:7   A.   The House of Shammai say, "Spices are crushed in a wooden crusher,

B.   "and salt in a cruse and with a wooden pot stirrer."

C.   And the House of Hillel say, "Spices are crushed in the usual way, in a stone pestle, and salt in a wooden pestle."

1:8. A.   He who picks out pulse on a festival-day —

B.   the House of Shammai say, "He makes his selection of food and eats it [right away]."

C.   And the House of Hillel say, "He makes his selection in his usual way, [putting it down using] his lap, a basket, or a dish;

D.   "but not [using] a board, sifter, or sieve [and preparing a large quantity, for the next day]."

E.   Rabban Gamaliel says, "Also: he swills and separates the husks."

1:9   A.   The House of Shammai say, "They send on the festival-day only [prepared] portions of [food] ."

B.   And the House of Hillel say, "They send domestic beasts, wild beasts, and fowl,

C.   "whether alive or already slaughtered."

D.   They send wine, oil, fine flour, and pulse,

E.   but not grain.

F.   And R. Simeon permits [sending] even grain.

The issue is whether one may act only in an ordinary way, M. 1:7, or even in an unusual way. The House of Shammai, M. 1:8, want the person to nibble but not make an ordinary meal. The Hillelites allow eating in a normal way, just as at a meal. M. 1:9 has the Shammaites take the view that the food must be ready for consumption on the festival-day; the House of Hillel regard it as adequate if the food is potentially edible on that day. The basic issue remains just as before. It concerns whether the scriptural reference to cooking is taxonomic and exemplary or ad hoc and exclusionary.[10]

So much for the main principles of classification: the basic conceptions, premises and self-evident rationality, of the Halakhic mode of thought and medium of analysis, its manner of identifying, framing, and solving problems. Have we discerned propositions that hold together the cases we have analyzed, and can we state those propositions in such a way that they may be shown right and true through other cases and problems altogether? Indeed we have, certainly we can.

By way of conclusion, let me repeat what is abundantly obvious. We have uncovered these basic principles of classification:

[1] All things bear intrinsic traits, inherent and definitive qualities,

[2] But all things stand in relationship to all other things, with the result that nothing is *sui generis*.

[3] It follows that the work of definition, which is to say, identifying the thing-ness of a thing, its true value for economic purposes, its right place in the order of nature and supernature for metaphysical ones, requires the comparison and contrast of one thing with other things.

---

[10] The other side of the argument concerning exclusion and inclusion within the classification of food-preparation is at M. Bes. 3:1-2. Hunting is not involved in food-preparation; therefore preparation of food on the festival excludes an act of hunting. M. Bes. 3:3 places another limitation; if there is no usable meat on a beast, on the festival it may not be slaughtered for use, and, moreover, there has also to be time to roast and actually eat a piece of the meat. That is an important exclusionary rule. M. Bes. 3:4 (+ 5) is in line with this exclusionary pattern. M. Bes. 3:6-8 then distinguish what is part of the process of food-preparation from what is not. Chapter Four, in particular M. Bes. 4:1-5, develops this same issue of excluding some actions and including others within the classification of food-preparation. Some must be done in a manner different from the ordinary way, so as to signify that the act is in connection with preparing food under a special set of rules. Some may not be done at all, e.g., for the former, moving food from here to there, chopping wood, and, for the latter, making utensils for use on the festival in connection with food preparation, building a stove, and the like.

[4] This we accomplish by finding how things are alike one another, so establishing a genus that encompasses more than a single thing, and how they contrast with one another, so defining the species of a common genus (work to be set forth in a later chapter). But at this point we note how the work of identifying a genus and accomplishing the speciation of a genus is done.

[5] That is by analyzing the traits of things and identifying those traits that are principal and so definitive, those that are subsidiary and not definitive.

[6] Then, among these traits, taxic indicators serve to define the classification into which things are assigned. What is at stake in this work? It is a nomothetic process, in which we uncover among the chaos of things the order stated by the rules that things conform to or reveal. And process then produces both the besought result in any given case and also the ultimate proposition, which is that things are orderly, conform to rules, make sense, exhibit a rationality that we can uncover. The process rests on these further propositions, upon all of which our initial foray has touched.

[7] Things that bear like taxic indicators fall into the same classifications and come under the same rule; things that bear unlike taxic indicators fall into the contrary classifications and come under the opposite rule.

[8] Taxic indicators appeal to abstractions, not only to concrete matters, and very commonly derive from fixed relationships, rather than from intrinsic and palpable traits of things.

IV. POLYTHETIC AND HIERARCHICAL CLASSIFICATION

The principles of classification require two important refinements, each in response to a considerable problem. The first problem is that species do not always correspond in every way, so appeal for taxonomic purposes to all shared taxic indicators is not feasible. Some supply the wrong signals. The second is that merely classifying things yields no interesting results, no principles susceptible of extension and generalization. The Mishnah's system of classification, within its larger theory of *Listenwissenschaft,* encompasses solutions to these two problems, the first through polythetic, the second through hierarchical, classification. And together, these two principles inform the whole and lead to the principal conclusions that the document, and the system it attests, wish to put forth. The modes of thought, as much as the medium of discourse, in every line express the systemic message.

To understand the former, we have to recall how the work of classification is carried on. Specifically, when things match, so that their indicative traits make possible that required comparison and contrast that permits us to reach conclusions about the like and the unlike, then a simple process of classification gets under way. We can compare one or three or six traits of one thing with corresponding types of traits of some other. If the six in both cases are the same, we classify both things under a single rule. If not, then one thing follows one rule, the other the opposite.

But, of course, not much in the here and the now to which practical logic and applied reason apply conforms to such a neat pattern. When we compare species of what we think, as a matter of hypothesis, form a common genus, we find that things are alike in some ways, unlike in others. Then do we have a common genus at all? And how are we to compare what is not precisely comparable with anything else? These two problems find solution in the conception of polythetic classification, the first of two fundamental complications of the basic principles of classification we have identified.

Why does a system of classification find it necessary to accommodate polythetic comparison? The reason is in the nature of things. We can easily demonstrate, things have so many and such diverse and contradictory indicative traits that, comparing one thing to something else, we can always distinguish one species from another. Even though we find something in common, we also can discern some other trait characteristic of one thing but not the other. If on the basis of one set of traits which yield a given classification, we place into order two or more items, on the basis of a different set of traits, we have a different classification altogether. But the formation of classifications based on monothetic taxonomy, that is to say, traits that are not only common to both items but that are shared throughout both items subject to comparison and contrast, simply will not serve. For at every point at which someone alleges uniform, that is to say, monothetic likeness, one can and will demonstrate difference. Then how to proceed? Appeal to some shared traits as a basis for classification: this is not like that, and that is not like this, but the two classes of things share in common an indicative trait, and common to them both, the indicative trait that both exhibit is such and so, that is to say, polythetic taxonomy.

The self-evident problem in accepting differences among things and insisting, nonetheless, on their monomorphic character for purposes of comparison and contrast, cannot be set aside: who says? That is, if I can adduce in evidence for a shared classification of things only a few traits among many characteristic of each thing, then what stops me from treating all the things alike? Polythetic taxonomy opens the way to an unlimited exercise in finding what diverse things have in common and imposing, for that reason, one rule on everything. Then the very working of *Listenwissenschaft* as a tool of analysis, differentiation, comparison, contrast, and the descriptive determination of rules yields the opposite of what is desired. Chaos, not order, a mass of exceptions, no rules, a world of examples, each subject to its own regulation, instead of a world of order and proportion, composition and stability, will result. That is the power of the present matter.

Polythetic classification therefore identifies among different species of a hypothetically-common genus some comparable traits, even while admitting the presence of other traits that are not comparable. We then compare like to like, in full knowledge that the whole of the one does not conform to the model of the whole of the other to permit that decision — wholly like, therefore one rule, wholly unlike, therefore the opposite rule — that the system finds the deepest and most satisfying logic of all. The method of polythetic classification rests upon the premise that things may intersect partially, and that that partial intersection suffices for analysis of the like and the unlike. It suffices because it yields, at points of commonality, the same law for different things. And the mode of thought as a whole aims throughout at the discovery of regularities and modalities of order, an order that is exhibited by the way things are.

Mishnah-tractate Baba Qamma 1:1-3 form a stunning exercise in polythetic classification, indeed shows precisely what is the discipline of such a taxonomical principle. Specifically, we recognize that there is a variety of indicative traits that characterize a given set of classes of objects or actions. If, then, we wish to form a single taxon to encompass them all, we may not be able to identify indicative traits that equally characterize all the items. So we find some few traits that are present throughout, and on the basis of these, we uncover the law common to all the items, hence not monothetic but polythetic classification. Before proceeding, let us examine the text itself.

MISHNAH-TRACTATE BABA QAMMA 1:1-3

1:1   A.   [There are] four generative causes of damages: (1) ox [Ex. 21:35-36], (2) pit [Ex. 21:33], (3) crop-destroying beast [Ex. 22:4], and (4) conflagration [Ex. 22:5].

      B.   [The definitive characteristic] of the ox is not equivalent to that of the crop-destroying beast;

      C.   nor is that of the crop-destroying beast equivalent to that of the ox;

      D.   nor are this one and that one, which are animate, equivalent to fire, which is not animate;

      E.   nor are this one and that one, which usually [get up and] go and do damage, equivalent to a pit, which does not usually [get up and] go and do damage.

      F.   What they have in common is that they customarily do damage and taking care of them is your responsibility.

      G   And when one [of them] has caused damage, the [owner] of that which causes the damage is liable to pay compensation for damage out of the best of his land [Ex. 22:4].

1:2   A.   In the case of anything of which I am liable to take care, I am deemed to render possible whatever damage it may do.

      B.   [If] I am deemed to have rendered possible part of the damage it may do,

      C.   I am liable for compensation as if [I have] made possible all of the damage it may do.

      D.   (1) Property which is not subject to the law of Sacrilege, (2) property belonging to members of the covenant [Israelites], (3) property that is held in ownership,

E.   and that is located in any place other than in the domain which is in
      the ownership of the one who has caused the damage,

F.   or in the domain which is shared by the one who suffers injury and
      the one who causes injury —

G.   when one has caused damage [under any of the afore-listed
      circumstances],

H.   [the owner of] that one which has caused the damage is liable to pay
      compensation for damage out of the best of his land [= M . 1:16] .

1:3   A.   Assessment [of the compensation for an injury to be paid] is in terms
            of ready cash [but is paid in kind — that is,] in what is worth money,

      B.   before a court,

      C.   on the basis of evidence given by witnesses who are freemen and
            members of the covenant.

      D.   Women fall into the category of [parties to suits concerning] damages.

      E.   And the one who suffers damages and the one who causes damages
            [may share] in the compensation.

I need hardly make explicit the way in which the passage exhibits the traits of
polythetic classification, since the matter is made explicit, the result being self-
evident. Things are not alike, but they have traits in common, and the common
traits then draw within a single rule diverse things (here: actions).

    Let us proceed to the continuation of the foregoing, which shows us how the
framers of a sizable portion of a tractate have taught the rules of polythetic
classification through a sequence of topically related cases. The work of organization
and exposition of the materials indeed is classificatory, in the sense that a vast
amount of information is set forth in a simple and clear pattern. The grid of the
distinction between half and full damages, on the horizontal plane, and the
distinctions among leg, tooth, and the like, on the vertical accounts for the whole, a
fine piece of taxonomic thought in that the classification of one set of variables
within the limits of a second and intersecting set of variables is what is accomplished.
Let us then contrast that complex mode of classification with the simple one to
which, in Chapter Four, we have become accustomed.

MISHNAH-TRACTATE BABA QAMMA 1:4

1:4   A.   [There are] five [deemed] harmless, and five [deemed] attested
            dangers.

      B.   A domesticated beast is not regarded as an attested danger in regard
            to butting, (2) pushing, (3) biting, (4) lying down, or (5) kicking.

      C.   (1) A tooth is deemed an attested danger in regard to eating what is
            suitable for [eating].

      D.   (2) The leg is deemed an attested danger in regard to breaking
            something as it walks along.

      E.   (3) And an ox which is an attested danger [so far as goring is
            concerned];

F.   (4) and an ox which causes damage in the domain of the one who is injured;

G.   and (5) man.

H.   (1) A wolf, (2) lion, (3) bear, (4) leopard, (5) panther, and (6) a serpent — lo, these are attested dangers.

I.   R. Eliezer says, "When they are trained, they are not attested dangers.

J.   "But the serpent is always an attested danger"

K.   What is the difference between what is deemed harmless and an attested danger?

L.   But if that which is deemed harmless [causes damage], [the owner] pays half of the value of the damage which has been caused,

M.   [with liability limited to the value of the] carcass [of the beast which has caused the damage].

N.   But [if that which is] an attested danger [causes damage], [the owner] pays the whole of the value of the damage which has been caused from the best property [he may own, and his liability is by no means limited to the value of the animal which has done the damage].

M. Baba Qamma 1:4, expanded and explained at M. 2:1, 2-4, 2:5, 6, classifies and organizes the diverse causes of damages within the grid defined by Scripture that injury done by what has been deemed harmless and causes damages is compensated at only half of the damages done, while injury done by an attested danger is compensated at the full estimate of the damages done. So much for polythetic classification, the less important of the two complicating principles of method.

Hierarchical classification embodies the purpose of the approach as a whole: not only to classify diverse things, which yields mere information. It is to establish a hierarchy of classes. That serves to make the point that things are not only orderly, but stand in hierarchical sequence to one another, everything in a single frame of order. This is worked out by showing that the rule applying in one class relates to the rule applying in some other: *all the more so*, in the case of what is of a higher station in the hierarchy to what is of a lower station, for example. The medium by which we move from *this*, to *why this, not that*, is through the argument, *if this, then surely that*, or *if this, then obviously not that*. On its own, that medium presents a mere point of logic.

What is at stake in classification? If we draw no conclusions, then nothing — by definition — happens. We have organized information. But if we do draw conclusions, then much happens, and we have so framed information as to produce conclusions of consequence. When we contemplate the Mishnah's conception of the realm of reality, the social order of humanity, the metaphysical order of nature and supernature, we ask, what makes all things move? How do we account not for a steady-state tableau, in which nothing happens, but for the realm of activity, in which, rightly ordered, everything happens the way it should happen? The answer to that question derives from the point at which classification is accomplished.

That is when we must ask, so what? And the point is, from classification we must draw conclusions, the rule that animates all rules. Then what conclusions are we to draw from our power to classify? They derive from hierarchization of the classes of things, as I said at the outset.

Let me say what is at stake in this question of the system's dynamic first in simple, syllogistic terms. In such an argument, we take two facts and produce a third not contained within the prior facts but through right logic generated by them. And that drawing of conclusions, that making of two things into a sum greater than the parts, defines the stakes of classification. For the mode of thought that we examine in its most concrete expressions serves not only to describe but to explain, not only to classify but to draw conclusions. How is this done? It is by moving from the classification to the comparison of classes of things: which stands lower, which higher? which imposes its rule upon another class altogether — or the opposite rule? To the method of *Listenwissenschaft,* for the Mishnah's mode of thought and argument, the source of power and compelling proof is hierarchization. Things are not merely like or unlike, therefore following one rule or its opposite. Things also are weightier or less weighty, and that particular point of likeness of difference generates the logical force of *Listenwissenschaft.*

Hierarchical classification serves a number of purposes. The main one is simply organize information in intelligible patterns, yielding *en passant* those doctrinal consequences that I promised. But the simplest and most common appeal to hierarchical classification as a mode of analysis hardly forms the basis for important secondary arguments or developments. At M. Hagigah 2:5-7 we have an absolutely classic hierarchical classification, as to the status of uncleanness, of [1] ordinary people, [2] abstainers (*Perushim* = Pharisees?), [3] those who eat heave offering (priests at home) and [4] those who eat holy things (priests in the temple). These are not merely classified but also set into relationship in regard to a variety of activities requiring cultic cleanness, with the relationships defined by various degrees of cultic uncleanness. Then conclusions can be drawn from the hierarchical classification of the persons encompassed here:

MISHNAH-TRACTATE HAGIGAH 2:5-7, 3:1-3

2:5   A.   They wash the hands for eating unconsecrated food, tithe, and heave offering;

       B.   and for eating food in the status of Holy Things they immerse;

       C.   and as to [the preparation of] purification water [through the burning of the red cowl, if one's hands are made unclean, his entire body is deemed to be unclean as well.

2:6   A.   He who immerses for the eating of unconsecrated food and is thereby confirmed as suitable for eating unconsecrated food is prohibited from eating tithe.

       B.   [If] he immersed for eating tithe and is thereby confirmed as suitable for eating tithe, he is prohibited from eating heave offering.

C. [If] he immersed for eating heave offering and is thereby confirmed as suitable for eating heave offering, he is prohibited from eating food in the status of Holy Things.

D. [If] he immersed for eating food in the status of Holy Things and is thereby confirmed as suitable for eating food in the status of Holy Things, he is prohibited from engaging in the preparation of purification water.

E. [If, however], one immersed for the matter requiring the more stringent rule, he is permitted to engage in the matter requiring the less stringent rule.

F. [If]] he immersed but was not confirmed, it is as though he did not immerse.

2:7   A. The clothing of ordinary folk is in the status of Midras uncleanness for abstainers [who eat unconsecrated food in a state of cultic cleanness].

B. The clothing of abstainers is in the status of Midras uncleanness for those who eat heave offering [priests].

C. The clothing of those who eat heave offering is in the status of Midras uncleanness for those who eat Holy Things [officiating priests].

D. The clothing of those who eat Holy Things is in the status of Midras uncleanness for those engaged in the preparation of purification water.

E. Yosef b. Yoezer was the most pious man in the priesthood, but his handkerchief was in the status of Midras uncleanness so far as eating Holy Things was concerned.

F. For his whole life Yohanan b. Gudegedah ate his food in accord with the requirements of cleanness applying to Holy Things, but his handkerchief was in the status of Midras uncleanness so far as those engaged in the preparation of purification water were concerned.

3:1   A. A more stringent rule applies to Holy Things than applies to heave offering,

B. for: They immerse utensils inside of other utensils for purification for use with [food in the status of] heave offering,

C. but not for purification for use with [food in the status of Holy Things.

D. [They make a distinction among] outer parts, inside, and holding place in the case of use for heave offering,

E. but not in the case of use for Holy Things.

F. He who carries something affected by Midras uncleanness [may also] carry heave offering,

G. but [he may] not [also carry food in the status of] Holy Things.

H. The clothing of those who are so clean as to be able to eat heave offering

I. is deemed unclean in the status of Midras uncleanness for the purposes of Holy Things.

J. The rule for Holy Things is not like the rule for heave offering.

K. For in the case of [immersion for use of] Holy Things one unties a knot and dries it off, immerses and afterwards ties it up again.

	L.	And in the case of heave offering one ties it and then one immerses.

3:2   A.   Utensils which are completely processed in a state of insusceptibility to uncleanness [and so when completed are clean] require immersion for use in connection with Holy Things,

      B.   but not for use in connection with heave offering.

      C.   A utensil unites everything contained therein for the purposes of Holy Things,

      D.   but not for the purposes of heave offering.

      E.   [That which is made unclean in] the fourth remove from the original source of uncleanness in the case of Holy Things is invalid,

      F.   but only [that which is made unclean in] the third in the case of heave offering.

      G.   And in the case of heave offering, if one of one's hands is made unclean, the other is clean.

      H.   But in the case of Holy Things one has to immerse both of them.

      I.   For one hand imparts uncleanness to the other for the purposes of Holy Things,

      J.   but not for the purposes of heave offering.

3:3   A.   With unclean hands they eat food which has not been wet down in the case of heave offering,

      B.   but not in the case of Holy Things.

      C.   He who [prior to interment of the deceased] mourns his next of kin [without having contracted corpse uncleanness] and one whose atonement rite is not complete [because an offering is yet required] require immersion for the purposes of Holy Things,

      D.   but not for the purposes of heave offering.

I cannot imagine more perfect composition of this genre of thought. All things hold together in a single pattern and the composition as a whole demonstrates that fact in terms of the most abstruse considerations. The facts concerning classification now yield more facts, once the process of comparison and contrast leading to an ordering of the classes gets underway.

But hierarchical classification shows more than merely the relationships between the things that are classified. That mode of thought and argument also yields a generalization that can pertain to cases bearing no resemblance to the one that has generated the principle. And therein we uncover the source of the power of hierarchical classification to motivate the entire system, imposing conclusions of a single order throughout the analysis of all relationships, whether in the natural or in the social world. The key then is the syllogistic power: the formation of new knowledge.

How does hierarchical classification create new knowledge. A good example derives from the demonstration of the rule of precedence.

MISHNAH-TRACTATE HORAYOT 3:6-8

3:6 A.   Whatever is offered more regularly than its fellow takes precedence over its fellow, and whatever is more holy than its fellow takes precedence over its fellow.

    B.   [If] a bullock of an anointed priest and a bullock of the congregation [M. 1:5] are standing [awaiting sacrifice] —

    C.   the bullock of the anointed [high priest] takes precedence over the bullock of the congregation in all rites pertaining to it.

3:7 A.   The man takes precedence over the woman in the matter of the saving of life and in the matter of returning lost property [M. B.M. 2:11].

    B.   But a woman takes precedence over a man in the matter of [providing] clothing and redemption from captivity.

    C.   When both of them are standing in danger of defilement, the man takes precedence over the woman.

3:8 A.   A priest takes precedence over a Levite, a Levite over an Israelite, an Israelite over a mamzer, a mamzer over a Netin, a Netin over a proselyte, a proselyte over a freed slave.

    B.   Under what circumstances?

    C.   When all of them are equivalent.

    D.   But if the mamzer was a disciple of a sage and a high priest was an am haares, the mamzer who is a disciple of a sage takes precedence over a high priest who is an am haares.

The principles of hierarchical classification are exemplified at M. Hor. 3:6-8. Precedence is accorded to the more regular or normal, to the male over the female (with exceptions deriving from the condition of the female), to the higher caste over the lower caste (with the exceptions deriving from the condition of all parties as to knowledge of the Torah).

Classification makes possible hierarchical classification, which for its part renders plausible argument on shared premises yielding firm results. Mishnah-tractate Negaim, on the disposition (classification) of those skin diseases under discussion at Leviticus Chapters Thirteen and Fourteen, provides a splendid and compelling exemplification of the power of classification to frame and solve problems. A profound problem of thought, extending backward into the Priestly Code in Leviticus, concerns the relationship of the holy and the unclean. That defines a point of contact between two utterly distinct realms, and how these then are to be drawn into relationship precipitates thought on hierarchization through not comparison but contrast: the principle of opposites and their relationship.

M. Negaim 13:10 concerns the relationship between the holy and the unclean.[11] The point is, the more susceptible to uncleanness, the higher the level of holiness,

---

[11]The comparison of religions yields many cases in which that which is subject to more restrictions also occupies a higher position in the hierarchy of the social and supernatural order alike.

and the higher the level of holiness, the greater the susceptibility to uncleanness.[12] So uncleanness and holiness in fact complement one another and generate, *mutatis mutandis,* precisely the same results. The upshot is that total opposites turn out to relate, to relate in the same way, and to produce the same effects. That is assuredly not an obvious or "commonsensical" position within the givens of the system, hence stands for a sum that transcends the parts.

MISHNAH-TRACTATE NEGAIM 13:10

A.   He was standing inside [an unclean house] but put his hand outside, with his rings on his fingers,

B.   if he remained for a time sufficient to eat a piece of bread,

C.   they are unclean.

D.   He was standing outside [an unclean house], and put his hand inside, with his rings on his fingers —

E.   R. Judah declares [them] unclean forthwith.

F.   And sages say, "[They are clean] until he will remain for a time sufficient for eating a piece of bread."

G.   They said to R. Judah, "If, when his entire body is unclean, he has not rendered unclean that which is on him until he will remain for a time sufficient to eat a piece of bread, when his entire body is not unclean, is it not logical that he not render what is on him unclean until he remains for a time sufficient to eat a piece of bread?"

The case of A-C has a clean man (not afflicted with saraat) enter an unclean house (afflicted with the disease), but, before he has stayed there any length of time, he sticks his hand out the window. The hand at that moment is still clean. If the man remains in the house long enough so that the rings, were they in the house itself, would become unclean, then the rings, though outside the house, become unclean. They are not separate from the man. What about the opposite case, Dff. Now we have the man outside, with his hand inside. Judah says the ring is unclean forthwith, not after the stated interval. Sages require the same interval as before, for the reason they give at G, an argument of hierarchical classification. Judah holds that since the man's body is outside, the rings are unclean as if they have come, on their own, into the house, and not because they are garments which the man is wearing. So he compares the case at hand to M. 13:9A-C, which follows, and sages to M. 13:9D-E:

---

[12]Mishnah-tractate Tohorot 1:9, 2:1ff. make precisely this same point.

Mishnah-tractate Negaim 13:9

A.   He who entered a house afflicted with plague,

B.   with his garments over his shoulder, and his sandals and rings in his hands-

C.   he and they are unclean forthwith.

D.   He was dressed in his garments, with his sandals on his feet and his rings on his fingers — he is unclean forthwith.

E.   But they are clean until he will remain for a time sufficient to eat a piece of bread —

F.   a piece of bread of wheat, and not a piece of bread of barley—

G.   reclining and eating it with condiment.

Now on what basis do I claim that the process of reasoning joins the opposites, unclean and holy, into a single unity? It is the framing of the issue through the amplification of the supplement to the Mishnah, the compilation called the Tosefta, that the matter is brought to explicit expression, as follows (with the citation of the Mishnah in bold face type):

Tosefta Negaim 7:9

[Cited verbatim from the Mishnah-passage above: And sages say, "[They are clean] until he will remain for a time sufficient for eating a piece of bread." They said to R. Judah, "If, when his entire body is unclean, he has not rendered unclean that which is on him until he will remain for a time sufficient to eat a piece of bread, when his entire body is not unclean, is it not logical that he not render what is on him unclean until he remains for a time sufficient to eat a piece of bread?"]

J.   Said to them R. Judah, "The reason is that the power of that which is susceptible to becoming unclean is greater to afford protection than the power of what is insusceptible of becoming unclean is to afford protection.

K.   "Israelites receive uncleanness and afford protection for clothing in the house afflicted with plague, but the gentile and the beast do not receive uncleanness and also do not afford protection for clothing in a house afflicted with the plague.

Judah's task, carried out at K, is to distinguish a case in which the entire body is unclean, when the rings are not unclean until an interval has passed, from the case in which the entire body is not unclean, in which case, he holds, utensils are supposed to become unclean forthwith.

His joining of uncleanness and holiness then follows: something which can become unclean also can afford protection and do so more readily than something which is insusceptible of becoming unclean at all. If Israelites are susceptible to becoming unclean, they also can afford protection for clothing. A person dressed in his sandals is unclean forthwith, but the sandals and garments he is wearing are still clean for a moment. But this applies only to Israelites. Gentiles or beasts, which are not subject to this form of uncleanness, entering the afflicted house will forthwith transfer contamination for garments or sandals which they are wearing." Then, as I said, there is a correspondence between one's status as to sanctification and one's susceptibility to uncleanness: the holier, the more sensitive to uncleanness. Then the two opposites form a single continuum and yield one point.

This argument and its numerous parallels are possible only within a system of classification, in which all thought is channeled into paths of comparison and contrast, inquiries into the genus and the species, the comparison of the species of a common genus, then the hierarchization of the results, one way or another. But hierarchical classification serves not only to relate opposites. It also allows for drawing conclusions that transcend the data on which the conclusions are based, which is to say, syllogistic argument. Let me give one fine instance of the way in which hierarchical classification makes possible that process of creative thought — *creative* being used in the exact sense of the word — derives from Mishnah-tractate Pesahim. In this case we consider the text, then its importance for our argument:

MISHNAH-TRACTATE PESAHIM 6:1-2

6:1   A.   These matters regarding the Passover sacrifice override [the prohibitions of] the Sabbath:

       B.   (1) slaughtering it, (2) tossing its blood, (3) scraping its entrails, and (4) burning its [sacrificial] pieces of fat,

       C.   But roasting it and rinsing its entrails do not override [the prohibitions of] the Sabbath.

       D.   Carrying it [to the Temple], bringing it from outside to inside the Sabbath limit, and cutting off a wen which is on it do not override [the prohibitions of] the Sabbath.

       E.   R. Eliezer says, "They do override [the prohibitions of the Sabbath]."

6:2   A.   Said R. Eliezer, "Now is it not logical [that these too should override the prohibitions of the Sabbath]?

       B.   "Now if slaughtering, which is prohibited under the category of labor, overrides [the prohibitions of] the Sabbath, these, which are [prohibited only] by reason of Sabbath rest [relying not upon the Scriptural prohibition of actual labor] — should they not override [the prohibitions of] the Sabbath?"

       C.   Said to him R. Joshua, "A festival day will prove [to the contrary. On festival days it is permitted to prepare necessary food, Ex. 12:16]. For they permitted work to be done on that day which is normally prohibited by reason of labor, but it is prohibited to do on that day [other actions] which are prohibited [merely] by reason of Sabbath rest."

D.   Said to him R. Eliezer, "Now what is the meaning of this, Joshua? How shall proof be derived from that which is an optional deed for that which is an obligatory one?"

E.   R. Aqiba replied and said, "Sprinkling [purification water on an unclean person] will prove the case. For it is an obligatory deed, and it is normally prohibited by reason of Sabbath rest, and it does not override [the prohibitions of] the Sabbath.

F.   "So you, do not be surprised concerning these matters, for even though they are obligatory deeds, and they are prohibited merely by reason of Sabbath rest, they should not override [the prohibition of] the Sabbath."

G.   Said to him R. Eliezer, "And upon this very fact I base my reasoning.

H.   "Now, if slaughtering, which is prohibited by reason of constituting an act of labor, overrides [the prohibitions of] the Sabbath, sprinkling [purification water on an unclean person], which is prohibited [merely] by reason of Sabbath rest — is it not logical that it [too] should override [the prohibitions of] the Sabbath?"

I.   Said to him R. Aqiba, "Matters are just the opposite. Now if sprinkling [purification water on an unclean person], which is prohibited by reason of Sabbath rest, does not override [the prohibitions of the Sabbath], slaughtering, which is prohibited by reason of constituting a prohibited act of labor — is it not logical that it too should not override [the prohibitions of] the Sabbath?"

J.   Said to him R. Eliezer, "Aqiba, you have uprooted that which is written in the Torah: At the twilight, at its appointed time (Num. 9:3) — whether this be an ordinary day or the Sabbath."

K.   He said to him, "Rabbi, bring me an 'appointed time' referring to these matters just as 'appointed time' refers to the actual act of slaughtering."

L.   A governing principle did R. Aqiba state, "Any form of labor which it is possible to carry out on the eve of the Sabbath does not override the Sabbath.

M.   "Slaughtering, which it is not possible to carry out on the eve of the Sabbath, does override the Sabbath."

On the Sabbath certain actions may be carried out in the preparation of the Passover sacrifice. Others may not. The issue then is the hierarchical classification of certain actions. If they fall into the category of a matter weightier than an action that may be carried out on the Sabbath, they fall into a hierarchical relationship with that action and all the more so may be done on the Sabbath: "if slaughtering, which is prohibited under the category of labor, overrides [the prohibitions of] the Sabbath, these, which are [prohibited only] by reason of Sabbath rest [relying not upon the Scriptural prohibition of actual labor] — should they not override [the prohibitions of] the Sabbath?" That argument then yields debate on whether or not the hierarchical classification is in fact a valid one. The issue is joined by the argument that there is no valid hierarchization at all, thus: "For they permitted work to be done on that day which is normally prohibited by reason of labor, but it is prohibited to do on that day [other actions] which are prohibited [merely] by reason of Sabbath rest." The unfolding of the argument then consists of challenges to the taxonomic premise of argument, e.g., "How shall proof be derived from that which is an optional deed for that which is an obligatory one?"

An exercise of hierarchization by appeal to traits inherent in the various classifications to be set into relationship, the exercise as a whole organizes information and transforms the data into a set of propositions — a deeply philosophical act. For at stake here is more than ordering and regularization of chaotic facts. It is the interest in the meanings of facts, why things are one way, rather than some other, why this, not that. In all, we want to know not only what propositions we may prove, but also what conclusions we must draw, from the classifications we can accomplish on the foundations of the traits of things. And that attitude of mind, yielding what we now call science, begins in hierarchical classification. To show how this process accomplishes its goals without even specifying a proposition to be demonstrated, we turn to a case in which merely collecting and properly classifying facts serves to yield a hierarchy, which is to say, an important proposition.

Let me here conclude with evidence that a complete tractate is devoted to the systematic work of hierarchical classification. For that purpose I present Mishnah-tractate Qiddushin. The rules cover the genus, the act of acquisition. The principle of the system as a whole is that things not only have indicative traits but also stand in relationship to all other things in a vast composition of order and regularity; and hierarchy is the upshot of order and regularity.

MISHNAH-TRACTATE QIDDUSHIN 1:1-8

1:1 A. A woman is acquired [as a wife] in three ways, and acquires [freedom for] herself [to be a free agent] in two ways.
   B. She is acquired through money, a writ, and sexual intercourse.
   C. Through money:
   D. The House of Shammai say, "For a denar or what is worth a denar"
   E. And the House of Hillel say, "For a perutah or what is worth a perutah."
   F. And how much is a perutah?
   G. One eighth of an Italian issar
   H. And she acquires herself through a writ of divorce and through the husband's death.
   I. The deceased childless brother's widow is acquired through an act of sexual relations.
   J. And acquires [freedom for] herself through a rite of Halisah and through the levir's death.
1:2 A. A Hebrew slave is acquired through money and a writ.

B. And he acquires himself through the passage of years, by the Jubilee year, and by deduction from the purchase price [redeeming himself at this outstanding value (Lev. 25:50-51)].

C. The Hebrew slave girl has an advantage over him.

D. For she acquires herself [in addition] through the appearance of tokens [of puberty].

E. The slave whose ear is pierced is acquired through an act of piercing the ear [Ex. 21:5].

F. And he acquires himself by the Jubilee and by the death of the master.

1:3 A. A Canaanite slave is acquired through money, through a writ, and through usucaption.

B. "And he acquires himself through money paid by others and through a writ [of indebtedness] taken on by himself," the words of R. Meir.

C. And sages say, "By money paid by himself and by a writ taken on by others,

D. "on condition that the money belongs to others."

1:4 1 A. "Large cattle are acquired through delivery, and small cattle through lifting, up'" the words of R. Meir and R. Eleazar.

B. And sages say, "Small cattle are acquired through an act of drawing."

1:5 A. Property for which there is security is acquired through money, writ and usucaption.

B. And that for which there is no security is acquired only by an act of drawing [from one place to another].

C. Property for which there is no security is acquired along with property for which there is security through money, writ, and usucaption.

D. And property for which there is no security imposes the need for an oath on property for which there is security.

1:6 A. Whatever is used as payment for something else,

B. once this one has effected acquisition [thereof] —

C. the other has become liable for what is given in exchange.

D. How so?

E. [If] one exchanged an ox for a cow, or an ass for an ox,

F. once this one has effected acquisition, the other has become liable for what is given in exchange.

G. The right of the Most High is effected through money, and the right of ordinary folk through usucaption.

H. One's word of mouth [dedication of an object] to the Most High is equivalent to one's act of delivery to an ordinary person.

1:7 1 A. For every commandment concerning the son to which the father is subject — men are liable, and women are exempt.

B. And for every commandment concerning the father to which the son is subject, men and women are equally liable.

C. For every positive commandment dependent upon the time [of year], men are liable, and women are exempt.

D. And for every positive commandment not dependent upon the time, men and women are equally liable.

      E.   For every negative commandment, whether dependent upon the time or not dependent upon the time, men and women are equally liable,

      F.   except for not marring the corners of the beard, not rounding the corners of the head (Lev. 19:27), and not becoming unclean because of the dead (Lev. 21:1).

1:8 A.   [The cultic rites of] laying on of hands, waving, drawing near, taking the handful, burning the incense, breaking the neck of a bird, sprinkling, and receiving [the blood]

      B.   apply to men and not to women,

      C.   except in the case of a meal offering of an accused wife and of a Nazirite girl, which they wave.

1:9 A.   Every commandment which is dependent upon the Land applies only in the Land,

      B.   and which does not depend upon the Land applies both in the Land and outside the Land,

      C.   except for Orlah and mixed seeds [Lev. 19:23, 19:19].

      D.   R. Eliezer says, "Also: Except for [the prohibition against eating] new [produce before the omer is waved on the sixteenth of Nisan] [Lev. 23:14]."

The six entries on human beings, and three on acquiring property — live, real, movable — set forth the nine categories in the order dictated by the pertinent traits listed in the successive predicates. At M. Qid. 1:8 we place into correct order men and women in relationship to various religious duties. Then at M. Qid. 1:9 the land is now placed into hierarchical relationship with other lands. Now what has happened here?

      The philosophical achievement at M. Qid. 1:1ff. is to collect and arrange in a coherent and intelligible manner diverse and otherwise unrelated facts. This is done by drawing into alignment, hence into a hierarchy, the diverse parties, on the one side, and the diverse facts, on the other. M. Qid. 1:7-8 presents six items on the liability of two classes of persons, women and men, to diverse kinds of commandments, which are then the predicate for the second construction. . M. Qid. 1:9 finally places into correct order the Land of Israel and other lands. I identify a profoundly philosophical mode of presenting information aimed at establishing an important proposition. For the upshot of the taxonomic exercise is hierarchization, and the setting forth of the relative positions of women, slaves, cattle, and property, on the on side, and men and women, on the other, surely constitutes an argument and a proposition, not merely a neutral repertoire of facts. And I should claim that all hierarchical exercises yield propositions of an imposing order indeed. But whence the principles of speciation?

v. THE GENUS AND THE SPECIES

      The Mishnah's framers' principle of speciation — like that of natural history as defined by Aristotle — appealed to the intrinsic traits, the nature, of things. The contrary claim, implicit throughout Sifra's critique of the Mishnah,[13] said that, without the revelation of the Torah, the human intellect can identify in the end only species, no genera. Sifra's authorship also maintained that many things never can become one thing except God makes them so and tells us in the Torah. To these allegations the framers of the Mishnah would respond by adducing the evidence at hand: things speak for themselves. They would (in this hypothetical argument) demonstrate that the created world exhibits not chaos but order and a regularity we can ourselves uncover. The critique of this position can be shown to contradict the facts of the palpable world, the creation of which, after all, the Torah describes.

These facts derive from every aspect and modality of all created existence: the natural world, society, language and culture, the life of the soul, the heart, the mind. All cohere. In nature and the nurtured world of culture, everywhere one turns to analyze the facts round about, the same simple givens emerge. Many things can be shown, through proper classification, comparison and contrast of pertinent traits, to be one thing. And all things merge in the hierarchy of being that one thing comprises. The contrary argument, that speciation properly carried out forms an obstacle to the composition (or recognition) of genera, appeals merely to cases, not to principles and forms an argument from example and episode, not well-examined generalization. So, I think, the authorship of the Mishnah will surely have wished to point out.

Our philosophers therefore will not have been witless for an answer to their most interesting critics. For, they can have responded, "But then how many cases do I need to adduce in evidence to demonstrate the falsity of classification by analysis of the intrinsic traits of things? And how many times do I have to demonstrate the fallacy of the claim that only Scripture provides the right categories?" The other side — Sifra's contrary-minded philosophers — can never conclude matters. For the possibility of making up cases is limited only by the recusant imagination. And no number of examples, even an infinity, proves anything; the imagination by definition is fecund. But, no principle subject to generalization beyond discrete cases having been proved, no universally applicable logic having been tested, no general rule having been established, the critique of the philosophy of classification by traits of things accomplishes no worthwhile goal. In the end it is simply not philosophical — so Sifra's authorship will have had to admit, had the philosophers of the Mishnah had their say.

The contrary view rests upon simple logic, not merely on complex cases, fabricated up one by one for the occasion. It is that claim we now have considered in full that everything has its thingness, its true category or class. It is the intrinsic or inherent traits of things themselves that define the true character of those things. It follows that we can so describe things as to identify the active and definitive, indicative traits. From there we can show that other things have (some of) these

---

[13]I briefly summarize my *Uniting the Dual Torah*, cited earlier.

same traits. Having identified a genus formed by appeal to intrinsic traits, we may proceed to speciate, pointing to differences between like and like. And the consequence of this labor of simple, logical formation of genera and differentiation of species is ineluctable. The fundamental principle that is applied here is that like things follow the same rule, unlike things, the opposite rule. In many ways the demonstration of the interplay of species of a common genus forms the complement to the analysis of interstitiality, to which, in due course, our attention must turn. Here the main point suffices: the work depends upon comparison and contrast. By definition, philosophical modes of thought appeal to rules of correct classification of things, and these rules are revealed for us through the presence or absence of taxic indicators.

To appreciate the power, indeed the closure, of argument accomplished by the philosophers of the Mishnah, we rapidly return to the upshot of our encounter with their practical logic. Here we shall see how speciation of a genus yields a hierarchy and produces the besought order of things, and, further, we note once more that happy union of rhetoric and logic with the philosophical task that yields in medium as much as in message the single systemic philosophy. If the claim that we have only species and no genus is to be sustained, then here is the kind of success — so our philosophers will have alleged — that has successfully to be overturned, this and every one like it.

To follow the case I have selected,[14] we have to remember that the common genus, "ruler," contains at least two species, high priest, and king. Then the high priest and the king form a single genus, but two distinct species, and the variations between the species form a single set of taxonomic indicators. The one is like the other in these ways, unlike the other in those ways. The remainder of Mishnah-tractate Sanhedrin Chapter Two shows the secondary amplification and discussion of the implication of the established principle, and that principle proves generative of further syllogisms, proposed and debated in the secondary details of the passage. Accordingly, in that exemplification of the working of the genus and the species we see a fine example of the generative logic of list-making, a taxonomy.

The study of the genus, national leader, and its two species, [1] king, [2] high priest shows how are they alike, how are they not alike, and what accounts for the differences. The premise is that national leaders are alike and follow the same rule, except where they differ and on that account follow each the opposite rule from the other. But that premise also is subject to the proof effected by the survey of the data consisting of concrete rules, those systemically inert facts that here come to life for the purposes of establishing a proposition. The whole depends upon three premises, already introduced: [1] the importance of comparison and contrast, with the supposition that [2] like follows the like, and the unlike follows the opposite, rule; and [3] when we classify, we also hierarchize, which yields the argument from

---

[14]And it is one of my favorites, because of its self-evidence and simplicity.

hierarchical classification: if this, which is the lesser, follows rule X, then that, which is the greater, surely should follow rule X. And that is the whole sum and substance of the logic of *Listenwissenschaft* as the Mishnah applies that logic in a practical way.

The upshot is simple. The power of taxonomic inquiry lies in its capacity to solve problems set by the infinite agenda of reality. No case in which speciation of a genus yields only species in the end is possible — pace Sifra's philosophers' position — because this method serves for all imaginable cases. Like scientific method, the theory of classification of genus and species in theory claims to extend to the outer limits of not knowledge but facts. That is why that mode of thought can solve all problems and therefore, *and thereby,* create new knowledge, just as syllogistic thought could and did create new knowledge in both Greek and medieval-Christian philosophy and science. A detailed examination of the workings of the philosophy would require a review of nearly all of the tractates of the Mishnah. For while only the majority of them attends to a fundamentally philosophical protocol, every one of them, without exception, draws upon the rhetoric and logic of *Listenwissenschaft* to make its points. That is what gives the document its uniform character throughout. But this uniformity of form and medium of thought is deceiving. For the power of the document flows from the mode of thought that it exemplifies and expresses, not the persuasive character of its rhetoric or the self-evidence of its logic or the ineluctable truth of its propositions; these comprise mere epiphenomena. Truth lies in right analysis, everywhere working its power of rationality. And that rationality consists in the simple view that much is little, many one, all susceptible of forming genera of one kind or another, every genus accessible of speciation.

To grasp the working of the mode of thought when it addresses very concrete problems of the genus and the species, let us review a variety of cases. Each one is meant to illustrate a stage in the unfolding of philosophical method. The first step in method of hierarchical classification is the simplest: showing that two or more things are one thing, and then demonstrating what difference it makes that one thing encompasses different things. This then shows us that species form a genus. At M. Nedarim 6:1ff. we have an exercise in showing the relationships between a genus and its species and also two species of a common genus. The matter is worked out over and over again, with a single result. We have to identify what is subject to a common genus, e.g., cooking covers roasting and seething, but also what is not within that genus. If one denies himself cooked food, he cannot eat what is loosely cooked in a pot but may eat what is solidly cooked in a pot, and so throughout.

MISHNAH-TRACTATE NEDARIM 6:1-6, 8-10

6:1   A.   He who takes a vow not to eat what is cooked is permitted [to eat what is] roasted or seethed.

B. [If] he said, "Qonam if I taste cooked food," he is prohibited from eating what is loosely cooked in a pot but permitted to eat which is solidly cooked in a pot.

C. And he is permitted to eat a lightly boiled egg or gourds prepared in hot ashes.

6:2 A. He who takes a vow not to eat what is cooked in a pot is prohibited only from what is boiled [therein].

B. [If] he said, "Qonam if I taste anything which goes down into a pot'" he is prohibited from eating anything which is cooked in a pot.

6:3 A. [He who takes a vow not to eat] what is pickled is prohibited only from eating pickled vegetables.

B. [If he said, "Qonam] if I taste anything pickled," he is prohibited from eating anything which is pickled.

C. [If he took a vow not to eat what is] seethed, he is forbidden only from eating seethed meat.

D. [If he said, "Qonam] if I taste anything seethed," he is prohibited from eating anything which is seethed.

E. "[He who takes a vow not to eat] what is roasted is prohibited only from eating roasted meat," the words of R. Judah.

F. [If he said, "Qonam] if I taste anything roasted," he is prohibited from eating anything which is roasted.

G. [He who takes a vow not to eat] what is salted is prohibited only from eating salted fish.

H. [If he said, "Qonam] if I eat anything salted," then he is prohibited from eating anything at all which is salted.

6:4 A. [He who says, "Qonam] if I taste fish or fishes," is prohibited [to eat) them, whether large or small, salted or unsalted, raw or cooked.

B. But he is permitted to eat pickled chopped fish and brine.

C. He who vows not to eat small fish is prohibited from eating pickled chopped fish. But he is permitted to eat brine and fish brine.

D. He who vowed [not to eat] pickled chopped fish is prohibited from eating brine and fish brine.

6:5 A. He who vows not to have milk is permitted to eat curds.

B. And R. Yosé prohibits [eating curds].

C. [If he vowed not to eat] curds, he is permitted to have milk.

D. Abba Saul says, "He who vows not to eat cheese is prohibited to eat it whether it is salted or unsalted."

6:6 A. He who takes a vow not to eat meat is permitted to eat broth and meat sediment.

B. And R. Judah prohibits [him from eating broth and meat sediment].

C. Said R. Judah, M'SH W: "R. Tarfon prohibited me from eating eggs which were roasted with it [meat]."

D. They said to him, "And that is the point! Under what circumstances? When he will say, 'This meat is prohibited to me.'

E. "For he who vows not to eat something which is mixed with something else, if there is sufficient [of the prohibited substance] to impart a flavor, is prohibited [from eating the mixture]."

6:6   A.   He who takes a vow not to eat meat is permitted to eat broth and meat sediment.

      B.   And R. Judah prohibits [him from eating broth and meat sediment].

      C.   Said R. Judah, "R. Tarfon prohibited me from eating eggs which were roasted with it [meat]."

      D.   They said to him, "And that is the point! Under what circumstances? When he will say, 'This meat is prohibited to me.'

      E.   "For he who vows not to eat something which is mixed with something else, if there is sufficient [of the prohibited substance] to impart a flavor, is prohibited [from eating the mixture]."

6:8   A.   He who takes a vow not to eat dates is permitted to have date honey.

      B.   [He who takes a vow not to eat] winter grapes is permitted to have the vinegar made from winter grapes.

      C.   R. Judah b. Beterah says, "Anything which is called after the name of that which is made from it, and one takes a vow not to have it-he is prohibited also from eating that which comes from it."

      D.   But sages permit.

6:9   A.   He who takes a vow not to have wine is permitted to have apple wine.

      B.   [He who takes a vow not to have] oil is permitted to have sesame oil.

      C.   He who takes a vow not to have honey is permitted to have date honey.

      D.   He who takes a vow not to have vinegar is permitted to have the vinegar of winter grapes.

      E.   He who takes a vow not to have leeks is permitted to have shallots.

      F.   He who takes a vow not to have vegetables is permitted to have wild vegetables,

      G.   since they have a special name.

6:10 1 A.   [He who takes a vow not to eat] cabbage is forbidden from asparagus [deemed a species of the cabbage genus].

      B.   [He who takes a vow not to eat] asparagus is permitted to have cabbage.

      C.   [He who takes a vow not to have] grits is forbidden to have grits pottage.

      D.   And R. Yosé permits it.

      E.   [He who takes a vow not to eat] grits pottage is permitted to have grits.

      F.   [He who takes a vow not to eat] grits pottage is forbidden to eat garlic.

      G.   And R. Yosé permits it.

      H.   [He who takes a vow not to eat] garlic is permitted to eat grits pottage.

      I.   [He who takes a vow not to eat] lentils is forbidden from eating lentil cakes.

      J.   And R. Yosé permits.

      K.   [He who takes a vow not to eat] lentil cakes is permitted to eat lentils.

L. [He who says, "Qonam] if I taste [a grain of] wheat or wheat [ground
up in any form]" is forbidden from eating it, whether it is ground up
or in the form of bread.

M. [If he said, "Qonam if I eat] a grit [or] grits in any form," he is
forbidden from eating them whether raw or cooked.

N. R. Judah says, "[If he said,] 'Qonam if I eat either a grit or a [grain
of] wheat,' he is permitted to chew them raw."

The matter is worked out over and over again, with a single result. We have to
identify what is subject to a common genus, e.g., cooking covers roasting and
seething, but also what is not within that genus. If one denies himself cooked food,
he cannot eat what is loosely cooked in a pot but may eat what is solidly cooked in
a pot, and so throughout. The upshot of these materials, continued at M. 6:4-5, is
carefully to show how the genus defines its species. M. Nedarim 6:6, 8-10 review
matters of the genus and the species. If I wanted to make up a rule book for students'
study of the rules of forming a genus, identifying the species, and then drawing
conclusions from the work, I cannot imagine a more effective mode of teaching
than the case at hand.

Mishnah-tractate Niddah 6:2-10 present what I conceive to be a climactic
exercise of taxonomy: the specification of species and their exceptions
(subspeciation). The unit is so well composed that I present nearly the whole of it,
since I think it provides fine evidence that philosophical the lesson that the framers
which to teach concerns the issue of subspeciation and how it plays itself out. Now
to our case

MISHNAH-TRACTATE NEDARIM 6:2-10

6:2 A. Similarly:

B . Any clay utensil that will let in a liquid will let it out.

C. But there is one which lets out a liquid and does not let it in.

D. Every limb which has a claw on it has a bone on it, but there is that
which has a bone on it and does not have a claw on it.

6:3 A. Whatever is susceptible to Midras uncleanness is susceptible to corpse
uncleanness, but there is that which is susceptible to corpse
uncleanness and is not susceptible to Midras uncleanness.

6:4 A. Whoever is worthy to judge capital cases is worthy to judge property
cases and there is one who is worthy to judge property cases and is
not worthy to judge capital cases.

B. Whoever is suitable to judge is suitable to give testimony, but there
is one who is suitable to give testimony but is not suitable to judge.

6:5 A. Whatever is liable for tithes is susceptible to the uncleanness
pertaining to foods, but there is that which is susceptible to the
uncleanness pertaining to foods and is not liable for tithes.

6:6 A. Whatever is liable for Pe'ah is liable for tithes, but there is that which
is liable for tithes and is not liable for Pe'ah.

6:7 A.   Whatever is liable for the law of the first of the fleece is liable for the
           priestly gifts, but there is that which is liable for the priestly gifts and
           is not liable for the first of the fleece.
6:8 A.   Whatever is subject to the requirement of removal is subject to the
           law of the Seventh Year and there is that which is subject to the law
           of the Seventh Year and is not subject to the requirement of removal.
6:9 A.   Whatever has scales has fins, but there is that which has fins and
           does not have scales.
     B.   Whatever has horns has hooves, and there is that which has hooves
           and does not have horns,
6:10 A.   Whatever requires a blessing after it requires a blessing before it, but
           there is that which requires a blessing before it and does not require
           a blessing after it.

The cases are so immediately accessible that we may turn forthwith to the question:
what do we learn about the genus and the species?

First, a genus may encompass species that differ in some ways from one
another, but that, nonetheless, fall within the common genus. This implicit affirmation
of polythetic taxonomy fully responds to the critique of Sifra's authorship of the
principles of identifying genera by appeal to the traits of things, not to the
classifications imposed by Scripture. Indeed, if I had to point to a single effective
reply in the form of a case, it is to this case. Then we see, in the speciation, what is
at stake. All bear one trait, there is one exception. It is the exception, within the
genus, that provokes us to recognize the speciation of the genus. And that is the
simple point that the authorship of this exquisite composition wishes to make.

Is speciation always the consequence of identifying a genus? Not at all. The
philosophers are quick to underline how many species, once formed into a common
class of things, in consequence of forming a genera may lose differentiating indicative
traits. That is to say, the genera serves to obscure points of difference among the
species, by itself imposing upon them all a single criterion of classification, which
is its own. This forms a stunningly subtle response to the critique that there are only
genera, only species. It is to say, to the contrary, once we know the genus, there are
no species, because other points of differentiation are not indicative! Here is a very
simple example.

MISHNAH-TRACTATE PESAHIM 1:6

1:6 A.   R. Hananiah, Prefect of the priests, says, "In the days of the priests
           they never refrained from burning meat which had been made unclean
           by an Offspring of uncleanness with meat which had been made by a
           Father of uncleanness,
     B.   "even though they [thereby] add uncleanness to its uncleanness [that
           of the meat made unclean by an Offspring of uncleanness]."
     C.   Added R. Aqiba and said, "In the days of the priests they never
           refrained from burning oil [in the status of heave offering] made

invalid by one who had immersed in that same day, in a lamp which had been made unclean by one who had contracted corpse uncleanness,

D.   "even though they [thereby] add uncleanness to its uncleanness [that of the heave offering oil invalidated by one who had immersed on that same day]."

M. Pes. 1:6(+7) makes an interesting taxonomic point. It treats as an encompassing genus, without further speciation, the classification of uncleanness. Once something is in that classification, we do not further classify; it is not only encompassing but also homogenizing, that is, a genus with no species. And that observation is in fact the point of the composition, which is explicit: "even though they [thereby] add uncleanness to its uncleanness [that of the meat made unclean by an Offspring of uncleanness]."

Thus far we have seen how the analytical thought based on the distinction of the genus and the species treats palpable things, with traits that we can touch and feel. But what about the speciation of ineffable abstractions, e.g., not fire but the intangible, heat? There should be no reason for the process of differentiation and reconstruction to limit itself to the concrete and the material, and indeed, we can find numerous cases of pure abstraction. One of them concern the physical problem, what is heat? If we can show the marks of the speciation of the genus, heat, then we may, in theory, expect the same analytical procedure to work in abstractions of any kind.

MISHNAH-TRACTATE SHABBAT 3:1-3, 5, 4:1

3:1   A.   A double stove which [people] have heated with stubble or straw —
       B.   they put cooked food on it.
       C.   [But if they heated it] with peat or with wood, one may not put [anything] on it until he has swept it out,
       D.   or until he has covered it with ashes.
       E.   The House of Shammai say, "Hot water but not cooked food [may one put on it on the eve of the Sabbath]."
       F.   And the House of Hillel say, "Hot water and cooked food."
       G.   The House of Shammai say, "[On the Sabbath] they take off [hot water placed thereon], but they do not put it back."
       H.   And the House of Hillel say, "Also: they put it back."
3:2   A.   An oven which [people] have heated with stubble or with straw-one should not put anything either into it or on top of it.
       B.   A single stove which [people] have heated with stubble or with straw, lo, this is equivalent to a double stove.
       C.   [If they heated it] with peat or with wood, lo, it is equivalent to an oven.
3:3   A.   They do not put an egg beside a kettle [on the Sabbath] so that it will be cooked.

B.   And one should not crack it into [hot] wrappings.

C.   And R. Yosé permits.

D.   And one should not bury it in sand or in road dirt so that it will be roasted.

3:5 A.   A kettle [containing hot water] which one removed [from the stove] —

B.   one should not put cold water into it so that it [the cold water] may get warm.

C.   But one may put [enough cold water] into it or into a cup so that [the hot water] will cool off.

D.   The pan or pot which one has taken off the stove while it is boiling —

E.   one may not put spices into it.

F.   But he may put [spices] into [hot food which is] in a plate or a dish.

G.   R. Judah says, "Into anything may one put [spices], except what has vinegar or fish brine [in it] ."

4:1 A.   With what do they cover [up food to keep it hot], and with what do they not cover up [food to keep it hot]?

B.   They do not cover with (1) peat, (2) compost, (3) salt, (4) lime, or (5) sand, C. whether wet or dry.

D.   or with (6) straw, (7) grape skins, (8) flocking [rags], or (9) grass, when wet.

E.   But they do cover up [food to keep it hot] with them when they are dry.

F.   They cover up [food to keep it hot] with (1) cloth, (2) produce, (3) the wings of a dove, (4) carpenters' sawdust, and (5) soft hackled flax.

G.   R. Judah prohibits in the case of soft [hackled flax] and permits in the case of coarse [hackled flax].

As we see, M. Shab. 3:1-3 work on an interesting distinction in the genus, heat. The law is that one may not cook a meal on the Sabbath, but he may keep a meal warm. How to use heat that is already present in the stove or oven from the eve of the Sabbath? That is the problem of speciation of the genus, heat. The answer is that one may not use materials that make coals, since these end up heating the food and not merely preserving pre-existing heat. Stubble or straw may be used. If the oven is heated with peat or wood, which yields coals, one may not put food on the oven until the coals have been removed or covered with dirt.

The later cases go over the same problem of the speciation of heat. At M. Shab. 3:5 the issue of differentiating among types of heat is turned on its head. One cannot heat a small volume of cold water but may pour in enough cold water to temper hot water. M. 4:1 takes up the same issues of the speciation of heat. The besought case is now self-evidently in hand: not only concrete genera, such as foods, are subject to speciation. The most abstract problems of imaginative thought, typified by the question, are there species of the genus, heat? assuredly fall within the capacities of the analysis of the genus and the species.

Abstractions of physics form one piece of evidence that this philosophy so works as to accommodate all manner of materials within its mode of thought. Abstractions of space of place present another piece of evidence for the same proposition. The problem at hand is the speciation of the genus, contained space. That seems to me still more impalpable than the genus, heat. Contained space, after all, may be minute or enormous, and therefore considerations of whether difference in volume yields difference in character have to be brought into play. Not only so, but contained space by definition involves position, and position is relative, invariably so, to something in some other position. A bottle and a room, a house and a cave — all are species of the genus, contained space. And that brings us to a remarkably exercise in the comparison and contrast of contained spaces, from a bee hive to a room, from a bottle to the belly of a dog, that is worked out in Mishnah-tractate Ohalot.

MISHNAH-TRACTATE OHALOT 9:1

A.   A hive which is in the midst of the house, and its mouth is toward the outside —

B.   about an olive's bulk of corpse matter is placed under it or on top of it, outside —

C.   whatever is directly opposite the olive's bulk, below it, or on top of it is unclean.

D.   And whatever is not opposite the olive's bulk, inside it, and the house is clean.

E.   In the house — unclean is only the house.

F.   In it — all is unclean.

Mishnah-tractate Ohalot Chapter Nine works out a detailed picture of the relationship between a utensil and a Tent. This work of comparison and contrast begins in the premise that a Tent and a utensil form a common genus, in that both of them contain and close off space. Then how do we classify an object that may constitute either a Tent or a utensil? We deal with a hire, made of a substance that is not susceptible to uncleanness. If the object is whole and can serve as a container, it is classified as a utensil. In relationship to corpse-matter, it then illustrates the rule governing a utensil. If the object is broken and cannot serve as a normal utensil, it is sufficiently large in and of itself to constitute a tent. The complications produced by these facts make for a vast and engaging chapter. We work out the hive as utensil, in various situations. If the airspace of the utensil and that of the house are not intermingled, we have one result; if they are, we have a different result. We then posit that the hive forms a tent, serving to spread contamination but not to provide for interposition; it is a utensil. It does interpose to protect its own contents.

We so arrange matters that we have sequences of cases that illustrate the diverse rules of classification of the object as utensil or tent and the way in which these rules apply to various situations, a truly brilliant composition of a grid of rules for the classification of cases.

MISHNAH-TRACTATE OHALOT 10:1, 11:1, 7; 12:1

A. A hatchway which is in the midst of the house, and there is in it a square handbreadth —

B. uncleanness is in the house —

C. that which is directly below the hatchway is clean.

D. Uncleanness is directly below the hatchway —

E. the house is clean.

F. Whether the uncleanness is in the house or in the [space] below the hatchway,

G. [if] one set his foot above it, he has combined the uncleanness.

H. Part of the uncleanness is in the house, and part of it is directly below the hatchway —

I. the house is unclean.

J. And that which is directly above the uncleanness is unclean.

11:1 A. The house which split —

B. uncleanness is on the outer side —

C. utensils which are on the inner side are clean.

D. Uncleanness is on the inner side —

E. utensils which are on the outer side —

F. The House of Shammai say, "Until there is in the split four handbreadths."

G. The House of Hillel say, "Any amount."

H. R. Yosé says in the name of the House of Hillel, "A square handbreadth."

11:7 A. A dog which ate the flesh of the corpse, and the dog died and was lying on the threshold —

B. R. Meir says, "If his neck is a handbreadth wide, he brings the uncleanness, and if not, he does not bring the uncleanness."

C. R. Yosé says, "We examine the uncleanness. [If the dog's belly is] from directly beneath the lintel and inside, [toward the house], the house is unclean. [If it is) from directly beneath the lintel and [towards the] outside, the house is clean."

D. R. Eleazar says, "[If] his mouth is inside, the house is clean; [if] his mouth is outside, the house is unclean, for the uncleanness exudes through his hind-parts."

E. R. Judah b. Beterah says, "One way or the other, the house is unclean."

12:1 A. A board which was placed over the mouth of a new oven and it projects on all its sides for a square handbreadth —

B. uncleanness is under it —

C. utensils which are on top of it are clean.

D. Uncleanness is on top of it —

E. utensils which are under it are clean.

F. And in the case of an old one, it is unclean.

G. R. Yohanan b. Nuri declares clean.
H. It was placed over the mouths of two ovens —
I. uncleanness is between them —
J. they are unclean.
K. R. Yohanan b. Nuri declares clean.

Chapter Ten presents us with a different set of problems of the commingling of space, now having to do with a house with a hatchway, a square handbreadth, open to the air, a kind of skylight. The hatch is of requisite space to permit the egress of uncleanness; since it is open to the air, it forms a separate and autonomous domain. Uncleanness affecting it will not affect the surrounding space of the house and vice versa. M. 10:1 presents the simple rule of the matter. We proceed to ask about a hatchway of less than a square handbreadth, that is, of less than requisite size for the egress of uncleanness; then we have uncleanness partially subject to the domain of the house and partly within the area of the hatchway, two hatchways, and the like — all issues of commingling, mixture and the distinction of space.

Mishnah-tractate Ohalot Chapter Eleven asks about the division of space, e.g., a roof of a house which has split. Is the space beneath deemed divided or united? Utensils under one part are not contaminated by uncleanness under the other; the space is not commingled once the Tent has split into two. M. 11:2 completes the matter and forms a transition to M. 11:3-7, which deal with whether or not a man can form a tent. That is to say, once we have compared a utensil to a Tent, we ask whether man falls into the same genus at all. He encompasses an empty space of requisite volume, that is, the contained space of the belly, so he does form a tent for the transmission of uncleanness. A man cannot form a tent for interposition, but a beast can, so M. 11:7. Now the contained space is the belly of a dog, joined in one direction by the esophagus upward to the throat and the mouth the other, the intestines to the anus. We have a dog which has eaten a piece of a corpse and died on a threshold. How do we determine whether the house is unclean? One principle is, does the dog form a tent over the corpse matter in its belly? Another is, where is the corpse matter located? A third is, where is the point of egress of the contamination to be found? Then from what part of the dog — mouth or anus — is the contamination going to exude? M. 12:1 pursues the issue of the analogy of the tent yet a step further. Now we have a board held up by a new, insusceptible oven. It forms a tent. The cases that follow then produce refinements. The issue is whether the oven itself interposes.

When I claimed that the fundamental mode of analytical thought was one of classification, I adduced in evidence not only cases but the traits of mind of the substantial part of entire tractates, Mishnah-tractates Berakhot., Qiddushin, and much of Sanhedrin, not to mention Mishnah-tractate Meilah to show the centrality of classification in imparting cogency to a tractate as a whole. Demonstrating how a complete tractate laid out principles permitted me to claim that I deal with a sustaining analytical method, not merely the happenstance of a single case. Can I show the same for the problem before us: the speciation of the genus? Indeed so. Let me now point to an entire tractate that through the medium of thought on the genus and the species works its way, beginning to end, through its topic.

The tractate is Yadayim, and the topic, the modes of cultic cleaning of hands for a meal in a state of cultic cleanness. Rather than give episodic cases, I rapidly describe the definitive chapter of the tractate as a whole. That account demonstrates how the analysis of the genus and the species, and the working out of the consequences of the principles of that mode of thought, take over and govern thought on an entire topical unit.

Mishnah-tractate Yadayim, in its legal passages, is philosophical in its modes of thought and in its repertoire of issues, because its mode of thought appeals to the species of a genus through analogical-contrastive modes of thought. The tractate on the purification of hands spins out its rules by appeal to the comparable ones of the rite of burning the red cow and mixing the ashes with water as described by Mishnah-tractate Parah. The reason for the comparison is simple. The rite of burning the red cow and making purification-water for the removal of corpse-uncleanness, described at Numbers 19:1ff., takes place outside of the Temple, yet involves a high degree of cultic purity. The rite of purifying hands likewise takes place outside of the Temple, and yet involves effecting cultic cleanness. That analogy forms of the two subjects a single genus. And the comparison and contrast — hands against the rite of the red cow — accounts for the formation of the singular rules at hand. So Yadayim is very much a philosophical tractate, because it is a tractate framed through analogical-contrastive thinking on the foundations of Mishnah-tractate Parah.

Since this tractate spins out its laws through comparisons and contrasts with the rules governing the preparation of purification-water for the rite of purification from corpse uncleanness, we ask, how, in particular, is the comparison of the species of the genus carried on? The answer is that the work is fully exposed only in one detail or another, a result that, by this point, can hardly surprise any reader. One instance is the requirement that in purification of hands, water must be contained within a utensil before it is poured out on the hands. Accordingly, that a utensil must be used is one systemically active detail, and, as a matter of fact, it is a detail borrowed from the rite of the red cow. It is not the only fact deriving from one species for the other by means of the operative and generative analogy. That water that has been used in connection with some act of labor may not be used for washing hands is another. Parallel to the rules on who may sprinkle purification-water is the issue of who may pour out water on the hands, but here it is a matter of contrast: it may be anyone, even an ape. Uncleanness of hands is removed by water, preparation of the water is to accord with rules pertinent to the purification-water of Mishnah-tractate Parah — when the matter is comparable, and to contrast with those rules when not.

MISHNAH-TRACTATE YADAYIM 1:1-3

1:1 A. [To render hands clean] a quarter-log of water do they pour for hands,
    B. for one,
    C. also for two.
    D. A half-log [is to be used] for three or four.
    E. A log [is to be used] for five and for ten and for a hundred.
    F. R. Yosé says, "And on condition that for the last among them, there should not be less than a quarter-log."
    G. They add [to the water used] for the second [pouring], but they do not add [to the water used] for the first [pouring of water over the hands].
1:2 A. With all sorts of utensils do they pour [water] for hands,
    B. even with utensils made of dung, utensils made of stone, utensils made of [unbaked] clay.
    C. They do not pour [water] for hands either with the sides of [broken] utensils, or the bottom of a ladling jar, or with the plug of a barrel.
    D. Nor should a man pour [water] for his fellow with his cupped hands.
    E. For they draw, and they mix [water with the ash of the red cow], and they sprinkle purification water, and they pour [water] for hands only with a utensil.
    F. And only utensils afford protection with a tightly fitted cover, and nothing affords protection from the power of a clay utensil [in the Tent of a corpse] except utensils.
1:3 A. Water which was unfit for cattle to drink
    B. [when it is located] in utensils, is unfit.
    C. [When it is located] on the ground, it is fit.
    D. [If] there fell into it ink, gum, or copperas, and its color changed, it is unfit.
    E. [If] one did work with it,
    F. or if he soaked his bread in it,
    G. it is unfit.
    H. Simeon of Teman says, "Even if he intended to soak [bread] in this and it fell into the second, it [the second] is fit."

Here in Mishnah-tractate Yadayim we have philosophical method in the mode of analogical-contrastive thinking. I see sustained work of classification in Chapter One, generating a set of rules bearing no philosophical interest whatsoever.

The exposition proceeds through an orderly exposition of the laws of washing hands: [1] the volume of water to be used (1:1); [2] the sort of utensil that is to hold the water (1:2); [3] the character of the water (1:3-5); [4] the persons who are employed. Is a fixed volume of water required, a quarter-log? M. 1:2 goes over the ground of M. Par. 5:5, thus underlining the analogical character of this tractate. For analogical-contrastive thinking, which is at work here, forms an important chapter in the philosophical mode of thought, which classifies data and so works out the correct rule governing things. This is done, in the present case, by appeal to the like and the unlike, and forms a profoundly philosophical exercise in rule-making through taxonomy. On that basis I treat the entire repertoire of rules of Chapter One as an exercise in philosophical thought of the analogical-contrastive order. Uncleanness of hands is removed by water, preparation of the water is to accord with rules pertinent to the purification-water of Mishnah-tractate Parah — when the matter is comparable, and to contrast with those rules when not. So here we have philosophical method in the mode of analogical-contrastive thinking.

Now, to conclude, if we ask ourselves, what is at stake in the work of identifying the genus and then comparing and contrasting its species? the answer is self-evident. At stake in the genus and the species is not merely the organization of information but the generation of new genera and new speciation, in more general terms, new syllogisms. And when that becomes plausible, then we have not merely method but message, expressed in detail to be sure. That is to say, what has become possible is the creation of not merely new information but new categories altogether. And that defines the ultimate act of creation.

Now that we grasp the stakes of show that species form genera, we proceed to the next logical question, which is, how then do we know one species from another?

VI. PRINCIPLES OF SPECIATION

Four principles or criteria of speciation are readily identified.

[1] The first concerns the formal or merely manifest as against the intrinsic or real traits of things, that is to say, the relationship between appearance and reality.

[2] The second derives from the definitive power of the function of things, as against their mere form, that is, not what they are but how they work.

[3] The third addresses reality now and reality then, which is to say, the relationship of the actual and the potential.

[4] And the fourth, and a very common one in the Mishnah's system, therefore held to be quite useful for the Mishnah's own systemic program, addresses the interplay between what one wants to have happen and what actually does happen: intention and outcome.

The reason that these four principles require detailed and protracted attention and are best shown to be subordinate and contingent upon the main task of the system, hierarchical classification, is simple. All four possess disruptive power within a system centered upon classification. Each can on its own serve as an argument against the entirety of the taxonomic structure. I say so because any one of these four distinctions of weight and ubiquity provides a variable, on the one side, and an unanswerable doubt, on the other. Let me explain what I mean by asking a sequence of exceedingly difficult questions.

How can I classify anything, if I cannot distinguish appearance from reality? And what takes precedence, what something is or what it does? And is the now definitive, or the becoming the main thing? Shall I dismiss teleology in all its forms? And, finally, where is there place, in a static account of things, for my wishes and intentionality?

All four of these principles thus serve to introduce movement into a philosophy of classification that wishes to account for the static order of things and to show how everything remains at rest in a well-composed universe. The solution to the problem of movement and disorder represented by imponderables and variables drew upon the system's own capacities. That is a mark of the power of the philosophy itself, just as — so we just noticed — the answer to the challenge of the fundamental taxic principle that the taxon derives from the things own qualities came from the system itself. The system-builders represented by the Mishnah solved their problem by transforming (potentially) destabilizing considerations into subordinated taxic indicators, that is to say, into principles of speciation. Let us now see in unusually rich detail how this was accomplished.

Showing how great issues found a subordinated place as principles of speciation begins with the simplest. It is the conception that appearance and reality have to be sorted out. The issue arises, of course, in the practicalities of applied reason, and that brings us to one among numerous cases in which our task is to determine whether how things really are or what they appear to be is the indicative variable. One such case derives from Mishnah-tractate Kilayim, the greater part of which serves to make the point that we speciate through resemblance. As with prior inquiries, served by entire tractates,[15] here too we shall review a whole tractate and show the cogency that derives from a philosophical reading of it.

With reference to the biblical prohibition of hybridization, Lev. 19:19, "You shall not let your cattle breed with a different kind, you shall not sow your field with two kinds of seed," and its parallel in Dt. 22:9-11, Mishnah-tractate Kilayim works on two philosophical problems. The first and paramount is the comparison and contrast of the species of a genus. The second is the consideration of attitude or intentionality, "It is man who both defines what constitutes a class and determines how to keep different classes distinct from one another...what appears to man as orderly becomes identified with the objective order of the world."[16]

Mishnah-tractate Kilayim 1:1, 4

1:1   A.   (1) Wheat and tares

       B.   are not [considered] diverse kinds with one another.

       C.   (2) Barley and two-rowed barley,

               (3) rice wheat and spelt,

               (4) a broad bean and a French vetch,

---

[15]Meilah, Qiddushin, Berakhot, for example.

[16]Irving J. Mandelbaum, *A History of the Mishnaic Law of Agriculture: Kilayim* (Chico, 1980: Scholars Press for Brown Judaic Studies), p. 1.

           (5) a red grasspea and a grasspea,

           (6) and a hyacinth bean and a Nile cowpea,

D.   are not [considered] diverse kinds with one another.

1:4 A.   And in [regard to] the tree:

B.   (1) Pears and crustaminum pears,

           (2) and quinces and hawthorns,

C.   are not [considered] diverse kinds with one another

D.   (1) An apple and a Syrian pear,

           (2) peaches and almonds,

           (3) jujubes and wild jujubes,

E.   even though they are similar to one another,

F.   they are [considered] diverse kinds with one another.

Mishnah-tractate Kilayim from 1:1 through 7:8 considers plants and the rule governing cultivating together different species of plants. The first consideration is resemblance. But it is not decisive when there are other traits of speciation. These items resemble one another and are not considered diverse kinds with one another, M. Kil. 1:1-4C. Other items, M. Kil. 1:4C-6 even though they resemble each other, are considered diverse kinds. M. 1:7-9 proceed to grafting one kind of plant onto another. M. 1:9E-3:7 proceed to sowing together different kinds of crops, first in the same space, then in adjacent spaces, and then. M.3:4-7, different kinds of crops in adjacent spaces.

MISHNAH-TRACTATE KILAYIM 2:6-7

2:6 A.   He who wishes to lay out his field [in] narrow beds of every kind [with each bed containing a different kind] —

B.   The House of Shammai say, "[He makes the beds as wide as the width of] three furrows of 'opening' [furrows ploughed for the purpose of 'opening' the field in order to collect rainwater],

C.   And the House of Hillel say, "[He makes the beds as wide as] the width of the Sharon yoke."

D.   And the words of these [one House] are near the words of those [the other House; there is little difference between the two measurements].

2:7 A.   [If] the point of the angle of the field of wheat entered into [a field] of barley,

B.   it is permitted [to grow the wheat in the field of barley];

C.   for it [the point of the angle of the wheat field] looks like the end of his field.

D.   If [his field] was [sown with] wheat, and his neighbor's [field] was [sown with] another kind,

E.   it is permitted to flank it [his neighbor's field] [with some] of the same kind [as that of his neighbor's field].

F.   [If] his [field] was [sown with] wheat, and his neighbor's [field] was [also sown with] wheat,

G. it is permitted to flank it [his field] [with] a furrow of flax but not [with] a furrow of another kind.

H. R. Simeon says, "It is all the same whether [a furrow of] flax seeds or [a furrow of] any kind [flanks the field] ."

I. R. Yosé says, "Even in the middle of his field it is permitted to test [the suitability of the soil for growing flax] with a furrow of flax."

At stake at M. Kil. 2:6-7 is not whether we actually are mixing crops, but whether it looks as though we are doing so. This is made explicit at M. Kil. 2:7C, for example: "for it [the point of the angle of the wheat field] looks like the end of his field." So long as each bed can be readily distinguished from another, different kinds may grow in the same field without producing the appearance of violating the law against diverse-kinds. So in this matter the law depends upon attitude and not upon actuality. The same considerations are operative through M. Kil. 3:7, e.g., M. 3:4: It is permitted to plant two rows each of chate melons or gourds, but not only one, since if it is only one, they do not appear to be planted in autonomous fields (Mandelbaum, p. 8). So too M. Kil. 3:3: "[If] the point of the angle of a field of vegetables entered a field of another [kind of] vegetables, it is permitted [to grow one kind of vegetables in the field of the other kind, for the point of the angle of the vegetable field looks like the end of his field, in line with M. 3:5D: "for whatever the sages prohibited, they [so] decreed only on account of appearances.

MISHNAH-TRACTATE KILAYIM 4:1

4:1 A. [The] bald spot of the vineyard —

B. House of Shammai say, '[It] need measure twenty-four cubits."

C. House of Hillel say, "[It need measure only] sixteen amah [square],"

D. [The] outer space of the vineyard —

E. House of Shammai say, "[It need measure] sixteen amah."

E House of Hillel say, "[It need measure only] twelve amah."

G. And what is [the] bald spot of the vineyard?

H. A vineyard which is bare in its middle.

I. If there are not there [in the bald spot] sixteen amah [square of space], [then) he shall not put seed into it.

J. [If] there were there [in the bald spot] sixteen amah [square of space], [then] they allow it [the vineyard] its area of tillage and he sows the rest.

We proceed, M. Kil. 4:1-7:8 to the issue of sowing crops in a vineyard. This is permitted if within or around a vineyard is an open space of the specified dimensions. If there is ample space between the vines, that space may be used. But if the appearance is such that the vines appeared mixed with grain, then the grain must be uprooted. The basic consideration is that grain or vegetables not create the appearance of confusion in the vineyard. Everything in the long sequence of rules derives from that single concern.

MISHNAH-TRACTATE KILAYIM 9:1-2, 8-9

9:1 A. Nothing is prohibited on account of [the laws of] diverse kinds except [a garment composed of a mixture of] wool and linen.

     B. Nor is anything susceptible to uncleanness through plagues except [a garment composed of either] wool or linen.

     C. Nor do priests wear anything to serve in the Temple except [garments composed of either] wool or linen,

     D. Camel's hair and sheep's wool which one hackled [combed] together —

     E. if the greater part is from the camels, it is permitted.

     F. But if the greater part is from the sheep, it is prohibited [to mix the fibers with flax].

     G. [If the quantity of camel's hair and sheep's wool is divided] half and half — it is prohibited [to mix the fibers with flax].

     H. And so [is the rule for] flax and hemp which one hackled together [if at least half of the hackled fibers are of flax, it is prohibited to mix them with wool].

9:2 A. Silk and bast silk are not subject to [the laws of] diverse kinds,

     B. but are prohibited for appearance's sake.

     C. Mattresses and cushions [composed of a mixture of wool and linen] are not subject to [the laws of] diverse kinds,

     D. provided that one's flesh not be touching them [while one sits or lies on them].

     E. There is no [rule permitting] temporary use in respect to diverse kinds [of garments].

     F. And one shall not wear [a garment of] diverse kinds even on top of ten [garments], even to avoid [paying] customs duty.

9:8 A. Nothing is prohibited on account of [the laws of] diverse kinds except [wool and flax which are] spun or woven [together],

     B. as it is written, "You shall not wear *shaatnez*" (Dt. 22:11) — something which is hackled, spun, or woven.

     C. R. Simeon b. Eleazar says, "It is turned away, and turns his Father in Heaven against him."

9:9 A. Felted stuffs [composed of wool and linen] are prohibited,

     B. because they are hackled [their fibers are hackled together].

     C. A fringe of wool [fastened] onto [a garment of] flax is prohibited,

     D. because [the threads of the fringe] interlace the web [of the garment].

     E. R. Yosé says, "Cords composed of purple wool are prohibited [to be worn on a garment of flax],

     F. "because one bastes the cord to the garment before tying [the ends of the cord together] ."

     G. One shall not tie a strip of wool to one of linen in order to gird his loins, even though a [leather] strap is between them.

Here the concern is to affirm the consideration of reality over appearance. The prohibition of mingling fibers of different species, with particular attention to wool and linen, occupies M. Kil. 9:1-10. Scripture's basic rule is amplified with special attention to mixtures, e.g., camel's hair and sheep's wool hackled together. Here we assign the traits of the dominant component of the mix to the entire mixture. Items that resemble wool and linen but are not of wool and linen, or that are not intended to serve as garments, are not subject to the prohibition.

The issue of intention is explicitly excluded. Even if one does not intend permanently to use a piece of cloth as a garment, it still may not be used at all if it is a mixture of diverse kinds, and so too at M. 9:2F. M. 9:4-10 complete the matter. Of special interest is M. 9:9, where the issue of connection is addressed. Here we have various mixtures that are prohibited because they are hackled together or interlaced. The entire tractate thus concerns the problem of appearance as against reality in connection with the mixture (commingling) of diverse species of plants, animals, and garments. The consideration of human attitude or intentionality enters in. There is no pericope that ignores one or another of these matters.

We recall that while some philosophical issues characterize the document overall, as the paramount ones of classification, mixture, and rules for hierarchical taxonomy has shown., others occur only episodically. A good example of the latter derives from the issue of the potential as against the actual. I resort to a less-than-felicitous neologism and call this philosophical principle merely "subject-specific," in that the document over all has not identified such principles as the source of its recurrent, generative problematic. One can learn a great deal about principles of classification, whatever particular topic comes to hand; one can learn something about the relationship of the potential to the actual — egg and chicken, acorn and oak — when certain highly particular issues arise. But there is no sustained effort to explore that philosophical problem as a problem of generalization with principles subject to generalization.[17]

One such problem has already passed our way. We recall that the issue occurs at M. Bes. 1:1, which takes up the issue of whether we regard what is going to happen as though it already has happened, or whether we interpret a potentiality as tantamount to an actuality. Even though, M. Bes. 3:2, we know that the nets for trapping a wild beast, fowl, or fish, set on the eve of the festival-day, enjoy the potentiality of trapping such a thing on the festival-day itself, one may not use such things as are caught, unless one knows for sure that they were caught prior to the festival-day. What is not designated in advance is not available for use. From our perspective, the interesting angle is that what is potential is not deemed as actual. But the entire tractate at hand does not devote itself to spelling out cases and problems concerning the potential and the actual. The important point about the matter is simple. It is a subordinated consideration, a mere taxic indicator in a philosophy of classification. The same episodic character assigned to the principle is seen at Mishnah-tractate Arakhin.

---

[17]Here then is a fine case of a principle that elsewhere sustains entire philosophical inquires, but here only contributes to the main point.

7:5   A.   He who purchases a field from his father, [if] his father died, and afterward he sanctified it, lo, it is deemed a field of possession (Lev. 27:16).

      B.   [If] he sanctified it and afterward his father died,

      C.   "lo, it is deemed a field which has been bought," the words of R. Meir.

      D.   R. Judah and R. Simeon say, "It is deemed a field of possession. "Since it is said, And if a field which he has bought which is not a field of his possession (Lev. 27:22)—

      E.   "a field which is not destined to be a field of possession,

      F.   "which excludes this, which is destined to be a field of possession."

      G.   A field which has been bought does not go forth to the priests in the Jubilee,

      H.   for a man does not declare sanctified something which is not his own.

      I.   Priests and Levites sanctify [their fields] at any time and redeem them at any time, whether before the Jubilee or after the Jubilee.

At M. Ar. 7:5 we have the issue of whether we deem what is going to happen as if it already has happened. The case is simple. If a person purchases a field from his father, is this deemed a field of possession, that is, one received by inheritance, at the point that the father dies? Yes, it is. All concur that if the father died and the man then sanctified the field, it falls under the rule of the field of possession. But if the man purchased the field and sanctified it and only afterward the father died, is it a field of possession? Meir holds that it is a field that has been bought, Judah and Simeon maintain that what is going to happen is deemed already to have happened. Therefore the field is deemed a field of possession.

Another *ad hoc* appearance of the principle concerns trading in futures, a classic case of assessing the reality of the potential.

5:7   A.   They do not strike a bargain for the price of produce before the market price is announced.

      B.   [Once] the market price is announced, they strike a bargain,

      C.   for even though this one does not have [the produce for delivery], another one will have it.

      D.   [If] one was the first among the reapers [of a given crop], he may strike a bargain with him

      E.   for (1) grain [already] stacked [on the threshing floor],

      F.   or for (2) a basket of grapes,

      G.   or for (3) a vat of olives,

      H.   or for (4) the clay balls of a potter,

      1.   or for (5) lime as soon as the limestone has sunk in the kiln.

J.   And one strikes a bargain for the price of manure every day of the year.
K.   R. Yosé says, "They do not strike a bargain for manure before the manure is on the dung heap."
L.   And sages permit.
M.   And one may strike a price at the height [of the market, the cheapest rate prevailing at the time of delivery].
N.   R. Judah says, "Even though one has not made a bargain at the cheapest rate [prevailing at the time of delivery], one may say to him, 'Give it to me at such-and — such a rate, or give me back my money'"

The point of M. Baba Mesia 5:7 is that one may not agree to pay in advance a fixed sum for a certain amount of produce if a market price has not yet been set. If the produce should prove to be more expensive, then the one who receives the money will lose out and turn out to have paid what is in fact interest on the advance. Once there is a market price, one may pay in advance for delivery later on; this is no longer speculating on futures in such a way that the creditor enjoys an unfair advantage in exchange for advance payment. At stake then is our assessment of what is potential; it is not deemed to be an actuality, such that an agreement is valid. Only when the potential crop has begun to actualize (so to speak) so that a market price has been set will the (further) potential crop be deemed an actuality. While the concern here is for usury, the consideration of the reality of the potential does enter in.

A fine case of the interplay of form as against function, as a matter of fact involving in a subordinated way the issue of intentionality, comes to us at Mishnah-tractate Shebi'it. There the matter of form vs. function is principal, since what we want to know is whether a person actually is working on his field in the Seventh Year and so is violating the law against doing so, or whether he merely appears to be working the land when he should not do so.

MISHNAH-TRACTATE SHEBI'IT 3:2, 4, 5

3:2 A.   [In accordance with the rule of M. 3:1], how much manure [may they bring out to a field during the Sabbatical year]?
B.   Up to three dung heaps per seah space [of land],
C.   each [dung heap containing no less than] ten baskets [of dung],
D.   each [basket containing a volume of no less than] a letek [fifteen seahs of dung].
E.   They may add to the [number of] baskets [above ten per dung heap],
F.   but they may not add to the [number of] dunghills [above three per seah space].
G.   R. Simeon says, "Also: [They may add to the number] of dung heaps."
3:4 A.   One who uses his field as a fold [for his flock during the Sabbatical year, which results in the spreading of manure throughout his field],
B.   makes an enclosure [that measures] two seah spaces in area.

C.   [After the enclosed area is filled with manure he creates a second fold adjacent to the first]. He removes three sides [of the original enclosure] and leaves the middle side [that is, the fourth side, in place. With the other three sides of the original fold he creates a second enclosure of the same size].

D.   The result is that he creates a fold [with an area] of four seah spaces.

E.   R. Simeon b. Gamaliel says, "[He may continue to create enclosures in this manner and so enlarge the area until it measures] eight seah spaces."

F.   If his entire field was four seah spaces in area,

G.   he sets aside a small section [of the field which he does not enclose in the fold]

H.   so as [to avoid] the appearance [of committing a transgression by manuring his field during the Sabbatical year].

I.   And he removes [manure] from within the enclosure and places it in his field in the accepted manner of those who handle manure [during the Sabbatical year, in accordance with the rule of M. 3:1-3].

3:5   A.   [During the Sabbatical year] a man may not begin to open a stone quarry in his field,

B.   unless it contains [enough stones to construct] three piles [of hewn blocks],

C.   each [pile] three [cubits long] by three [cubits wide] by three [cubits] high,

D.   [so that] their measure is [equivalent to] twenty — seven stones. [That is, each pile must contain no less than twenty — seven blocks, each measuring one cubic cubit).

M. Sheb. 3:1-4:1 turns to the problem of cultivating the land during the Seventh Year, with special attention to the difference between actually doing so and appearing to do so. There are acts of labor that will not necessarily benefit the field in the Seventh Year, but which may appear to others to do so. For example, one may store manure in the field. But what if this actually enriches the soil during the Seventh Year? Then doing so is prohibited. So how are we to do the work in such a way that we do not appear to be manuring the field? One brings out three dung heaps per seah of land, each of considerable size; then people will not think that it is to manure the field, the heaps being too few and too scattered, so M. Sheb. 3:2. Along these same lines, one may not appear to clear the field for planting (M. Sheb. 3:5-4:1). One can open a stone quarry, so long as it does not appear that the farmer is clearing the land of stones and so preparing it for cultivation. One who tears down a stone fence in his field may remove only the large stones, to indicate that he is not clearing the land, so M. 3:6-7.

While the issue on the surface concerns the interplay of form and function — the form of the action, tilling the field in some way, as against its consequences, which in these cases may be nil — Newman states, "The sanctity of the Seventh Year depends in the last analysis upon the actions and will of the people of Israel."

From a philosophical perspective, what is important is the power of intentionality (here: will) in solving taxonomic problems, assigning to the class of forbidden or prohibited actions things that the attitude of the community at large deems to be work associated with the Seventh Year or not."

When we ask about the interplay of form versus function as taxic indicators, we draw close to the consideration of intentionality. For when we want to know whether an object's functionality determines its classification, we have to find out to whom, and for what, the object is deemed to function. And that requires us to investigate the attitude of the craftsman who made the object or the owner who has the right to determine its use. A simple example of the interplay of form and function concerns defective clusters. These are defective specifically because they do not have the form that is normal to clusters of grapes, that is, with shoulders and a pendant.

MISHNAH-TRACTATE PE'AH 7:7

7:7 A. [As regards] a vineyard [the produce of which] is entirely defective clusters —

B. R. Eliezer says "[The produce] belongs to the householder."

C. R. Aqiba says, "[It] belongs to the poor."

D. Said R. Eliezer, "[Scripture states], When you harvest the grapes of your vineyard, you shall not strip it bare of defective clusters afterward (Dt. 24:21).

E. "If there is no harvest [because the entire yield is defective clusters], how can there be defective clusters [left after the harvest]?"

F. Said to him R. Aqiba, "[Scripture states], And you shall not strip your vineyard bare of defective clusters (Lev. 19:10).

G. "[This verse applies] even if [the produce of the vineyard is] entirely defective clusters, [such that there will be no harvest] ."

H. [In Aqiba's view, then,] why does [Scripture] state, When you gather the grapes of your vineyard, you shall not glean it of defective clusters afterward (Dt. 24:21)?

I. [This verse teaches that] the poor may not [claim] the defective clusters before the harvest.

M. Pe. 7:7 asks whether the classification of defective clusters depends upon objective facts or subjective attitudes. The taxonomic question is worked out by our definition of the meaning of "defective," parallel to the sense of the word "forgetting." Is there an objective standard — a fixed form — for the shape of a well-formed cluster? In that case, the farmer must give all clusters that do not conform. Then the whole of the vineyard may go to the poor. Eliezer holds that the category of defective cluster applies because of the farmer's evaluation or attitude. We take account of the function of the grapeclusters; if they so function as to constitute the whole of the crop, then they cannot fall into the class of defective grapeclusters. If there will be no crop at all, then whatever the condition of the grapeclusters, they cannot be rejected. The farmer cannot anticipate leaving the entire crop to the poor; his intentionality will then be taken into account.

Intentionality forms a subsidiary taxic indicator, not a principal and generative systemic component. The consideration of the role of attitude is complex, because sometimes intentionality forms a taxic indicator, and sometimes not. The way in which intentionality makes its appearance is equally complex. Sometimes specific word-choices signal the presence of that consideration, oftentimes not. But the one fundamental trait of a subsidiary component of a larger system is its subordination to other, more urgent issues. The matter of intentionality is contingent and stipulative, not uniform, not formative and certainly not ubiquitous. Indeed, the only principle that operates throughout is the one that everything can be classified in some few ways. Beyond that point, all considerations are relative to something beyond themselves, which is that one thing.

Nonetheless, intentionality does form a major taxic indicator, and, unlike considerations of the potential and the actual, or of form versus function, that indicator does form the operative consideration — the taxic indicator — for large segments of entire tractates. One important example is Mishnah-tractate Kelim, which, overall, deals with the impact of intentionality or attitude upon the classification of objects. At stake is the status, as to cultic cleanness, of useful objects, tools or utensils. The main point as to the taxonomy of objects — within the classes, unclean, clean — is that when an object has a distinctive character, form, use, or purpose, it is susceptible to uncleanness, so that, if it is in contact with a source of uncleanness, it is deemed cultically unclean. If it is formless, purposeless, or useless, it is insusceptible.

Three criteria govern the determination of what is useful or purposeful. First come properties deemed common to all utensils, whatever the material. Second are qualities distinctive to different sorts of materials. Third is the consideration of the complex purposes for which an object is made or used, primary and subsidiary, and the intention of the user is determinative. As is clear, intentionality is not the only issue, but it is a primary one.

As to cleanness or uncleanness of objects, we classify those made of one set of materials, wood, leather, bone, and glass, as against those made of the other, clay and alum crystal. The former when flat are clean, when made into a receptacle, unclean (that is, susceptible to uncleanness), and if broken, they are clean or insusceptible. The latter have a separate rule as to becoming unclean and conveying uncleanness, which is to say, through their contained airspace. If broken, they are clean. The upshot is to classify, as to uncleanness, things of the same genus, that is, utensils, but of different species, that is, speciated by material. How the matter works itself out in detail is readily described. Once we have introduced the consideration that the utensil that is broken is insusceptible, M. Kel. 3:1-8, we proceed to specify the sort of breakage that renders the object insusceptible, e.g., how big a hole in a receptacle. The size of the whole depends upon the use of the utensil, with the result that the process of classification is further refined by appeal to the purpose that a utensil ordinarily serves. The basic conception is that, with a clay utensil, when broken, without regard to the size of the crack or perforation, it is insusceptible. What is the case with linings of plaster added to utensils? If required by the utensil, they are intrinsic and will share in the uncleanness of the utensil; that is, they are connected or joined, because of their function. If not necessary to the functioning of the utensil, they are extrinsic and not joined and if the utensil is contaminated, they are unaffected, so M. Kel. 3:5-8. Let us turn to a specific text to show us in situ how the matter spells itself out.

MISHNAH-TRACTATE KELIM 5:1-2

5:1 A. A baking oven —
      B. "Its beginning [is] four [handbreadths].
      C. "And its remnants [are] four," the words of R. Meir.
      D. And sages say, "Under what circumstances? In the case of a large one, but in the case of a small one —
      E. "Its beginning is any size at all, and its remnants [to remain susceptible] are the larger part [of the original oven]."
      F. From when its manufacture is complete [it becomes susceptible to uncleanness].
      G. What is the completion of its manufacture?
      H. When one will heat it sufficiently so that sponge cake may be baked in it.
      I. R. Judah says, "When one will heat the new [oven] sufficiently so that in an old one, one may bake sponge cakes."
5:2 A. A [double] stove —
      B. 1. Its beginning is three [fingerbreadths]. 2. And its remnants are three. 3. When its manufacture is completed.
      C. When is the completion of its manufacture?
      D. When one will heat it sufficiently to boil on it the smallest of eggs, broken and put in a saucepan.
      E. The ordinary stove — [if] one made it for baking, its measure is according to that of a baking oven [= four].
      F. [If] one made it for cooking, its measure is according to that of a double stove [= three].
      G. [As to] the stone which projects: from the baking oven, a handbreadth, or from the stove, three fingers, is a connector.
      I. [As to] that which extends from the ordinary stove: [If] one made it for baking, its measure is according to that of an oven; [if] one made it for cooking, its measure is according to that of a double stove.
      J. Said R. Judah, "The handbreadth was stated only with reference to [the space] between the oven and the wall."
      K. [If] two ovens were side by side, one gives [assigns as a handle] a

handbreadth to this one and a handbreadth to that one, and the remainder is clean.

The issue of M. Kel. 5:1-2 is the point at which an oven is deemed useful. The general rule is that when an object is fully manufactured, then it is susceptible to uncleanness. But in the case of a clay oven, the oven may be used even before it has reached its full dimensions. Hence we want to know when it is useful, even prior to the completion of its processing. On the other end, if one is breaking down the oven, at what point is it completely useless. And, along these same lines, what are the appendages of the oven that are essential for using it, hence connected and part of the object, and which ones are not essential and therefore not connected? The criterion of classification throughout is function, not form: use, measured by a common consensus on the matter. So the recurrent taxonomic principle is usefulness, but that is adapted to the consideration of purpose or intentionality.

Here is a fine case in which classification is affected — and effected — by issues of attitude and will.

Mishnah-tractate Kelim 15:1

15:1 A. Utensils of wood, utensils of leather, utensils of bone, utensils of glass:

B. when they are flat, they are clean.

C. And when they form receptacles, they are unclean.

D. [If] they have been broken, they are clean.

E. [If] one made from them [from their shards or remnants, new] vessels, they receive uncleanness from now and henceforward.

F. "The chest, the box, and the tower (cupboard), a straw hive, and a reed hive [basket], and a tank of an Alexandrine ship

G. "which have [flat] bottoms

H. "and hold forty seahs in liquid measure, which are the same as two kors in dry measure

I. "lo, these are clean.

J. "And all other utensils, whether they hold or whether they do not hold [something],

K. "are unclean," the words of R. Meir.

L. R. Judah says, "The tub of a [water] wagon and the food chests of kings, and the tanner's trough, and the tank of a small ship, and the ark,

M. "even though they hold [the requisite volume],

N. "are unclean,

O. "for they are made to carry only what is in them.

P. "And all other utensils —

Q. "those that hold [the requisite volume] are clean.

R. "And which do not hold are unclean."

S. Between the opinion of R. Meir and that of R. Judah, the difference concerns only the baking trough of the householder.

The taxonomic principles affecting wooden utensils are stated at M. Kel. 15:1A-E. When flat they are insusceptible, when formed into a receptacle, they are susceptible. But when flat ones are designed regularly to function in some useful way, they are susceptible too, e.g., flat baking boards. The issue of the susceptibility of heavy boxes is at stake. They are not ordinarily moved, so are deemed fastened to the ground and insusceptible. But they function so as to carry what is in them, so the intention of the maker is decisive, and they are useful specifically because they may be moved about even though that is not common; hence they will be unclean. Here is a case in which intentionality forms the taxic indicator. M. 15:2-3 distinguish along the same lines between the intentionality of a craftsman or a householder. If an object is for a craftsman, it is designed for a single specific function and is susceptible. If for a householder, the object may equally serve diverse uses and is not specific to a single use. It therefore is insusceptible, having no "name" unto itself. Here we have an absolutely classic problem of classification: appeal to function, appeal to intentionality, appeal to form — all within a single grid, formed of wooden objects.

The importance of intentionality also is limited by its contingency. For the role of intentionality finds its measure in particular in the taxonomic power of that consideration to affect a variety of cases. Where it works, it works, where it does not work, it is abandoned. But then we have also to explain, within the conception of the contingency of intentionality, why that is a consideration at all. For intentionality is one potentially organizing principle that is not at all specific to the types of cases at hand, e.g., the classification of objects by reference to the intentionality of the craftsman or owner. Quite to the contrary, the attitude of a farmer is shown to be consubstantial with the attitude of God, with the result that God responds to the intentionality of the farmer.

That is the fact that shows us the systemic promise of the issue of intentionality, explaining why it matters at all. That fact furthermore underlines how radical is the initiative of subordinating intentionality within a system of classification. When we come to Mishnah-tractate Ma'aserot, we see the extraordinary power imputed to intentionality in the classification of the natural world, now with reference to the ownership of the land and its produce.

MISHNAH-TRACTATE MA'ASEROT 1:1

1:1 A. A general principle they stated concerning tithes:
     B. anything which is (1) food, (2) cultivated, (3) and which grows from the earth is subject to [the law of] tithes
     C. And yet another general principle they stated:
     D. anything which at its first [stage of development] is food and which at its ultimate [stage of development] is food [e.g., greens] —
     E. even though [the farmer] maintains [its growth] in order to increase the food [it will yield] —

F. is subject [to the law of tithes whether it is] small or large [at all points in its development].

G. But anything which at its first [stage of development] is not food, yet which at its ultimate [stage of development] is food [e.g. , the fruit of trees]

H. is not subject [to the laws of tithes] until it becomes food.

The main problem of M. Ma'aserot 1:1ff. is taxonomic. At what point does a crop enter the status of being subject to the removal of tithes and offerings? Prior to that point, it is classified as not liable, afterward, liable. This is subdivided into two categories, as Jaffee says: "when in the course of a crop's growth may it be used to satisfy the obligation to tithe? When, further, in the course of the harvest of the crop, must the tithes actually be paid? The answer is that the produce may be tithed as soon as it ripens; it then becomes valuable. But only when the householder by an action claims his harvested produce as personal property must the crop be tithed; that is in general when untithed produce is brought from the field into the home. Hence when the farmer, by an act that expresses his attitude, lays claim on the crop, then God responds by demanding his share of that same crop, owing to him as owner of the Land of Israel. In general, therefore, at stake is the interplay of classification and intentionality. The basic conception holds that when one takes possession of produce and deems it of value, then God's share is owing.[18]

The same metaphysical power of intentionality is shown in play in a completely distinct area, which is, when water has the power to impart the status of susceptibility to uncleanness to dry produce. The theory is that dry produce is insusceptible; that theory derives from Lev. 11:34, 37, as sages read the verses. Then, appealing to the notion of opposite, produce that has been wet down is susceptible to uncleanness. But that is the fact, sages maintain, only when the farmer has deliberately wet down the produce or has affirmed that he wants it to get wet. That point is made in the following rather odd item:

MISHNAH-TRACTATE MAKHSHIRIN 6:1

6:1 A. He who brings up his produce to the roof because of the maggots,

B. and dew fell on it —

C. it is not under the law, "If water be put".

D. If he intended such, lo, this is under the law, "If water be put".

E. [If] a deaf — mute, an imbecile, or a minor brought it up, even though he gave thought that dew should fall on it —

F. it is not under the law, "If water be put",

G. because they have the power of deed but not the power of intention.

---

[18]Martin Jaffee, *Mishnah's Theology of Tithing: A Study of Tractate Ma'aserot* (Chicago, 1981: Scholars Press for Brown Judaica Studies), p. 1.

On the very surface, the issue of Mishnah-tractate Makhshirin concerns classification, specifically, whether or not a crop has been rendered susceptible to uncleanness by reason of the application of water, in line with the received reading of Lev. 11:34, 37. As we see, the attitude of the farmer forms the principal indicator. If he did not want the crop wet down, then whether or not it has been wet down, it remains insusceptible. M. Makh. 6:1-3 make the simple and generative point that liquid that is used unintentionally is insusceptible, that is to say, liquid that is not wanted has no affect on crops on which it is poured. Only liquid that is used deliberately, that is, that is wanted, has the effect of changing the status of dry produce and rendering it susceptible to uncleanness.

Lest the reader suppose that intentionality plays its primary role in the classification of things as to susceptibility to uncleanness, we turn forthwith to an entirely distinct topic, the conduct of the cult, and to problems of classification in which cleanness is not at stake.

MISHNAH-TRACTATE MENAHOT 1:1, 3

1:1 A. All meal offerings from which the handful was taken not for their own name are valid [for offering up, and, in the case of the residue, for the priests' eating].

      B. But they have not gone to their owner's credit in fulfillment of an obligation,

      C. except for the meal offering of a sinner and the meal offering of jealousy [of a suspected adulteress] [which, if improperly designated, are invalid].

      D. The meal offering of a sinner and the meal offering of a suspected adulteress (1) from which the handful was taken not for their own name, (2) [or which] one put into a utensil, and (3) conveyed and (4) offered up not for its own name,

      E. or for its own name and not for its own name,

      F. or not for its own name and for its own name,

      G are invalid.

      H. How so [in a case of doing one of the afore-listed actions) is it for its own name and not for its own name?

      I. [If one did one action] (1) for the sake of the meal offering of a sinner and (2) [another action] for the sake of a freewill meal offering.

      J. Or [how do we define a case of doing one of the afore-listed actions] not for its own name and for its own name?

      K. For the sake of (2) a freewill meal offering and for the sake of (1) the meal offering of a sinner.

1:3 A. [If] he put in too much oil [M. 9:3] or put in too little oil or put in too little frankincense [M. 13:3], it is invalid.

      B. He who takes up the handful of meal offering [with the improper intention] to eat its residue outside,

      C. or an olive's bulk of its residue outside,

D.   to burn a handful thereof outside,

E.   or an olive's bulk of a handful thereof outside,

F.   or to burn its frankincense outside —

G.   it is invalid. But extirpation does not apply to it.

H.   [If he takes up the handful of meal offering with the improper intention] to eat its residue on the next day,

I.   or an olive's bulk of its residue on the next day,

J.   to burn a handful thereof on the next day,

K.   or an olive's bulk of a handful thereof on the next day,

L.   or to burn its frankincense on the next day,

M.   it is refuse. And they are liable to extirpation on its account.

N.   This is the general principle:

O.   [In] every [case in which] one (1) takes the handful of meal offering, or (2) puts it into a utensil, or (3) conveys it, or (4) offers it up, [with the improper intention] to eat something which is usually eaten [the residue] or to offer up something which is usually offered up [the meal offering]—

P.   outside of its proper place,

Q.   it is invalid. But extirpation does not apply to it.

R.   [If one does so with the improper intention to eat the residue or to offer up the meal offering] outside of its proper time, it is refuse. And they are liable on its account to extirpation.

S.   [And the foregoing rule applies] on condition that that which renders the offering permissible is offered in accord with its requirement.

T.   How is that which renders the offering permissible offered in accord with its requirement?

U.   [If] one took the handful in silence [without improper intention] and put it into the utensil and conveyed and offered it up [with the improper intention to do so] outside of its proper time,

V.   or [if] one took the handful of meal offering [with the improper intention of eating that which is eaten or offering up that which is offered up] outside of its proper time, and [then] put it into a utensil and conveyed and offered it up in silence [without improper intention],

W.   or [if] one took the handful and put it into a utensil and conveyed and offered it up [with the improper intention to eat that which is eaten or to burn that which is burned] outside of its proper time [only] —

X.   this is a case in which that which renders the offering permissible is offered up in accord with its requirement.

The pertinent issue in Mishnah-tractate Menahot is the impact of intentionality upon the designation of a meal-offering for a given purpose. The meal has to be designated for a specific purpose, e.g., as the meal offering of a sinner, and it must serve for the particular purpose at hand, e.g., the sin that has come to light. In the case that the meal-offering is presented under some other designation, that is, "not for its own name," than the one for which it was set aside, it is a valid offering but does not fulfil the obligation of the sinner. The issue, then, is the impact of intention upon the classification of a substance that has been made holy. The substance retains its sanctification, but does not serve the purpose that was meant for it. M. Menahot 1:1-2 present this conception.

M. Menahot 1:3-4 go on to the issue of the improper intention on the part of the priest to eat the residue of the meal offering or to offer up the handful outside of the correct time or place, respectively. If while effecting one of the four principal actions in connection with preparing the meal offering, which are taking the handful, putting it into a utensil, bringing it to the altar, and offering it up, the priest should form the intention of eating his share or burning the handful outside of the courtyard, the improper intention has classified the meal offering as invalid. And that is without respect to the actual deeds of the priest. If he has the notion, while doing any one of these four actions, of eating or burning the meal outside the proper time, the offering is rendered refuse.

This conception is qualified. What has been stated is the rule if what renders the offering permissible for priestly use has been offered properly. If it has not, then there is no consideration of refuse at all. One authority holds that if the improper intention concerning time comes before the improper intention concerning location, we invoke the rule of refuse. In any event we have an otherwise valid offering. But if one has improper intention concerning place, he invalidates the meal offering before he has given play to his other improper intention, which concerns time and which alone brings into play the rules of refuse. Why, he asks, should we declare an already invalid meal offering to be refuse at all? The entire chapter therefore works on the interplay of intentionality and classification of meal offerings.

Intentionality classifies not only intangible things, that is, whether or not something is suitable for the cult. It affects also quite material considerations. One of these is the violation of the Sabbath, which is a matter of action, and which, in the theory of this mode of thought, bears weighty sanctions. Deliberate violation of the Sabbath may involve the death-penalty (whether imposed on earth or in Heaven is not an issue here). Yet actions are classified, vis à vis culpability, not only with respect to concrete deed but also, and especially, with respect to the attitude of the actor. Considering the practicality of these issues, we cannot dismiss the power of intentionality by maintaining it is really an abstraction that concerns intangible and socially irrelevant matters.

MISHNAH-TRACTATE SHABBAT 2:5

2:5   A.   He who puts out a lamp because he is afraid of gentiles, thugs, a bad spirit,

       B.   or if it is so that a sick person might sleep,

       C.   is exempt [from liability to punishment].

       D.   [If he did so], to spare the lamp, the oil, the wick,

       E.   he is liable.

F.   And R. Yosé exempts [him from liability to punishment] in all
      instances except for [one who does so to spare] the wick, because he
      [thereby] makes [it into] charcoal.

M. Shab. 2:5 sets forth through the contrast of two cases the stunning conception
that the violation of the Sabbath is a matter of not only action but also intention or
attitude. If one carries out an action, it may or may not fall into the classification of
Sabbath-violation. If one's intent is not for one's own benefit, then the action is not
culpable. If it is for one's benefit, e.g., to produce material gain, then the action is
culpable. So intentionality forms the indicative point of differentiation.

    I cannot imagine a more profound statement of that principle of the taxonomic
power of intentionality than the one in hand. The basic issue here is whether or not
one is liable for doing an act of labor which is not needed in itself but only to effect
some extrinsic purpose. The sparing of the wick is an act of labor done for itself.
The deeds of A, B, are done for an extraneous and permissible purpose; since the
purpose, that is, intentionality, is valid, the deed done to effect that intentionality is
not culpable. We take account of what one intends as well as what one does in
interpreting the prohibition of acts of labor. M. Shab. 10:4 once again introduces
the consideration of intentionality. If one intended to violate the law but did not
actually do so, he is exempt from punishment. If he intended to transport an object
in front of him in the normal way but it slipped around behind him and was carried
in an unusual way, he is exempt. If he intended not to violate the law but did so, he
is liable. M. 10:5 adds that if one performs a prohibited act of labor for some
purpose other than the commission of that act of labor itself, he is exempt from
liability. If it is permitted to carry an object and one by the way carries a container
for that object, he is not liable.

    But matters are considerably more complex than these simple cases suggest.
The following introduces an interesting refinement.

MISHNAH-TRACTATE SHABBAT 3:6

3:6   A.   [On the Sabbath] they do not put a utensil under a lamp to catch the
            oil.
      B.   But if one put it there while it is still day, it is permitted.
      C.   But they do not use any of that oil [on the Sabbath],
      D.   since it is not something which was prepared [before the Sabbath for
            use on the Sabbath].
      E.   They carry a new lamp, but not an old one.
      F.   R. Simeon says, "Any sort of lamp do they carry, except for a lamp
            which is burning on the Sabbath."
      G.   They put a utensil under a lamp to catch the sparks.
      H.   But [on the Sabbath] one may not put water into it,
      I.   because he thereby puts out [the sparks].

The interest of the framers of this tractate in defining the correct purpose of things and in identifying the intentionality that has affected things, by appeal to that correct purpose, for use on the Sabbath, comes to the fore at M. Shab. 3:6, a somewhat odd item. The principle here is somewhat more complex than it would appear on the surface. The reason is that the oil has been set aside for use in the lamp. That act of intentionality has established the character of the oil. It cannot then be carried. When the oil drips into the dish, the dish too cannot be carried. The dish formerly was available for use; it now has been prohibited, and so its status has been changed, and that cannot be allowed. If the dish was designated prior to the Sabbath for the particular purpose that it now is made to serve, however, then it is permitted for use in that way. That explains the principle of M. 3:6A.

The parallel point concerns an old lamp. It is not used, because it is undesirable. It falls into the classification of that which has not been set aside for Sabbath use. The new lamp may be used. So the passage overall works on the principle of the classification of objects — permitted, prohibited for Sabbath use — through the prior act of intentionality. We have to revert to Mishnah-tractate Besah to locate discussions of the interplay of intentionality and classification of so sustained and penetrating a character. What has been designated or classified in advance for use on the Sabbath may be handled, but what has not been so designated may not be handled. At M. Shab. 4:2 too therefore the question of an act of intentionality is worked out. A hide is available for use with or without food, since it may be spread out and serve for reclining; it is a utensil the intrinsic purpose of which is to do just that. Wool shearings are purposed for weaving or spinning, acts not done on the Sabbath. They cannot be used on the Sabbath. If they are used to cover a dish and keep it warm, the dish may be removed but not restored. Here again the conception of a prior act of intentionality that classifies an object and endows it with its purpose and hence its distinctive character vis à vis the Sabbath is paramount.

A still more engaging issue is how intentionality interacts with separate considerations of the Sabbath entirely. A person is liable for transporting an object across the boundaries from private to public domain. But there is an intervening principle of taxonomy that tells us whether or not the action is culpable. If someone transports something that is not held to be of worth or value, that is, an object of no consequence, then transporting the object produces no consequences and does not impose liability.

MISHNAH-TRACTATE SHABBAT 7:3

7:3 A. And a further general rule did they state:
   B. Whatever is suitable for storage, which people generally store in such quantity as one has taken out on the Sabbath—
   C. he is liable to a sin offering on its account.

D. And whatever is not suitable for storage, which people generally do not store in such quantity as one has taken out on the Sabbath —

E. only he is liable on its account who stores it away [and who then takes it out].

M. Shab. 7:3 goes on to review a taxonomic principle involving intentionality. Then at M. 7:4 we have a list of the minimum volume or quantity of various sorts of food stuffs for the transportation of which a person is liable. These are minimum amounts of food for which an animal or a human being will find meaningful use, e.g., a mouthful of food and the like. The upshot is that the attitude or intentionality of a human being is taken into account.

But intentionality is subjected to objective limitations, for the matter at hand is not left to subjective considerations, e.g., what an individual person may deem or worth or not of worth. There is a limit as to subjectivity in the objective quantities held to be of value to anyone, if not to a given person. The consideration, then, of what is deemed to be valuable is not left in the hands of the private person. The issue of intentionality or inadvertence is introduced in these terms: "This is the general principle: All those who may be liable to sin offerings in fact are not liable unless at the beginning and the end, their [sin] is done inadvertently. [But] if the beginning of their [sin] is inadvertent and the end is deliberate, [or] the beginning deliberate and the end inadvertent, they are exempt — unless at the beginning and at the end their [sin] is inadvertent."

The taxonomic power of human intentionality extends to the classification of produce as holy or common. Given the Halakhah's acute practical interest in priestly perquisites, that fact makes all the more surprising the subordinated position of intentionality in the system as a whole. Here is a case in which intentionality determines whether something is subject to the taboos of sanctification:

MISHNAH-TRACTATE TERUMOT 1:1-2

1:1 A. Five [sorts of people] may not separate heave offering,

B. and if they separated heave offering, that which they have separated is not [valid] heave offering:

C. (1) a Heresh, (2) an imbecile, (3) a minor,

D. and (4) one who separates heave offering from [produce] which is not his own.

E. (5) A gentile who separated heave offering from [the produce of] an Israelite,

F. even with permission —

G. that which he has separated is not [valid] heave offering.

1:2 A. A Heresh

B. who speaks but does not hear

C. may not separate heave offering,

D.   but if he separated heave offering, that which he has separated is [valid] heave offering.

E.   The Heresh of which the sages spoke under all circumstances is one who neither hears nor speaks.

Mishnah-tractate Terumot refers to the designation (separation") of a portion of the crop as heave-offering, that is, as rations for the priests. That produce is deemed sanctified, holy only for the priests' consumption and related purposes. At stake at M. Terumot 1:1-2, 3 is how produce is classified so that part of it falls into the category of heave-offering, that is to say, is sanctified. The Israelite is central to the process of classification, that is, sanctification. So Avery-Peck states: "The holy heave offering comes into being only if man properly formulates the intention to sanctify part of his produce and indicates that intention through corresponding words and actions. The centrality of human intention in this process is illustrated by the fact that individuals deemed to have no understanding, e.g., imbeciles and minors, and therefore no power of intention, may not validly designate heave-offering."[19] No produce is intrinsically holy. All depends upon the intentionality, as to classification, of the householder. That accounts for the interest at M. 1:1-2 in an act of classification accomplished through full intentionality of someone with the power of intentionality. The indicative traits of those excluded from the process then bear the generalization.

The taxonomic power of intentionality furthermore comes into play when it comes to violating the sanctity of heave-offering. If a non-priest has eaten heave-offering, how do we classify the act? If he has done so intentionally, he is subjected to one set of sanctions, and if unintentionally, a different set of sanctions, as specified at M. Terumot 6:1D: the principal and added fifth are restored to the priesthood. The added fifth is a fine through which the non-priest makes atonement for misappropriating the sanctified produce (Avery-Peck, p. 193). The task is to indicate who is liable to pay the principal and added fifth, and what produce may be used for that purpose. While the whole of Chapter Six works on these questions of detail, what generates the questions to begin with is the power of classification deriving from intentionality.

VII. CONCLUSION

We now differentiate hermeneutics of the topics covered in Chapters One through Six from the Halakhic hermeneutics that govern the interpretation of all topics: the particular from the generic hermeneutics.

---

[19] Alan J. Avery-Peck, *The Priestly Gift in Mishnah. A Study of Tractate Terumot* (Atlanta, 1981: Scholars Press for Brown Judaica Studies), p. 3.

The particular hermeneutics, we have seen, covers the matter of the potential and the actual, the considerations of the form and function of things, the conception of intentionality as a heuristic principle — all of them autonomous and free-standing modes for ordering what was not at rest but in motion and for explaining things or persons or actions. The particular hermeneutics thus answered the call of the topical classification that defines the category-formations of the Halakhah. The uniform task assigned to each is readily determined. It was to serve as a taxic indicator within the process of classification. Thus whether or not we consider the potential or only the actual character of a thing would determine the classification of that thing. The function, not only the form, of a thing would define its classification. The attitude or intentionality of an actor would take part in the classification of the act or its consequences.

While each of these considerations can have formed on its own the foundation for a vast structure and system of explanation and application to diverse cases, none did. All of them contributed to the system's claim to self-evidence by showing that the system found a place for every conceivable variable and point of differentiation. And that implicit and tacit judgment, the utilization of great conceptions for the system's small purposes in taxonomy, showed the power of this mode of thought to encompass all things. That is how generative conceptions of thought were absorbed within the system and made to contribute to its plausibility. None of these conceptions made the system work. All of them prove episodic and local.

What of the generic hermeneutics, and what then holds the whole together? *It is the generic hermeneutics that transforms the particularity of the topic and its teleology into the generalization of the principle and its negotiation of abstract relationships.* Generic hermeneutics — as much as the theological system of the Aggadic documents — transcends the documentary boundaries of the Halakhic documents, Mishnah through the Bavli. These documents relate in three ways, they are autonomous of one another, connected to one another, and continuous with one another. Here is the source of continuity: not only theological, but philosophical and logical.

To spell this out: in terms of my continuing study of the composition of Rabbinic Judaism, showing the singularity of its documents and asking how the documents intersect and interact and ultimately make a single coherent statement, I differentiated text, context, and matrix. In the present setting, the category-formations form the text, each read on its own, within its own logic, in accord with a theory of the particular hermeneutics that emerges in a hypothetical process of analogical-contrastive reasoning. The various specific types of generic hermeneutics then establish the context, transcending the limits of the category-formations but not encompassing them all together and all at once. The matrix, we now realize, is what I have defined in this chapter's picture of the Halakhic modes of analytical thought that everywhere govern. The system finds it possible to speak all together and to set forth a single statement when the deepest layers of rationality are reached, the foundations of all thought penetrated.

But while I claim to have accomplished one part of the work, I have yet to turn to the more difficult. I have treated the category-formations as the starting point and have not attempted, yet, to discern the rationality that defines their foundations. That is to say, the two distinct hermeneutical constructions that impart sense and order to the Halakhic category-formations prove essential to the Halakhic structure and system. They permit us to explain all things but the main thing, which is the thing itself. I mean the Halakhic category-formations themselves. That question is answered in *Why This, Not That?*[20]

---

[20] *Why This, Not That? Ways Not Taken in the Halakhic Category-Formations of the Mishnah-Tosefta-Yerushalmi-Bavli.* Lanham, 2003: University Press of America. Second printing, revised, of *The Comparative Hermeneutics of Rabbinic Judaism.* Volume Eight. *Why This, Not That? Ways Not Taken in the Halakhic Category-Formations of the Mishnah-Tosefta-Yerushalmi-Bavli.* Binghamton, 2000: Global Publications. ACADEMIC STUDIES IN ANCIENT JUDAISM series.

Jacob Neusner

The Aggadic Role in Halakhic Discourses. Lanham. February 2001. University Press of America. Academic Studies in Ancient Judaism series. Volume I

The Aggadic Role in Halakhic Discourses. Lanham. February 2001. University Press of America. Academic Studies in Ancient Judaism series. Volume II

The Aggadic Role in Halakhic Discourses. Lanham. February 2001. University Press of America. Academic Studies in Ancient Judaism series. Volume III

A Theological Commentary to the Midrash. Lanham. April 2001. University Press of America. Academic Studies in Ancient Judaism series. Volume I. *Pesiqta deRab Kahana.*

A Theological Commentary to the Midrash. Lanham. March 2001. University Press of America. Academic Studies in Ancient Judaism series. - Volume II. *Genesis Raba.*

A Theological Commentary to the Midrash. Lanham. April 2001. University Press of America. Academic Studies in Ancient Judaism series. Volume III. *Song of Songs Rabbah*

A Theological Commentary to the Midrash. Lanham. April 2001. University Press of America. Academic Studies in Ancient Judaism series. Volume IV. *Leviticus Rabbah*

A Theological Commentary to the Midrash. Lanham. June 2001. University Press of America. Academic Studies in Ancient Judaism series. Volume V *Lamentations Rabbati*

A Theological Commentary to the Midrash. June 2001. University Press of America. Academic Studies in Ancient Judaism series. Volume VI. *Ruth Rabbah and Esther Rabbah I*

A Theological Commentary to the Midrash. June 2001. University Press of America. Academic Studies in Ancient Judaism series. Volume VII. *Sifra*

A Theological Commentary to the Midrash. July 2001. University Press of America. Academic Studies in Ancient Judaism series. Volume VIII. *Sifré to Numbers and Sifré to Deuteronomy*

A Theological Commentary to the Midrash. August 2001. University Press of America. Academic Studies in Ancient Judaism series. Volume IX. *Mekhilta Attributed to Rabbi Ishmael*

The Unity of Rabbinic Discourse. January 2001. University Press of America. Academic Studies in Ancient Judaism series. Volume I: *Aggadah in the Halakhah*

The Unity of Rabbinic Discourse. February 2001. University Press of America. Academic Studies in Ancient Judaism series. Volume II: *Halakhah in the Aggadah*

The Unity of Rabbinic Discourse. February 2001. University Press of America. Academic Studies in Ancient Judaism series. Volume III: *Halakhah and Aggadah in Concert*

Texts without Boundaries. Protocols of Non-Documentary Writing in the Rabbinic Canon, Lanham, 2002: University Press of America. Academic Studies in Ancient Judaism series. Volume Two. *Sifra*

Texts without Boundaries. Protocols of Non-Documentary Writing in the Rabbinic Canon, Lanham, 2003: University Press of America. Academic Studies in Ancient Judaism series. Volume Three. *Sifré to Numbers.*

Texts without Boundaries. Protocols of Non-Documentary Writing in the Rabbinic Canon, Lanham, 2003: University Press of America. Academic Studies in Ancient Judaism series. Volume Four. *Sifré to Deuteronomy.*

Texts without Boundaries. Protocols of Non-Documentary Writing in the Rabbinic Canon, Lanham, 2004: University Press of America. Academic Studies in Ancient Judaism series. Volume Five. *Genesis Rabbah.*

Texts without Boundaries. Protocols of Non-Documentary Writing in the Rabbinic Canon, Lanham, 2004: University Press of America. Academic Studies in Ancient Judaism series. Volume Six. *Leviticus Rabbah.*

Texts without Boundaries. Protocols of Non-Documentary Writing in the Rabbinic Canon, Lanham, 2004: University Press of America. Academic Studies in Ancient Judaism series. Volume Seven. *Pesiqta deRab Kahana.*

Texts without Boundaries. Protocols of Non-Documentary Writing in the Rabbinic Canon, Lanham, 2004: University Press of America. Academic Studies in Ancient Judaism series. Volume Eight. *Esther Rabbah and Ruth Rabbah.*

Texts without Boundaries. Protocols of Non-Documentary Writing in the Rabbinic Canon, Lanham, 2004: University Press of America. Academic Studies in Ancient Judaism series. Volume Nine. *Song of Songs Rabbah.*

Texts without Boundaries. Protocols of Non-Documentary Writing in the Rabbinic Canon, Lanham, 2004: University Press of America. Academic Studies in Ancient Judaism series. Volume Ten. *Lamentations Rabbah.*

Texts without Boundaries. Protocols of Non-Documentary Writing in the Rabbinic Canon, Lanham, 2004: University Press of America. Academic Studies in Ancient Judaism series. Volume Eleven. *Mekhilta Attributed to Rabbi Ishmael.*

Texts without Boundaries. Protocols of Non-Documentary Writing in the Rabbinic Canon, Lanham, 2004: University Press of America. Academic Studies in Ancient Judaism series. Volume Twelve. *Abot deRabbi Natan.*